CHARLEMAGNE

Manchester University Press

CHARLEMAGNE
EMPIRE AND SOCIETY

edited by Joanna Story

Manchester University Press
Manchester and New York

distributed exclusively in the USA by Palgrave

Published by Manchester University Press
Oxford Road, Manchester M13 9NR, UK
and Room 400, 175 Fifth Avenue, New York, NY 10010, USA
www.manchesteruniversitypress.co.uk

Distributed in the United States exclusively by
Palgrave Macmillan, 175 Fifth Avenue,
New York, NY 10010, USA

Distributed in Canada exclusively by
UBC Press, University of British Columbia, 2029 West Mall,
Vancouver, BC, Canada V6T 1Z2

British Library Cataloguing-in-Publication Data is available

Library of Congress Cataloging-in-Publication Data is available

ISBN 978 0 7190 7089 1 paperback

First published 2005

First reprinted 2010

Printed by Lightning Source

CONTENTS

List of illustrations   *page* ix
List of contributors   xi
Preface   xiii
List of abbreviations   xv

Introduction: Charlemagne's reputation *Joanna Story*   1

1 The long shadow of the Merovingians *Paul Fouracre*   5

2 Charlemagne the man *Janet L. Nelson*   22

3 Einhard's Charlemagne: the characterisation of greatness *David Ganz*   38

4 Charlemagne's imperial coronation and the Annals of
     Lorsch *Roger Collins*   52

5 Charlemagne's government *Matthew Innes*   71

6 Charlemagne and the aristocracy: captains and kings *Stuart Airlie*   90

7 Charlemagne's church *Mayke de Jong*   103

8 Charlemagne's 'men of God': Alcuin, Hildebald, Arn
     Donald A. Bullough   136

9 The Carolingian renaissance of culture and learning
     Rosamond McKitterick   151

10 Charlemagne and the renewal of Rome *Neil Christie*   167

11 Charlemagne and the world beyond the Rhine *Timothy Reuter*   183

12 Charlemagne and the Anglo-Saxons *Joanna Story*   195

13 Charlemagne's coinage: ideology and economy *Simon Coupland*   211

14 Rural settlement hierarchy in the age of Charlemagne
     Christopher Loveluck   230

15 Urban developments in the age of Charlemagne *Frans Verhaeghe*
     with Christopher Loveluck and Joanna Story   259

Bibliography   289
Index   317

LIST OF ILLUSTRATIONS

1 Charlemagne's Europe   *page* xvii
2 Northern Francia (places mentioned in the text)   xviii
3 Carolingian Italy   xix

4 The composition of the Lorsch Annals   59
5 Vienna, ÖNB Cod. 515, fol. 1v, the Lorsch Annals, 795   61
6 Vienna, ÖNB Cod. 515 fols 3v–4r, the Lorsch Annals, 800–2   62

7 (a) Pre-reform coinage of Charlemagne   214
  (b) Monogram coinage of Charlemagne   219
8 Origin of Charlemagne's monogram coinage found at Dorestad
  (stray finds only)   222
9 Portrait coins of Charlemagne   225

LIST OF CONTRIBUTORS

Stuart Airlie is Senior Lecturer in History at the University of Glasgow

Donald Bullough was Professor of Medieval History at the University of St Andrews from 1973 to 1991

Neil Christie is a Senior Lecturer in Archaeology at the University of Leicester

Roger Collins is Fellow in the School of History, University of Edinburgh

Rev. Dr Simon Coupland is a vicar in Kingston-upon-Thames, Surrey

Paul Fouracre is Professor of Medieval History at the University of Manchester

David Ganz is Professor of Palaeography at King's College, University of London

Matthew Innes is a Reader in History at Birkbeck College, University of London

Mayke de Jong is Professor of Medieval History at the University of Utrecht, The Netherlands

Christopher Loveluck is a Lecturer in Medieval Archaeology at the University of Nottingham

Rosamond McKitterick is Professor of Medieval History at the University of Cambridge

Janet L. Nelson is Professor of Medieval History at King's College, University of London

Timothy Reuter was Professor of Medieval History at the University of Southampton from 1994 to 2002

Joanna Story is a Lecturer in Early Medieval History at the University of Leicester

Frans Verhaeghe is Professor of Archaeology at the Free University of Brussels, Belgium

PREFACE

This book began as a response to a weekend conference on Charlemagne in the anniversary year of his imperial coronation, in February 2000, hosted by the Department for Continuing Education at the University of Oxford. Maggie Herdman's enthusiasm for hosting the meeting at Rewley House was reflected in the popularity of the conference and the response of colleagues to the suggestion that a book of this type would make a most welcome addition to the literature on Charlemagne and his world.

Carolingian studies have undergone something of a renaissance in the past 20 years or so and courses on Early Medieval Europe and the Age of Charlemagne are now commonplace in university curricula in the UK and USA. Crucial to this has been the increased quantity of contemporary primary sources translated into English, which enable students to engage directly with this most formative period of European history. This book seeks to fill a gap in the secondary literature on Charlemagne by bringing together a variety of scholarly voices and approaches to focus on key issues concerning his life and his world. Here, we bring together the fruits of recent scholarship but also seek to pick out areas and issues that are less well understood, showing the way – we hope – to future generations of early medieval historians and archaeologists.

The editor of this book owes a great debt to all the contributors, and to Jonathan Bevan of Manchester University Press, for their patience and fortitude in the face of adversity and delays. The untimely deaths of two contributors and colleagues has left a gap that is keenly felt; I am very grateful to the families of Tim Reuter and Donald Bullough for permission to publish their papers posthumously, and to Jinty Nelson, David Ganz and Simon MacLean for their help in bringing those papers to publication. Additionally, Julia Smith and Tom Noble provided many shrewd comments and careful advice on the book at an early stage in its production. My students at the University of Leicester have also been important, providing feedback and consumer comments on many of the ideas and articles included here.

Thanks are also due to the British Academy for their sponsorship of Chris Loveluck's Post-doctoral Research Fellowship at the University of Southampton during which he wrote his paper, to the Österreichische Nationalbibliothek (Bildarchiv) in Vienna for their permission to publish plates from ÖNB Cod. 515, to the Koninklijk Penningkabinet, Leiden and to Mark Blackburn of the Fitzwilliam Museum, Cambridge for their permission to publish photographs of coins in their collections, and to Catherine Story for her maps.

Finally, this book is dedicated to the memory of Donald Bullough and Tim Reuter, both of whom died in 2002. Their wise words on the Age of Charlemagne have taught us much.

Joanna Story
Leicester

ABBREVIATIONS

AB	*Annales Bertiniani* / Annals of St-Bertin
AF	*Annales Fuldenses* / Annals of Fulda
AKG	*Archiv für Kulturgeschichte*
AL	*Annales Laureshamenses* / Lorsch Annals
AM	*Annales Mosellani* / Moselle Annals
AMP	*Annales Mettenses Priores* / Earlier Annals of Metz
AQ	*Ausgewählte Quellen zur deutschen Geschichte des Mittelalters*
AX	*Annales Xantenses* / Xanten Annals
BAV	Biblioteca Apostolica Vaticana
BSFN	*Bulletin de la Société française de numismatique*
CBA	Council for British Archaeology
CC	*Codex Carolinus*
CCM	*Corpus Consuetudinum Monasticarum*
CCSL	Corpus Christianorum Series Latina
CLA	*Codices Latini Antiquiores*
CSEL	*Corpus Scriptorum Ecclesiasticorum Latinorum*
DA	*Deutsches Archiv für Erforschung des Mittelalters*
EHD	Whitelock, *English Historical Documents*
EHR	*English Historical Review*
Einhard, *VK*	Einhard, *Vita Karoli Magni*
EME	*Early Medieval Europe*
FS	*Frühmittelalterliche Studien*
HWJ	*History Workshop Journal*
HZ	*Historische Zeitschrift*
JEH	*Journal of Ecclesiastical History*
JML	*Journal of Medieval Latin*
JMP	*Jaarboek voor Munt- en Penningkunde*
JRA	*Journal of Roman Archaeology*
KPK	Koninklijk Penningkabinet, Leiden

ABBREVIATIONS

LHF	*Liber Historiae Francorum*
LP	*Liber Pontificalis*
MGH	Monumenta Germaniae Historica

Capit. Episc.	*Capitula Episcoporum*
Capit.	*Capitularia*
Conc.	*Concilia*
DD	*Diplomata*
Dip. Germ.	*Die Urkunden der Deutschen Karolinger*
Dip. Imp.	*Diplomata Imperii*
Dip. Karol.	*Diplomata Karolinorum*
Epp.	*Epistolae*
Epp. Sel.	*Epistolae Selectae in usum Scholarum*
Fontes	*Fontes Iuris Germanici Antiqui in usum scholarum ex Monumentis Germaniae Historicis separatim editi*
Leges	*Leges Nationum Germanicarum*
PLAC	*Poetae Latini Aevi Carolini*
SS	*Scriptores*
SSRG	*Scriptores Rerum Germanicarum in usum scholarum separatim editi*
NS	nova series
SSRL	*Scriptores Rerum Langobardicarum et Italicarum*
SSRM	*Scriptores Rerum Merovingicarum*

MIÖG	*Mitteilungen des Instituts für Österreichische Geschichtsforschung*
MOnG	*Mitteilungen der Österreichischen numismatischen Gesellschaft*
NChr	*Numismatic Chronicle*
n.s.	new series
P&P	*Past and Present*
PBSR	*Papers of the British School at Rome*
PL	*Patrologia Latina*
QK	*Quellen zur karolingischen Reichsgeschichte*, 3 vols, AQ vols V–VII, Darmstadt (1955–60)
RFA	*Annales Regni Francorum* / Royal Frankish Annals
RFA(Rev.)	*Annales qui dicuntur Einhardi* / Revised Version of the Royal Frankish Annals (traditionally attributed to Einhard)
RN	*Revue Numismatique*
Settimane	*Settimane di studio del centro italiano di studi sull'alto medioevo*
TRHS	*Transactions of the Royal Historical Society*

1 Charlemagne's Europe

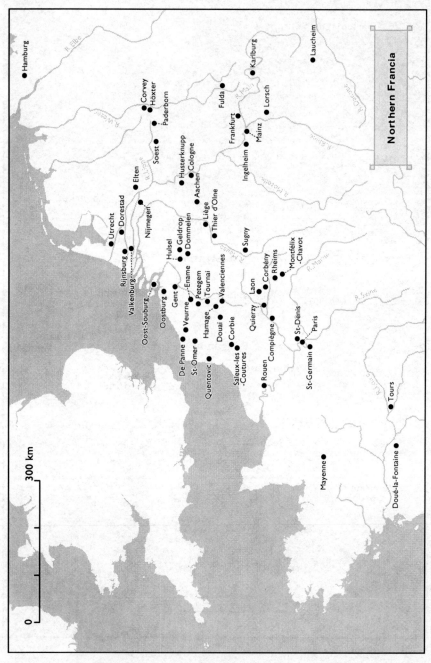

2 Northern Francia (places mentioned in the text)

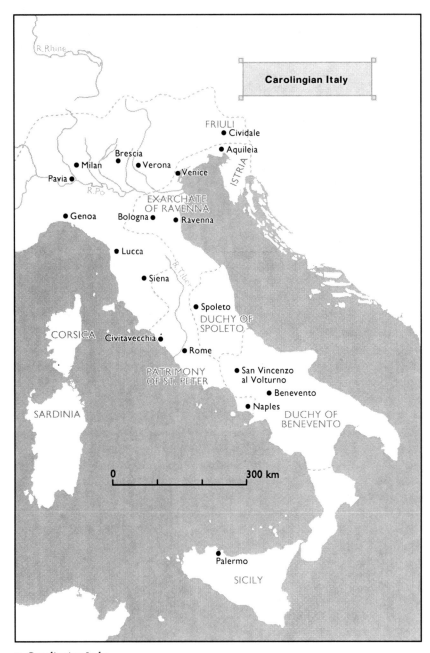

Carolingian Italy

R.Rhine

FRIULI
● Cividale

● Aquileia

Brescia
● Milan ● ● Verona
Pavia ● ● Venice

ISTRIA

EXARCHATE
OF RAVENNA
● Genoa Bologna ● ● Ravenna

● Lucca

● Siena

● Spoleto
DUCHY OF
SPOLETO

CORSICA Civitavecchia ●
● Rome

PATRIMONY
OF ST. PETER
● San Vincenzo
al Volturno
● Benevento
● Naples
DUCHY OF
BENEVENTO

SARDINIA

R.Po

R.Tiber

0   300 km

●
Palermo

SICILY

3 Carolingian Italy

CHARLEMAGNE'S REPUTATION

Joanna Story

In spring 775, an Anglo-Saxon scholar called Cathwulf wrote a letter to Charlemagne, celebrating the recent conquest of the Lombards by Frankish armies and the growing reputation of the young king. 'God has raised you', he said, 'to the honour of the kingdom of Europe's glory', and although Charlemagne was not yet thirty years old, Cathwulf predicted greater glory even than this if he continued to honour God and to serve the Church.[1] Cathwulf's letter is the earliest source to attribute Europe-wide influence to Charlemagne, but it was an idea that appealed to other Carolingian scholars, who returned to the theme as Charlemagne's reputation grew. The most forthright of these was the poet who composed the panegyric epic *Karolus magnus et Leo papa* not long after 800, and in it proclaimed Charlemagne as the 'beacon' and 'father of Europe' (*pharus Europae ... rex, pater Europae*).[2] The 'Europe' that the poet had in mind was not simply the kingdoms of the Franks and the Lombards that Charlemagne ruled; it included implicitly those Christian peoples beyond his borders, whose governance was illuminated by Charlemagne's equitable and far-reaching Christian kingship that was balanced perfectly by the spiritual authority of the papacy in Rome.

But, as the *Karolus* poet knew well, this idealised symbiosis of spiritual and temporal authority had been seriously undermined in April 799 by a bungled attempt to assassinate Pope Leo III and by the accusations of corruption levelled against him by his enemies in Rome. Leo's flight to Charlemagne's palace at Paderborn in early summer 799 (later eulogised by the *Karolus* poet) precipitated the series of events which culminated in the coronation of Charlemagne as emperor by the pope in the basilica of St Peter in Rome during the Christmas celebrations the following year. As the king rose from his prayers before the high altar, Leo placed a crown on his head, and he was acclaimed as emperor by the congregation in the manner of the emperors of ancient Rome. By taking on the

1

imperial title, Charlemagne not only revived the office of emperor in the West (not known there since 476) but, more seriously, challenged the supremacy of the Byzantine emperors in Constantinople, who claimed an unbroken succession from Constantine and Augustus.

Charlemagne's imperial coronation in Rome on Christmas Day 800 has always been regarded as one of those 'before-and-after' moments, a defining event that epitomises the spirit of an age and which shapes the historical interpretation of the period as a whole. It was controversial at the time, and has remained so. It took a decade for the Byzantines to recognise Charlemagne's imperial rank, and Einhard, Charlemagne's courtier and biographer, continued to protest even after the emperor's death that Charlemagne had 'disliked [the title] so much that, if he had known in advance of the pope's plan, he would not have entered the church that day'.[3] The question of whether Charlemagne owed his rank to the pope and thus owed his authority to rule to the Church in Rome, raised fundamental questions about the source of political authority, and became central to assessments of Charlemagne's achievements and reputation in later centuries. In the early sixteenth century, for example, Machiavelli recognised in the events of 799/800 the beginnings of the inexorable rise of papal power. Instead of sitting in judgment over a corrupt pope, Charlemagne had received from him the rank of emperor, creating a precedent for later holders of that office; 'by these means', Machiavelli reasoned, 'she [the papacy] constantly extended her authority over temporal princes'.[4]

Charlemagne's reputation has resonated down the twelve centuries since his imperial coronation and every age has found a Charlemagne to suit its needs. Since the tenth century, stories of his deeds have been retold and Charlemagne has been recast variously as a crusader to the Holy Land; as saint, pilgrim and relic collector; as an ideal lawgiver and the founder of universities; as a precursor of Reformation thought on icon and relic worship; as a slave-owning despot and genocidal murderer of the Saxons; as ancestor of French monarchs; or as founder of the first Germanic Reich and, thus, inspiration for the Third.[5]

There is a Charlemagne for every age and political expediency, but since 1945 it has been Charlemagne's credentials as the 'Father of Europe' that have held a particular attraction for politicians seeking a pan-European figurehead, most notably in the award of the *Karlspreis* ('Charlemagne Prize') given annually since 1950 to the statesman who has contributed most to the cause of European stability and unity. Charlemagne's kingdom, which had at its peak stretched across most of modern-day France, Germany and Italy, was a useful metaphor for Europe after the Second World War, where old enemies were to be allies and a vision of European economic unity and political cohesion was slowly becoming a reality. For example, in 1965 the 800th anniversary of Charlemagne's canonisation was marked by a major exhibition in Aachen sponsored by the Council of Europe, and a comparison between the lands of Charlemagne's Empire and the 'current European Economic Community' was explicit.[6]

Thirty years later, in 1996, Chancellor Kohl of Germany and President Chirac of France were patrons of an exhibition on the Merovingian Franks. It was shown in Berlin (former East Germany), Mannheim (former West Germany) and Paris (France), and had as its theme, 'The Franks: pioneers of Europe', underlining the common Frankish ancestry of the French and reunified German nations.[7] This was followed in 1999/2000 by a major series of exhibitions celebrating 'Charlemagne: the making of Europe'. Prompted by the 1200th anniversary of Pope Leo's trip to Paderborn, and the completion of extensive excavations at Charlemagne's palace there, the core exhibition at Paderborn was followed by an impressive series of comparative exhibitions in York (Britain), Brescia (Italy), Barcelona (Spain), and Split (Croatia).[8]

Each of these exhibitions, in its own way, reflected the trend towards regionalism within European identity at the turn of the twenty-first century. The last of these, 'Croats and Carolingians', sought to demonstrate through the material culture of the ninth and tenth centuries that the origins of the Croatian nation state are to be found in the western, Catholic tradition – the polar-opposite to the eastern, orthodox roots of Serbia. The Barcelona exhibition, 'Catalunya in the Carolingian age' implicitly recognised the regionality of modern Spain; the historical and linguistic ties of Catalunya lie northwards, to the Pyrenees and beyond. In Brescia we saw 'The future of the Lombards; Italy and the construction of Charlemagne's Europe', which placed northern Italy at the heart of the European project. And, though impressive in detail, the comparative scale of the UK exhibition, 'Alcuin and Charlemagne: the golden age of York', made the parochial British attitude concerning ties with Europe hard to miss.

When the US President, William Jefferson Clinton, received the Charlemagne Prize in June 2000, his speechwriter borrowed the *pharus* metaphor of the *Karolus* poet to account for the persistence of Charlemagne's reputation and his continued relevance to the twenty-first century, 'Twelve centuries ago, out of the long, dark night of endless tribal wars, there emerged a light that somehow has survived all the ravages of time, always burning brighter, always illuminating Europe's way to the future'.[9] Although historians may not choose to credit Charlemagne with such powers of percipience, his reputation undoubtedly has had remarkable staying power. This mythologising began in his lifetime: Cathwulf and the *Karolus* poet both wrote with an eye to posterity as much as to their patron, and the popularity of Einhard's *Life of Charlemagne* meant that it was his carefully-crafted account of the king that provided a template for Christian kingship throughout the Middle Ages.

The chapters in this book, however, are concerned more with Charlemagne's lifetime than with his afterlife in popular imagination and folk histories. The themes chosen are central to the evaluation of his reign and its impact on communities within and beyond Francia. Readers new to the period will find here much about text-based and archaeological sources, as well as syntheses of research and interpretations, old and new. For those for whom the period is more familiar, this volume provides a forum for a variety of voices whose individual perspectives on the age of Charlemagne collectively produce a new perception of the period. There are many other topics and themes that could have been included – on Spain and Byzantium, for example – but as it stands this book demonstrates not just the vibrance of modern scholarship but also how much more there is to be said about Charlemagne's empire and the societies over which he ruled.

Notes

1 Cathwulf, *Letter to Charlemagne*, MGH *Epp.* IV, pp. 502–5; Leyser (1992); Garrison (1998a); Story (1999).
2 *Karolus magnus et Leo papa*, MGH *PLAC* I, pp. 366–79, lines 12, 504; Dutton (1993), no. 12 and Godman (1985a), no. 25.
3 Einhard, *VK*, ch. 28.
4 Machiavelli, *The History of Florence*, I.11; trans. Detmold ed. (1882), I, p. 26.
5 Geary (2002); Becher (1999a), pp. 135–49; Morrissey (2003); Anderson (1991).
6 Braunfels, ed. (1965) and (1965–67).
7 Wieczorek (1996).
8 Stiegemann and Wemhoff, eds. (1999a) and (1999b); Garrison et al. eds. (2001); Camps, ed. (1999); Bertelli and Brogiolo, eds. (2000); Milosevic, ed. (2000). See also Bertelli et al. eds. (2001).
9 www.karlspreis.de.

THE LONG SHADOW
OF THE
MEROVINGIANS

Paul Fouracre

There is no entry in the *Guinness Book of Records* for the dynasty that ruled the longest in early medieval Europe. Were such an entry to exist, the Merovingian rulers of Francia, who survived for 274 years, would top the list. Second would be the line of Ecgbert of Wessex: they were around for 264 years, if we discount the Danish interlude, that is. And in third place, at 236 years, would come the Carolingians. Trailing well behind would be Mercians, Salians, Ottonians and Amals, not to mention those families of rulers whose success was too brief or too intermittent for historians to refer to them as 'dynasties' at all. Of these dynasties, only the Carolingians are on record as having disparaged their predecessors. The question of why the Carolingians felt the need to do so is the concern of this chapter.

To heap scorn on their predecessors was, of course, an obvious strategy for a new dynasty that wished to justify what amounted to a *coup d'état* against their legitimate overlords. But when we unpack the derogatory statements that Carolingian writers made about the Merovingians, we find that, though their general purpose is obvious, the detail of the attacks upon the Merovingians still requires careful consideration. We must explain, above all, why Carolingian authors should have situated the collapse of Merovingian power in the late seventh century, a time when the regime seems to have been in relatively good shape, rather than in the time of Charles Martel, the leader whose triumphs really put the old dynasty in the shade.[1]

Kings in name only

Einhard's characterisation of the Merovingian dynasty as decrepit is unforgettable. The Merovingians, he says (in the opening chapter of his *Life of Charlemagne*) 'had lost all power' years before King Childeric III was deposed by Charlemagne's father Pippin in 751. They had lost everything except 'the empty title of king'. Real power rested with the leading officials of the court, the 'mayors of the palace'. The kings merely had to 'act the part of a ruler', that is, in receiving ambassadors and presiding over assemblies, but being directed in this by others. Finally, the ruler cut a ridiculous figure, travelling from the single farm he owned, to the annual assemblies and back again on a lumbering ox-cart.[2] Although it is acknowledged that Einhard was being unfair on this last point (the Merovingians were not being ridiculous when they rode on ox-carts; they were continuing late-Roman practices of transporting the governor's writing office),[3] his picture of the last Merovingians as mere figureheads – *reges inutiles* ('useless kings') or, more familiarly in French, the *rois fainéants* ('do-nothing kings') – retains a powerful hold on the imagination.

We find the same image of useless Merovingians in the *Annales Mettenses Priores* (the Earlier Annals of Metz), a kind of Carolingian house-history composed about the year 805, thus nearly a generation earlier than Einhard's *Life of Charlemagne*.[4] In the Earlier Annals of Metz the image is much more elaborate and it is reinforced with quasi-historical detail. The work begins with the rise to power of Charlemagne's great-grandfather, Pippin of Herstal, first in Austrasia and then throughout Francia. The first section relates how Pippin's father Ansegisel had been killed by a man called Gundoin. When Pippin grew up, he tracked down and killed Gundoin, thereafter taking power in Austrasia. This episode has been rejected as legend, and it is true that, unlike the rest of the text, one cannot identify any written source upon which the story might have been based. But one can find a plausible historical context for the tale.[5]

Gundoin was a member of a family which had long been rivals to that of Pippin. Pippin's family had been driven from power in the early 660s, and had been replaced by Gundoin's family as leaders of the Austrasian nobility. It thus seems highly likely that Pippin would have had to overcome Gundoin in order to become leader. In starting with the Gundoin slaying, the author of the Earlier Annals of Metz began his, or her, history in the mid-670s at the latest, and with the focus squarely upon Pippin of Herstal. Pippin's family were the natural leaders of Austrasia, Gundoin had been a murderous interloper and Pippin had put things right. The author then constructed a careful justification of the extension of Carolingian (or 'Pippinid') power over the rest of Francia by detailing the unfortunate consequences of Merovingian inaction. We learn at some length, therefore, how in the year 687 it was necessary for Pippin to fight against the Merovingian king, Theuderic III, in order to wipe out the injustices which had grown up under the indolent kings and their arrogant and greedy mayors of the palace. After his victory in 687 at the famous battle of Tertry (made famous, incidentally, by this very work), Pippin himself became mayor and proceeded to rule the Frankish lands in all but name. Dutifully he oversaw the accession of Theuderic's sons, but 'giving these men the name of kings, he kept the reins of the whole realm and governed with the highest glory and honour'. It was Pippin who conducted the kings to the annual assemblies and stage-managed them, and it was Pippin who dealt with the ambassadors of foreign peoples.[6] This is the scenario which Einhard reduced to a few sentences about the kings who 'had lost all power'.

Both texts prepared the way for the Carolingians to take the royal title by stressing that under the last Merovingians power had become divorced from royalty. It was the duty of the Carolingians to reunite the 'name' of king with the power that a king should exercise. As the Earlier Annals of Metz had it, the Merovingian charade had become not just embarrassing, but also morally indefensible because it led to injustice. In a very long section explaining why it was necessary for Pippin to invade Neustria and attack the Merovingian king, Theuderic III, and his mayor, Berchar, we learn that many Neustrians had fled to Pippin to escape the oppressive regime of their own land.[7] In particular, many had been wrongly deprived of inheritances. Finding it impossible to obtain justice in Neustria, they petitioned Pippin to take up their cause. The latter's invasion was thus seen to be in the name of justice, and the Battle of Tertry itself was the judgment of God.

It would, however, be the pope (the ultimate arbiter of Christian power and morality) who in effect called time on the Merovingians by switching his support to the Carolingians as the family more fit to rule, because it was the most powerful in the land. By the time the Earlier Annals of Metz were composed, this idea was already at least a generation old. It is in the *Continuations of the Chronicle of Fredegar* that we first meet the notion that it was the pope who sanctioned the transfer of royalty from Merovingians to Carolingians.[8] The passage in question was probably written no later than 751, and certainly not later that 768.[9] It amounts to a statement that after having sent an embassy to Rome, Pippin and his wife Bertrada were made king and queen on the order and authority of the pope, as well as with the agreement of the Franks. By the late 780s, at the latest, this short statement had been embellished so that it voiced the kind of concerns about the divorce of name and power that we meet in later sources. According to the Royal Frankish Annals, in 749 the Frankish legates (who are now named) asked the pope, Zacharias, a specific question: 'whether it was good or not that the kings of the Franks should wield no power, as was the case at the time'. Pope Zacharias's reply was that 'it was better to call him king who had the royal power than the one who did not'.[10] He then commanded by virtue of his apostolic authority that Pippin be made king. The agreement of the Franks was no longer mentioned.

It thus seems clear that by the time of Charlemagne, and probably by the time he became king in 768 – so, well before Einhard wrote – the picture of the last Merovingians as names without power, whose royal title was transferred to the Carolingians by order of the pope, was already well established. The Royal Frankish Annals, which provide the definitive version, celebrated Carolingian success so consistently and so unconditionally that it is thought that they were more or less the mouthpiece of the new regime.[11] If so, it follows that their account of the transfer of royalty in 751 amounts to what we might term 'an official line'. The same line, albeit in garbled form, and misplaced, appears in an early ninth-century Byzantine text, *The Chronicle of Theophanes*. Theophanes (d. 818), placed the 753–54 visit of Pope Stephen II to Francia in the years 723–24, and tells how Stephen raised Pippin to the throne. He describes the Merovingians in basically the same terms later used by Einhard, but adds that they 'did nothing except eat and drink inordinately'. Their famous long hair he misinterpreted as bristles sprouting from their backs, like pigs. He also apparently thought that it was Pippin, rather than Pippin's father Charles Martel, who was victor over the Arabs. This may suggest that, having been formulated at the Carolingian court, this version of events then travelled outwards with Frankish ambassadors to other peoples.[12]

Justifying the illegal

The determination of the Carolingians to put out a clear, consistent and coherent message about how, and why, they had come to power, is perfectly under-standable. The Merovingians, as we have seen, had ruled longer than any other family in Europe. The holding of political office, the operation of the law courts, the summoning of assemblies and armies, and the practice of religion were all sanctioned by royal authority. The Merovingians were, in short, a chief source for the legitimation of power in Francia. The other source was God, but divine approval could not so much legitimate power as be cited as justification for holding or taking it. What the Carolingians did to the Merovingians was strictly illegal: they forcibly deposed the king, and they must have been aware that a seventh-century ancestor of theirs had been put to death for deposing his lord, a Merovingian. The Carolingians were never in a position to question the legitimacy of Merovingian royalty, but sought instead justification on moral grounds for the transfer of that royalty to themselves. The Merovingians had become so feeble that they ignored the harm being done to their subjects. It was therefore incumbent upon the Carolingians, as the stronger power, to make themselves kings in order to secure justice, that is, to make sure that the Franks were ruled justly, and to protect the weak. Pippin fought the Battle of Tertry to uphold the rights of those who had been unjustly exiled from Neustria. After the battle, according to the Earlier Annals of Metz, he 'set right all the confiscations which in those regions had come about over many years through the greed and injustice of the leaders'. When peace had been restored, he then turned to the 'well-being of the churches, orphans and widows'.[13] This sense of moral obligation would remain a guiding principle of Carolingian government thereafter, for it served as a reminder of the new dynasty's right to rule.

For the papacy, the concept of justice related primarily to the 'rights of St Peter' (*iusticia beati Petri*), that is, to the protection of the property and rights of the papacy.[14] In the mid-eighth century this meant above all protection from the Lombard rulers of Italy, and it was the wish to gain the support of the Franks against the Lombards that led the popes to support the Carolingians. This is clear from the earliest letters in the *Codex Carolinus*, the Carolingian copy of correspondence between the ruling family and the papacy. Five of the first eight letters in the collection, from the period 739–56, beg for help against the Lombards. The strongest support for the new dynasty came in fact not in 749 or in 751, but in 754 when Pope Stephen II anointed Pippin, Bertrada, and their sons Charles and Carloman, and declared that henceforth the Franks should choose their kings only from this family.[15] Stephen's declaration was the last move in a successful campaign to get Pippin to commit himself to intervening in Italy to protect the rights of St Peter. In the minds of Carolingian authors this rather pragmatic endorsement, with its very concrete aim, would be understood as unconditional support freely and justly given.

Given the problems of establishing their own legitimacy, it is easy to see why the Carolingians felt the need to justify the deposition of the last Merovingian in terms of the dynasty's loss of power and its inability to deliver justice. And equally one can understand how they read into the practical negotiations with the papacy a more abstract statement of moral support. In the Earlier Annals of Metz we can see in some detail how a more elaborate justification was crafted from a reading of earlier texts. Important here is the late seventh-century *Passio Leudegarii* (The 'Passion', or death, of Leudgar, bishop and martyr of Autun).[16] Although this work had nothing to say about the ancestors of the Carolingians, it did provide a graphic example of a greedy and wicked mayor, Ebroin (d. *circa* 680), and a clear warning about how an unscrupulous mayor (Ebroin, again) might keep a king in the background and 'just use his name' which would allow the mayor 'to do harm to whomsoever he wished, with impunity'.[17]

Chief among Ebroin's sins was the persecution unto death of the hero of this work, Bishop Leudegar. Ebroin's persecution of Leudegar is remembered in the Earlier Annals of Metz, and becomes one of the sources of injustice which Pippin was driven to correct. There was another reason to suggest that Pippin triumphed over Ebroin's legacy, for back in the 670s Ebroin had soundly beaten Pippin in battle.[18] After he became mayor, Pippin is portrayed as the opposite of Ebroin. As we have already seen, he used his position of dominance over the king to do good. He protected the weak and fought for justice, restoring to their inheritances all those whom Ebroin had unjustly exiled. The *Passio Leudegarii*, in short, provided just the material that was needed to portray a political establishment in urgent need of fresh blood and reform.

Two other sources strongly influenced the narrative of the Earlier Annals of Metz. These are the *Liber Historiae Francorum* (LHF for short) and the *Continuations of the Chronicle of Fredegar*. The *LHF* is a Neustrian chronicle, roughly the last third of which dealt with the history of the Franks in the seventh and early eighth centuries. It closes in the year 721, although the author said that he, or she, was writing in 727. This work is strongly in favour of the Neustrian Franks and their Merovingian kings.[19] The *Continuations of Fredegar* cover the period from about 650 to 768.[20] Up to 721 the *Continuations* followed the narrative of the *LHF* fairly closely, although they toned down some of the latter's pro-Merovingian sentiment, and left out the episode in which a Carolingian ancestor was put to death for treason. After 721, the *Continuations* tell a story of unqualified success for the Carolingians, starting with the military triumphs of Charles Martel and leading up through the coronation of Pippin in 751 to his victories as king, and the successful handing on of power to the next generation in 768.

The Earlier Annals of Metz contested the pro-Neustrian and pro-Merovingian narrative of the *LHF*, and this is one reason why the author spent so much time on the events of the later seventh and early eighth centuries. We can see this, for instance, in the passage quoted earlier in which Pippin dutifully made the sons of Theuderic III kings. The passage comes at the end of a description of the just and pious way in Pippin ran the kingdom, and as we saw, it concludes first with the statement that it was Pippin who gave the title of king to the sons, and second with a reiteration of the fact that it was Pippin who 'governed with the highest glory and honour'. Here the author seems to have been reacting against the *LHF*, which singled out one of Theuderic's sons, Childebert III (*r.* 695–711) as a rather special king. He was 'celebrated', and a 'famous and just lord ... of good memory', for which there is supporting evidence in the form of original charters, which not only show people from all over Francia attending Childebert's court, but also record judgments made by his assemblies against Pippin's family itself.[21] Childebert, it is clear, was no *roi fainéant*, and he was certainly not Pippin's poodle. Hence the need to say that he was.

Charles Martel

Once the narrative passed beyond the period covered by the *LHF*, the author of the Earlier Annals of Metz could relax. He or she followed the text of the *Continuations* with few additions, for the fiercely pro-Carolingian sentiments of this account could scarcely be improved upon. It followed the career of Charles Martel (Pippin of Herstal's son, and Charlemagne's grandfather) from the point at which he stood alone against the Neustrians, Frisians and Saxons to his death in 741, before which he divided all the Frankish territories between his sons, as if he were a king. On the way there were campaigns against all the peoples who had once obeyed the Merovingians but who had slipped away as the dynasty had decayed. And most famously, in the year 733, Charles Martel fought and beat the Arabs at the battle of Poitiers, a moment over which the *Continuations* lingered in triumph.[22] After 741, the account turns to the heroic struggles of Charles Martel's sons. They subdued the Aquitainians, Alemans, Bavarians and Saxons, who had revolted as soon as Charles Martel was dead. Then one of the sons, Carloman, departed the scene to become a monk in Italy. This act, say the *Continuations* strengthened the position of the other brother, Pippin.[23] Four years later, this strength would be recognised by the pope, who, as we have seen, sanctioned the transfer of royalty to Pippin as one who already had the power of king.

On the face of it, the narrative of the mid-eighth century – as we read it in the *Continuations* – seems to provide much more promising material for the Carolingian rewriting of history than that of the earlier period in which the Earlier Annals of Metz set the decline of the Merovingians and the rise of the Carolingians. Certainly more was known about the time of Charles Martel, even given the fact that the author had good sources for the era of Pippin of Herstal. Einhard did stress the importance of Charles Martel as one who crushed despots and defeated the Arabs, but this he placed after the description of the last Merovingians. He also made it clear that Charles Martel inherited his power from Pippin of Herstal. It was thus Pippin who had rescued the Franks from the ailing regime of the Merovingians. Charles Martel then took the next step in eliminating those despots who still troubled the Franks, and in driving back the Arabs.[24]

For the author of the Earlier Annals of Metz, why could Charles Martel and his sons not be portrayed as model rulers? After all, they won all their battles, reasserted Frankish control over a host of peoples and saved Francia from the 'pagan' Arabs? To situate the triumph back in the later seventh century, moreover, actively created problems. It may have been the need to counter the pro-Merovingian narrative of the *LHF* which focused Carolingian attention on Pippin of Herstal's triumph in 687 and, as we have seen, the *Passio Leudegarii* did provide material relating to this period which could be spun in the direction of the Carolingians. But to build up Pippin's regime as the perfect antidote to the tyranny of Ebroin, left the author of the Earlier Annals of Metz with the difficult task of explaining how the regime fell apart as soon as Pippin was dead. For after his death at the end of 714, his family was thrown out of power in Neustria and probably in southern Austrasia too. It was attacked on all sides, and there was a struggle within the family, which led to Charles Martel being imprisoned by his step-mother Plectrude, Pippin's widow.[25] It is really at this point that the rise of the Carolingians begins, in the person of Charles Martel and in the form of incessant military campaigning for a whole generation. In this sense, the age of Pippin of Herstal was a false dawn. So why concentrate upon it? One answer could be that the time of Charles Martel was just too difficult to deal with other than in terms of a narrative of military successes. Unlike the earlier period, it was within the horizon of living memory, and memories of Charles Martel are likely to have been particularly bitter.

The figure of Charles Martel presents plenty of problems to the modern historian too. We know from the *LHF* that he was born about the time of the battle of Tertry, and that he was a son of Pippin.[26] From the *Continuations of Fredegar* we learn the name of his mother, Alpaida, but we know nothing more about her and we are left guessing about who might have been related to Charles on his mother's side.[27] The indications are that Charles Martel was a rather insignificant member of the Pippinid family, and that it was only the death of the three leading males of the family and the crisis which followed in 715 that propelled him to the forefront. He may therefore have been regarded as something of a *parvenu* and there was certainly fierce resistance to him, not least from members of his own family.

There are interesting parallels between Charles Martel and the old Neustrian mayor of the palace, Ebroin, whom the Earlier Annals of Metz set up as the paradigm of the bad ruler. Both Charles and Ebroin were military strongmen, who used force to stay in power. They both broke with the political consensus through which the mayors of the palace brokered the interests of regional leaders and the concerns of royal government. What followed in both cases was a marginalisation of the kings, and violent intervention in the provinces. This meant exiling or even killing recalcitrant bishops and an alienation from the palace of leading provincial magnates, though we are, of course, much better informed about what happened to the bishops than to the secular leaders. When excluded from the palace, both leaders set up their own Merovingian kings. Ebroin raised a boy called Clovis to the throne in 675,[28] and Charles Martel raised up another called Clothar in 717.[29]

Clovis was discarded as soon as Ebroin had fought his way back to power and had control of the established king, Theuderic III. Clothar died rather conveniently as soon as Charles Martel had beaten his Neustrian enemies in 718 and had arranged for the return of the rightful king, Chilperic II. In both cases, this was puppetry on a grand scale 'just using the names', without paying due respect to royal lords. But Charles Martel went even further than Ebroin here, for when in 737 King Theuderic IV died, Charles continued as mayor of the palace without a king, but still used his name. No Carolingian source tells us this, but we can detect the interregnum from charters, including one issued by Charles himself, which are dated according to the number of years since the death of Theuderic. Charles's last charter, drawn up the month before he died (October 741), is dated 'in the fifth year after the death of King Theuderic'.[30]

Under both men, persecuted church leaders became saints – that is to say, their victims were seen as having suffered for the Church and accounts of their ordeals were recorded in Saints' Lives. In Ebroin's case we saw this in relation to Bishop Leudegar, whose sufferings were set down in the *Passio Leudegarii*. Charles Martel's saintly nemesis was Eucherius, bishop of Orléans, who was exiled in 733. Although he was not killed, he died in exile, and the *Vita Eucherii* was composed shortly after his death.[31] To become a villain in a Saint's Life was likely to result in a permanent stain upon one's reputation. Where Ebroin was concerned, we have already seen how, 125 years after the event, his persecution of Leudegar still figured in the Earlier Annals of Metz as a terrible example of evil. Even at the end of the ninth century, Ebroin's name could still evoke shades of the diabolical. In the *Chronicle of Ado*, a work from southern Burgundy, one of Ebroin's victims, blinded by the mayor, was praying by the bank of the River Rhône when he heard the sound of his tormentor being rowed to hell.[32]

The same work makes an oblique reference to Charles Martel, in that it laments the destruction of the Church in the region at the hands of the Franks, telling of one Bishop Willicarius of Vienne who could bear its suffering no longer and chose to retreat into a monastery.[33] Willicarius was very probably one of the bishops driven out by Charles, along with Eucherius of Orléans. The *Chronicle of Ado* here relates what is a very familiar scene. It is one in which churches lost much of their lands to greedy laymen who were the followers of Charles Martel. This picture of 'secularisation' becomes almost standard in those later ninth-century narratives which deal with the period. The ultimate source for this perception was the *Vita Eucherii* which told of how Charles Martel distributed the lands of the church of Orléans to his followers (*satellites*).

It was Hincmar, the highly influential archbishop of Rheims from 845 to 882, who was responsible for making Eucherius's experience stand for Charles Martel's treatment of the Church in general. In a letter of 858 written to the kings of East and West Francia, Hincmar claimed 'that of all the kings and princes of the Franks', Charles Martel 'was the first to take property away from the Church and to divide it up'. This statement he underlined with an account of a vision which Eucherius was supposed to have had in exile. It was of Charles Martel's tomb in the monastery of St Denis, which was found to be empty, but bore the scorch marks left by the dragon which had dragged him off to hell, his sin being the way in which he had treated the Church.[34] In a later work, the *Vita Rigoberti* (the Life of Rigobert of Rheims, another bishop who had been driven out by Charles Martel), Hincmar labelled Charles *non rex sed tyrannus* ('not a king but a tyrant'), as one who had unjustly wielded power.[35] Einhard had used the term *tyranni* for the despots whom Charles Martel crushed; that Hincmar should use the term for Charles himself reflects the very strong conviction in the later ninth century that he had indeed robbed the Church. Ebroin had likewise been termed a *tyrannus* in the *Passio Leudegarii*. Of the two, Charles Martel was surely the bigger tyrant.

Though both men would enter written memory as personifications of injustice, it can be argued that in reality Charles Martel did far more than Ebroin to break up the political establishment. It would, in other words, have been very difficult to portray him, as the Earlier Annals of Metz did his father Pippin, as one who preserved order and restored justice. Ebroin's tyranny was short-lived, and though he drove out one particular political faction, order and consensus was soon restored. It was in this sense a regime in good working order that Pippin won for himself at the Battle of Tertry, seven years after Ebroin's death.

What happened after Pippin himself died at the end of 714 is too complex a story to explain in detail here, but there are a few points that do bear directly upon Carolingian perceptions of the past. The first is that there was resistance to the leadership of Charles Martel from Pippin's widow Plectrude and her grandsons. Charles Martel, we know, was imprisoned by Plectrude. Even after he had escaped at the end of 715, had marshalled resistance against forces invading Austrasia and beaten his Neustrian enemies in battle in 717, he still had to turn his forces on Plectrude before she would yield up Pippin's treasure and effectively acknowledge his position as leader.[36] It was not until 724 that her grandsons were dealt with, and one of them apparently remained a threat as late as 741 when Charles died.[37] The second point is that from his escape in 715 to his death in 741 hardly a year went by without Charles Martel having to fight, and in several years he fought more than one enemy. He clearly he had a lot of enemies, and it was nearly always necessary to use force to get them to accept his authority. After he died, many of those he had fought, beaten and subdued, refused to accept the authority of his sons, and the fighting began again.

The author of the Earlier Annals of Metz explained this fighting (beginning again in the time of Pippin of Herstal) as necessary and justified in order to bring back into the fold those peoples whom Merovingian indolence had allowed to slip into independence, and it is still often said in history textbooks that it took the vigour of the Carolingians to reverse the separatist tendencies of the Frankish regions. A more subtle modern view is that those who resisted Charles Martel were not trying to break away from the kingdom of the Franks, but were fighting to preserve their privileges within the Merovingian order. The Agilolfing dukes of Bavaria, for instance, claimed the right to rule as office-holders of the Merovingian kings. Bavarians could be ruled only by members of the Agilolfing family, who had been appointed to that task by the Merovingians. But since the Agilolfings had also married into the Carolingian family, this made them very difficult to deal with.[38] In addition, magnates in the peripheral regions had strong family links with magnates elsewhere in the kingdom, and it is thought that as Charles Martel defeated the leading families in Austrasia and Neustria, resistance was carried on by their relatives in other regions, where there also gathered refugees and enemies from earlier encounters.[39]

Not surprisingly, therefore, the fighting seems to grow fiercer, the deeper into the regions it progressed. Nor is it surprising that in 743 when Charles's sons Pippin and Carloman were hard-pressed by the revolts, they found it expedient to raise up another (and the last), Merovingian king, Childeric III, the son of Theuderic IV who had died back in 737. No Carolingian narrative tells us of Childeric's accession, and again, we must deduce it from charter material; in a charter he issued in July 744, Childeric addressed Carloman as the one 'who placed us upon the throne of the kingdom'.[40] Raising another Merovingian to the throne was surely designed to take the wind out of legitimist opposition.

Nevertheless, force was still needed to crush the leaders on the periphery. In so doing, the Carolingians clawed their way to that position of supremacy that Pope Zacharias was said to have recognised.

We have seen that Einhard, and the author of the Earlier Annals of Metz, wished to portray the ancestors of Charlemagne as leaders who took power in order to preserve order. They were shown to have honoured the kings and to have treated the magnates justly. The Earlier Annals of Metz go further and stress the selflessness of Pippin in taking on the impious regime of Theuderic and Berchar, his arrogant mayor. One can now see why it was preferable to set this ideal behaviour in the late seventh rather than in the mid-eighth century. Charles Martel could be then be portrayed as a military hero who recovered and defended what Pippin had achieved. The *Continuations of the Chronicle of Fredegar* did this by comparing Charles to the Old Testament warrior and judge Joshua, which invited further comparison between the Franks and the Israelites. No more justification for Charles's attacks upon his neighbours was needed. He was simply righteous, and all his enemies were, by implication, the enemies of the Lord. This was very much a post-Merovingian way of thinking, and one perfectly suited to a regime forged in battle.

Conflict within the Carolingian family in the mid-eighth century was another good reason for situating that family's triumph in the time of Pippin of Herstal. It could also be that later Carolingian authors were as ignorant as we are about Charles Martel's maternal ancestry. Concentrating on the family in the seventh century was a way of giving him illustrious ancestors, including women. By the time the Earlier Annals of Metz were written, St Arnulf of Metz (an early seventh-century leader whose cult was growing strongly in Metz in the later eighth century) was being claimed as one of the family's ancestors, and the family had another saint in Pippin's aunt, Gertrude, abbess of Nivelles (d. *circa* 653). Not only, therefore, was Pippin of Herstal an ideal leader, but his family included two saints. This was one less than the Merovingians could boast, but better, for whereas Pippin's saintly forebears were of ancient Frankish lineage, the Merovingian saints were all queens of non-Frankish origin. It was, in short, a family worthy of royalty. But Charles Martel had tried to destroy all but his branch of it, and after his death the history of the family becomes even less salubrious.

Skeletons in the Carolingian cupboard

In his *Life of Charlemagne*, Einhard said that it would be impossible to write about the birth or childhood of Charlemagne, for of this there was no written record, nor anyone still living who knew about it.[41] This seems unlikely. Surely Einhard could at least have told of how in the year 753, Charlemagne, then only five years old, had been sent out to accompany Pope Stephen for the last hundred miles of his journey to the Frankish court. We know of this because Stephen II's biography tells us that it happened, and this is a work which was also available to Einhard.[42] It is more likely that Einhard did not wish to talk about Charlemagne's birth and childhood because there were too many skeletons in the family cupboard. Let us briefly examine the remains, for the final phase of the family's history, before 754, holds the key to the way in which they wished to present the past.

Charles Martel had two wives (in sequence) and an unknown number of concubines. By them he had at least seven children. Three children born to concubines seem never to have been close to power. Three other sons were included in his plans for the division of the Frankish lands. The other child, a daughter, Chiltrude, put herself outside the immediate family by running off with Odilo the duke of Bavaria.[43] This was seen as terrible scandal and, because she and Odilo had a son (Tassilo) who inherited the duchy, the match later caused great problems for Charlemagne when he decided to crush Bavarian independence.[44] Carolingian involvement with Bavaria was in fact deep, for Charles Martel's second wife, Swanahild, was of Bavarian, and even Agilolfing, stock. It was said to have been at Swanahild's urging that Chiltrude (who was not her daughter) ran off to Bavaria. Swanahild and Charles Martel had a son, Grifo. In 741 both Grifo and Swanahild were driven out by Pippin and Carloman, Charles's sons by his first wife. After several attempts to fight back, Grifo was killed in 753.[45]

Carloman was the older brother. In 741 he was about thirty-three years old, and married with at least one son. Pippin was aged about twenty-six, and unmarried. He would not marry for three more years, nor have a son, the future Charlemagne, until 2 April 748.[46] It has been argued that as things stood before Charlemagne's birth, it would have seemed certain that in the future Carloman's descendants would be the ones to lead both the family and the Franks. Charter evidence has been quoted to suggest that it was Carloman who was the prime mover in raising Childeric III, and that he did this to protect his sons within a reconstituted palace community. One cannot prove this on the basis of a single charter, and it seems much more likely that the motive for raising another king was, as suggested earlier, the defeat of those rebelling against the Carolingians as unlawful rulers. Nonetheless, the suggestion that Carloman might have seen the reconstitution of the Merovingian palace as a way of protecting his interests is a plausible one.

In 747, after the defeat of the rebels, Carloman went to Rome, leaving his sons in the care of Pippin and Childeric. The oldest son, Drogo, was almost certainly of majority age in 747. There are indications that he now became mayor of the palace to Childeric, and given that Pippin had no children, Drogo's position was at this stage strong.[47] All this changed with the birth of Charlemagne on 2 April 748. Pippin now began to manoeuvre against Drogo, persuading Pope Zacharias to keep Carloman in Italy as a monk (this had not necessarily been Carloman's intention in going to Rome), and at the same time seeking Zacharias's support for some plan to make himself king. Getting rid of Childeric was, in this view, the key to dissolving the order left by Carloman and in elevating Pippin beyond the other members of the family. It took two more years of preparation before Pippin took this last step in 751, but there remained significant resistance to the move. Drogo and Grifo were still at large, and in 753 it was necessary for the pope, Stephen II, to write to the other Frankish leaders telling them to support Pippin or suffer perdition. He then, as we know, came in person to Francia. Carloman followed him, possibly to rally support for Drogo, although an early ninth-century, revised version of the Royal Frankish Annals said that he came to Francia to plead the cause of the Lombards.[48] In this version, an unwilling Carloman was ordered by his abbot (of Monte Cassino) to oppose the pope's request for help against Lombards; an interpretation which had the virtue of explaining Carloman's action in terms of necessary monastic obedience. But on his arrival he was put under house arrest, and died in 755. Also in 753 Drogo and an unnamed brother were tonsured and sent to a monastery, and Grifo was killed. It was now that Pope Stephen solemnly anointed Pippin, his wife Bertrada and their sons, declaring that henceforth the kings of the Franks should be chosen from their seed only.

This scenario, which has been reconstructed from charter evidence rather than from pro-Carolingian narratives, is rather conjectural. It is nevertheless persuasive in suggesting that the *coup d'état* of 751 was aimed as much at ensuring Pippin's dominance within the Carolingian family as it was at redressing the imbalance of power between Merovingians and Carolingians. It was, in this view, only in the generation after 754, when this one branch had become so pre-eminent that it determined the identity of the whole family, that authors close to the Carolingians began to rewrite history in terms of Merovingian decadence, and Carolingian moral superiority that went back to the seventh century. The events leading up to 754 were, by contrast, not ones which could be used to cast glory upon Charlemagne's family.

Writing off the Merovingians

Let us close by seeking to understand the denigration of the Merovingians in the wider historical context. We have seen that Pippin of Herstal's victory at the Battle of Tertry did not mark the end of the old order, but actually served to strengthen it by ending the exclusion of Austrasians from the Merovingian palace. A break did come, however, with prolonged conflict in the time of Charles Martel and his sons. The power of the old elite in Neustria, Burgundy and southern Austrasia was broken. The ducal families of Alsace, Alemannia, Aquitaine, Frisia, Thuringia and eventually Bavaria, lost their power and privileges and disappeared. These regions and others, such as Hesse, Provence and Rhaetia, were then more fully incorporated into the Frankish kingdom. Some Franks close to the Carolingians were given important positions in these new provinces, and at the same time the native nobilities of the peripheral regions were more firmly tied into the centre both by the demands made upon them by the rulers, and through their own desire to emulate Frankish ways, and to share in the success and prosperity of the new regime.

In the later Merovingian period, although Aquitaine was in economic and cultural terms much on a par with the central region of Francia, the areas which lay in what is now Germany, were not. Catching up with the centre amounted to the foundation of monasteries and the organization of a fledgling Church into bishoprics, the use of charters to record property transactions, the spread of coinage and the introduction of Frankish local government led by counts. The effect of such developments in social terms was a strengthening of the position of the local nobility, whose property rights came to be better defined and who could prosper by serving the Franks. Settlement patterns changed as peasants were grouped to work estates which gave the nobles a more direct income, and the church led the way in the organisation of land and people in this manner. Nobles became patrons and clients of local churches and monasteries, and this further reinforced their social power. These shifts were in progress before the Carolingians arrived. Indeed, one could reason that it was because the local nobility had become better resourced, and better armed as a consequence, that the peripheral regions were able to resist the Carolingians so effectively. But by the same token, once their resistance had been broken, the way was open for a rapid integration into the mainstream of Frankish culture. By the mid-Carolingian period there was no longer much cultural difference between centre and periphery in the Frankish empire.[49]

It is important to identify this new constituency as a possible audience for accounts of Merovingian failings and Carolingian virtues. Another factor here was the sudden disappearance in 751 of the position of mayor of the palace. In the past the mayor had been a figure of mediation between king and nobility. He was usually the representative of the most powerful faction of magnates, and his role should be understood within the context of factional politics. The Carolingians crushed other political factions and kept the mayoralty for themselves. Then when Pippin was elevated from mayor to king he in effect combined both roles, dealing directly with the magnates. There were no longer any factional groupings, and no prime-ministerial figure who could be used to check the powers of the ruler. All attention now focused on the king. Even the ruling family had been narrowed down to that focus. In this sense there was indeed a new order after 751, but it was one in constant need of justification and historical explanation, not least to those most recently recruited to the regime.

The denigration of the Merovingians was part of a much larger ideological campaign to justify and reinforce Carolingian power. Ideas of justice, papal support, divine sanction, orthodoxy and purity in religion, military success, moral correction, reform and wisdom range through all genres of Carolingian writing.

By the time the Earlier Annals of Metz were composed, the perception of the past was also determined by the recent experience of Charlemagne's coronation as emperor, and it is important to remember that the audience of this work would have had the elevation of Charlemagne in mind when they heard how the Carolingians became kings. The description of Pippin of Herstal's triumph was peppered with the language of empire.[50] Success was thereby the ultimate justification for the Carolingians, and they contrasted their vigour with the torpor of the Merovingians to show that they deserved their success.

In a passage written after Charlemagne's death, the so-called 'Revised' version of the Royal Frankish Annals commented on the year 790, a year in which unusually there was no military campaign. Nevertheless, 'so it would not seem that he had grown idle and soft with leisure', Charlemagne sailed up the River Main and down again.[51] What a contrast with the Merovingians. Was it not over-kill to keep on drawing the contrast, over sixty years after the disappearance of the old dynasty? It seems not, for in those intervening years the Carolingians had made themselves the focal point not just of political life, but also of religious and cultural life. As rulers they had become much more ambitious, claiming the right to intervene in more and more areas of their subjects' lives. In a regime in which custom still determined most aspects of social behaviour, every new step required justification, and none more so than the massive break with the past which was made when the Carolingians deposed the last Merovingian.

Everything they did thereafter had to justify that act. We have seen that the Carolingians thought long and hard about how to explain what had happened, and we have suggested why they placed the triumph a good half-century earlier than one might have expected. The attacks upon the reputation of the Merovingians were very successful, but nothing could alter the fact which made the denigration necessary, namely, that in terms of survival and continuity of rule the Merovingians achieved more than any other West European dynasty of the period. Within a generation of 751, the Carolingians began to take Merovingian names for their children, for these were proper royal names (Louis = Clovis; Lothar = Clothar). The Merovingians may have been 'shadow kings', but their shadow was long indeed.

Notes

1 Fouracre (2000); Jarnut et al., eds. (1994).
2 Einhard, *VK*, c. 1.
3 Wood (1994), p. 102.
4 *Annales Mettenses Priores (AMP)*, 687–725; trans. Fouracre and Gerberding (1986), pp. 350–70.
5 Werner (1980), pp. 100–11.
6 *AMP*, 687–90; trans. Fouracre and Gerberding (1996), pp. 353–62.
7 *AMP*, 687; trans. Fouracre and Gerberding (1996), pp. 353–8.

8 Fredegar, *Continuations*, c. 33; trans. Wallace-Hadrill (1960), p. 102.

9 Collins (1994) and (1996), pp. 112–17 on dating the text.

10 RFA, 749.

11 McKitterick (1997) and (2000).

12 *Chronicle of Theophanes*; trans. Mango and Scott (1997), pp. 556–7.

13 AMP, 691; trans. Fouracre and Gerberding (1996), pp. 359–60.

14 *Codex Carolinus (CC)*, no. 6 (755), p. 489 for the first use of the phrase.

15 CC, no. 11, at p. 505.

16 *Passio Leudegarii*, MGH SSRM V, pp. 249–363; trans. Fouracre and Gerberding (1996), pp. 215–53.

17 *Passio Leudegarii*, c. 5; trans. Fouracre and Gerberding (1996), p. 222.

18 *Liber Historiae Francorum (LHF)*, cc. 43–53, pp. 215–328; trans. Fouracre and Gerberding (1996), p. 91, placing the battle of Bois-du-Fays ('Lucofao') between 676 and 679. Also Gerberding (1987), pp. 79–83.

19 Gerberding (1987).

20 Fredegar, *Continuations*, trans. Wallace-Hadrill (1960), pp. xliii–xlv; Collins (1996).

21 LHF, c. 50; trans. Fouracre and Gerberding (1996), p. 94; Fouracre (1984).

22 Fredegar, *Continuations*, c. 13; trans. Wallace-Hadrill (1960), pp. 90–1; Fouracre (2000), pp. 87–8, 148–9.

23 Fredegar, *Continuations*, c. 30; trans. Wallace-Hadrill (1960), pp. 100–1.

24 Einhard, *VK*, c. 2.

25 Fouracre (2000), pp. 57–78.

26 LHF, c. 49; trans. Fouracre and Gerberding (1996), p. 93.

27 Fredegar, *Continuations*, c. 6; trans. Wallace-Hadrill (1960), p. 86. On Alpaida's family see, Gerberding (1987), pp. 117–20; Fouracre (2000), pp. 55–6.

28 *Passio Leudegarii*, c. 19; trans. Fouracre and Gerberding (1996), pp. 235–6.

29 LHF, c. 53; trans. Fouracre and Gerberding (1996), pp. 95–6.

30 Fouracre (2000), pp. 165–6.

31 *Vita Eucherii*, MGH SSRM VII, pp. 46–53.

32 *S. Adonis Viennensis Chronicon*, PL 123, col. 117.

33 *Ibid.*, col. 122.

34 Hincmar, *Epistola Synodali Carisiacensis*, MGH Capit. II, no. 297, p. 432. On the secularisation issue, see Reuter (1994) and Fouracre (2000), pp. 122–37.

35 *Vita Rigoberti*, c. 12, MGH SSRM VII, p. 69.

36 LHF, cc. 51–3; trans. Fouracre and Gerberding (1996), pp. 94–6.

37 Collins (1994), pp. 229–35.

38 *Leges Baiwariorum*, MGH Leges sectio I.5, pp. 312–13; Airlie (1999), pp. 93–119.

39 Geary (1985).

40 MGH *Dip. Imp.* I, no. 97, pp. 87–8.

41 Einhard, *VK*, c. 4.

42 LP, 'Life of Stephen II', c. 25; trans. Davis (1992), p. 63.

43 Fredegar, *Continuations*, c. 25; trans. Wallace-Hadrill (1960), p. 98.

44 As demonstrated in Carolingian writing on the deposition of Tassilo; Airlie (1999); and Reuter, ch. 11 (pp. 183–94), this volume.

45 RFA, 741–53; Fredegar, *Continuations*, c. 35, trans. Wallace-Hadrill (1960), p. 103, which refers to Grifo only to record his death.

46 Becher (1992) corrects the date of Charlemagne's birth from 743/44 implied by the RFA and Einhard.

47 The missionary Boniface was unsure in 747/48 whether to attend the synod of Pippin or that of Drogo; Boniface, *Epistulae*, no. 53, trans. Emerton (1940), pp. 141–2.
48 RFA *(Rev.)* 753; trans. Scholz (1970), p. 40.
49 Fouracre (2000), pp. 176–80.
50 Fouracre and Gerberding (1996), pp. 340–3.
51 RFA *(Rev.)* 790; trans. Scholz (1970), p. 69.

2

CHARLEMAGNE
THE MAN

Janet L. Nelson

The sense of knowing a historical personage may be an occupational illusion of historians. Can we seriously hope ever to know Charlemagne the man? The relatively plentiful contemporary records, evoking a vivid impression of Charlemagne's agency – that is, his intent in action – and an age stamped by that singular life, conspire to produce a confident 'yes'. Yet the absence of substantial writings produced by Charlemagne himself, the worryingly uneven evidential coverage of his sixty-five years, the court origins and propagandistic purposes of so much of the source-material, and the apparent dearth of the kind of information that is a biographer's staple fare – about the subject's early upbringing, mental formation and family relationships, about his sexuality and friendships and innermost beliefs – all this impels a deeply pessimistic 'no'.[1] The historian's dilemma is refracted in recent anxieties over Einhard's *Life of Charlemagne*, since what used to be the modern narrator's standby begins to seem nowadays a construct so idiosyncratic as to reveal much more about Einhard than about his larger-than-life subject.[2]

The dilemma has been mirrored more generally in commemorations of twelve-hundredth anniversaries in 1999 and 2000, in which Charlemagne has been harnessed more or less cheerfully to the imperatives of a new European age. Today's historians, untrammelled by Einhard's sense of personal indebtedness to his nurturer, mostly evade the task – and question the very feasibility – of life-writing about Charlemagne. Some of them string select aspects of the reign on a loosely chronological thread, while a few boldly forgo chronology in favour of strong themes and contextualisation.[3] A rare 'biography' focuses on the political environment, enveloping life in his times.[4] Mapped onto the larger dilemma is, still, an older argument concerning this subject's identity: German or French? *Karl der Grosse* or *Charlemagne*?[5] If in this chapter (and this book) the name 'Charlemagne' is preferred, that reflects no conviction about the man's intrinsic

Frenchness, but simply what's become his normal moniker in English. Perhaps a British historian writing for an anglophone public finds it easier than French or Germans to consign the argument about Charlemagne's 'national' affiliation to the history of historiography and to the agendas of twelfth-century myth-makers and nineteenth- and twentieth-century apologists for modern states.

Other arguments, though, are not so easy to sidestep: about the advisability of seeking to understand the past in terms of an individual rather than of socio-political structures and processes; about the usefulness, or otherwise, of approaching an age through a man. The attribution of agency even to a twentieth-century Great Leader has required very careful qualification in the light of constraining structures and multiple interacting agents and agencies.[6] As attempted by an archaeologist or a numismatist for Charlemagne *c.* 800, the reconstruction of agency can seem over-optimistic.[7] If eighteenth-century regimes were only beginning to acquire the statistical information on which to predict or manipulate supply and demand, how could Charlemagne be credited with an economic policy or public–private initiatives?

Or does that rhetorical question mask a teleological false assumption? Agency does not necessarily diminish, the further back you go.[8] Debate is in order, certainly, as to the extent of Charlemagne's success in carrying out what he intended. There is plenty of evidence that practice fell short of ideal. Yet the self-same evidence leaves no doubt of Charlemagne's aims and intentions across a wide range of issues, not least those of trade and coinage; and an approach that privileges the sequential, while accommodating the thematic, allows the possibility of discerning cause and effect, and hence of measuring policy's effectiveness. To insist on a personality's evolution over time, moreover, is emphatically not to indulge in worship of a Great Man, but to set a life firmly in context and, as the person catches and is caught in a series of moments, to follow the grain of a life as lived.

A man who reached sixty-five, a man whose geographical range of action expanded dramatically in the course of his adult years, a man who propelled as well as experienced major changes in the way public affairs were conducted, a man interested in both thought and practicalities, and in their mutual impact: such a man's personality was bound to evolve over the decades as he matured, and grew old. Set such a man within a family and you appreciate social determinants of changes in experience and perception, as child became man, son and brother became father and grandfather, took joy in partnership and offspring, suffered repeatedly the grief of personal loss.[9] Superimpose – as you might place transparencies showing churches and palaces on a physical map – changing constellations of friends, colleagues, counsellors and servants, and make due allowance for their individual and collective influence. Superimpose, again, the cultural beliefs and values this man carried in his head from early socialisation, and allow for change and adaptation here too, as new personal encounters and priorities, over time, had their effects. Acknowledge back-projection, local colour, and special pleading in *The Deeds of Charlemagne*, but be prepared to uncover Charlemagne's humour beneath Notker's.[10]

One of this chapter's two starting-points is the conviction that evidence of sufficient quantity and quality exists to permit the building of such a multi-layered account in Charlemagne's case, and hence to perceive him not only shaped by, and responding to, given structures and circumstances, but possessed of a strong sense of his own identity and a personal drive to shape and inspire his world. Half of Einhard's *Life* is about its subject's 'interior and domestic life', and these chapters reveal things about Charlemagne's sexuality and his spirituality that can be checked against – and confirmed by – other sources.[11] A second starting-point is my sense of professional obligation to respond to the challenge of post-modernism. Pieces of evidence must be understood in terms of the texts in which they are embedded, of course, and narratives must be deconstructed to expose authorial intents: these are old skills of the historian's trade. The upshot, though, is not the identification of mere 'discourse(s)', layer on layer of fictions, or a series of explainings-away, but the capture of glimpses of a living man, and through those the plausible reconstruction of a reality: a life lived in the context of ideological and material cultures which historians, like archaeologists, must insist is recoverable. In what follows, I discuss three bits of evidence, relating respectively to episodes in 756, 774 and 785. None is by any means a new discovery, but all are still in need of being more fully charted. They suggest, as I hope to show, recurring themes of memory, identity, subjectivity and intentionality that linked the phases of Charlemagne's life and defined it as a whole.[12]

Charlemagne loses his first milk-tooth

Episode one frames Charlemagne in the mid-750s, the early years of the reign of his father, Pippin, as king. That the evidence for Pippin's accession is so 'difficult' – that is, skewed, gap-ridden and contradictory – betrays the difficulties faced by writers who at the time and afterwards tried to explain and justify his *coup d'état*. I begin with that event because it changed Charlemagne's life and prospects for good. Since the turn of 741–42, Pippin and his elder brother Carloman had held power in Francia together, as mayors of the palace. Carloman was already married, and had offspring. Pippin, who had till then remained single, married in (probably) 744, but by July 747 no child had appeared. Meanwhile, the brothers had installed another in the long line of Merovingian kings, for the Frankish aristocracy would acknowledge the legitimacy only of a member of the dynasty that had ruled their ancestors since Clovis (481–511).[13]

From 747, events moved fast for Pippin. Late that summer, he apparently agreed a deal whereby Carloman would enter monastic retirement at Monte Cassino in central Italy while Pippin would protect the succession claims of Carloman's son (or sons).[14] Perhaps at the very moment that agreement was made,

24

Pippin knew that his wife was pregnant with the child who was to be born on 2 April 748, and who grew up to be Charlemagne. Pippin began overtly to plan for assuming the royal title and consigning the Merovingian king (and his son) to a monastery. Aristocratic support from lay magnates and higher clergy was cultivated; approval was gained from Pope Zacharias. In 751, bishops consecrated Pippin as king in a ritual which for the Franks was a notable innovation, and magnates acknowledged him in the traditional style.[15] Pope Stephen II confirmed the new dynasty by (re-)consecrating not only Pippin but his wife and sons too in 754.[16] By early August of that year, Carloman was dead, and his sons had disappeared from the written record.

Rosamond McKitterick has made a forceful case for regarding the stress that the Royal Frankish Annals (RFA) place on papal approval of the new dynasty as an invention aimed at legitimating Pippin's *coup* a generation after the event, that is (probably) in the later 780s.[17] But the *Second Continuator of Fredegar* is an independent source for the events of 750–51, and not just earlier than the RFA but a strictly contemporary witness, if Roger Collins is right to argue (and I think he is) that the *Second Continuation* was produced in the household of Pippin's uncle, Count Hildebrand, for presentation to Pippin in (or soon after) 751 and the *Third* was produced in the household of Hildebrand's son for presentation to Pippin's sons in (or soon after) 768.[18] It is worth spelling out the further implication that Charlemagne and his brother were brought up on the stories in Fredegar and the *Continuations* and hence were, from earliest boyhood, connoisseurs not just of Frankish history but of recent Frankish history as a well-tailored version of Carolingian family history.

Pippin's rise to power emerges from recent research as dark, contested and violent, far from the smooth progression presented by the RFA and by so much modern historiography.[19] Not until the mid-750s could Pippin could have felt relatively secure in his new monarchic title. Supernatural support had been invoked throughout these testing years, not only from St Peter (via the pope) but from two of the three traditional Frankish patron saints, Martin and Denis.[20] Germain completed the trio, and his patronage would confirm Pippin's grip on the key region of Paris and the Seine basin.[21] According to the *Translatio* of St Germain (*translatio* here having the technical sense of an account of the removal of a saint's body to a new tomb, with accompanying miracles), written in the early ninth century, or at least based on some early ninth-century material, the saint appeared in a vision to a woman-devotee of his cult and demanded that his body be 'translated' as promised twenty years before by Pippin's father Charles Martel.[22] The woman told the abbot, and the abbot reported this to Pippin, who gladly agreed and summoned a large assembly to attend the event. The date, specified with some care, was 755.

The author of the text stated at this point that he had not been present, but heard the story from many who were, 'of whom I mention here only one most excellent authority, namely, the Lord Charles the most glorious emperor, who was present as a seven-year-old at his father's act of piety and diligently, with admirably good memory, recalled what he saw and reported it with admirable fluency'. The *Translatio* continues in what purport to be Charles' own words, with an account of the inability of Pippin and his great men, or the bishops, or the monks themselves, to lift the saint's sarcophagus, and the general distress that prevailed until 'someone said that certain possessions of the monastery located within the royal *villa* of Palaiseau had been subjected to various depredations by royal revenue-collectors (*fiscalini*) and that the saint demanded an end to these afflictions'. Pippin thereupon not only declared that the wrong would be righted but handed over the whole *villa* of Palaiseau to the saint.

The sarcophagus was now moveable. But there was a further hitch because the carrying-poles, which had been made very long so that as many people as possible could share in the pious labour, prevented the sarcophagus from being lowered into the hole prepared for it. Everyone suggested cutting the poles, but Pippin objected: 'The sarcophagus might be damaged. Some safer plan must be found'. No sooner had he spoken than the sarcophagus moved of its own accord and, 'while everyone was stupefied and put their hands to their mouths in their alarm, it slipped rapidly off the poles and dropped into the hole. ... When they all looked into the hole, they saw that the sarcophagus, which they'd feared shattered, was safe and sound. Clearly this was the work of angels! And while everyone marvelled, I [*remember this is still Charlemagne speaking*], while playing about as boys will, slipped down by accident into the hole. And there I soon lost my first tooth'.[23]

Several generations of modern scholars have agonised over the reliability of this tale. Internal evidence shows that the *Translatio* cannot be later than 846, and it is clearly a St-Germain production. The nineteenth-century editor Georg Waitz, seeing no inherent difficulty in dating the saint's 'translation' to 755, was tempted to believe that the account was indeed based on Charlemagne's oral testimony, near the end of his life, to an event he recollected. Yet there were problems about the date. First, Charlemagne – if born in 742, as Waitz and virtu-ally all scholars till recently believed – could not have been 'a seven-year old' in 755. That problem has disappeared with Matthias Becher's convincing demon-stration that Charlemagne was born in 748.[24] A second difficulty was mid-ninth-century evidence that the *translatio* occurred on a Sunday (25 July), which would preclude the *Translatio*'s '755' and indicate 756 as the year.[25] Thus Bruno Krusch, mocking other scholars' 'credulity', argued that 'Charlemagne's' story of the *translatio* was 'historically worthless', interpolated into an existing collection of St Germain's miracles simply to justify the monastery's claim to Palaiseau. Krusch's solution, separating *Translatio* from miracles, involves the awkward presumption that the original text began with a miracle-story setting the scene for a *translatio* which it then failed to describe.[26]

By comparison, the argument that the *translatio* occurred in 756, not 755 – and hence when Charlemagne was eight, not seven – even if correct, seems to me relatively unimportant, just as it is relatively unimportant that, as any dentist or parent will tell you, the first milk-tooth though most commonly lost at seven is quite often lost at six or eight. For, from the standpoint of a medieval narrator, the age of seven was significant because it marked the end of infancy – the years 'when', as Isidore put it, 'the teeth are not yet well fixed' – and the beginning of the second period of a male child's life, that of *pueritia*, boyhood, also known as 'years of discretion' – at which point, as Isidore said, 'the teeth are changed'.[27] In Charlemagne's memory, it was the symbolic age that counted. St Germain's *translatio* was recalled by him as the occasion when his boyhood began, and in its very beginning was subjected to discipline. It was, in other words, a signal moment, and as it happened a very public one, in the boy's life. The story was a kind of confession.

A child's loss of his first tooth is still an event invested with some meaning in most European cultures. I have failed to find any early medieval case-material except for this story. If it was a ninth-century monk's fabrication, then it would have been a highly unusually one for which no written source can readily be suggested. The mid-ninth-century material from St-Germain suggests a *translatio* of the saint's remains not too long before. It may be that it was Charlemagne himself who filtered Pippin's grant of Palaiseau into his memory of that event. For although there is no evidence for Charlemagne's making a visit to St-Germain in his later, imperial years, a credible context does exist for his transmission of the *translatio* story, and his part in it, to a member of the St-Germain community. In 811 the list of witnesses to Charlemagne's will, a roll-call of those closest to the emperor at that time, included a man who must shortly before have received his abbacy by royal fiat, Irmino of St-Germain.[28] This, Irmino's first appearance in the sources, is an indication of Charlemagne's ongoing interest in St Germain.[29] A decade or so later, Irmino was to take an interest in Palaiseau when his abbey's famous polyptych was being compiled; and Charlemagne was commemorated at St-Germain in its earliest extant necrology.[30]

What is rehearsed in 'Charlemagne's' story of the loss of his first tooth, and what is portrayed as making it particularly memorable and meaningful for him, is a rite of passage within which the natural event figured as a little miracle on its own. Why should not that scene (with even a shade of scene-stealing?) – in which his, his father's and the Frankish elite's shared and public devotion to the saint were entwined with the child's private experience – have figured, or surfaced, in the ageing Charlemagne's memory of his own young life? That the story was retailed at all suggests that contemporary adult responses were understanding, if not indulgent, rather than shocked. Most members of monastic communities, after all, would once have been child-oblates, offered to the monastery by parents or kin at or about the age of seven, and they may also have recalled the association of oblation with the onset of *pueritia* and their own loss of baby-teeth.[31] Charlemagne's tale would reveal, yes, a well-trained memory and a gift for narrating; yes, an alert and responsive, confident and engaging personality; but also the man's recollection of his child-self as one whose life was already associated, at a remembered natural transition-point, with supernatural contact, and of natural loss that was also a means to supernatural strengthening.

Charlemagne at the shrine of St Peter

The conquest of the Lombard kingdom was no foregone conclusion, in terms either of Charlemagne's own intentions or of military probabilities. According to Einhard (who in this case had no apparent reason to dissemble), the Franks in Pippin's reign had been unenthusiastic about campaigning in Italy in the interests of the papacy.[32] Both of Pippin's campaigns of the 750s had been followed by swift negotiations and rapid Frankish withdrawals. Charlemagne in 773 was another reluctant warrior in Italy, despite strong incentives to intervene. In 770, when he co-ruled the Frankish kingdom with his brother Carloman, Charlemagne's alliance with the Lombards was sealed by his marriage to the daughter of the Lombard king Desiderius.[33] Carloman's death on 4 December 771, at the age of twenty, threw Frankish politics into confusion at the same time as it offered Charlemagne rich possibilities of extended power.

Carloman's share of the kingdom did not just fall into Charlemagne's lap. Carloman had left sons whose mother, Gerberga, was determined to uphold their claims and had the support of some important magnates. Charlemagne saw that the way to win over a majority of his late brother's leading men was to enter into a new marriage-alliance that would supply a power-base in or alongside what had been his brother's kingdom; further, to attack the Saxons' great shrine and so acquire quick moveable returns in the form of plunder, to be redistributed among the Frankish aristocracy, perhaps especially those of the middle Rhine--Main region where there had long been friction between Franks and Saxons. A new bride meant, of course, repudiating the Lombard princess, against canon law and after scarcely more than a year of marriage. For Charlemagne, canon law may have held less deterrent force than fear of the consequences of dishonouring the Lombard king and people; but the potential gains must have seemed to him to outweigh those risks.

The unceremonious return of the Lombard princess to Desiderius's court at Pavia was an unforgivable insult to Lombard honour. Coincidentally, Gerberga's arrival, with her sons, at that same court, offered Desiderius the means of revenge against Charlemagne. He determined to take up the claims of Charlemagne's nephews, hoping to persuade the pope to consecrate them kings of the Franks.[34] The pope was new, since Stephen III had died on 24 January 772. There was nothing foreordained about a Frankish-papal alliance, nor unthinkable about a

Lombard-papal one. For a while in 771, Stephen III had in fact been the ally of Desiderius, his 'most excellent son', while Carloman, isolated and increasingly hostile towards his own brother, had allegedly authorised his *missus* to attack Rome.[35] The biographer of Stephen's successor, Hadrian, presents him as consistently hostile to Desiderius, yet shows that he continued to negotiate for over a year, while conciliating rival factions in Rome.

Papal politics remained reactive, and fluid. Only in the spring of 773 did Desiderius lose hope of persuading Hadrian to come to Pavia to consecrate the Frankish princes. By then, Charlemagne's successful Saxon campaign in 772 had won him additional Frankish support against any claims on his nephews' behalf, hence strengthened his hand in dealing with Desiderius, and encouraged Hadrian to hope that direct Frankish intervention in Lombardy and in Rome would do more to give effect to a maximalist reading of 'St Peter's' territorial rights than a Lombard alliance was ever likely to. In the summer of 773, however, even after a Frankish assembly had approved the decision to invade Lombardy, Charlemagne still made repeated attempts to resolve the crisis peacefully: twice over, he offered Desiderius 14,000 *solidi* to make peace. After being rebuffed on the second occasion, Charlemagne offered to withdraw if Desiderius would hand over 'no more than three sons of Lombard judges as security for the restoration of the cities' claimed by the papacy.[36] Only when the offers had been indignantly refused did the campaign continue in earnest, and in September a two-pronged Frankish attack across the Mont-Cenis and Mons Iovis (Great St-Bernard) passes caused Desiderius to pull his forces back into the strongholds of the Lombard plain. It was a strategy that had worked well for the Lombards in the 750s, as the prelude to negotiated settlement.

Charlemagne's priority was to capture his nephews, and this he achieved in February or March. But it is not clear that Verona, the stronghold where the boys had been held, was also captured: perhaps, instead, the city leaders handed them over in a special deal. The Franks took some cities in northern Lombardy; but there was as yet no wholesale Lombard abandonment of Desiderius.[37] As the siege of Pavia dragged on, Charlemagne's position must have become increasingly risky. His absence from Francia meant leaving a key region exposed to Saxon counter-attack[38] while, six months into the siege of Pavia, feeding and supplying his army would have been becoming increasingly difficult. These were the circumstances that led, in late March 774, to a decision that may be interpreted, despite the note of 'victory' struck by the papal biographer, as one of desperation: Charlemagne moved south via Tuscany to Rome.[39] The papal biographer stresses that he took in his entourage a number of notables, evidently including some Lombards. Yet these were not so many as to slow a rapid march. 'So fast was his journey that he presented himself at the homes of the apostles [i.e. Rome] on Holy Saturday itself [2 April – was it a coincidence that the date was also Charlemagne's birthday?]. The blessed Pope Hadrian [had] heard that he was coming and was struck by great amazement and rejoicing that the king of the Franks had come so unexpectedly; he sent all the judges [i.e. the leading men of Rome and perhaps other nearby cities] to meet him at the place called Novae, some 30 miles (50 km) from this city of Rome. There they welcomed him with banners'.[40]

It was the first time that any Frankish king had come to the Holy City, and encountered at first hand 'not just a topographical concept but a very complex reality'.[41] This visit was surely a crucial event in Charlemagne's life. As a boy of five he had become acquainted with Pope Stephen II in Francia, and thereafter over some twenty years he had received a string of letters from a sequence of popes, but to meet Peter's successor at Peter's shrine was an altogether more intense and memorable experience. The processions Hadrian organised to welcome him to 'the hall of the apostle' were carefully organised 'as for greeting an exarch or patrician'. At daybreak on Holy Saturday, Hadrian received Charlemagne at the top of St-Peter's steps and they embraced each other. Taking the pope's right hand, the king entered the church itself to pray 'near the apostle's tomb'; then they 'went down together to St Peter's body and ratified their oaths to each other'. Only then did Charlemagne enter Rome, though he spent that night back at St-Peter's. The next day, Easter Sunday, king and pope feasted together at the Lateran; and for the next two days Charlemagne followed the usual Easter itinerary used by the pope. Probably at some point during these crowded days, Hadrian presented Charlemagne with a copy of the just-revised classic canon law-book of the sixth-century Dionysius Exiguus, hence called the Dionysio-Hadriana: a gift that would resonate in the *Admonitio generalis* of 789.[42]

The climax of Charlemagne's visit came with his meeting with Hadrian at St-Peter's on the Wednesday after Easter. After receiving from the pope a copy of what he declared to be an agreement made by Stephen II and Pippin in 754, Charlemagne had two copies made on the spot by his notary Etherius. The first was ratified by his own hand, and subscribed by his leading men.

> They placed it first on St Peter's altar and then in his holy *confessio* [the area in front of the altar above the saint's tomb], and both the king of the Franks and all his judges handed it to St Peter and to his holy vicar Pope Hadrian, promising under a terrible oath to maintain everything included in that donation. The Christian king of the Franks had Etherius write out a [further] copy of the donation; then with his own hands, he placed it inside over St Peter's body, beneath the gospels which are kissed there, as a firm security and an eternal reminder of his name and that of the kingdom of the Franks.[43]

Charlemagne then took away with him a further copy of the donation 'made out in the holy Roman church's office'.

Over the past century and more, inordinate amounts of more or less legalistic exegesis, frequently driven by more or less confessional zeal, have been expended on this passage.[44] What Hadrian asserted, and Charlemagne acknowledged, were the rights of 'St Peter' (that is, the papacy) to an enormous swathe of territory in

Italy. In my view, the seriousness of Charlemagne's position just before Easter 774 is a key factor in explaining why he agreed to such terms. For the Franks, whether or not persuaded by the papacy's legal claims, or impressed by the Donation of Constantine,[45] Hadrian's support was politically indispensable at that moment. Yet the mainspring of Charlemagne's response to Hadrian's *démarche* on 6 April lay neither in law nor in politics but in the experience of physical contact – and ongoing contact – with St Peter's remains.

Popes had long known how to convey a sense of this experience, even when the beneficiaries had never come to Rome. Gregory I had sent privileged recipients tiny pieces of cloth that had been in contact with Peter's tomb, and filings from his chains.[46] In 770, Stephen III had sent Charlemagne and Carloman a strongly-worded letter of protest which he had previously 'placed in the *confessio* of St Peter and offered the sacrifice and victims to our God upon it'.[47] The *confessio* was like a numinous oven, whence that letter had emerged hot with holy power. But, on 6 April 774, the crucial document did not emerge: it remained on Peter's body 'as a firm security ... for the names [that is, the honour, status and rights] of himself and of the kingdom of the Franks'. In placing the document there, and leaving it there like a battery on permanent charge, Charlemagne believed that he had ensured that he and his people would always be connected to St Peter's aid and protection. In that confidence, he left Rome and returned to the siege of Pavia, which fell less than two months later.

According to Hadrian's biographer, 'God's wrath had raged furiously against all the Lombards inside that city and many were lost by disease and annihilation, so it was God's will that His Excellency the king of the Franks captured the city'.[48] That reading of events was surely shared by Charlemagne himself. He had gained his 'firm security'. His grateful devotion never cooled, nor did the heat of that remembered moment at Peter's *confessio*. What Hadrian thought to be the terms of Pippin's 'donation' were never to be carried out, despite a long sequence of plangent appeals. As far as Charlemagne was concerned, his obligations to protect Peter's Church were indeed scrupulously fulfilled, on a higher plane than the merely geographical. In Charlemagne's mind, that fulfilment was inseparable from continuing manifestations of divine blessings secured by Peter's intercession.[49] Einhard's testimony to Charlemagne's 'cherishing of St Peter's church above all other holy places', and 'having nearest his heart ... the wish to defend and protect the church of St Peter and to beautify and enrich it ... above all other churches', faithfully echoed his master's voice.[50] The visit to St Peter in 774 stamped the rest of the reign: each of three further visits, in 781, 787 and 800–1, reaffirmed and reinforced what was 'nearest his heart'.

Charlemagne remembers St Arnulf

Paul the Deacon, a Lombard born and bred, may have regretted his time in Francia. The visit was an enforced one, prolonged by the scholar–monk's desire to see his own brother freed from Frankish custody.[51] As soon as this aim had been accomplished, Paul was off again to Italy. Yet during his brief years in Francia, Paul evidently became a member of the court circle. When Bishop Angilramn of Metz, one of Charlemagne's chief counsellors, commissioned Paul to write the *Deeds of the Bishops of Metz* sometime about 783 or 784, it may have seemed natural for the author–courtier to seek oral as well as written evidence, not least concerning Bishop Arnulf, ancestor of Charlemagne himself.[52] Perhaps it did not take Paul long to realise that in Charlemagne he had a potential fund of information. In the *Gesta*, one story in particular is credited to 'that assertor of the whole truth, the distinguished king Charles'.[53]

Arnulf, 'moderator of the palace' for the Merovingian king, was doing penance for 'certain excesses'. Whether these were sexual acts or warlike ones is unspecified (the second only are attested, though celebrated rather than criticised, in a seventh-century source, the *Vita Arnulfi*).[54] Crossing a bridge over the River Mosel one day, Arnulf took a ring from his finger and threw it into the river saying, 'I shall consider myself free from the bonds of my offences on the day when I get back this ring which I now throw'. Some time later, Arnulf, who had meanwhile become a bishop, received as a gift a fish which he ordered to be prepared for the evening meal. The cook while gutting the fish found a ring. He took the ring to Arnulf, who immediately recognised it as the one he had thrown into the Mosel, and thanked God accordingly for having remitted his sins. Paul adds – and perhaps the gloss is his informant's – that Arnulf resembled the biblical judge and war-leader Gideon in seeking a sign from God, but that the enemies whom Arnulf had vanquished were mightier than Gideon's.[55] The focus then shifts to Arnulf's dealings with his two sons, only one of whom was blessed (like the biblical Jacob) by his father, and destined to succeed him. Paul does not claim that Charlemagne had also supplied the information here, not even when he says that the name of one of the sons, Anschisus, 'is believed to be derived from Anchises, the father of Aeneas 'who had come long ago from Troy to Italy', yet it's more than likely that Charlemagne had access to the likely source of this tale, the *Chronicle of Fredegar*.[56]

In a characteristically arresting paper, Walter Goffart drew attention to the coincidence of Paul's production of the *Deeds*, and in particular the stories of Arnulf's penance and of his two sons, with 'a notable though not very long hiatus in Charles's life [which] had just taken place', namely the five-month gap between the death of his third wife[57] Hildegard on 30 April 783, and his next marriage, by 6 October, to Fastrada. In a series of subtle arguments – the most important of which is that 'Anschisus-Jacob symbolizes Charles the Younger',[58] the first of Charlemagne's sons by Hildegard – Goffart makes an intriguing case for seeing in the *Deeds* the essentials of a succession-plan made by Charlemagne. The plan was new-ish, Goffart contends, in so far as it excluded Pippin son of Himiltrude, that is, Charlemagne's eldest son (though on Goffart's view, that exclusion had already been decided on in 781), and it prefigured the future, in so far as it bound Charlemagne to 'abstinence' – or at least 'conscious planning' for 'greater abstinence' – from 783 on.

The hiccup there is revealing, for the weak point in Goffart's argument is of course the fact of Charlemagne's remarriage, which was followed, predictably enough, by the births of two babies within the next five years or so. That both babies would be girls could surely *not* have been predicted; and that means that there was no sort of 'guarantee' of the Young Charles's sole succession to Francia. My own view is that Goffart is half-right: Paul does preserve the gist of a 'plan', but it was not Charlemagne's, whether in 783 or 781. Hopes and schemes about the succession must have flitted around the court as soon as there were plural potential heirs, and the factions that surrounded those heirs, especially nobles connected with the heirs' maternal kin, probably did most to encourage such rumours. If any 'plan' can be read from Paul's work, it would be that of supporters of the Young Charles who, unlike his younger brothers in 781, ruled no firmly defined (sub)kingdom, and would have no royal title of his own till Christmas Day 800. Yet no-one, least of all when Charlemagne himself had recently got married again, and (as Goffart fails to mention) to a woman he was clearly very fond of, could have expected the paterfamilias to pin himself down to sexual abstinence, 'greater' or otherwise.

If the 'early design for the succession' is discarded, there remains much of interest in the story of Arnulf's penance and the miraculous return of the ring as told by Charlemagne. It could at the same time suggest Charlemagne, a latter-day Gideon, as Arnulf's antitype. Paul states explicitly that Charlemagne was Arnulf's *trinepos* (great-great-great-great grandson),[59] and implicitly that he fulfilled the promise of Arnulf's blessing on his own descent-line. The ring inside the fish is a folk-motif, yet one that's transformed here by context into a thoroughly christian sign. The 'whole truth' of which Charlemagne tells is compounded of different layers and meanings. Thus the picture Paul paints of his patron is not just of a garrulous narrator of barbarian histories, nor in any simple sense of a purveyor of oral traditions.

Instead, Paul's Charlemagne had reflected long and hard on the history of his lineage, allowed a place for religious preoccupations in his ancestor's secular career, appreciated the significance of penitence and remission, and was ready to interpret an exceptional event as a divine sign. This is rare and precious testimony, then, to a thinking man, convinced that God intervened directly in the affairs of his own family, and willing to read biblical typology therein. From here it was a short step to believing (Paul's words at this point may or may not echo Charlemagne's own) that his was a family chosen by God to bring forth 'men so stalwart and strong that the realm of the Franks will be most worthily transferred to their descent-line'. Such confidence did not solve the problem of intra-familial conflict, but perhaps it helped close kin to live with tensions that were inevitable.

Conclusions

The three episodes I have briefly analysed here are mere soundings into a large terrain but, like the stories in Notker's *Deeds*, they are much more than merely anecdotal. For each episode there is a key source which, when carefully weighed and set in context, reveals a personality impressionable, driven and determinedly driving towards self-set objectives: the observant, eager boy in 756, the devoutly ambitious young monarch in 774, the anxious yet confident family-manager in 785. The sequence is complicated by cross-cutting chronologies of recollecting and connecting: the boy remembered by the man in his sixties; the monarch at St Peter's tomb understanding anew a relationship that stretched back to boyhood and grasping its implications for future glory and duty; the father recalling family lore about his ancestor's predestined fatherhood and pondering the consequences of his own actual one. Each moment shows Charlemagne retrospective, responsive and in formative action. Each needs to be understood in a life's continuum.

These three successive moments, unusually vividly documented, are not unrepresentative. The impression of an individual with, from an early age, a strong sense of his own identity emerges from other sources for other moments in this life. It was an identity grounded in and bounded by a cluster of relationships and reciprocal rights and duties: first and foremost with family, living and dead and yet unborn; with friends, faithful men, counsellors, courtiers, clergy and monks, officers, agents, subordinates, dependants, servants, and the Frankish people at large; last but certainly not least with supernatural beings – God and, more directly, the saints who were special patrons and friends of the man himself, of his dynasty and of the Franks. Impelled by well-remembered commitments, guided by signs recognisable to contemporaries as well as himself, sustained by regularly-reaffirmed acknowledgment from friends and followers, Charlemagne performed consistently as a leader of men. Responsiveness to others' expectations, visible in the episodes of 756, 774 and 785, characterised the various phases and forms of Charlemagne's activities.

Beneath responsiveness, though, was a quality intrinsic to the man, his hallmark: one that communicated itself to others, and at critical moments – political decision-making, wartime – imposed itself on them. Einhard called it by the classical term *constantia*: constancy, steadiness, unswerving determination, a long-term following-through of intent in action. I think that *constantia* endowed Charlemagne's varied activities with consistency in his own mind and in others' minds, and made of his life something he and others perceived as coherent even as it was ongoing. This was so despite the often (and necessarily) improvised, opportunistic nature of Charlemagne's actions, whether in politics or in warfare or in religious patronage or propitiation. For Charlemagne not only had an evolving vision of a larger project in which all the details could fit, but he gave his contemporaries a sense of partnership in that project, and reconstructed Frankishness in terms of it.

If his *constantia* was an imperial virtue, the Franks too were constant, an imperial people. And since virtue, now, was also Christian virtue, all were enrolled not just in the defence of the Church and rights of St Peter but in a collective 'correction' (Charlemagne's preferred word) that extended into the everyday obligations of religious, political and social life. This ideological mass conscription was Charlemagne's answer to the ideological crisis entailed by his father's *coup*. Charlemagne's personal quest for self-knowledge and self-realisation, which emerges most clearly in texts of his imperial years but can be seen as following-through aspirations expressed fitfully much earlier in his life, was generalised over time into a cultural programme. Charlemagne, then, delivers as promised? Yes, because so too, in the end, do sources that, if not the fictions despaired of by postmodernists, are certainly 'difficult' for historians. Handled (I hope) with care and (I confess) a touch of optimism, they have turned out to put us in touch with Charlemagne the man.

Notes

1 Nelson (2000b). For help and criticism I am very grateful to Jo Story, Paul Fouracre, David Ganz and Julia Smith, and especially to the late Tim Reuter.

2 Innes and McKitterick (1994), pp. 203–10; Kempshall (1995); Dutton (1998), pp. xviii–xxiv, 15–39; Krüger (1998).

3 Becher (1999a); Barbero (2000); Favier (1999).

4 Hägermann (2000).

5 Werner (1995).

6 Kershaw (2000).

7 Hodges and Whitehouse (1983), pp. 102–11, 173–6; Hodges (2000), pp. 93–118; Hendy (1988).

8 Parker (1998); Gillingham (1999); Stafford (1998).

9 Nelson (2002b).

10 Notker, *Gesta Karoli* I, 34, II, 5, MGH *SSRG*, NS XII, pp. 47–8, 53; see Barbero (2000), p. 142; Ganz (1989); Innes (1998a); Wickham (1998b), pp. 248, 255; Nelson (2001a) and (2001b).

11 Nelson (2000b), p. 130.

12 Nelson (2001c).

13 Becher (1989).

14 Becher (1992).

15 Fredegar, *Continuations: Second Continuator of Fredegar*, c. 33; trans. Wallace-Hadrill (1960), p. 102.

16 *Liber Pontificalis (LP)*, 'Life of Stephen II', c. 27, trans. Davis, p. 64, where the consecrations are dated to January 754. The *Clausula de unctione Pippini Regis*, whose author

claims to be writing in 767, dates the consecrations precisely to 28 July, but Stoclet's demonstration – in (1980) and (2000) – that it was written well over a century after the event inclines me to accept the date indicated by the papal biographer. The consecrations are attested in *CC* no. 11, at p. 505.

17 McKitterick (1997) and (2000).
18 Collins (1994), pp. 235–46.
19 Collins (1998b); Nelson (2002b); Fouracre, ch. 1 (pp. 5–21) in this volume.
20 MGH *Dip. Karol.* I, nos. 4–8.
21 MGH *Dip. Karol.* I, no. 122 (Charlemagne, 779), referring to an earlier grant by Pippin.
22 *Translatio S. Germani*, c. 2, MGH *SS* XV(i), pp. 5–6.
23 *Ibid.* c. 6, p. 8.
24 Becher (1992), pp. 50–4, Becher (1999b), pp. 42–3, and Hägermann (2000), p. 638, accept the *Translatio* account; Fried (2000) rejects it.
25 Heinzelmann (1979), p. 115, n.22; Fried (2000), pp. 575–9.
26 *Miracula S. Germani*, MGH *SSRM* VII, pp. 368–71.
27 Isidore, *Etymologiae* XI.ii.9, *PL* 82, col. 416, and *Liber Numerorum*, *PL* 83, col. 188.
28 Einhard, *VK*, c. 33.
29 MGH *Dip. Karol.* I, nos. 71 (772), 122 (779), 154 (786).
30 Molinier, ed. (1902), p. 250.
31 de Jong (1996), pp. 31–3, 44–5, 62–4, 71–2.
32 Einhard, *VK*, c. 6.
33 Nelson (1998).
34 *LP*, 'Life of Hadrian', cc. 9, 23, trans. Davis (1992), pp. 126–7, 133; Löwe (1956).
35 *CC*, no. 48.
36 *LP*, 'Life of Hadrian', cc. 28, 30, pp. 494–5, trans. pp. 135–6.
37 *LP*, 'Life of Hadrian', cc. 32, 34, trans. Davis (1992), pp. 136, 138.
38 RFA, 773/4.
39 *LP*, 'Life of Hadrian', c. 35, trans. Davis (1992), p. 138.
40 *Ibid.*
41 Schieffer (2000), p. 281.
42 Bullough (1991), pp. 14, 133, 142.
43 *LP*, 'Life of Hadrian', c. 43, trans. Davis (1992), p. 142.
44 Noble (1984), pp. 83–6, 138–40; Davis (1992), pp. 107–14, though neither accounts for the absence of evidence for the so-called 'Treaty of Quierzy' earlier than the 'Life of Hadrian'.
45 Noble (1984), pp. 134–7; Brown (1995), p. 328.
46 McCulloch (1976), pp. 145–84. In MGH *Epp.* IV, no. 30, Gregory claimed that Pope Leo I had demonstrated the potency of such secondary relics.
47 *CC*, no. 45. Buc (2001), p. 71.
48 *LP*, 'Life of Hadrian', c. 44, trans. Davis (1992), p. 142.
49 See, for example, Theodulf of Orléans, *Libri Carolini*, ed. Freeman (1998), pp. 98 and 126, or Charlemagne's letter to Pope Leo III, MGH *Epp.* IV, no. 93, pp. 136–8.
50 Einhard, *VK*, c. 27.
51 Goffart (1988), pp. 329–47; McKitterick (1999) and McKitterick (2004), pp. 60–83. For Paul's plea for his brother, see Godman (1985a), no. 1, pp. 82–3.
52 Goffart (1986).
53 Paul the Deacon, *Gesta episcoporum Mettensium*, MGH *SS* II, p. 264. For Old Testament models, see Garrison (1998a) and (2000a).

54 *Vita Arnulfi episcopi Mettensis* c. 4, MGH *SSRM* II, p. 433.
55 Paul the Deacon, *Gesta*, p. 264.
56 See above, n.18.
57 Goffart (1986), p. 79, but see Nelson (1991), pp. 197–202, and Nelson (2002b).
58 Goffart (1986), p. 83.
59 'One generation too many', Goffart (1986), p. 77, n.62.

3

EINHARD'S CHARLEMAGNE:
THE CHARACTERISATION
OF GREATNESS

David Ganz

Because we believe Einhard, we may not understand him. His biography of Charlemagne has convinced readers that 'Charles was great, that his achievements were remarkable and not to be matched, and that he was deservedly famous, for he waged war with great skill and success and almost doubled the size of the kingdom which he had inherited'.[1] But Charlemagne's greatness was not merely that of the warrior: he cultivated the liberal arts, he improved his kingdom and adorned its churches, and he loved his children. And somehow Einhard has convinced us that because we can learn what Charlemagne ate and drank and how he dressed and what his voice sounded like, we can come closer to him than to other early medieval people. Einhard's inclusion of personal details inspired the two biographers of Louis the Pious, and started the recording of such details, the construction of a way of life – what Einhard calls 'habits and interests' (*mores ac studia*) and 'the manner of his life' (*vitae modus*) – which seemed to complement and even to explain the deeds of a hero. Einhard created Charlemagne, and in so doing he set an agenda for a new sort of biography, the ways of life of medieval rulers.[2]

Yet because Einhard has so shaped our picture of Charles the Great, we are in danger of overlooking Einhard's originality. All too often, Einhard is seen according to the programme instigated by Walahfrid Strabo, who supplied a preface to the *Life* in the 840s.[3] Walahfrid's preface gives a brief biography of Einhard, praising his learning, his exemplary character and his truthfulness. He was the man to whom Charlemagne told his secrets. He preserved his splendid reputation even during the reign of Louis the Pious. This should confirm the truth of what he tells us.[4] Walahfrid then explains that he has supplied titles and divisions to help the reader to find specific topics more easily. But Einhard, by contrast, was not interested in setting himself in the foreground of his work, in affirming either his wisdom or his political acumen, much less in letting his reader find specific topics.

Einhard's biography lacked any chapter divisions: it formed a concise and structured whole. Indeed, no ninth- or tenth-century manuscript of the *Life* has any
divisions beyond Einhard's preface, the start of the text (*Gens Merovingicarum*) and
the beginning of Charlemagne's will.[5]

Walahfrid's intervention began the process of judging whether Einhard was a
reliable historian. Scholars with a superior knowledge of the events of Charlemagne's reign have not been slow to detect error and bias. Ranke memorably
noted that Einhard's little book is full of historical errors, and German historians
have since diligently repeated his maxim.[6] For Ranke, Einhard's duty was to convey *die exacte Wahrheit*, 'that precise truth', which had replaced eloquence, beauty
and moral instruction as the goal of historical writing. And once Einhard's errors
had been identified it became necessary to explain the bias which had caused them.

Einhard's aim

Instead of investigating Einhard's bias or his silences, this essay tries to explain
what sort of work he was writing. Our best guide to Einhard's ideology is the
meticulous exploration of his vocabulary, learning what associations the words he
selected might have had by finding out what words and phrases he borrowed
from other writers. His biography is amazingly laconic: a very great deal is left
unsaid. So his sparse vocabulary is made to carry a particular weight in an enterprise which is both highly original and enormously ambitious. The idea that
someone other than a saint might merit a Latin biography was entirely new: early
medieval biographies were fittingly written to commemorate saints and to
encourage others to imitate their lives. But Einhard is writing to commemorate
someone whose deeds 'can scarcely be imitated by the men of our age'.[7] And he is
writing a biography which, he asserts, demands Ciceronian eloquence: 'to write
and account for such a life what was required was Ciceronian eloquence, not my
feeble talent, which is poor and small, indeed almost non-existent'.[8]

Traditionally, Christian writers had rejected Ciceronian eloquence for the
simplicity of those fishermen to whom Christ had preached his Gospel; John Cassian
expressed his rejection of such 'Ciceronian eloquence' using the same phrase,
Tulliana facundia, that Einhard echoed with approval.[9] Like Cassian, the Merovingian *Passion of Praeiectus* affirmed that its readers should not look for Ciceronian
eloquence in that saint's life, but for the purity of Holy Church.[10] So Einhard was
asking to be assessed by standards which had long been regarded as inappropriate
for the Christian reader. He follows the teaching of Alcuin's *Rhetoric*: 'for our
eloquence to attain the authority of the ancients we need to read their works and
let them provide us with a model'.[11] Einhard had been Alcuin's student at court,
and it is clear that he had read the *Rhetoric*, and been inspired to read those
rhetorical works of Cicero on which Alcuin had drawn. The *Rhetorica ad Herennium*
(regarded as a work of Ciceronian eloquence, and of which Einhard had a copy)

affirms that the orator should speak either out of a compelling sense of duty, or from the earnest wish that everyone should call to mind the virtues of the individual whom he is commemorating.[12] Einhard's preface establishes his obligation, and the prodigious merits of his hero. This programme of eloquence in the praise of rulers, and its Ciceronian authority, are ultimately a part of Alcuin's legacy.

In following Alcuin, Einhard had embarked on a new kind of writing, as he states in his preface: 'if it will be possible to avoid angering with a *new* book those who criticise the old masterpieces composed by the most learned and eloquent of men'. The book is new because it is the biography of a lay contemporary ruler. It draws on 'the old masterpieces' because it quotes Cicero and Suetonius, and these 'old masterpieces' include works of classical and not of Christian culture. Whatever the impact of the biography as a picture of a ruler, Einhard's literary agenda proved influential: we have good grounds for believing that the *Life* of Charlemagne was studied by young monks, including Lupus of Ferrières and Gottschalk.[13] Walahfrid set Einhard in the context of a revival of learning 'in a misty and so to speak blind expanse with a new radiance almost completely unknown to this barbarous land before Charlemagne returned the kingdom to brilliance and sight.'[14] Alcuin's student Hraban Maur praised Einhard's eloquence in the epitaph which he composed for Einhard,[15] and Lupus affirmed that Einhard 'had attained the seriousness of Cicero and other ancients, supplying elegance of thoughts to be found in ancient authors'.[16] When Walahfrid wrote a preface for Thegan's biography of Louis the Pious, he noted that it was ill-written: style had become a necessary feature of biography. In 839 Wandalbert of Prüm quoted from Einhard's preface in the preface to his own *Life* of St Goar, mentioning 'those who judge the deeds of the present to be inferior to the past and not worth commemoration in writing'.[17] So before his death in 840 Einhard's text had already become so influential that its values could shape the writing of a saint's life, the very genre it had reacted against.

We need to acknowledge that Einhard's text was not as fixed for its Carolingian readers as we now regard it. Thegan and the Astronomer (both biographers of Louis the Pious) and the scribes of the ninth-century copy of the *Life*, now Vienna, ÖNB 473 (as Reimitz has shown), all regarded Einhard's *Life* as a text which might be excerpted or adapted to suit their needs. At St-Gallen at the end of the ninth century, Notker Balbulus supplied a remarkable supplement which circulated in manuscripts together with Einhard's *Life*, and which subverts Einhard's secular picture of Charlemagne.[18]

Since our earliest surviving copies of the *Vita Karoli* date from some fifty years after its composition, this early evidence of reception can provide as important a guide to the text as does the evidence of transmission.[19] And both of these must be used to supplement modern accounts of what Einhard was doing: our own views of his intention cannot but be anachronistic, reflecting our sense of what Einhard's values should have been.

The text of the *Life* was made accessible to Carolingian readers in several different ways. Surviving copies sometimes have the brief verse preface in which Louis the Pious's librarian Gerward presented the work to Louis, 'to praise him and his eternal memory and to raise Louis's famous name to the stars'.[20] No copy with Gerward's verses also has Einhard's own preface, a preface which may first have been directed to Gerward himself. The unique title of the preface in a London manuscript, British Library Cotton Tiberius C.XI, *Einhardus carissimo G. suo salutem*, seems to preserve a trace of that presentation copy ('Einhard, greetings to his dearest friend G.') and resolves the problem of whom Einhard was addressing in the preface when he wrote *en tibi librum*. *Tibi* is most commonly used to a specific individual and not to a 'general reader'.[21] So Einhard may have sent one version of the *Life*, with a preface explaining what he was trying to achieve, to a friend at Louis's court.

Vita et conversatio

It is important to be precise about what sort of work Einhard thought he was writing. It is a *Vita* – telling how its subject lived – both in his preface and in the title given to the work in all the early manuscripts. In the remarkable ninth-century manuscript Vienna, ÖNB 473, which seems to have been copied from an earlier exemplar, the Royal Frankish Annals are combined with Einhard's account of Charlemagne's private life. At the join between Annals and *Life* the titles read, *Finiunt Gesta Domini Karoli Magni et praecellentissimi Francorum imperatoris. Incipit Vita eiusdem principis* ('Here end the Deeds [*Gesta*] of the Lord Charles the great and most excellent emperor of the Franks. Here begins the Life [*Vita*] of that same prince').[22] All of this is followed by the *Gesta* of Louis the Pious from the Royal Frankish Annals, the two separated by a blank recto and an elaborate title in monumental capitals. McKitterick has suggested that this manuscript was copied to legitimate the rule of Charles the Bald as a worthy successor to a series of Frankish rulers.[23] It also contains an important genealogy, which glosses over the deposition of the last Merovingian ruler and the coronation of Pippin.

So the annals supply the *Gesta*; the *Life* is something different. This distinction was not always perceived by Einhard's readers: Walahfrid calls the work *Vita et gesta*, Lupus calls it *Gesta*, as does Louis the Pious's librarian Gerward.[24] But Einhard is clear: he is writing about the *Vita et conversatio et ex parte non modica res gestas* ('life and way of life, and his many accomplishments'), the *actus et mores caeterasque vitae illius partes* ('deeds, habits and other aspects of his life').[25] Charlemagne's deeds have become a part of his life.

The pairing *Vita et conversatio* had clear origins in hagiography. Jerome wrote about the *Vita et conversatio* of Paul the desert hermit;[26] the robber saint Moyses and the harlot Mary of Egypt each had a shameful life (*vita*) until their conversion to a pious way of life (*conversatio*).[27] Everyone lives a life, but only those who achieve such a conversion live a life worth imitating. *Conversatio* is a term with religious overtones and is twice used by Einhard in that sense. He uses the word to describe how Charlemagne's uncle left his kingdom for a monastery 'driven by a desire to lead a contemplative life' and how his sister Gisela had 'from her girlhood chosen the religious life'.[28]

Vita et conversatio stand in contrast to the *gesta*, the events recorded in Carolingian annals. The annal form, deriving from Isidore and Bede, was the recording of what was worthy of memory at home or in war, by land or sea. The annal appeared anonymous and objective. By the reign of Louis the Pious, annals were regarded as 'most ancient practice, habitual for kings from then to now to have the deeds and events written down for posterity to learn about'.[29] The *Gesta* of Bishop Aldric of Le Mans treat annals as an official and final record.[30] The Royal Frankish Annals, and their revised version, were a widely circulated and official version of Frankish history, year by year from 741 to 829. This sense that annals were widely known is important, for Einhard not only drew on the Royal Frankish Annals, but he also implicitly assumes their presence as a narrative record to supplement his diachronic approach to personality.

Despite their apparent objectivity, the Royal Frankish Annals present a continuous narrative which is validated by divine intervention. Battles are won 'by God's aid' in 773–76, 778–79, 783–84, 786, 788 and 791; all these references to divine assistance were removed in the Revised Annals.[31] The Royal Frankish Annals also use adjectives, frequently superlatives, to describe Charlemagne. In 769, during his dispute with his brother, he is *benignissimus* ('most benign'), he is frequently *gloriosus* and, when making peace with the Saxons, he is *gloriosissimus* ('most glorious') in 794, *praeclarus* ('illustrious') in 775, *mitissimus* ('most gentle') when dealing with Tassilo in 787. He is *clementissimus* ('most merciful') in 778 and 788, *prudentissimus piissimus* ('most prudent and most pious') in 787, and in 788 *Dei dispensator* ('steward of God'). Einhard in his preface used two such superlatives to describe Charlemagne: he is 'most excellent' and 'most famous'. *Excellentissimus* was the standard epistolary formula for addressing a ruler. *Famosissimus* can be found in Cassian and Rufinus, and soon became a stock epithet for Charlemagne.[32] But Einhard did not rely on repeating these adjectives. He chose to characterise Charlemagne with a more complex framework of terminology.

Einhard's preface justifies his work. It is a tribute to his patron, his *nutritor* ('foster father'), the term which Augustine used of Ambrose and Bede of Abbot Ceolfrith. Einhard's claim to write truth is also the traditional claim of the hagiographer, an eyewitness of the miraculous events he is recording for posterity. And the deeds of Charlemagne, like those of the saints, could not be passed over in silence. In an account of the translation of the relics of Marcellinus and Peter, Einhard again claims the truthfulness of the eyewitness to justify his account of miracles as reliable. At the start of the Christian era, Cyprian had described Paul's vision of Christ, during his ascent into heaven, as having 'the truthfulness born of sight'[33] and this wording is used in other accounts of miracles. But the eye-witness had a place in the writing of history as well as hagiography. For Isidore of Seville, annals dealt with events of which a generation had had no personal experience, but history had to be written from direct experience, by someone who had seen what he was to write down.[34] So Einhard's claim to eyewitness testimony may express the way his biography would differ from the traditions of the annals. The Astronomer's *Life of Louis* states that he (like Einhard) is an eyewitness and can supply a fitting praise. The new genre of royal biography was to be the work of members of the ruler's circle, men who could write with a proper eloquence.

A famous Russian story tells of how Lenin, on his deathbed, left two envelopes as his legacy to his country. One was labelled, 'To be opened if things get bad', and the second, 'To be opened if things get very bad'. It soon became necessary to open the first envelope, which contained the message 'Blame me'. As things grew worse and worse, the time came to open the second envelope. That message read 'Do as I did'. On the accession of Louis the Pious legates were sent throughout the kingdom to do justice and to remove the oppressors of the people, the oppressors being officials whom Charlemagne had appointed. But in the 820s Charlemagne had become the model ruler, no longer the oppressor.[35] In the *Admonitio ad omnes regni ordines* issued between 823 and 825 Louis claimed to be following the example of his father and his ancestors: 'We do not doubt that it is known to all of you by sight or by repute that our father and forefathers, after they were elected by God to this, especially strove that the honour of the holy church of God and the status of the kingdom should remain fitting. And we do as best we can following their example.'[36]

Krüger has recently suggested that the 'Admonition' was inspired by the *Vita Karoli*: there are further parallels in the discussion of the proper reception of foreign embassies, and the repair of bridges.[37] I am less certain. In 827 Ansegisus described Charlemagne as the 'king and ruler of the kingdom of the Franks and the devout defender and humble supporter of the holy church'.[38] His collection of Charlemagne's capitularies is also, like Einhard's *Life*, an explicit defence against the threat of oblivion. Charlemagne had become a legacy, not simply to be explored with the exuberant superlatives of the Royal Frankish Annals or the *Magnus et Orthodoxus* ('Great and Orthodox') of the inscription – perhaps composed by Einhard – which was carved on Charlemagne's tomb, but also to be used as a stick to beat others with. In 837, Louis the Pious was accused of not having followed the example of Charlemagne.

The biography is presented as a tension between Einhard's professions of humility and modesty and his claims for Ciceronian eloquence. That Ciceronian eloquence becomes the means of eclipsing a Christian language and a Christian set of values, which cannot readily accommodate the ruler Einhard wanted to portray. Of course Einhard's hero is an explicitly Christian ruler, concerned to protect Christians throughout the world and to worship God in a fitting way. His victory over the Saxons depended on his condition that the Saxons abandon the cult of demons and their native rites to take up the sacraments of Christian faith and worship. But throughout the biography these Christian values are implicit: the pope made Pippin king – and made Charlemagne and Carloman succeed him – by God's will. Charlemagne is granted rule over the holy places in Palestine and he restores the churches throughout his kingdoms. He had been brought up a Christian from his youth and he went to church morning and evening, and for the night office. He was concerned with the splendour of the church at Aachen and with the church of St Peter. And at the end of his life his decision to make Louis co-emperor seemed divinely inspired.

Löwe suggested that Einhard's account of Charlemagne as protector of the church and of Rome may reveal an awareness of the implications of the *Donation of Constantine*.[39] But while we may recognise such subtle nuances in Einhard's text, that text is not the exemplary biography of a Christian ruler of the kind which Thegan and the Astronomer provided for Charlemagne's son. It is Thegan, not Einhard, who describes the dying Charlemagne correcting the gospels.[40] It is the Astronomer who reminds us that Charlemagne died as the most pious emperor.[41] Einhard resisted such explicit Christian language, because his sense of greatness could not be simply Christian. And contemporaries were prepared to challenge any picture of Charlemagne as a virtuous Christian emperor.[42]

Some modern readers have regarded the *Vita Karoli* as a treatise on kingship, albeit implicit. But any reader of Carolingian treatises about kingship would be amazed by the silences which fill the *Vita Karoli*. Einhard has little to say about how best to govern a Christian people, or about *consilium* ('counsel'), the virtue which pervades Smaragdus's *Via Regia*. A tradition which goes back to Book V of Augustine's *City of God*, explicitly quoted by Jonas of Orléans in Chapter 17 of his *De Institutione Regia*, praises emperors not for the length of their reign or their peaceful death or their defeat of enemies, for these things have been granted to worshippers of demons. Happy rulers, Augustine explained, rule justly and remember that they are men. They are happy if they fear God and if they love His kingdom.[43] Einhard tells us that the *City of God* was Charlemagne's favourite book: he surely shared Augustine's uncertainty about which emperors were to be praised. If we look at the royal biographies by Thegan and the Astronomer their pages are full of biblical quotations.

We get closest to Einhard's explanatory scheme in an aside in the account of the Saxon war: 'Charlemagne was able to endure and to bear anything, not yielding in adversity nor assenting to a false-smiling fortune in prosperity'.[44] Einhard may have found his false-smiling Fortune in Boethius, but not in any Christian source. The suggestion that humans can be deceived by Fortune set a distance between human endeavour and human understanding of God's purposes. It is a part of Einhard's classical vocabulary, and may derive from Suetonius' *Life of Nero*.

For Regino of Prüm, at the end of the ninth century, Fortune was the best means of explaining the vicissitudes of history.[45]

But the prime agent of historical explanation in the *Vita Karoli* is Einhard's elaborate terminology of personality. Alcuin had said that an orator may secure the benevolence of his audience if he describes the acts of his protagonists as done bravely, wisely and with moderation.[46] This is how Charlemagne's acts are described. Even his appearance is seen as the reflection of his authority and dignity. And it is the use of such abstractions which shapes Einhard's picture of Charlemagne. Instead of the adjectives used in the Royal Frankish Annals, Einhard makes the ethical dimensions of his hero into nouns – independent qualities. Those nouns do not include the *clementia* and *liberalitas* of the Annals – 'clemency' for Tassilo, 'liberality' when Charlemagne ransomed monks sold in Spain in 807. Hellmann noted how Suetonius had used epithets to characterise particular instances of imperial behaviour.[47] For Einhard, Charlemagne was characterised by epithets such as *pietas*, a term covering both love of neighbour and religious devotion. He showed *reverentia* ('reverence') for his mother, *patientia, constantia, prudentia* ('patience, constancy, prudence') and most of all *magnanimitas, magnitudo animae* or *animositas*, that is 'magnanimity' and 'perpetual constancy of mind in adversity' as in prosperity, which the mutability of the Saxons could not defeat or wear out. It is Charlemagne's 'magnanimity' which conquers the quarrelsomeness of the Byzantine emperors.[48] *Magnanimitas* is above all a Stoic virtue, though much praised by Cicero.

The Lives of the Caesars

Einhard wrote, alarmed lest his patron and friend be effaced by the shadows of oblivion. Behind that fear lay a reference to *Ecclesiastes* (9:5–6): 'The living know that they shall die but the dead know not any thing, neither have they any more a reward, for the memory of them is forgotten. Also their love and their hatred and their envy is now perished, neither have they any more a portion forever in any thing that is done under the sun'. To resist that oblivion, Einhard turned to the biographical material he found in Suetonius's *Lives of the Caesars*. Einhard is utterly silent about this source, a rare text in the Carolingian age. Nor does he follow Suetonius quite as slavishly as some modern readers have thought.[49] Yet Suetonius offered him a model which avoided historical narrative. As he explicitly stated, his order is 'not by time but by topic'.[50] Focusing on the anecdotal detail that reveals the individual, Suetonius could document the ruler's qualities and defects to assess his performance within a series of categories.[51] Einhard turned to Suetonius as a source for the structure as well as the vocabulary of biography. Like Suetonius, Einhard describes his ruler's *gens* ('people'), his wars, the territories conquered, the public works, the navy, the private life, marriages, children, relations, how the children were brought up, friendships, appearance, dress, food and drink, rest, eloquence and studies, death, burial and portents. The only two sections without any Suetonian parallel are the imperial coronation and the coronation of Charlemagne's son Louis.

But, while Suetonius supplied the model, Einhard was not as slavish a follower as Bernheim or Halphen have suggested.[52] Set beside most of Suetonius, Einhard's text is incredibly laconic. He moves in a world of monumentality and silence, a world in which his terms convey a different weight and resonance from Suetonian ones.

For Einhard is using ethical terms which are not religious but political. They constitute Charlemagne's inner essence and they mean that the range of anecdote found in Suetonius can be omitted. We rarely feel close to Charlemagne in this biography: his own words are mentioned only four times. We learn that he could not do without the company of his daughters, that he complained about fasts, that he often told the sacristans not to allow anything unworthy to be brought to or left in the church at Aachen, and that if he had known about the imperial coronation he would not have entered St-Peter's.[53] With the possible exception of that last comment (which may be no more than a profession of modesty), none of these is as revelatory as the words of emperors recorded by Suetonius. Nor are there many facts not to be found in other sources. If Walahfrid was correct and Charlemagne told Einhard his secrets, very few have found their way into this *Life*. Einhard never explicitly defends his hero, except in the account of the two conspiracies against Charlemagne where we are told that 'Charles consented to his wife's cruelty and so moved away from his natural benignity and mildness. For the rest of his life he ruled with the highest love and esteem of everyone, and not the least charge of cruelty or unfairness was ever brought against him by anyone'.[54]

It is a biography in which use of the first person is exceptionally rare. We have Einhard's account of why he is silent about Charlemagne's birth, infancy and boyhood. He will lay out and demonstrate Charlemagne's deeds, his *mores* and the aspects of his life, omitting nothing which is fitting or necessary. In an important aside Einhard explains why he does not supply details of the difficult crossing of the Alps: 'I would relate here how difficult it was to enter Italy over the Alps and what a struggle it was for the Franks to overcome unmarked mountain ridges, upthrust rocks and rugged terrain, were it not my intention in this book to record the manner of his life rather than the details of the wars which he waged.'[55]

Einhard may be recalling the accounts of the crossings of the Alps in Livy and Orosius, but he had crossed the Alps himself and could have given an eloquent account. Instead there are systematic, if summary, accounts of the wars. In every case we learn why the war was started and how it was concluded. The fullest account is of the Saxon war, and it shows how Einhard explains Charlemagne's most difficult achievement:

> The Saxons, like all of the nations dwelling in Germania are by nature fierce and given over to the worship of demons and opponents of our religion. There were

more immediate causes: the open frontier and the constant slaughter, theft and arson, which so enraged the Franks that they resolved on open war. The war lasted for thirty-three years, prolonged by the treachery [*perfidia*] of the Saxons. Finally the Saxons were united with the Franks into one people.[56]

In the Royal Frankish Annals readers could learn how in a single year Charlemagne might fight Spaniards, Saracens, Saxons and Slavs. In the *Life* his campaigns target separate peoples, and so the expansion of the kingdom of the Franks becomes a series of victories or treaties, suggesting a grand strategy rather than a policy of plunder.

Einhard had found such a model in Suetonius, but his terminology is not merely Suetonian. After the account of the final campaign, against Gottfried, King of the Northmen, Einhard has a remarkable passage, which deserves to be quoted in full:

These were the wars that that mighty king waged with great skill and success in many lands over the forty-seven years he reigned. In those wars he so splendidly added to the Frankish kingdom, which he had received in great and strong condition from his father Pepin [Pippin], that he nearly doubled its size. Previously the so-called eastern Franks had occupied no more than that part of Gaul bounded by the Rhine, the Loire, the ocean and the Balearic Sea and that part of Germany bounded by Saxony, the Danube, Rhine and Saal (the river that divides Thuringians and Sorabians). In addition to these areas, the Alemannians and Bavarians fell under the control of the Frankish kingdom. Charles himself, in the wars just described, first added Aquitaine, Gascony, and the whole range of the Pyrenees until the river Ebro, which has its source in Navarre, passes through the fertile fields of Spain, and joins the Balearic Sea under the city walls of Tortosa. Next he conquered all of Italy, which runs more than a thousand miles from Aosta to lower Calabria, which forms the border between the Beneventans and the Greeks. Then he subdued Saxony, which comprises a large part of Germany and is thought to be twice as wide as the land occupied by the Franks, but similar to it in length. After this he added both Pannonia, Dacia on the far side of the Danube, and also Istria, Liburnia and Dalmatia. However, for the sake of friendly relations and preserving the pact between them he allowed the emperor of Constantinople to keep certain coastal cities. Then he subordinated and made tributary all the rough and uncivilised peoples inhabiting Germany between the Rhine and the Vistula rivers, the ocean and the Danube. They almost all speak a similar language, but are very different from each other in custom and appearance. Among these peoples the Weltabi, Sorabians, Abrodites and Bohemians are of special importance, and he came into armed conflict with all of them. Other peoples who far outnumbered them, simply surrendered.[57]

This ethnogeography derives not from Suetonius but from passages in Orosius and Isidore, though some details seem to depend on Pliny's *Natural History*.[58] Solinus is the source for the length of Italy.[59] The name of the Weltabi is found in the Revised Royal Frankish Annals for 789, but the Sorabi and the Abroditi are first mentioned there in 822. Liburnia and Dalmatia feature together in the annal for 821. In its ethnic terminology this passage thus reflects the concerns of Louis the Pious's court circle. And the geography was visible to that circle: Louis had kept the silver table with a map of the world which Charlemagne had owned and had willed to be divided at his death.[60] Paul the Deacon, in his *History of the Bishops of Metz*, had stated that Charlemagne had extended his kingdom as never before.[61] Einhard, writing long after Paul, was able to use his knowledge of classical geographical writings to give a detailed picture of Charlemagne as the 'Father of Europe'.

Einhard's geographic excursus is his fullest tribute to Charlemagne's imperial achievement. It reveals his own interest in Germany and the Germans, an interest explicit in his preface, in which he described himself as 'a German without training in the language of Rome'. Two passages in the *Vita Karoli* have excited the interest of Germanists: Einhard's listing of Charlemagne's German names for the months and the winds, and his command 'that the very old Germanic poems in which the deeds and wars of ancient kings were sung should be written down. He began a grammar of his native language'. Suetonius had recorded the calendar reforms of Caesar and Augustus, but Einhard's detail about the Germanic Christian calendar is remarkable. In his account of the translation of relics to his monasteries he recorded miracles in which Germanic speakers were possessed by devils speaking fluent Latin and in which deaf and mute boys spoke German and Latin.[62] He makes it quite clear that Latin was the language of Christianity, but that German was the native tongue of his own compatriots. So the Christianisation of the Saxons, which ended their violation of divine and human laws and speeded their union with the Franks, was the model for the progress Charlemagne brought to the *barbaras ac feras nationes*, the 'rough and uncivilised' Germans between Rhine, Vistula and Danube. This vision of Christian kingship is echoed in the coronation *Ordines*, where the peoples ruled are to keep faith and love and charity and are victorious in peace.[63]

Power and a private life

Ultimately Einhard's Life of Charlemagne is very much about the implications of power, though the justification of royal power is set in the opening sections about the rise of the Arnulphings. The Merovingians are without vigour, they have only the vain name of king, in contrast to the wealth and power of the mayors of the palace. The rulers whom Charles Martel fights are called 'tyrants', rulers without any divine right to their thrones.[64] In contrast Charlemagne and Carloman are made kings by an assembly of the Franks on condition that they divide the kingdom equally, and they both accept these conditions. Einhard, as a Frank from east of the Rhine, portrays Charlemagne as a Frankish ruler wearing Frankish clothing and subject to Frankish conditions of consent. The power of the Franks was always suspect to the Greeks and Romans.[65] In the Beneventan war, Charlemagne is concerned for the *utilitas gentis* the 'best interests of the people'.[66] Charlemagne's friendships with foreign rulers increased the glory of the kingdom. The association of Louis with Charlemagne as co-emperor in 813 was for the *utilitas regni* ('best interests of the kingdom'), and it both enhanced his reputation and inspired fear in surrounding peoples. Kingdom and nation, especially the nation of the Franks, have a part in Einhard's world; his focus on Charlemagne should not hide his national pride.

Yet it is the account of Charlemagne's private life which has attracted readers. The thick neck, the bulging belly, the weak voice for so large a man, even the limp can all be found in the lives of the Caesars, but they were not the stuff of early medieval biography. It is the measure of Charlemagne's greatness that these details do not damage him. And they are enhanced by Einhard's care to make his hero into another intellectual: enjoying the *City of God*, educating his children in the liberal arts as well as the Frankish ones, learning grammar and astronomy and even trying to write with his tablets under his pillow. The 'leisure and learning' which Einhard found in Cicero and exhorted his readers not to abuse had become the hallmark of the civilised rule of his hero. Tiberius had also most diligently cultivated the liberal arts, and Einhard probably found the word 'talkative' (*dicaculus*) – which he uses to praise Charlemagne's eloquence – in the *Scriptores Historiae Augustae*.[67] But he was reporting on the court life in which he had shared, where poets were prized and courtiers discussed comets. This revival of learning was admired by Walahfrid and Lupus: it has become Charlemagne's undisputed legacy.

Einhard's biography is the work of a courtier erecting a monument to his patron. And that monument, like the arch erected over the grave, called Charles 'the great' (*Karoli magni*).[68] Such an epithet was neither common nor self-evident, though posterity had no hesitation in adopting it. In 841 Nithard could write of Charlemagne 'deservedly called great by all nations'. The best modern analysis of historical greatness remains Burckhardt's lectures *Das Individuum und das Allgemeine,* given in 1870–71 as a part of his course on the study of history.[69] Burckhardt recognised that the concept of greatness is both relative and indispensable, and explicitly warned against a need for submission and admiration, which lead to the worship of false idols. We risk confusing power with greatness and thinking ourselves much too important. But the great man is unique and irreplaceable, his relationship to his age a sacred marriage, his understanding of his age free from the noise of the moment.[70] Einhard has no such philosophical reflections: his vision of greatness derived from his classical models and required the eloquence of Latinity. But by proclaiming that Charlemagne was 'the most outstanding and deservedly famous king ... the greatest of all the men of his time' and recording his deeds, 'which people now alive can scarcely equal' he ensured that Burckhardt, and lesser historians, would have to acknowledge Charlemagne's greatness.

His biography was an effort to provide a fitting praise: 'Could I keep silent about the splendid and exceedingly brilliant deeds of a man who had been so kind to me and could I allow his life to remain without record and proper praise as if he had never lived?' Jerome had decreed that the acts of the saints should not be passed over in silence. Einhard affirmed that the cohorts of the saints could make room for someone even greater than them.

Notes

1 Nithard, *Hist.*, 1.1; trans. Scholz (1970), pp. 129–30.
2 Einhard, *VK*, cc. 4, 6.
3 Walahfrid, *Preface*, MGH *SSRG*, pp. xxviii–xxix; trans. Dutton (1998), pp. 7–8.
4 Dutton (1998), p. 8.
5 The chapter divisions used in all Latin and English editions of Einhard, *VK*, derive from the 1521 edition published in Cologne by Hermann, Count of Neuenar (1492–1530). Walahfrid's chapter headings and divisions are included as notes in Holder Egger's edition (1911). Löwe (1974) notes that the chapter headings and Walahfrid's reorganisation of the text obscure our understanding of Einhard's intentions.
6 Ranke (1854); Wattenbach and Levison (1953), p. 273; Hellmann (1932), p. 54.
7 Einhard, *VK*, Preface.
8 *Ibid.*
9 Cassian, *De coenobiorum institutis*, XII.19; ed. Ramsey (2000), p. 265.
10 *Vita Praeiecti*, MGH *SSRM* V, p. 226.
11 Alcuin, *Disputatio de rhetorica*, c. 37, p. 132.
12 Kempshall (1995); Krüger (1998), pp. 134–7.
13 Löwe (1983); Lambot, ed. (1945), p. 89.
14 Walahfrid, *Preface*; trans. Dutton (1998), pp. 7–8.
15 Hraban Maur, *Epitaphium Einhardi*; MGH *PLAC* I, pp. 237–8; trans. Dutton (1998), p. 10.
16 Lupus, *Epistolae*, no. 1 (830); trans. Dutton (1998), pp. 166–8.
17 Wandalbert, *Vita et miracula Sancti Goaris*, ed. Steine (1981), pp. 2–3, 94.
18 Ganz (1989).
19 I have identified 112 surviving manuscripts of the *Vita*. The date of its composition is much discussed; I believe that Einhard revised his text, but that a first version was already circulating in the mid-820s. See also Tischler (2001).
20 Gerward, *Preface*; trans. Dutton (1998), p. 4. Gerward was probably the author of the *AX*; Löwe (1951).
21 Ganz (1997).
22 Reimitz (2000a), pl. 10.
23 *Ibid.*, p. 70.
24 Walahfrid, *Preface*, trans. Dutton (1998), p. 7; Lupus, *Epistolae*, no. 1, trans. Dutton (1998), p. 167; MGH *PLAC* II, p. 126; trans. Dutton (1998), p. 4.
25 Einhard, *VK*, Preface, c. 4.
26 *PL* 30, col. 302.
27 *PL* 74, col. 367.
28 Einhard, *VK*, cc. 2, 18.
29 Smaragdus, *Vita Benedicti*, Preface, MGH *SS* XV, p. 201.
30 *Gesta Aldrici*, PL 115, col. 92. The *Gesta* also echo Einhard's strictures on prolixity.
31 Collins (1998a).

32 Jonas of Orléans, *Historia translationis S. Hucberti*, *PL* 106, col. 389.

33 Cyprian, *Ad Fortunatum*, c. 13; *CSEL* III, p. 346.

34 Isidore, *Etymologiae*, bk I.xliv.

35 The *VK* was certainly composed after 817. Löwe (1983) argued for a date in the late 820s and gives a full account of all previous dating attempts. Krüger (1998) suggested that the *VK* was being quoted in charters of Louis the Pious issued in 823. It is important to note that, in a manuscript culture, the date of composition is not the date at which a work was circulating to a wide readership.

36 MGH *Capit.* I, no. 150, pp. 303–7.

37 Krüger (1998), p. 144.

38 Ansegisus, *Liber legiloquus*, Preface, MGH *Capit.* I, no. 137, p. 275.

39 Löwe (1974), pp. 12–13.

40 Thegan, *Gesta Hludowici imperatoris*, c. 7.

41 Astronomer, *Vita Hludowici imperatoris*, c. 20; trans. Cabaniss (1961), pp. 52–3.

42 Dutton (1994); Hägermann (2000), pp. 577–81.

43 Jonas, *De institutione regia*, c. 17, quoting Augustine, *City of God*, V.24.

44 Einhard, *VK*, c. 8.

45 Löwe (1973), pp. 149–79.

46 Alcuin, *De rhetorica*, c. 20, ed. and trans. Howell (1965), p. 100.

47 Hellmann (1932), pp. 49–61.

48 Einhard, *VK*, c. 28.

49 Innes (1997a). The verso of the last leaf of the Tours copy of Suetonius (Paris, BNF lat. 6115) has a very rubbed ninth-century text, including a discussion of tyranny, which has not yet been edited.

50 Suetonius, *Vita Augusti*, c. 9.

51 A. Wallace-Hadrill (1995), p. 22.

52 Halphen (1921), pp. 91–8.

53 Einhard, *VK*, cc. 19, 24, 26, 28.

54 Einhard, *VK*, c. 20.

55 Einhard, *VK*, c. 7; Einhard, *Translatio*, I.7–8; trans. Dutton (1998), pp. 77–8.

56 Einhard, *VK*, c. 7.

57 Einhard, *VK*, c. 15.

58 Orosius, *Libri Historiarum contra paganos*, I.2; Isidore, *Etymologiae*, XIV; Pliny, *Natural History*, III.5.6.

59 Solinus, *Collectanea rerum memorabilium*, II.23.

60 Thegan, *Gesta Hludowici*, c. 8.

61 Paul the Deacon, *Gesta episcoporum Mettensium*, MGH *SS* II, p. 265.

62 Einhard, *Translatio* III.14, 17–18; trans. Dutton (1998), pp. 103–4, 106–7.

63 Jackson (1995), pp. 53, 59–60, 63, 64, all dating from Charlemagne's reign.

64 Fouracre, ch. 1, pp. 5–21, in this volume.

65 Einhard, *VK*, c. 16.

66 Einhard, *VK*, c. 10.

67 Tiberius, *Vita Hadriani* 20.8.1; '*dicaculus*' is very rare, as Gottschalk noted, and is not found in Cicero or Suetonius; Lambot, ed. (1945), p. 489.

68 Einhard, *VK*, c. 31.

69 Ganz, ed. (2000), pp. 274–305.

70 *Ibid.*

4

CHARLEMAGNE'S IMPERIAL CORONATION AND THE ANNALS OF LORSCH

Roger Collins

Sources for Charlemagne's imperial coronation

While most of Einhard's account of Charlemagne in his *Vita Karoli* is still generally trusted, sometimes uncritically so, his description of Charles's reactions to receiving the imperial title has long been questioned.[1] Einhard reports that the king went to the city of Rome in 800, 'to restore the very disturbed state of the Church', and spent most of the winter there. No account is given of how he came to receive the imperial title, and even the location and exact date of his elevation are implied rather than stated explicitly. The nature of the proceedings and the rituals involved in this process of emperor-making are not described at all. All that is revealed clearly in the very brief section of the work devoted to these events, is that Charles subsequently claimed that he was not pleased by what had occurred and that, if he had known in advance what was to happen, he would not have entered the church that day, despite its being one of the great festivals of the Christian year.

Charles's reluctance to accept the imperial coronation, as reported by Einhard, has no doubt rightly been interpreted as a manifestation of the tradition of the refusal of power, both secular and ecclesiastical, that was a marked feature of political good behaviour in late antiquity.[2] Secular rulers, from the emperor Julian in 360 to the Visigothic king Wamba in 672, are described in the narrative sources as obstinately refusing imperial or royal office, but finally agreeing when threatened with death as the only alternative. In a very similar way, those called to offices of power and status in the Church were expected to put up a show of resistance, before in the end allowing themselves to be persuaded into acceptance. How far such refusals represented a purely literary convention or to what extent they actually had to be acted out in practice is not known, but it is clear that they constituted the accepted way to describe how praiseworthy individuals might have been expected to respond when called upon to undertake high office.

For such a response to be credible, however, there had to be no element of premeditation or planning in the making of the offer. The intended recipient of an office of authority had to be unaware that this was about to be thrust upon him. For there to have been too long a lead-up to this point, even if it were kept concealed from the central figure himself, would strain credulity. The decision to select the individual to be so honoured thus also had to seem to be a sudden, and possibly an inspired, choice. In the case of Charlemagne and the imperial coronation, not only does Einhard's account of his supposed personal reluctance to accept his new status fit this model, but the apparent lack of prior planning and discussion of the decision to revive the western imperial title in his favour clearly belongs to the same tradition. If Charles was to be presented as regretting being tricked into his change of status, then there could be no suggestion that the revival of the imperial office in the West had been seriously discussed in the period leading up to his acceptance of it. Thus, to preserve the decencies of correct political behaviour, the complex and lengthy decision-making processes that might be expected to have preceded Charles's taking of the title of emperor cannot be expected to feature in the narrative sources of this time.

As a result, Einhard gives but the briefest account of the events leading up to the imperial coronation. He reports simply that the populace of Rome had attacked Pope Leo III, blinding him and cutting out his tongue, forcing him to flee to Charles to beg for help. It was to rectify the damage done to the Church by this episode that the Frankish king came to Rome early the following winter.[3] As an outline of these events, Einhard's version is not mendacious, but it is compressed to the highest degree. Much fuller versions of all or some of these episodes can be found in other sources, including the *Annales Regni Francorum* (properly translated, the 'Annals of the Frankish Kingdom', but commonly known as the Royal Frankish Annals and hereafter abbreviated to RFA), various other sets of shorter Frankish annals, the unfinished or truncated verse panegyric known as *Karolus magnus et Leo papa* (The Paderborn Epic), and the biography of Leo III in the *Liber Pontificalis*. Several of the letters of Alcuin, formerly a prominent member of Charles's entourage and by this time abbot of St-Martin at Tours, also throw light not just on some of these events but also on the inspiration behind the idea of reviving the imperial title.[4]

None of these texts is very substantial, or in itself gives a full and convincing account of what happened, let alone of the motivation behind the actions of the primary participants. In consequence, and not surprisingly, it has become customary for scholars seeking to interpret the causes and significance of the imperial coronation of 800 to try to produce a synoptic version of events, using elements culled from all the available sources. Thus, one text might be called upon to provide a date for a particular episode, while another might be used to suggest the motive behind it. Taking bits and pieces of information from all these sources ultimately produces an apparently seamless narrative that can be used to justify one or other of a number of possible explanations for what happened. That the sources themselves give often contradictory accounts of particular parts of the story, or omit some aspects of it while favouring others, need not matter when such an approach is adopted. Omissions can be passed over in silence when one text provides the information that another lacks, and contradictions vanish when the historian can pick and choose at will amongst the various elements on offer from multiple sources. The result is, of course, intellectual blancmange, that is about as appetising and nourishing as its gastronomic namesake.

Behind each and every source was a creative intelligence that worked upon the information available, deciding what to include and what to omit. Each author was also prey to the dissemination of misinformation and subject to the ignorance caused by a lack of information. What is required, in place of the approach outlined above, is a thorough examination of each of these sources of evidence, in an attempt to try to understand just how much each compiler or author actually knew, and why they wished or were persuaded to describe some events in the way that they did and to omit others entirely. It cannot be assumed that each text depended upon full and reliable information or that motives did not exist to limit or distort the image presented of one of the most significant episodes in the history of the age. The individual perspective, both ideological and chrono-logical, of the composers of these sources thus requires analysis to isolate the distinctive features, both strengths and weaknesses, of their accounts.

The compositional history and tradition of each text also requires study, so as to establish as best we may when it was first composed and what possibilities existed for subsequent stages of editing or altering its account. For example, while it is often taken for granted that the RFA were at this time being compiled on an annual basis, and that they therefore provide a virtually contemporary account of the events they describe, no extant manuscript of this work can lead its reader back beyond the stage of the completion of the final version of the text, in other words no earlier than the form in which it existed after the year 829. Thus, at least three decades of editorial alteration or 'improvement' may exist between the first writing of the RFA annal for 800 and the state in which it is available to us today.[5]

The Lorsch Annals

The kind of detailed analysis of each of the sources relating to Charles's imperial coronation suggested here would require more extended treatment than is possible in a single chapter. A beginning, though, can be made by looking at one particular text that has been recognised as having a unique contribution to make to our understanding of these events. This is the set of annals known since the late eighteenth century as the *Annales Laureshamenses* or 'Annals of Lorsch' (*AL*).[6] The *AL* are much less substantial than the well-known RFA, but some of the inform-ation to be found in the *AL* is not available from any other Frankish annal or chronicle source. Above all, the *AL* provides specific information on the important questions of when and where the decision about offering the imperial title to Charlemagne was made, as well as giving an explanation of the grounds on which the offer was made and why he was willing to accept it.

Among the unique details that this text provides is the claim that the question of reviving the imperial title in Charlemagne's favour was raised and discussed at an assembly held in Rome following his arrival.[7] This, no doubt correctly, has been identified with the assembly that, according to the RFA, began its meetings seven days after the Frankish ruler arrived in the city on 24 November. In other words the assembly started on 30 November or 1 December – over three weeks before the crowning of Charlemagne as emperor on Christmas Day 800. The *AL* are the only source that contradicts Einhard's statement about Charles's ignorance of what was going to happen when he entered St-Peter's that day, and show instead that the matter had been debated and decided upon at the beginning of the same month. These annals might thus seem particularly deserving of credence.[8] If so, this must depend upon analysis of their compositional history and an intensive sifting of their testimony on the events surrounding the imperial coronation.

While none of the so-called minor Frankish annals have benefited from a modern critical edition or much scholarly study, the *AL* have long aroused more interest, largely because of the hypothesis that a fragment of a manuscript (now in Vienna), containing the final section of the work, was the compiler's original codex or at least provided evidence of contemporary, year-by-year composition of the annual entries of which the work is comprised.[9] This has been used to support the widespread view that many Frankish annal compilations, above all the RFA, enjoyed at least some periods of contemporaneous year-by-year composition, rather than retrospective compilation covering a period of several years. The *AL* thus bear a heavy burden of historiographical responsibility, despite the limited and ambiguous nature of the evidence of their own manuscript tradition.

The composition of the Lorsch Annals and the St-Paul manuscript

In its fullest form, the *AL* consist of a set of annals that, following a brief chronological introduction, cover the period from the year 703 up to the year 803.[10] This complete run of annals is found only in the sole surviving quire of an otherwise lost codex.[11] In the late eighteenth century it belonged to the monastery of St-Blasien in the Black Forest, in south-western Germany, and in 1790 it was edited by the librarian of the house, Aemilianus Ussermann (d. 1794).[12] The Napoleonic Wars led in 1809 to the relocation of the monks of St-Blasien and their library to the monastery of St-Paul im Lavanttal, in Carinthia (Kärnten), in southern Austria. However, when in 1820 the editor of the newly founded Monumenta Germaniae Historica, G.H. Pertz, sought to use this manuscript to prepare a new edition of the work for the first volume of the Monumenta's *Scriptores* series, it could not be found and was presumed to have been lost.[13] Pertz therefore had to make do with the text of the manuscript as contained in Ussermann's edition.

Fortunately, the St-Paul manuscript of the *AL* had not been permanently lost; it was rediscovered and used in 1889 by Eberhard Katz to produce a new edition of the *AL*, intended to emend and improve earlier versions.[14] Only his edition provides a first-hand description of the manuscript, with suggestions as to its date and provenance. A marginal note referring to the burial of Charlemagne's brother-in-law Gerold in the abbey of Reichenau has been taken to support a Reichenau provenance, and Katz's dating of the codex to the ninth century remains unchallenged.[15] The only other text contained in the manuscript is part of an Easter table, using (unusually) the nineteen-year cycles of Theophilus of Alexandria, covering the period from 777 to 835, which might suggest, though not prove, that it was written before the latter date.[16]

The compositional history of the text that, in its full form, is uniquely preserved in the St-Paul manuscript is complex but revealing. As has long been recognised, the text of the entries for all the years from 703 up to and including 785 is not unique to this set of annals.[17] Almost exactly the same material appears in at least two other contexts. One of these is the set of annals known since the nineteenth century as the *Annales Mosellani* or Moselle Annals (*AM*), which cover the years 703 to 798.[18] These are preserved exclusively in a late eleventh- or early twelfth-century manuscript from northern France; a reference on fol. 81 to the compilation of Domesday Book means that it must post-date 1086, the year in which that text was compiled.[19] The other is the work known as the *Fragmentum Chesnianum*.[20] This is a group of annals, covering the years from 768 to 790, set between a copy of the *Chronicle of Fredegar* (in its second version) and part of the RFA (for the years 791 to 806), in a late ninth- or tenth-century manuscript from Rheims.[21] While the *Fragmentum* begins only in 768, the text of all the annals for the years before 786 is virtually identical in all three works. The implication, long accepted, is that this represents an earlier annalistic stem that was borrowed and separately continued after 786 by the compilers of the *AL* and the other two sets of annals. This is confirmed by the presence at the end of the *AL* entry for 785 of a calculation of the number of years that had passed between the death of Pope Gregory the Great in 605 and 'the present'.[22]

Numerous references to events and persons connected with the monastery of Lorsch in the *AL* annals from 764 to 785 make it virtually certain that the act of compilation in 785 was carried out there.[23] The related house of Gorze also features, but such references are not as frequent or extensive as for Lorsch. In particular, the obits of all the abbots of Lorsch up to the year 784 are included in the annals, while the death of only one of those of Gorze is mentioned. It was the prominence of information relating to Lorsch that led to the full set of annals, from 703 to 803, being given the title of *Annales Laureshamenses* or Lorsch Annals. This encouraged Kurze to identify the compiler of the *AL* as Richbod, abbot of

Lorsch (from 784) and bishop of Trier (791–804), whose death in 804 might explain the sudden cessation of annal-keeping with the entry for 803.[24] However, the references to the monastery and its abbots end with the annal for 785, and it must be concluded that it was only the stem compilation which finished in that year that was the genuine Lorsch product. Nothing in the post-786 section of annals demonstrates any Lorsch connection. Additionally, neither of the two extant manuscripts containing all that we now have of the *AL* was written at Lorsch, so it is highly unlikely that the text in its completed form was a Lorsch work or that Richbod was its author.[25] At least, though, it is possible to establish the existence and isolate the text of the earlier compilation of annals made in Lorsch in 785, which provided the stem from which the rest of the *AL* developed. Despite the risk of causing confusion with the numerous other historical compilations that are also rightly or wrongly ascribed to Lorsch, it might be helpful to call this stem text the Lorsch Annals of 785.

As previously mentioned, the *AL* are not alone in attaching their own unique record of the years 786 to 803 onto the stem formed by the Lorsch Annals of 785. The *Fragmentum Chesnianum* and the Moselle Annals do the same. Thus, while the *Fragmentum* and *AL* are textually very close for the years 768 to 785, they diverge completely in the middle of their respective annals for 786, and show no further link.[26] The fact, however, that they share a common opening section of the entry for 786 would suggest that rather than using the Lorsch Annals of 785 in their original form and as completed in that year, they were both actually using a copy of the 785 compilation that had received a short continuation on into 786. Textually it is easy to demonstrate that the *Fragmentum*, while generally briefer than *AL*, did not derive its text of the Lorsch Annals of 785 (with the 786 continuation) directly from *AL*. The two works owe their close relationship and textual similarities to a shared indebtedness to the common source. The third compilation that depended upon the Lorsch Annals of 785 for its account of the years up to that date, the Moselle Annals, is different in this respect; it lacks an entry for 786 (which thereafter consistently puts out its chronology by one year), and does not contain the material common to the *AL* and *Fragmentum* relating to the events of that year. It thus seems likely that it used a copy of the original version of the Lorsch Annals of 785 as the basis of its continuation, rather than one with the 786 extension.[27]

What this adds up to is more interesting than the laborious processes involved in making these deductions. That is to say, it would seem that a surprising number of annal compilations were being initiated in the mid-780s. One was completed in Lorsch in 785, and was given a short continuation in 786. From this, three other sets of annals derived; one from the 785 version (*AM*) and two from that of 786 (*AL* and the *Fragmentum*). Interestingly, none of these carried on for very long. The *Fragmentum* ends with its entry for 790, *AM* terminates in 798, and *AL* carries on only to its brief annal for 803. It is notable too that several other 'minor' annal compilations also come to an end at the same period. These include three textually closely-linked sets of annals that are all partly related to the Lorsch Annals of 785 through the use of a common source for their entries for the years up to 759.[28] These compilations – known as the *Annales Nazariani* (Annals of St-Nazarius), the *Annales Guelfybertani* (Wolfenbüttel Annals) and the *Annales Alamannici* (Alemannic Annals) – end with accounts of the years 790, 791 and 799 respectively, though the latter two enjoyed various ninth-century continuations.[29]

These chronological coincidences, if that is what they be, are not the only point of contact between all these texts when taken as a whole. What is also particularly notable is the nature of their contents. They avoid any reference to purely local concerns and events, unlike the Lorsch Annals of 785 (and indeed many other medieval chronicles and annals). Deaths of abbots are not recorded and hardly a bishop is mentioned. Instead, attention is devoted consistently to the major political and military events taking place in the Frankish realm, and above all to the deeds of its ruler and his family. Although there are indications that the works were being written in ecclesiastical centres, their concerns are pre-eminently secular (even allowing that manifestations of divine favour or displeasure might be expressed through the outcome of secular events). Equally notable are those aspects of royal activity that are not mentioned; legal and administrative matters, including the issue of several weighty and significant capitularies, never feature in these records. Above all, while most of these annals – and several other sets not mentioned here – are clearly being independently compiled, with marked variations between them in terms of language and details chosen for inclusion, they display a remarkable consistency in terms of the nature of their contents, and that can hardly be coincidental.

It may be that the flurry of annal-making in the 780s, which might well be extended to include the RFA themselves (the first section of which consists of a compilation of annals extending up to the year 788), was somehow officially sponsored. Otherwise, it is hard to understand in the light of previous practices why so many different sets of annals should be compiled at different locations, more or less all at the same time, while also being so consistent in the nature of the information they include and that which they exclude. The termination of virtually all of them in the 790s or in the years up to 806, despite subsequent stages of continuation in some cases, is equally striking, and can hardly be coincidental. How this unprecedented spate of annal-making and its cessation came about is not easy to understand, in the absence of specific references in capitulary legislation or other sources to the promotion or discontinuation of such record-making processes. That the RFA start to continue their stem text of *c.* 788 some time about 794, and then display several marked changes in their literary and other characteristics about 807/8, cannot fail to be pertinent in this context.[30] It is at least a possibility that the making of annals, of a particular type and content, in many of the major ecclesiastical centres of the Frankish realm, was encouraged by Charlemagne and his court from the later 780s onwards, only to give way to an attempt to promote a single 'authorised' and centrally produced record in the form of the RFA by about 807/8 at the latest. It is thus significant that the continuation of the *Annales Guelfybertani* covering the years 791 to 805 is no more than an epitome of the entries of the RFA for the same period, and that the *Fragmentum Chesnianum* is followed without any break by the text of the RFA for the years 791 to 806.[31]

Some of the conclusions so far reached with respect to the relationships between the various sets of Carolingian annals, and the text tradition of *AL* can be rendered graphically by the diagram in Figure 4:

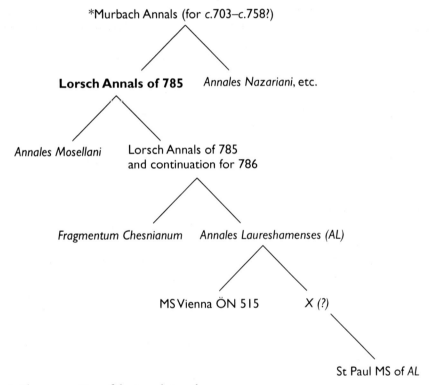

4 The composition of the Lorsch Annals

The Vienna manuscript

The only other manuscript containing a portion of the *AL*, Vienna Österreichische Nationalbibliothek MS 515, has often been used as evidence that at least some of the entries for the years 786–803 were composed annually and were thus genuinely contemporary with the events described, possibly even the author's own copy.[32] This manuscript is a fragment of an otherwise lost codex and consists of only eight folios. The first five contain the final entries of *AL*, comprising part of the entry for the year 794, followed by all the annals up to the concluding one for 803. The script used for writing most of the extant folios, and certainly all of the *AL*, has been dated to around the year 800, thus making it contemporary with the text being copied.

The manuscript was once thought to come from Lorsch itself, but a reassessment of the script has suggested an origin in an unidentified scriptorium further up the Rhine, possibly in the Lake Constance region, geographically close to Reichenau, the probable home of the St-Paul manuscript.[33] The Vienna codex was found in Reichenau itself by Wolfgang Lazius in 1551, but there is no evidence that it had originated there. The relationship between the Vienna fragment of *c.* 800 and the St-Paul manuscript of perhaps a quarter-century later is close but not immediate. There are some errors in the St-Paul codex that could not have arisen if it were a direct copy of the Vienna one; at least one intermediary stage must be postulated. That both extant codices containing *AL* come from the Reichenau/Lake Constance area, and are close in date to the original point of compilation, supports the suspicion that the work was first put together in this region. Another lost copy, however, must have made its way westwards to the Spanish March, where it served as an important ingredient in the still little-understood Chronicle of Moissac.

The view that the Vienna manuscript was the *AL* author's own copy of his work, alongside various refutations of this view, has led to a number of contradictory claims being made about the testimony of this fragment. Perhaps because of this uncertainty as to its status, it has attracted comparatively little scholarly interest in recent years.[34] Evaluation of the importance of the Vienna manuscript, and the text it contains, depends on close palaeographic analysis. Unterkircher detected four different scribal hands in the five extant folios whose work can be summarised as follows: Scribe A (fol. 1r, fol. 1v line 18 to fol. 2v line 13); Scribe B (fol. 1v lines 1–18, fol. 2v line 14 to fol. 3r line 1); Scribe C (fol. 3r line 2 to fol. 4r line 17); Scribe D (fol. 4r line 18 to the end of the work on fol. 5r, line 10).[35] The rest of folio 5 was originally left blank, probably for further continuations of the annals that were never written. In the late tenth century the remainder of fol. 5r was used for some Old High German verses, and then a few short liturgical pieces were added on fol. 5v.

If these changes of scribal hand are compared with the text, then the division of annals between Unterkircher's four scribes appears as follows: Scribe A wrote what has survived of the annal for 794, then the second part of the annal for 795 (Figure 5, lines 18–27) and all of the annals for 796 and 797; Scribe B wrote the first part of the annal for 795 (Figure 5, lines 1–18); Scribe C copied the annals for the years 799 to 801 (Figure 6); while Scribe D was responsible for those for 802 (Figure 6, fol. 4r lines 18–27) and 803. Thus the changes of hand generally, but not universally, coincide with the beginning of new annals. While this variety of hands is not encountered in other manuscripts containing annals, it may mean no more than the scribes taking turns, marked by the limits of the individual annals,

xxviii + DCCXCV· Sed & etiam tunc apud aquis palatio domnus rex
celebrauit pascha· & infidelitas unde consueuerat a parte saxanorum
exortaest· quia ad domnus rex supal & remeſuenire uo luiſſet nec ipſi
ad eum pleniter uenerunt· nec eis solarium ut ipſe iuſſerat mittens miſe
Tunc iterum cognita infidelitate eorum rex cum exercitu ſuo ſuper eos
ueniens aliis et pacifice robuſtam uenientes ex parte ſaxanorum· & cum eo
inſolatio ſuo ipſum rex expleuerunt· & ipſe cum exercitu ſuo ad albia
puenit· ſed aliis circa palude ſalue & cum uiſi huiuſmodingas ad eum pleniter
nonuenerunt· domnus rex tamen reſedens apud bardunuuih·
tantam multitudinem obſidum inde tulit· quartum nunquam in diebus ſuis
aut in diebus patris ſui aut in diebus regum francorum inde aliquando tu
.... ſed & tunc omnes ad ſe uenientes excepto his quos iam ſupra
.... & his qui mercſalbe erant· ipſi ad eum pleniter
adhuc nonuenerunt· eo quia ſ ſum domni regis uiuit & in rege abor ridas
ceſſerunt· ideo non credebam q dingratia eius puenire potuiſſ
Ceteri autem omnes pacifice uenerunt & iuſſionem ſuam promitt
implere· & quia domnus rex iterum credens ſuis nullu uoluntate
...ficient fidem ſuam ſeruando· Tunc ecclecquis pollectio de
terra aue ....lus qui dem nomine rodcenus
ad domnum regem aemonen ....ſuit quod domnus
rex honorifice ſuſcepit & bcep ....& eos qui cum
eo uenes & cum magno honore & domr ..... remea
ſer· ſed pro bnyce· & in eo anno apeſt ....aere vvnl
hoſecag magna multitudo p quib; domnus rex omp......
gretu er egent & diſtribui ipſu theſeco ....
ſe abbatibus & comites necnon & lanuie ..... fil
ſuos de coda theſauro mirifice honoreuit· & ip ſo

5 Vienna, ÖNB Cod. 515, fol. 1v, the Lorsch Annals, 795

61

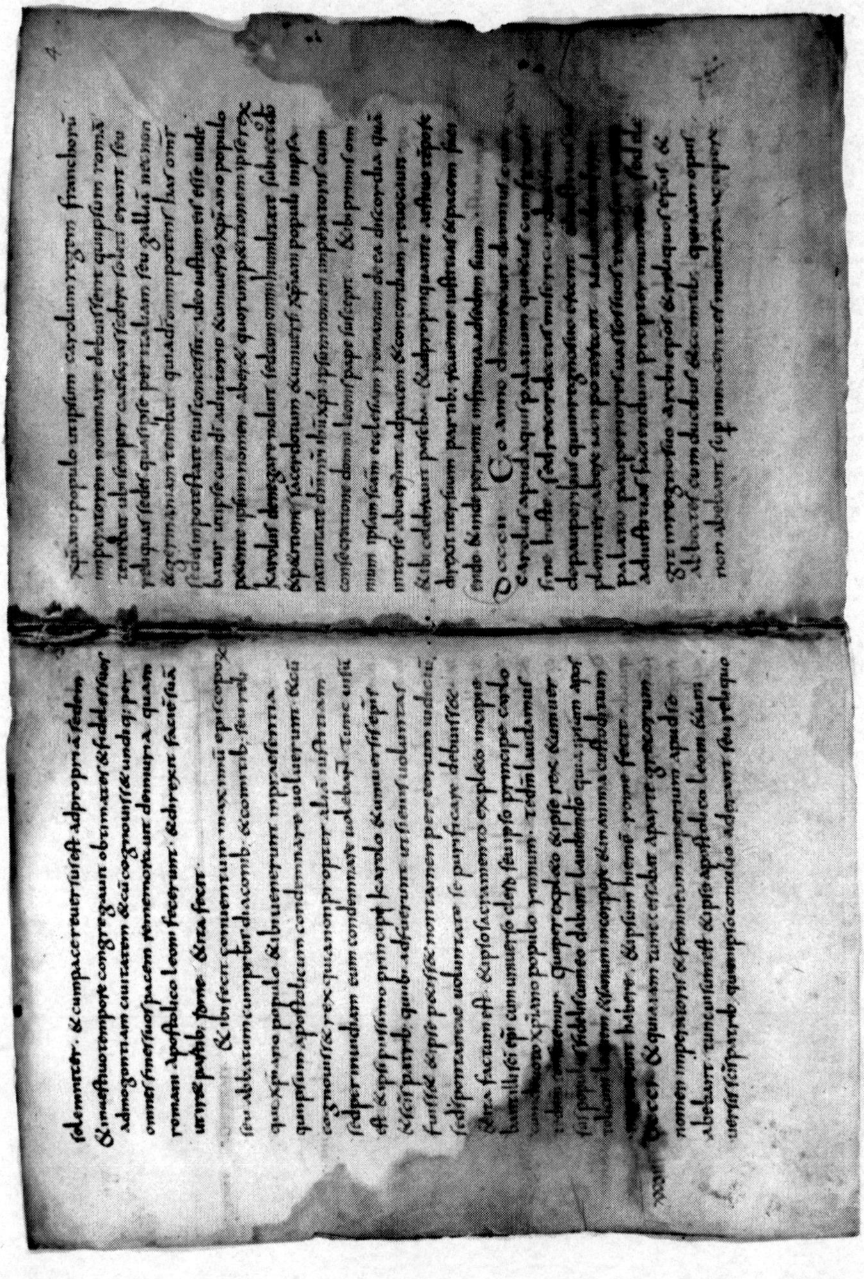

6 Vienna, ÖNB Cod. 515, fols 3v–4r, the Lorsch Annals, 800–2

in copying out a text that was before them. This is certainly one way in which the evidence of this manuscript has been interpreted.[36] However, such an explanation would make most sense if the work were being done more or less continuously. Other evidence suggests that the copying of individual annals was taking place over a relatively protracted period of time, with significant intervals – of months or even years – falling between each session of writing.

Unterkircher's distinction between the first two scribes, A and B, is undoubtedly correct, but the case for his scribes C and D is far less persuasive. Scribe A's work is clearly distinguishable; among other things he used an older 'oc' form of the letter 'a', deriving from the early or pre-caroline minuscules, which cannot generally be found in the other sections of this manuscript. The distinctions between Unterkircher's scribes B, C, and D are far less clear-cut and certain. There is quite a lot of variation in letter forms within the sections of text assigned to the supposed scribes, and it is thus not at all easy to establish a clear view of their individual peculiarities. Another possible scenario is that the differences noticed by Unterkircher represent not so much changes in personnel but rather ones in time and in pens. In other words, the sections assigned by Unterkircher to scribes B, C, and D could all have been written by the same person, but over an extended period of time, with intervals between periods of writing.[37]

The series of stages that can be distinguished in the writing of the manuscript, which represent changes of scribe or gaps between scribal activity in the writing-up of the text of the annals, are as follows. The surviving portion of the entry for 794 was written up at one time, but the entry for 795 was copied in two stages and by two different scribes (Figure 5, fol. 1v – change of hand at line 18). The second part of the 795 annal was written in the same stint as that for 796. The annals for 797, 798 and 799 were written up individually, but probably by the same man. The crucial entries for the years 800 and 801 were then copied together. The 802 entry was written separately (Figure 6, fol. 4r, lines 18–27), or possibly at the same time as the short account of 803, with which the work ends. The rest of the folio 5 was left blank to accommodate subsequent annals, possibly including some more material on the year 803, but for whatever reason the project was not pursued any further.

Certain textual errors to be found in the Vienna manuscript make it likely that this cannot be the author's original manuscript. The erasure on fol. 3v (line 7) may be particularly significant; because of the coincidence of the word *fecit* the scribe was led into thinking he had finished the annal for 800, and began writing the heading for that for 801, before discovering there were another 17 lines of the 800 annal to copy (Figure 6, fol. 3v, lines 7–23). But the evidence for intermittent periods of scribal activity linked directly to the writing-up of the individual annals does imply that it was a copy of an exemplar that was itself in the process of periodic expansion. This suggests, as does the palaeographic view of its dating, that the Vienna fragment was very close indeed to the original compilation, both in time and place, reflecting directly the compositional processes of the latter.

These would involve something like the annual writing-up of new entries for each year, probably soon – though not necessarily immediately – after their completion.

The latter reservation is prompted by the fact that there is at least one feature of the text itself that would militate against the conclusion that this was a process of exactly contemporary recording. In reporting the coup in Rome against Leo III in April 799, the annal for that year adds the comment that the conspirators responsible were now in exile. As this judicial sentence was not passed on them until early in the year 801, it can only have been after that point that the entry for 799 was prepared.[38] *AL*'s account of the imperial coronation and the events immediately preceding it could therefore only have been composed after Charles's return to Francia in 801. However, this may thus provide us with evidence of how the new emperor's title and the justification for his taking it were first presented to those Franks who had not been with him in Italy, and who might have had reservations about what had happened and what it meant.

The Lorsch Annals and the imperial coronation

A comparison between the accounts of the *AL* and RFA for the crucial years 799–801 is revealing. As in so many other cases, when two such sets of Frankish annals are compared what is most obvious is how different they are, in respect of what their compilers decided to include or to omit, despite similarities in the general nature of their contents and the pattern of events they describe.[39] In its entry for 799, the RFA began by reporting how the pope was taken captive during the Major Litanies, was blinded and had his tongue cut out, but was subsequently able to make his escape by climbing over a wall and taking refuge with Charles's *missi*, Abbot Wirund and Duke Winigis of Spoleto. Meantime, Charlemagne himself was *en route* to Paderborn while his eldest son, Charles the Younger, had been sent to negotiate with the Slavs and to receive the submissions of the Saxon *Nordliudi*. Charlemagne received the exiled pope at Paderborn and sent him back to Rome, before himself setting out back to his winter residence at Aachen. There he received an envoy from the Byzantine governor of Sicily, and others coming from the inhabitants of the Balearic islands, who wished to place themselves under his protection. A monk sent from Jerusalem by the patriarch also arrived at court, bringing the king relics from the Holy Sepulchre and the keys of the city. Various other military events were also recorded in this annal for 799, including a campaign in Brittany and Avar revolts.[40]

In contrast the *AL* have a more limited tale to tell: the Romans cut off Pope Leo's tongue, but did not blind him, as they had initially intended; no account is given of Leo's escape; Charlemagne's residence in Paderborn is mentioned, as is the pope's reception there, but no reference is made to wider Saxon affairs or to the activities of the young Charles. But more detail is given about Leo III's return to Rome than was the case with the RFA; the *AL* say he was sent back with great honour, accompanied by the king's *missi*, who then rounded up those in the city who had plotted again the pope, and sent them to Charlemagne. The annal also reports a forced deportation of Saxons and the building of a remarkably large church in Paderborn, neither of which is mentioned in the RFA.[41]

In general, though, the *AL* have a much more restricted focus, concentrating almost entirely on events that in retrospect can be seen to be leading up to the imperial coronation, and at the same time giving emphasis to features that support a particular interpretation of that event. In this context it is important to note firstly the very marked emphasis placed in this annal on the honourable reception and treatment afforded to Leo by Charlemagne, and secondly the difference in character of this annal in comparison with those that precede it in *AL*. The omission of virtually all military and diplomatic affairs, as otherwise recorded in the RFA, is not a characteristic of *AL* in its annals for the year 786 to 798. Their sudden omission here, in favour of the unnecessarily laboured account of the pope's visit to Paderborn, is a sure sign that the annalist is trying to convey an ideologically charged message; there is 'spin' to be detected here.

Comparison of the annals for the year 800 underlines the differences between the two sources. The RFA start with the sending of Charlemagne's envoy to Jerusalem, his visit to the Channel ports and the orders he gave there for the construction of a fleet. A detailed listing is given of his subsequent itinerary between his Easter court at St-Riquier and the holding of an assembly at Mainz in August. Thence Charles is said to have crossed the Alps to Ravenna, where he planned a campaign against the recalcitrant Duke of Benevento, before proceeding to Rome. A detailed description follows of his reception by the pope at the twelfth milestone outside the city and his subsequent arrival at St-Peter's on 24 November. Then comes the account of the assembly on the 30 November, at which the king gave his reasons for his coming to Rome, and Pope Leo swore on oath that he was innocent of the accusations levelled against him. On the same day, the king's envoy, sent out at the start of the year, returned from Jerusalem accompanied by two Palestinian monks bringing the keys of the Holy Sepulchre and of Calvary as a gift for the king. The annal ends with the king celebrating Christmas, but makes no mention of the imperial coronation on that day.[42]

The *AL*, in a much briefer annal, record that the king had toured his estates and the resting places of the saints at the beginning of the year; his son Pippin was with him, and his youngest son Louis came to meet him at Tours. The death there of his wife Liutgard is reported in both the RFA and *AL*, though only the former gives the exact date. At a subsequent assembly in Mainz (the one that the RFA assigns to the month of August) Charlemagne recalled the injury done to the pope the previous year and, the *AL* annal says, therefore decided to go to Rome. No details are given of his route or initial reception, but more information is provided than is to be found in any other source about the great assembly, attended by bishops, priests, abbots and counts. Here Leo's accusers appeared and he himself took an oath of compurgation (purification); Charlemagne himself then led the assembly in the singing of the *Te Deum*. The annal for 800 ends at this point, although the account of this assembly resumes at the start of the annal for 801.[43]

Comparing the two annals, it is easy to see that *AL* presents the decision to go to Rome as the explicit outcome of the assembly held in Mainz in August, and provides only a very sketchy account of Charlemagne's movements earlier in 800, making no connection with later events. The *AL* ignores all other diplomatic and military events, and fails to mention the nature and date of Charlemagne's reception in Rome, or the arrival of the envoys from Jerusalem. On the other hand, this source provides a much fuller account of the nature and purposes of the great assembly in Rome, without giving a date for it, and thus perhaps obscuring its chronological relationship to the ensuing imperial inauguration on Christmas Day.

The description of this council continues in the opening section of the *AL*'s annal for 801. The *AL* state that the 'name of emperor' (*nomen imperatoris*) was currently lacking amongst the Greeks, who were now subject to 'female imperial rule' (*femineum imperium*) under Irene. As a consequence, the pope and others present at the assembly decided to give the title of emperor to Charlemagne, who was now master of Rome and of all of the other former imperial residences in Italy, Gaul and Germany.[44] The king was 'unwilling to deny their request' and, as a result, he was consecrated emperor by the pope on Christmas Day. Staying on in Rome until Easter, he then returned to Francia via Ravenna.

Once again, the *AL* version of the events of 801 is far balder than that of the RFA. Its focus is more limited, but it gives special emphasis to particular episodes. The RFA annal has a much more detailed and wide-ranging account of the year 801; it reports Charlemagne's coronation, and the trial and sentencing of those who had conspired against the pope. The dispatch of his son Pippin against the Beneventans is recorded, as are some of the details of the king's itinerary in Italy on his way back to Francia, including the fact that at Pavia he was met by an embassy from the Abassid caliph, Harun al-Rashid, and presented with the gift of an elephant. The RFA annal also reports that in the course of the year an earthquake damaged Rome, that there was widespread pestilence in Gaul and Germany, and that the Franks captured the city of Barcelona.[45] This triumph is, along with Pippin of Italy's conquest of the Beneventan town of Chieti and all other military and diplomatic events of the year, entirely absent from the *AL* account.

Comparison with the RFA for the years 799–801 indicates that the *AL* account is throughout highly selective, far more so than is the case with its annals for the preceding years, and is focused almost entirely upon events relating to the taking of the imperial title. The *AL* entries for the years 799–801 are clearly tendentious in a number of ways. Firstly, although this source has been used to disprove Einhard's contention that Charlemagne did not know what was going to happen to him when he entered St-Peter's on Christmas Day in the year 800, the purposes of the two accounts are actually identical. The *AL* go out of their way to emphasise the lack of longer-term planning preceding Charlemagne's receipt of the imperial title. The annal for 800 claims explicitly that it was only at the August assembly in Mainz that the king, 'recalled the injury inflicted upon the *apostolicus* Leo by the Romans and set his face to going to Rome'.[46] In other words, it was not until this late stage that the decision to go to Rome was taken and, by implication, Charlemagne's activities earlier in the year had no bearing upon what would follow. No chronology is provided for his arrival in Rome, nor for the holding of the great assembly.

This great assembly can hardly have been spontaneous or unplanned; although no details are given in any source about the precise number of participants, the *AL* stress that it was the largest possible gathering (*conventum maximum*), consisting of 'bishops and abbots, with priests, deacons, counts, and the rest of the Christian people'. While major military expeditions, such as the 791 campaign against the Avars, could involve the participation of the greater prelates as well as lay magnates of the realm, the presence in Rome of the large number of ecclesiastical dignitaries suggested by the *AL* account could hardly have been unpremeditated or unplanned. Although not stated, it seems reasonable to assume that this involved Italian as well as Frankish clerics and nobles, all of whom would have had to make their way to Rome with the king or to have been there by the time of his arrival.

The limited and closely focused narrative of *AL* in the annals for the years 799–801 is equally tendentious in its treatment of the pope. Thus, a disproportionate amount of the entry for 799 is devoted to describing the quality of Leo's reception at Paderborn: 'And the lord king received him with honour and honoured him with many gifts and honours and afterwards sent him back to his own seat with peace and great honour; and the *missi* of the lord king escorted him in honour'.[47] No hint is given that Leo came as a suppliant in need of Charlemagne's assistance, let alone that those who had conspired against him in April had made serious accusations against him.

Similarly, the assembly held following Charlemagne's arrival in Rome in 800 is presented in the *AL* as having one primary purpose, that of justifying Leo. On hearing the charges, which are never specified, and with no other evidence presented, the king is said to have decided that there were no just motives for the accusations and that the complainants were acting only out of malice. It therefore seemed appropriate to him and to 'all the bishops and holy fathers there present' that the pope should take an oath. This, however, the annalist stressed, was not something that was imposed on him. As the annalist put it, the assembly decided that, 'if such was his will and he himself so requested, he ought to cleanse himself, but of his own free will, not through judgment on their part'.[48] This exactly matches the concern expressed by Alcuin in a letter of 799 to Archbishop Arn of Salzburg, and reflects a sixth-century view that there was no judicial authority, ecclesiastical or secular, superior to that of the pope and thus capable of sitting in judgment on him.[49]

Leo's oath, taken 'of his own free will', thus marked the end of the attempt to depose him, and was also intended to clear him from the stain of the accusations made against him by his enemies; but what these charges had been the *AL* studiously avoided stating. The point of this was to ensure that the man who only three weeks later would crown the new emperor was untainted by scandal and above reproach. How far Charlemagne and the other participants in the assembly actually felt this to be the case cannot be known, but this process had made him into if not an ideal, then at least an acceptable, bestower of the imperial crown.

In conclusion, it seems that the *AL* account represents the earliest version of the taking of the imperial title as explained to the Franks once Charlemagne had returned from Italy in 801. Given arguments for the 'official' character of Frankish annal-making in the 780s and 790s, *AL*'s account may be the nearest we can come to the view held by Charlemagne and his advisers in 801/2 of what had happened in Rome in the winter of 800 – or, at least, how they wished those events to be seen by the Franks. In contrast to the RFA and Einhard, the *AL* stressed that the decision to offer Charlemagne the title had been taken by a great council of the leaders of the clergy and the laity, and was thus not purely or primarily a papal initiative.

The reasoning behind their action was also explained: the imperial title was vacant because the Eastern Empire was under *femineum imperium*, and Charlemagne was master of all of the former imperial seats in the West. This recognised the Roman and Byzantine idea of the indivisibility of the empire. With no legitimate emperor in the east, it was possible for the man who ruled the *sedes imperii* in the west to be elevated to the imperial dignity without any suggestion of usurpation, or the need to secure recognition from Constantinople.[50] There is no hint here of a papal right to select and invest the emperor, as expressed in the forged *Donation of Constantine* (compiled, probably in Rome, in the second half of the eighth century).[51] In 801 Pope Leo's standing may still have been weakened by the accusations made against him in 799, and his role as the consecrator of the new emperor had therefore to be fully vindicated by an account of what had befallen his opponents and how he had cleared himself of the charges they had made against him, whilst keeping his unique pontifical authority intact.

All these factors that seemed so important in 801 declined in significance in the years that followed. The overthrow of the Empress Irene by Nicephorus I in 802 and the ensuing Byzantine refusal to recognise Charlemagne's title undermined the constitutional nicety of the unitary and indivisible empire. Pope Leo's position became increasingly secure, perhaps assisted by the carefully cultivated growth of the legend that he had been miraculously cured from blinding at the hands of his attackers in 799 – something that the *AL* account explicitly denies.[52] At the same time, the idea that the imperial title was in the gift of an assembly may have become increasingly unattractive as Charlemagne's plans for his succession matured from 806 onwards.

Thus, when the RFA account of these years was compiled or edited, about

807/8, significant changes can be found in the way that the events of 799–800 were described; the role of the assembly in offering the title to Charlemagne disappears completely, and in consequence greater prominence was given to his formal investiture by the now rehabilitated pope. At the same time it seems that it was no longer necessary for any justification to be found for why he took the imperial office. Much more of the diplomatic exchanges and gift-giving that surrounded the process could be included by the RFA, though without any hint being allowed that they indicate rather longer-term planning of the coronation than it would be proper to admit. It was the echoes of these traditions, rather than the much closer ones of *AL*, that were to be reflected in Einhard's *Vita Karoli* written two decades later.

Notes

1 Levillain (1932), pp. 5–19; Schramm (1951); Folz (1974), pp. 148–9.
2 Béranger (1948).
3 Einhard, *VK*, c. 28.
4 Hentze, ed. (1999).
5 Collins (1998a), pp. 191–213. On the similarly important date of 751 see McKitterick (2000).
6 Wattenbach and Levison (1953), II, pp. 187–9.
7 *Annales Laureshamenses (AL) (3)* 800, p. 44; *AL (2)*, p. 38. Folz (1974), pp. 136–42.
8 Fichtenau (1953).
9 Lambech (1669), vol. 2, pp. 377–81. Despite Fichtenau's doubts (1953), pp. 309–27, it was endorsed by Hoffmann (1958), pp. 76–90. See Bullough (1970), p. 65.
10 A start-date in 703 may imply that the earliest element began as a continuation of a copy of Bede's 'Minor Chronicle', contained in his *De temporibus*, which ended in that year. There are no grounds for believing that *AL* ever extended beyond 803, despite Ganshof's thoughts (1970), p. 673 on its similarity to the Chronicle of Moissac (which extends to 818); a change of style and geographical focus suggest that the Moissac text relied for the period 803–18 on a different source.
11 Benediktinerstift St-Paul im Lavanttal, Cod. 8/1; Stiegemann and Wemhoff, ed. (1999a), pp. 38–40. The contents of the remainder of the manuscript are unknown.
12 *AL (1)*, ed. Ussermann (1790), pp. lxxiii–lxxx.
13 *AL (2)*, ed. Pertz, MGH *SS* I, pp. 22–39, at 20. Pertz claimed to have had the help of the abbot and librarian of St-Paul in the hunt for the codex, but whether it had genuinely been misplaced or whether the monks deliberately prevented him from getting access to it will never be known.
14 *AL (3)*, ed. Katz (1889), pp. 11–12 for a short account of the codex. My thanks to Richard Corradini for a copy of this rare edition.
15 *Ibid.*, pp. 20–1.
16 Unterkircher (1967), p. 18.
17 Halphen (1921), pp. 26–36.
18 *Annales Mosellani*, MGH *SS* XVI, pp. 491–9; partial trans. King (1987), pp. 132–7.
19 St-Petersburg, National Library of Russia, MS O.v.IV.1, fols. 65v–72v; Staerk (1910), I, p. 283; Lappenburg noted the reference to Domesday Book.

20 *Fragmentum Chesnianum*, ed. Duchesne (1636), pp. 21–3.

21 Rome, Bibliotheca Apostolica Vaticana, MS Reg. Lat. 213, fols. 149–51 (*Fragmentum*), fols. 151–7v (RFA). Its text of RFA is in Kurze's 'B' class (p. ix) and is close to that used for the extension of the *Annales Tilliani*; Collins (1996), p. 125.

22 *AL (3)* 785, p. 34; trans. King (1987), p. 137.

23 These references are found most extensively in *AL*; they have all been omitted from the *Fragmentum*, and only some are preserved in *AM*.

24 Kurze (1913), pp. 26–7, followed by Fichtenau (1953) and Folz (1974).

25 Above n.11. On the other codex, MS Vienna ÖN 515, see below.

26 Easily shown by the parallel texts in MGH *SS*, I, pp. 30–4.

27 Contra Halphen (1921), pp. 31–2, 36 who presents all three texts as deriving from the 785 core.

28 This common source no longer exists independently; it is thought to have been compiled at Murbach (founded in 727) and extended up to the year 751; Lendi (1971). 'The Lorsch Annals of 785' depended on a defective copy of it: they lack some details (recorded in other sets of annals that used the Murbach source) especially in the entries for the 740s, and their chronology is a year out for most of the 750s.

29 Lendi (1971), pp. 18–26; Wattenbach and Levison (1953), pp. 188–9.

30 Collins (1998a).

31 Above, n.21. *Annales Guelfybertani*, MGH *SS* I, pp. 40–4; on the unique copy of these annals at Wolfenbüttel, see Bischoff (1940), p. 21.

32 *CLA* X, no. 1482.

33 Bischoff (1974), pp. 53, 79, 120–1, and Bischoff (1965), p. 36.

34 See McKitterick (1997), pp. 117–18.

35 Unterkircher (1967), pp. 13–17.

36 Bullough (1970), p. 65.

37 Other distinctions can be noted, such as changes in the strength and colour of ink (eg: fol. 3r, lines 21–2 and fol. 5r, lines 5–6) suggesting several writing stints. Both these changes in ink correspond to changes in annal: that for the year 800 starts on fol. 3r line 22, and that for 803 on fol. 5r, line 6.

38 *AL (3)* 799, p. 43; for their exile in 801, see RFA 801; trans. King (1987), pp. 94, 143.

39 See Collins (2002).

40 RFA 799; Becher (1999a).

41 *AL (3)* 799, p. 43; *AL (2)*, pp. 37–8; trans. King (1987), p. 143.

42 RFA 800.

43 *AL (3)* 800, pp. 43–4; *AL (2)*, p. 38; trans. King (1987), p. 144.

44 *AL (3)* 801, p. 44; *AL (2)*, p. 38.

45 RFA 801.

46 *AL (3)* 800, p. 44; *AL (2)*, p. 38; trans. King (1987), p. 144.

47 *AL (3)* 799, p. 43; *AL (2)*, p. 37; trans. King (1987), p. 143.

48 *AL (3)* 800, p. 44; *AL (2)*, p. 38; trans. King (1987), p. 144.

49 Alcuin, *Ep.*, no. 179, MGH *Epp.* IV, pp. 296–7; trans. Allott (1974), no. 102.

50 On Frankish-Byzantine-papal relations at this time, see Classen (1988).

51 Noble (1984), pp. 134–7.

52 RFA 799 is categoric that Leo was blinded; RFA *(Rev.)* 799 is more circumspect. The fullest account is in *LP*, 'Life of Leo III', c. 13; trans. Davis (1992), p. 186.

5

CHARLEMAGNE'S GOVERNMENT

Matthew Innes

The problem of early medieval government

Einhard, in his biography of Charlemagne, discussed his hero's career under a series of rubrics: his deeds at home and abroad, his habits (*mores*) and cares, and his administration of the kingdom.[1] The first section is a lengthy account of Charlemagne's many wars and his relations with neighbouring rulers, and is followed by a description of Charlemagne's 'life and *mores*'. This forms the most memorable part of the book, covering personal appearance and deportment, relations with his family and life at court: here was a portrait of the moral character of the ruler, and the moral worth of the man. The final section, covering Charlemagne's administration of the kingdom before moving on to discuss his death, has proved the most problematic for most modern commentators.

Einhard's treatment of the administration of the kingdom began with Charlemagne's care for the 'Christian religion' and his dealings with Rome and the popes including the imperial coronation, and went on to cover Charlemagne's actions 'after taking up the Imperial name', particularly his provision of written law for all the peoples under his rule, and his care to have the Frankish cultural heritage recorded in writing. The lack of attention to the nuts and bolts of administration, and to the mechanisms by which Charlemagne was able to govern an empire which stretched from the Ebro to the Elbe, is striking. Ganshof, the most respected modern student of Carolingian government, even went so far as to suggest that Einhard was here reflecting the 'insufficiency' of Charlemagne's administration, and that 'most of Charlemagne's efforts to provide the Frankish monarchy with a more effective *administratio* took the form of *ad hoc*, partial measures, which he did not regard of being of general application'. Ganshof thus saw Einhard's account as reflecting the roots of political failure, which he believed he could detect in the decades after 800 in the absence of a dedicated, centralised administration.[2]

We should pause before we endorse Ganshof's judgement, and the pessimistic view of the Carolingian empire it suggests. Einhard's biography is a clever literary work that needs to be handled carefully as historical evidence. Nonetheless, Einhard's lack of any real interest in what we would understand as government is typical of the Carolingian sources in general. Indeed, Einhard's concentration on Charlemagne's care for the 'Christian religion' corresponds with the official line propagated on royal coinage. The focus of Einhard's *Life* is not, therefore, merely a literary foible; it relates to contemporary patterns of thought.

Some historians have even gone so far as to claim that the Carolingians lacked any clearly defined concept of the state: contemporary writers of histories and annals tended to focus on the king's role within his household and at the court, and his care for the Church, without ever really identifying an area of governmental activity independent from either or encompassing both.[3] Of course, eighth- and ninth-century rulers were capable of discussing and reflecting upon the activities that allowed them to rule their realms. Indeed, by the first decades of the ninth century, some Carolingian writers – and the advisers responsible for a handful of royal documents and legislation – were able to revive the classical term *res publica*, literally 'the public thing', to refer to the apparatus of royal power. More usually, however, when discussing the activity of ruling, Carolingian writers used general and fairly generic terms, notably *regnum*, 'kingdom'. Even the closest we have to a textbook on Carolingian government, a booklet of advice penned by the elder statesman Hincmar, archbishop of Rheims, for a young king in 882, focuses on the conventional virtues expected of a Christian king, and on the management of the palace: it saw the society of the royal court as a microcosm of the kingdom, able to encompass the society of the realm through the annual assemblies to which the leading men of the kingdom flocked. Government was here a matter of 'ordering the palace', to quote the tract's title.[4]

In a milieu as deeply infused with Christian morality as Charlemagne's court, any division between the ethics of private life and of public office was unthinkable. Kings were answerable to God for their care of their people, and by the reign of Louis the Pious the ideology of divinely-granted ministry (*ministerium*) was explicitly applied to all those holding office, whether secular or ecclesiastical: all were helpers in the emperor's God-given ministry, and so answerable to God and the emperor for its fulfilment. The leaders of the Christian people were charged with the creation of moral and social order within society: there was no real sense that their actions constituted a separate sphere of government over and above normal social action.

So, to return to Einhard's depiction of Charlemagne, our surprise that the subjects discussed could constitute the 'administration of the kingdom' rests primarily on the difference between the categories of political thought current in the Carolingian period, and those that inform our own understanding of the relationship between state and society. There is a real danger in allowing these differences in basic ideological categories to shape our interpretation, and to go on to argue that Carolingian government was 'insufficient' and doomed to failure, simply because Carolingian government differs from our modern expectations. Modern notions of the state have arisen in a world where developments in communications and economics have created technologies of power that were unavailable to Charlemagne. To analyse Charlemagne's government, we need to understand the possible strategies for ruling in an early medieval society, as well as the severe limitations on the centre to control the localities.

The rules of the game

The advancement of a moral (as opposed to an institutional) understanding of ruling – a phenomenon with deep roots in late antiquity – suffused the basic categories of thought about political power in the Carolingian period. However, it would be a mistake to treat early medieval statehood as a problem in intellectual history alone. After all, these ideological categories were potent precisely because they made sense to those who were at the heart of politics, and because they had practical implications for the exercise of power. Without a substantive infrastructure of royal rights that provided the muscle to rule the provinces, exercising political power over time and space posed real problems for early medieval kings.

Like the rulers of the other barbarian kingdoms that emerged in place of the Roman Empire in the west, the Merovingian kings who established the Frankish kingdom in Gaul in the decades around AD 500 inherited much of the administrative infrastructure of the late Roman state. In the late Roman period, the system of tax assessment and allocation – the dominant mechanism for the circulation of wealth – had determined the essentially symbiotic relationship between cities and the imperial government, a relationship which allowed landowners to entrench and legitimate their local power by acting as the intermediaries between imperial demands and agrarian realities.[5] Similarly, in the early Merovingian period the survival of much of this infrastructure meant that local elites were involved in a process of negotiation and competition for office, the ultimate arbiter of which was the royal court. Not that this was wholesale continuity: the bulky apparatus of late Roman imperial and provincial government more or less vanished, leaving city-based practices associated with the assessment and collection of revenue and the performance of public burdens; landowners increasingly aspired to control two new positions which were emerging as crucial, those of bishop and count.

Although some historians have recently made claims for long-term continuity, it is clear that by the seventh century this system was in terminal decline thanks to privileges granted to important churches and the conviction that free Franks should be exempt from taxation. A new, typically early medieval, political system, in which local power lay unmediated in the hands of landowners, who were directly and personally responsible for ruling their localities, emerged. Local communities conducted their affairs through public meetings, at which necessary decisions were made collectively; local power was a matter of using the influence that landed wealth allowed to sway these occasions. The position of count, with its responsibility for the administration of justice and the performance of military service, was of crucial importance in the secular sphere: not only did it grant legitimacy to its holders, but it enabled them to levy fines and ultimately mobilise force against those who were deemed to have failed in their obligations to the community. Because landowning elites were too poor and insecure to go it alone, and needed allies and legitimacy to sustain their positions in their communities, local and regnal politics were inextricably tied together.

Struggles in any locality were mediated through the court, which granted office, privileges and land. The success with which the seventh-century Merovingian rulers, particularly in Neustria, were able to create a viable political system is only just beginning to emerge. Even during royal minorities, disputed successions or periods of personal royal weakness, politics remained a matter of competition for position at court. Indeed, the ancestors of the Carolingians were only able to rise to dominance in the late seventh and early eighth centuries by establishing themselves at the heart of this system through their position as mayors of the palace and their control of the Neustrian court; without this position, their vast landed wealth in Austrasia could not be translated into legitimate political authority.[6]

This political system, focused on the Merovingian court, proved remarkably durable: after all, it was not until 737 that the Carolingians felt able to do without a Merovingian king on the throne, and it was not until 751 that they replaced the Merovingian dynasty. However, the rising dominance of the Carolingian family at the court, and the civil war of 714–19 from which Charles Martel emerged victorious, fractured allegiances and broke the ties which normally bound court and localities together, particularly around the fringes of the Merovingian world.[7] Hence Martel, his son Pippin, and his grandson Charlemagne, had to devote much time and energy to 'reconquest', a political necessity given the possibility that these peripheral principalities could harbour rivals and threaten the Carolingians' tenuous legitimacy. The result was almost constant campaigning: annalists noted with surprise those years in which there was no campaign.

This activity lay at the heart of Carolingian political success in the eighth century, as Einhard himself acknowledged. Military success brought with its lucrative spoils in plunder, tribute and land, which the Carolingians were able to redistribute as they chose; it also generated charisma, and created a cohesion among those who together enjoyed success under Carolingian leadership. Joining the war-trail was the easiest way to gain the goodwill and notice of the rulers, and campaigning became a key engine of social mobility even for relatively humble landowning families. The annual assembly at the Marchfield, which marked the beginning of the campaigning season, was moved to the month of May under Pippin, becoming the central political institution. Whilst on campaign, Carolingian rulers were able to build bonds of association and loyalty which entrenched their dominance of the political community.[8]

For much of Charlemagne's reign the basic expansive dynamic continued. But expansion could not go on forever. In fact, by the end of the eighth century the pace had slowed, as Charlemagne made a series of conscious and sensible strategic decisions about when and where to stop. The end of expansion necessitated a new frontier policy of marcher commands coupled with political and cultural influence on the empire's neighbours.[9] It also created a fundamental need for change within the empire, as the mutual loyalties of the war-trail could no longer glue together the Carolingian political system. By the 780s, the wealth, status and contacts brought by military success had given rise to a change in political style; Charles led armies in person less frequently, and the Church reforms and cultural revival begun under Carloman and Pippin gained in political profile. With the defeat of the Avars in 793, the golden age of expansion was over. New mechanisms to integrate local elites into the Carolingian system were needed. In place of the annual campaign, royal courts emerged as the central political stage. In a sense, this was a move back towards the seventh-century system of court-based politics, but in a different social context and above all on a far, far larger scale.

In the last decades of the eighth century we see the construction of a series of new, purpose-built palace complexes in a novel, monumental idiom at Aachen, Ingelheim and Frankfurt. Whilst the range and pace of the royal itinerary decreased considerably from the 790s, the new palaces were not intended to function as sedentary capitals. Rather, situated in the Carolingians' political heartlands, these were to be the central places in the new system, where elites who had previously fought shoulder-to-shoulder with the king now came to meet their ruler. Charlemagne now seldom travelled south of the Loire, or east of the Rhine–Main valleys, but expected elites from the outlying provinces to visit him in the heart of the empire. What had previously been the relatively spontaneous and unselfconscious rites of the war-trail were formalised as institutions of government: individuals were required to attend the annual assemblies, bringing gifts to order. Links between the king and local elites were fostered through the granting of office at court to key figures from across the empire, and by reinvigorating the old practice of having promising youngsters spend a politically formative period of their careers at court.[10]

But, on a local level, Carolingian expansion had done little to alter the basic realities of the power of landowners: it had simply allowed the Carolingians to fashion an extensive coalition across western Europe. The increased size of the political community led to a marked vertical differentiation within landowning elites. At the top of the hierarchy, a small group of families emerged, which did well out of Carolingian patronage, gaining lands and offices scattered right across Europe. The size of the empire also necessitated regional differentiation, between the royal heartlands – whose political topography was defined by palace complexes and sites for assemblies – and those provinces which experienced the royal presence intermittently and indirectly, through the annual trek of influential landowners to the assembly, their return bearing news of the royal will, and their ties of friendship and kinship with the personnel of the court.

The creation of sub-kingdoms in Aquitaine and Italy under Charlemagne, and Bavaria under Louis the Pious, meant that this geography was not static, nor articulated in terms of distance from a single fixed centre, even in the period of the 'unification' before the political divisions of the latter two-thirds of the ninth century. And beyond the old Frankish core of the Merovingian realm and its peripheral principalities lay the marches, where the basic institutions of Carolingian power were subject to significant alterations. But in the localities between the core and the marches remarkably little changed, as even those landowning families who had initially been lukewarm or even hostile eventually aligned themselves with the Carolingians, whilst newcomers implanted with Carolingian backing soon merged into local society. Once expansion had stopped, the maintenance of this coalition was only assured if its members continued to feel the need to plug into the Carolingian system, establishing a regular and reliable interface with the court to ensure the continued flow of favour. The challenge for Charlemagne, then, was to integrate the local power of landowners into the formal structures of a new empire that could no longer be fuelled by the spoils of war alone. [11]

The rhetoric of reform

The prime source for Charlemagne's attempts to meet this challenge is a series of documents known as capitularies. [12] Written records of the decisions of kings in consultation with assemblies, their title comes from the habit of writing up records chapter by chapter (Latin *capitula*), borrowed from the conventions governing the records of Church councils. The genre has Merovingian precedents: there are surviving sixth- and seventh-century royal decrees which were issued at assemblies, often in conjunction with Church councils, and the promulgation of decrees played a significant role in late Merovingian politics. [13] The development of a programme of Church reform and the holding of a series of Church councils seems to have provided a similar stimulus under the early Carolingians.

Under Pippin, the decisions – some secular and some ecclesiastical – of the assembly which met at Ver in 755 were issued in this form, while under Charlemagne the decisions of a council held at Herstal in 779, in response to a grave political crisis, were likewise recorded as *capitula*. But from the time of the

Admonitio generalis (General Admonition) of 789, such records become more regular, reaching their peak in the first decades of the ninth century, when several for each year survive. Although we should not forget the possibility of losses, this pattern of surviving evidence does seem to reflect changes in actual practice. The issuing of written decrees from annual assemblies held at palaces in the heartlands of the empire also clearly relates to the changing patterns of contact between the king and the provinces, evident in the development of the royal court and the palace system.

We should be aware that the material that we tend to lump together as 'capitularies' is fairly heterogeneous, and that in contemporary usage the term 'capitulary' is not used frequently as a technical term for chapter-by-chapter records. Narrative sources as a rule do not use the term, preferring to talk in general terms about the holding of assemblies, the making of decisions and the issuing of laws. There was a clear consciousness that there was a particular kind of record appropriate for the instructions given and decisions made at royal assemblies, as the development of conventions of form, and reference back to earlier examples of the genre, make clear. But the boundaries of the genre were blurred: it encompassed royal orders of general application, letters of admonition and instruction for specific officials, the results of the deliberations of assemblies on secular and ecclesiastical affairs, lists of approved additions and alterations to extant written laws, administrative memoranda, even surveys of royal estates. This blurring was encouraged by the explosion in the quantity of surviving written material concerned with the transmission of the royal will and the exercise of royal rights, an explosion which itself is indicative of a renewed emphasis on the use of the written word in the operation of government.[14]

What were the implications of this attempt to articulate a programme of reform? Debate has centred on the status of the capitularies as law. Were they merely *aides-mémoires* recording decisions made orally, or did the written record itself have constitutive force? Were they expressions of the royal will, or records of the consent of those present at the assembly? Questions such as these, about the precise legal status of the written text, may owe more to the interests of modern constitutional lawyers than to early medieval realities. In any case, it is clear that by the end of the eighth century there was an expectation that an assembly's decisions would be recorded in an authoritative, written form. In legislation from the early ninth century, arrangements were made for copies to be distributed to interested parties and stored in the palace archives, and royal officials were enjoined to read and reread their copies. By the reign of Louis the Pious, copies of capitularies and other legal texts were distributed from the palace, while a high-placed royal official, Ansegisus, abbot of St-Wandrille, put together a compilation of capitulary rulings, which was soon used as a source of reference in subsequent legislation.[15] That is, by the end of Charlemagne's reign, the creation of a written record was central to the issuing of these instructions.

The fundamental problem facing those involved in Carolingian legislation was the communication of the decisions of assemblies across the whole empire, not the location of constitutional power in king or people, or the priority of oral proclamation or written law. When capitularies stressed the consent of those present, they were underlining the status of the law, not least because consensus could be seen as the expression of God's will: thus those present were bound together as a body which agreed and approved of the decisions they had reached collectively.[16] In this, as in the vagaries of its preservation and the frequent repetition of some clauses, Carolingian legislation is similar to the imperial law of the late Roman emperors, on which it was partly based. In both cases, the difference from modern law is not a result of inefficiency or ineffectiveness, but results from a fundamental difference in the function of law-giving. These rulers were exhorting and persuading the landowners on whom they relied to put law into action.

The key issue – particularly in dealing with the legislation of Carolingian rulers who lacked the dedicated administrative infrastructure which their Roman predecessors had possessed – was the ability of the court to make the exhortations of the capitularies heard in more distant places. This has been a matter of hot and polarised debate that has been at the heart of different judgements on Carolingian government. Those wishing to advance a pessimistic argument have presented the capitularies as mere royal wish-lists, while those who are more optimistic have used the capitularies as the basis for a description of a centralised state. The problem is that far too often such debate has involved ultimately circular arguments, using sources written at the court as the basis for contentions about the success or otherwise of the court in having its way locally. To move on, we need to develop new strategies for interrogating the local evidence as to the impact of the court and its programme.

One important focus of research has been the sizeable number of Carolingian manuscripts in which capitulary legislation survives, the vast majority neither written nor preserved at the royal court. In spite of the problems of identifying original functions and owners, the manuscript evidence does point to a wide diffusion and an interest which went beyond the academic foibles of ecclesiastical intellectuals.[17] A related argument stresses the sheer volume of capitularies, and the internal evidence within them for the exhortation and examination of local agents and the circulation of written instructions. If the success of an early medieval government rested on the ability of the centre to maintain effective and regular contact with its agents in local areas, the very existence of such material on this scale suggests that Carolingian government was able to meet the most pressing challenge it faced.

The key to understanding change in local areas lies, however, in source material which is only beginning to be appreciated for the light it can shed on the operation of government: the rich seam of legal documents preserved in their thousands through monastic archives right across Europe. This charter evidence allows us to build up a detailed picture of the working of Carolingian society, the role of royal officials in the localities, and the interplay of office and landed power. The categories of nineteenth-century editors, who processed the evidence for us and drew a clear distinction between royal and private documents, has led historians to neglect the rich evidence for the activities of royal officials in implementing royal decisions on specific issues in the provinces. For example, in 777 two counts and two *vassi dominici* were despatched by the king to effect the transfer of a piece of land to the monastery at Fulda, and to make a written record of the local meeting and the boundaries of the transferred land. The records from Lorsch note in 782 that a local boundary dispute was resolved by one side taking their complaints to the palace to obtain a royal document allowing them to hold a local inquest; another local boundary dispute was resolved in 795 by a count who called a local meeting *ex pracepto domni Karoli regis* ('on the precept of the lord king, Charles').[18]

True, none of these cases directly show the contents of a capitulary being enforced. Searches for the explicit citation of written law in general, let alone capitularies, in the charter evidence has largely been conducted in vain, particularly in Europe north of the Alps. This need not necessarily reflect ignorance of the law: it is quite possible that disputes were settled within the general framework of rules laid down in the law without the explicit citation of specific rulings regarding particular cases.[19] In any case, the presence or absence of direct citations of written legislation in local documents is an imperfect means of testing the impact of the capitularies. It assumes that capitularies were primarily written statements of law, complementing the written law-codes of the Franks and the other peoples within the empire; although some capitularies did exactly that, the main concern of the majority was the instruction of royal officials in the provinces. And, as we have seen, the charters offer a vivid picture of the mechanisms of contact and feedback between the court and these local areas.

The impact of reform

The charter and manuscript evidence helps us to understand what constituted Carolingian government beyond the centre, and how capitularies functioned as instruments of power. For one thing, a significant number of the surviving manuscripts bear explicit witness to communication between the court and royal officials. The great capitulary of 802, for example, survives in three different versions, addressed to three different pairs of royal officials, operating in the regions around Orléans, Paris and Rouen respectively; a sizeable number of other capitularies survive in a version directed to a specific official.[20] More significantly still, written reports sent back to court by local officials are often documented, as stated in many charters and envisaged in a number of capitularies from the later part of the reign: most remarkably, in Charlemagne's reply to a series of queries sent him by an official.[21] Given that such pragmatic documents, likely to be of very little lasting import or interest, are among the least likely to survive, the existence of the number that do is telling evidence for the increasing importance of written instruments as the means of communication between the king and his local agents.[22]

There is also some significant evidence for the communication of the contents of the capitularies from royal officials to communities. Some surviving manuscripts of a capitulary emending the Frankish laws from 803 include a prologue describing how Count Stephen made its contents known in the public court in the city of Paris, and a copy of the document subscribed by those present.[23] This process of communication – the provision of a written copy to a small number of royal officials who expounded and explained the decisions made at court to the communities they ruled – was the norm envisaged in the capitularies. The controversy over the importance of writing in the capitularies has long obscured the very particular mixture of written and oral communication, of writing and exhortation, on which this medium of political education rested.[24] After all, in 803 Charlemagne commanded that his *missi* should submit written reports back to him on the various admonitions they had delivered in the places they had been.[25]

In fact, similar concerns about communication and education informed the most important and best-documented innovation of the reign, the implementation of a universal oath of fidelity to the king.[26] Although there was a Merovingian precedent for the swearing of an oath of loyalty to the king by all free men, by the beginning of Charlemagne's reign such oaths were only sworn by important members of local elites who were personal recipients of the ruler's goodwill and, therefore, 'faithful men' of the king. In 789 Charlemagne moved to extend the practice to all free men, who were to swear loyalty, on holy relics, to the king in the person of his local representative. This move was a reaction to perhaps the most serious revolt of the reign, in 785–86, by a group of magnates from the provinces east of the Rhine. They had formed a conspiracy which aimed at murdering the king if he entered their region again, and this had been cemented by swearing oaths of mutual solidarity. Charlemagne punished the ringleaders with blinding and the confiscation of lands, and made them swear loyalty to him on holy relics. Further legislation clarified the meaning of the oath and the procedures by which it was sworn.

The implementation of the universal oath of fidelity was not simply an attempt to ensure loyalty through the kingdom. Charlemagne also outlawed the swearing of mutual oaths of group solidarity, mindful of their use in conspiracies: associations or gilds for a variety of purposes were to be allowed, but without the swearing of oaths. Although Charlemagne encouraged the development of relationships of lordship and personal dependence for the purposes of social cohesion, sworn armed followings (*trustes*) were outlawed. There were also recurrent attempts to limit the ability of individuals to raise armed posses to use in pursuit of legal rights through the feud, since these might likewise create powerful horizontal bonds that bypassed the king.[27] Social bonds secured by supernatural glue were to descend vertically from the king to all, and horizontal groupings were not to be exclusive, nor to create obligations that came between the individual and his lord king.

The oath was a means of projecting the persona of the king into places where contact with the king had previously been indirect and mediated through local elites. As the oath was sworn, royal officials were to ensure that those taking it understood its meaning, and to offer sermonising explanations of its significance. In 802 Charlemagne proclaimed 'that it should be publicly expounded to all, in such a way that every person can understand, how important and how many are the matters that this oath comprehends', before going on to list the obligations implicit in the oath – not only specifics such as respect for the king's property, orders and rights, but also generalities such as fidelity to the king in all matters, that 'everybody should personally strive … to maintain himself fully in God's service', that all should show care for the Church, widows, orphans and pilgrims, and to practise just judgment and avoid injustice. 'All this is binding, because of the oath to the Emperor'.[28]

A surviving return from an Italian *missus* gives an idea of the type of context in which the oath was sworn: a public meeting attended by 180 men, their names listed.[29] One charter written on 20 August 802 in the public court at Freising in Bavaria shows the impact of the political education classes run by the *missi*, and directly echoes the official explanation of the oath in the 'General Capitulary to the Missi' issued earlier that year: local witnesses give testimony 'as we promised this year in our oath of fidelity to the lord Emperor Charles … without any fraud or deception but most truthfully'. This document may be remarkable but it is not unparalleled.[30] The implementation of the oath of loyalty signified a fundamental shift in the structure of the kingdom, from a pyramid of self-standing segments held together by personal relationships between their leaders and the king, to a clearly defined hierarchy, at which power at all levels was articulated with reference to paramount obligations to the king as ruler of a Christian society.

One of the obligations created through the swearing of the oath was the promotion of just judgment: in 802 Charlemagne had explained that implicit in the oath were obligations to ensure that litigation 'is to be carried out in all respects in accordance with justice and the law; and by no means is anyone to be allowed to thwart justice by bribery, favour, some contrivance of evil flattery or the protection of relatives; no-one is to agree anything with anyone unjustly, but everybody is to aim, with all zeal and willingness, at the accomplishment of justice'.[31] Such concerns pervade the capitularies. Injunctions about the conduct, location and timing of local courts abound; the processes of local alliance-making and sociability, of feasting, hunting and gift-exchange, were to be firmly separated from the actual administration of justice, which was to be conducted so as to be accessible and fair to all, with special care to be given to the cases of the poor, widows and orphans. A vision of a Christian community, united by charity towards all, thus informed a programme for the reshaping of the public meetings – through which elites had dominated their localities – into institutions through which the justice of a Christian king was made available to all.[32]

These are precisely the kind of injunctions whose effectiveness will always remain unknown on account of the lack of any surviving evidence. For example, we have no way of knowing whether counts observed injunctions that banned them from cutting short their court hearings to allow the local elite to go hunting. Nonetheless, the charter evidence can shed some light on two developments, which Ganshof saw as central to an attempt to create a more efficient and professional system of justice: the use of sworn inquests by royal officials to establish fact, and the creation of a new class of experts to oversee the conduct of justice, the *scabini*.[33] Investigation of the workings of justice on a local level as revealed in the charter evidence has revealed that neither of these measures transformed the institutional basis of justice; rather, they established firmer links between the social elites who dominated local courts and the ambitions of the king as guarantor of justice. Justice on a local level had always rested on the collective testimony of the dominant elements in the community, and the line between these traditional practices of oath-swearing and the sworn inquest was a fine one indeed.[34]

Additionally, it is difficult to see the *scabini* as agents of a revolution in justice. The official title given to those men who oversaw and underwrote the local operation of justice changed, as the new term *scabinus* was adopted in the capitularies from the 780s, and was slowly and intermittently taken up thereafter in documents produced at a distance from the court. But this change of vocabulary did not reflect a wholesale change in function or personnel, and the identity of the groups of the local well-to-do who oversaw the conduct of justice changed little in the Carolingian period. What the capitularies do insist is that local notables see themselves as holders of an office for which they were accountable to king and God, and to conduct themselves accordingly. Close investigation of the diffusion of the title has shown how, for some local landowners at least, this ideology was a valuable way of cementing local status by creating a direct alignment with the king.[35]

Hierarchies of power

We should abandon misleading modern assumptions that the capitularies constitute statute law aimed at reshaping the practices of an administrative machine, and instead see them as a mechanism designed to encourage a new, hierarchical relationship directly linking local communities and the king. Local leaders who had overseen the business of their communities were instructed in their duties as explicitly royal officials who were unambiguously accountable for their actions. Look at the famous injunction of 802, in which Charlemagne decreed that judges should give judgement according to written law. Unlike modern historians who have discussed this legislation, Charlemagne himself did make a comparison between written law and unwritten local custom: he contrasted just judgment according to the written law with the personal initiative (*arbitrium*) of the judge.[36] Justice was to be practised according to universal rules set down in writing, and counts were to act as unequivocally royal officials in a political hierarchy in which power descended from above, not simply as local leaders owing personal loyalty to the king. Landowners were to see themselves as office-holders bound in a hierarchical relationship with their king, not simply the local great and good dealing with their own affairs according to time-honoured traditions; legislation encouraged communities to complain about their leaders if they did not conduct themselves according to the Carolingian programme.

The charter evidence hints at the diffusion of these ideas. In August 795, for example, those assembled at a meeting held at a *tumulus* in the Odenwald recounted the past history of their community in terms of the counts who had previously held a 'ministry in the service of the king'; a decade or so earlier, those transacting a property deal in Hesse located the land and men concerned as lying 'in [Count] Swicgar's rule', using the vernacular equivalent of the Latin *ministerium*, Old High German *ambath*. Borgolte's work on the province of Alemannia (roughly modern Switzerland and southern Germany) has shown the determination of the Carolingians to create a network of counties that were to be understood as royal offices, not family property or personal dominion.[37]

Crucial in effecting the programme of the capitularies were a group of royal officials known as the *missi dominici* – literally, 'the lord's sent ones'. *Missus* was traditionally a label for *ad hoc* royal agents sent on specific, short-term missions, normally a relatively humble or young man engaged in the king's personal service at the palace. The activities of these young men engaged in the personal service of the king were paralleled by the increased use of *vassi dominici* – again, initially young men under direct royal lordship – in overseeing royal rights across the kingdom. The capitularies suggest a gradual increase in the use of *missi dominici* in the last decades of the eighth century, and an expansion of the tasks they were given, culminating in the 'Programmatic Capitulary' of 802, in which a system of pairs of *missi*, one churchman and one layman, covering the Frankish heartlands of the Empire, was created, and a 'job description' covering the responsibilities of the *missi* on their annual tour outlined.[38]

The *missi* have often been depicted as a nascent professional administrative class of dedicated royal officials. However, it is absolutely clear that most *missi* were chosen from the ranks of local landowners. One observer of the capitulary legislation in 802 – in which the system of *missi* was regularised – also commented that, after this date, *missi* were no longer chosen from amongst 'the poorer *vassi* from the palace'.[39] Detailed study of the charter evidence for the activities of the *missi* has suggested that local contacts and knowledge were vital in being able to intervene effectively. The *missi* were *de facto* leaders of a region, and kings tended to alternate the position within the small circle of dominant local families, thus tying them into the governmental programme and affecting a political balance. These families were now competing for royal favour and the position of *missus* that allowed them to be 'top dog' locally; previously they had enjoyed positions of quasi-princely regional dominance that were self-standing and not dependent on the king's favour, and did not involve the implementation of a political programme for the king. The structure of regional power was thus reworked from a self-standing pyramid to a hierarchy of power descending from, and defined by, the court.

The *missi* were the primary royal agents responsible for overseeing the implementation of the rulings of the capitularies; a significant number of capitularies are addressed directly to them, either generally or to named individual *missi*. They were to oversee the activities of counts, particularly in the administration of justice. This included the handling of particularly complex or difficult local disputes, for which there is plentiful charter evidence to illuminate the workings of the system. Two areas of governmental activity absolutely crucial to the regime were increasingly reserved for the *missi*: the taking of the oath of loyalty and the levying of military service. Like the oath, military service was a crucial mechanism of interaction between king and local elites, and was reorganised under Charlemagne through the *missi*.

In the period of successful expansion before 800, the attraction of the war-trail was such that there was no need for rules and regulations about the obligation to serve; local elites wanted to fight, to gain contact with a king and a share of the spoils, and the practical arrangements of recruitment and equipment were carried on through the agencies of these elites in their localities. In a new context of defensive warfare after 800, the sociology of military service changed. Legislation about military service was sparse until the first decade of the ninth century, when it exploded, providing clear rules outlining which classes of people were responsible for military service and for supporting those on military service. By placing the administration of these rulings in the hands of the *missi*, military arrangements were removed from the arena of *ad hoc* arrangements and alliances within communities where they had been previously organised; lists of those liable were to be compiled and local evidence shows that the new system was put into effect.[40]

The implementation of the system of *missi* went hand-in-hand with the reform of the Church for, as we have seen, *missi* worked in pairs, a leading ecclesiastic alongside a figure chosen from the secular elite: there is a remarkable letter to the bishop of Toul from his archbishop ordering a general mobilisation, and showing how the Church hierarchy provided an excellent mechanism for the operation of government.[41] In fact, in some areas the position of ecclesiastical *missus* devolved to the dominant bishop, very often the provincial metropolitan or archbishop. The use of *missi* as links between the court and the region thus paralleled and, indeed, built on the simultaneous creation of a regular Church hierarchy, and the implementation of Church governments through a system of archbishops.

In fact, Carolingian Church reform was part and parcel of the restructuring of the political system. In the late Merovingian period, local elites had used the Church to entrench their dominance, building mutually supportive relationships with favoured churches, which had often been founded or endowed – and so controlled – by their kin; rural monasteries became centres of family power, while some families were able to establish control of bishoprics. Hand-in-hand with Carolingian control went the dismemberment of these matrices of local power. Excess Church land was to be effectively controlled by the king, and granted out in life-tenure on the king's word in return for the payment of an annual rent to the Church that retained ownership. The resources of over-mighty bishops were further redistributed to provide endowments for local counts.

The late Merovingian practice of granting important monasteries immunity from the actions of local officials was combined with the gift of royal protection, and so the great monasteries of the realm were subjected to royal lordship; indeed, grants of immunity and protection show Charlemagne following a predatory policy in those areas outside the traditional Merovingian heartland, and acquiring lordship over monasteries in southern Gaul and the provinces east of the Rhine by hook or by crook in the decades after 780.[42] The development of a programmes of ecclesiastical and monastic reform, and the implementation of regular synods and assemblies, transformed the position of abbots and bishops from that of leaders of their own institutions to that of officials in an empire-wide Church whose job was the implementation of an empire-wide programme of reform and agreed standards. These measures not only allowed kings to tap the Church's wealth and power, but also transformed abbots and bishops into royal officials, who were used in secular as well as ecclesiastical matters. Charlemagne, once again, created a regular hierarchy of power, and implanted direct royal lordship into every locality.

The politics of office

The creation of a hierarchy of power, and the connection of the 'small worlds' of the localities to the person of the king, did not create a free-standing administrative apparatus, independent and separate from the local dominance of landowners; this was impossible in a world where royal resources were only quantitatively different from those of local elites. In fact, local elites exercised a form of public power at a local level; Carolingian government rested on the interaction between two tiers of public power, that of local elites and that of kings.

In Carolingian usage, to exercise legitimate power was to be 'public', while to be 'private' was to be 'deprived' of legitimate power: holding the 'public faith' that was involved in ruling legitimately would transform a private individual into a public person. Although critics might accuse some powerful individuals of putting their individual interests before the care for the public good, modern distinctions between an individual's public or official role and their private interests had little place in these categories of thought, precisely because it was impossible to perform an office properly without drawing on the power created by individual landed wealth.[43] There were occasions on which royal patronage led to the rise of 'new men' into the ruling class, or implanted members of the landed elite as officials in areas where they had no local contacts. But on these occasions, newcomers always and everywhere quickly acquired the landed muscle they needed to carry out their jobs, by fair means or foul: to stay an outsider and attempt to rule was an impossibility. The implantation of new men inevitably tended to lead to disruption, resentment and, more often than not, to the abuse of position in order to provide landed wealth; it was neither desirable as a rule, nor conducive to good government.[44] We cannot, therefore, measure royal power or governmental success by the frequency of the imposition of outsiders, which was always rare in any case.

Central to the Carolingian programme was a reshaping of the relationship between those elite families that had long dominated their localities and the king. The political capital generated by three generations of successful expansive warfare allowed a fundamental reorientation of the political structure of the empire. Where previously aristocrats had been loosely bound into personal relationships with the king, and their localities thus tied to the court only indirectly, now kingship was directly related to the localities themselves, and the status of local landowners as holders of an office responsible for implementing a programme of administrative reform was explicitly stated. The new ethics of office reverberated into the rural communities which made up the empire; hence they were echoed in legal documents recording local property transactions.

Pessimists about the value of the capitularies and the impact of Charlemagne on the empire have often written with the benefit of a peculiar kind of hindsight. Knowing that the empire would be a conglomeration of kingdoms by the middle decades of the ninth century, and that the Carolingian dynasty would soon after lose its monopoly on these kingships, they have sought the roots of these later problems under Charlemagne.[45] The problem with such an approach is that the shadow thus cast by later developments is more likely to obscure than illuminate. Our understanding of the ninth-century Carolingian world is currently under-going rapid and radical revision, and recent research has made it clear that the succession problems of the Carolingian dynasty and the division of the empire into a conglomeration of Carolingian kingdoms did not lead to the collapse of the political system within those kingdoms.[46] In fact, the inevitability of political division between a fraternity of Carolingian kings had always been acknowledged, notably by Charlemagne himself in his own plans for the succession. Louis the Pious only inherited a 'united empire' because his brothers all predeceased their father, and he too planned for a future of multiple kingships, albeit with his eldest son enjoying the authority of the imperial title. In fact, a system of competing Carolingian kings proved viable until the last two decades of the ninth century, when a lack of Carolingians led to political crisis.

If we look at the relationship between kings and landowning elites, the politics of the ninth century centred on the disposition of royal office. Louis the Pious and his sons faced different problems from those addressed by Charlemagne, but they were powerful and effective rulers whose ability to govern their kingdoms was not in doubt. In fact, contemporaries complained about the tyranny of kings who sought to 'hire and fire' key countships, and they regarded royal restraint in the granting and taking away of office as a cause for praise and celebration.[47] The first high-profile sackings of counts had occurred under Louis the Pious, fomented in the convoluted politics of the last years of his reign, but under rulers such as Charles the Bald and Louis the German the withdrawal of royal endowments and public office was central to the exercise of kingship. When we read of local civil wars, as royal appointees sought to remove their predecessors as count, this does not reflect the growth of autonomous landlord power in the localities, but the unceasing efforts of kings to treat countships as offices. By the tenth century, kings had lost the power to intervene in this manner: this was a result of the decreased resources of kings, who were now happy simply to secure alliance and allegiance from local elites. Even then, countships were not seen as family property in the manner of an estate, but rather as legitimate princely office devolved from God.

Ruling an early medieval kingdom did not centre on ensuring the efficient running of a self-standing administrative machine. Central to good kingship was the ability to broker strong relationships with local elites and the Church. Practices of elite sociability such as hunting, feasting and praying, and the ritual conventions that governed the behaviour of kings and elites when they met on these occasions, were the fundamental practices in early medieval politics through which 'the rules of the game' were articulated and negotiated.[48] These activities, faintly visible in the sources, were central to Charlemagne's rule and that of his successors. But the issuing of written instructions to royal agents and the articulation of a programme of reform meant that Carolingian kingship was not only a matter of the war-trail and the hunt.

Notes

1 Einhard, *VK*, Preface, c. 4. On the organisation of the *VK*, see Hellmann (1932); Innes (1997a): Ganz, ch. 3 (pp. 38–51) in this volume.

2 Ganshof (1971), pp. 4–5. Cf. Löwe (1974), Staubach (1984).

3 Fried (1982); Nelson (1988); Innes (1997b) esp. pp. 851–5.

4 Hincmar, *De ordine palatii*, MGH *Fontes* III, pp. 32–99; trans. Dutton (1994), pp. 485–500.

5 On this and what follows see, Wickham (1984); Fouracre (1992); Innes (2000a); W. Davies (1988), esp. pp. 201–10, and for the problem of the medieval 'state' see now R. R. Davies (2002).

6 Wood (1994), pp. 255–73; Fouracre and Gerberding (1996), pp. 1–26; Rosenwein (1999), pp. 74–95.

7 Fouracre (2000).

8 Reuter (1985); Bullough (1985a); Innes (2000a), pp. 143–53.

9 Reuter (1990); Noble (1990).

10 On the court, see Bullough (1985b); Airlie (1990) and (2000); Innes (2003). On relations between kings and aristocrats, see Le Jan (1995); Airlie (1995).

11 The fundamental study is Werner (1980). On royal and aristocratic topographies, see Innes (2001a). On local workings see Innes (2000a); Brown (2001). On the marches, see Smith (1992) and (1995a).

12 The seminal study is Ganshof (1959), with McKitterick (1989), pp. 23–75; Mordek, ed. (1986), pp. 25–50 and Mordek (1995); Wormald (1999), pp. 30–92.

13 Wood (1990) and (1994), pp. 102–19.

14 Ganshof (1971), pp. 125–42; McKitterick (1989), pp. 25–37, and (1993); Nelson (1990).

15 It is not clear if Ansegisus acted on private initiative or official instructions. Similar issues about the relationship between individual initiative and public policy surround the writing of capitularies generally: see Lupus' letter to Hincmar (Lupus, *Epistolae*, no. 43) and the capitularies drafted by Einhard (see Mordek (1990)).

16 Nelson (1983).

17 McKitterick (1989), pp. 23–75; Wormald (1999), pp. 53–70; Mordek (1995).

18 Stengel, ed., *Fulda charters* (1913–58), no. 83; Glöckner, ed., *Codex Laureshamensis* (1929–36), no. 6a and 228.

19 Innes (2000a), pp. 111–18, 129–39.

20 *Capitulare Missorum Specialia*, MGH *Capit.* I, no. 34, trans. King (1987), pp. 243–4; MGH *Capit.* I, nos. 24, 31, 85, trans. King (1987), pp. 258–60.

21 MGH *Capit.* I, no. 58. Similar reports back to the palace abound in the charters, e.g., Bitterauf, ed. (1905) I, no. 143.

22 Garrison (2000b).

23 MGH *Capit.* I, no. 39.

24 For a vivid description of the reading aloud of royal exhortations, see Eigil, *Vita Sturmi*, c. 12.

25 *Capitulare Missorum*, c. 25, MGH *Capit.* I, no. 40, p. 116.

26 Ganshof (1971), pp. 111–24; Becher (1993); further bibliography in next note.

27 For example, the *Capitulary of Herstal* (779), MGH *Capit.* I, no. 20, c. 14 (*trustes*), c. 16 (oaths and gilds), c. 22 (feud); trans. King (1987), pp. 203–5. See Le Jan (1995), pp. 122–30; Geary (1995), pp. 584–5; Althoff (1990), pp. 119–33, 149–67.

28 *Capitulare Missorum Generale* (802), cc. 2–8, MGH *Capit.* I, no. 33, pp. 92–3, trans. King (1987), pp. 234–5.

29 MGH *Capit.* I, no. 181; see Ganshof (1971), p. 134.
30 Bitterauf, ed. (1905), I, no. 186, and see Brown (2001). Also, for example, Wartmann, ed. (1863), I, no. 187: sworn testimony given 'according to our faith and the oath which we gave to the lord king'.
31 MGH *Capit.* I, no. 33, c. 8, p. 93; trans. King (1987), p. 235.
32 For a basic description, see Ganshof (1968). For more recent interpretations, see Fouracre (1995b); Le Jan (1997); Brown (2001).
33 Ganshof (1968), pp. 76–9, 107; Estey (1951).
34 Davies and Fouracre, eds. (1986), pp. 60–1, 200–1.
35 Three examples from 782: *Codex Laureshamensis*, ed. Glöckner (1929–36), no. 228; MGH *Dip. Karol.* I, no. 148; Guérard, ed. (1859), no. 31, also Albanes and Chevalier, eds. (1899), no. 41. On these see, Innes (2000a), pp. 182–5; Geary (1994).
36 MGH *Capit.* I, no. 33, c. 26, p. 96, trans. King (1987), p. 239; Geary (1995), pp. 600–1.
37 *Codex Laureshamensis*, ed. Glöckner (1929–36), no. 6a, 3684b/3066, and MGH *Dip. Karol.* I, no. 142; Borgolte (1984).
38 MGH *Capit.* I, no. 33; trans. King (1987), pp. 233–42.
39 *AL* 802, trans. King (1987), pp. 144–5. For *missi*, Hannig (1983) and (1984).
40 Reuter (1985); Innes (2000a), pp. 143–56.
41 Frothar of Toul, *Epistolae*, no. 2, MGH *Epp.* 5, p. 277.
42 McKitterick (1983), pp. 41–5, 53–64; de Jong (1995); for case-studies, see Innes (1998b); Rosenwein (1999), pp. 97–134. The fundamental work here is that of Josef Semmler.
43 Innes (2000a), pp. 254–9.
44 Airlie (1990), pp. 197–9.
45 Cf. Collins (1998b), pp. 171–4.
46 On local power, see Innes (2000a), pp. 195–240. On court politics, see Maclean (2003).
47 Regino of Prüm, *Chronicon*, s.a. 876, MGH *SSRG* 50, p. 110.
48 On rituals and 'rules of the game', see Althoff (1997) and Buc (2001).

6

CHARLEMAGNE AND THE ARISTOCRACY CAPTAINS AND KINGS

Stuart Airlie

In the year 782, the long series of campaigns against the Saxons that predated Charlemagne's reign, but which was brought to grim conclusion by him, took a turn for the worse. Under the leadership of Widukind, the Saxons threw off the Frankish yoke and rose in fierce revolt. Leading members of the Frankish aristocracy, entrusted by the king with hostilities against the Slavs, turned aside from that task and moved against the contumacious Saxons. They were joined by reinforcements led by a man called Theoderic, a relative (*propinquus*) of the king himself, and they prepared to fall upon the rebels. This must have been a formidable military force, led as it was by highly placed members of Charlemagne's following, including such officers of the court as the chamberlain, the count of the stables and the count of the palace, not to mention Theoderic. This was a man who had risen high from his first appearance in our sources as a vassal of the king in 775 and who was a hard man, 'a reckless warrior to the end of his life' as Donald Bullough has described him. But perhaps it was because the leaders of this force were so eminent and victory seemed so certain that disaster ensued. The leaders who had been joined by Theoderic worried that the glory of the victory would fall to him as the king's relative and so they charged on without him. They and their forces were cut to pieces. A late but very full account in the Revised version of the Royal Frankish Annals tells us that the chamberlain, the count of the stables, four counts and a score of other distinguished noblemen fell, along with those of their followers who stood by them till the end.[1]

Mutual rivalry and jealousy among commanders is not confined to medieval armies, as the personality clashes of Montgomery and Eisenhower in the Second World War show. Nonetheless, this episode reveals something of the tension between the Carolingians and their great aristocratic followers, tensions that usually resulted, it should be said, in creative achievements for the Franks. The grip of the Carolingian dynasty on power was not as tight in the 780s as it was later to become. As we shall see, in 785 Charlemagne was to face something much more threatening than the 'prima donna' attitudes of essentially loyal commanders, in the form of a conspiracy against his rule and life led by disaffected aristocrats from the eastern territories. The Carolingian family had held the throne only since 751. It had a good record of showering prestige and treasure on its followers through military victory, but that record was not unbroken; in 778 Carolingian forces had been defeated in Spain and Saxony.[2]

Even loyal followers of the king, among whom we should count the unfortunate casualties of 782, could feel resentful towards members of the royal house, whose promotion and prestige could be seen to have been won at their expense. The aristocracy was not simply an instrument for the king's hands; it was a partner. As such, its value to the king is demonstrated in the bloody sequel to the Saxon defeat. Charlemagne himself journeyed east, rounded up those Saxons identified as responsible for the rebellion and presided over their killing (some 4,500 in a single day, according to the Revised version of the Annals).[3] With this act of mass brutality, Charlemagne re-asserted Frankish mastery and avenged the death of his friends who had fallen in his service. Followers had to be honoured in death as they had to be rewarded in life and it was the fierce rhythms generated by bonds of lordship such as this that led Wallace-Hadrill to stress the stark otherness of Carolingian political culture: 'what scholars call [Charlemagne's] personality as a statesman never existed'.[4]

The respect paid by the king to his followers, as seen in this episode, shows that early medieval kingdoms such as Charlemagne's should not be seen as subject to the exclusive power of the royal ruler but governed by a largely co-operative oligarchy, in Reuter's phrase. Such a picture is the result of intense scholarly work on the early medieval aristocracy, particularly since 1945, work that has done much to correct excessively king-centred views of political history. It may be, however, as Reuter has suggested, that the scholarly stress on collective action and co-operation is itself now threatening to harden into an orthodoxy that may merit critical scrutiny.[5] This need not mean that we must return to a view of royal power and aristocratic power as being mutually hostile. Royal authority was a key element in the Frankish world. But the right of one particular family – the Carolingian family itself – to royal rule was not something that could be taken for granted. It was thus a significant achievement for the Carolingians to persuade the aristocracy that service to them was an integral component of aristocratic identity and part of the aristocratic ethos.

Magnates as team players

We can imagine the members of the aristocracy assembled in ranks behind Charlemagne, by looking at the list of witnesses to his will, drawn up in 811.[6] The list consists of thirty great men of the empire. The first fifteen names are those of the great archbishops, bishops and abbots, and this should remind us that it is not always easy or indeed helpful to our understanding of the period to draw too sharp a distinction between the clerical and secular elites, which stemmed from the same aristocratic families. Abbot Adalung was abbot of Lorsch, an abbey that had originally stood rather apart from the Carolingians; but the presence of Adalung, who was connected to the abbey's founders, testifies to the success of its incorporation into the Carolingian system.[7] Archbishop Arn of Salzburg belonged to a Bavarian aristocratic family and his presence in the witness list testifies to the successful absorption of Bavaria into the Carolingian empire.[8] All this does not mean that we should see such clergy exclusively as political figures. Nor should we understand the virtual monopoly of high clerical office by the aristocracy as simply the exercise of its claims to authority by other means. The denunciation of 'secular-minded' clergy by Alcuin may point to the existence of secular values among churchmen but it also shows that they were expected to behave differently, and the careers of many show that they did so.[9] Indeed, as we shall see, the rough warriors of the secular elite could also be men of cultivation and were certainly members of a Christian culture.

We cannot, in the confines of this chapter, survey all fifteen of the secular witnesses to the will but a glance at three of them makes instructive points. It is worth noting that one of them, Wala, was himself a Carolingian. Like Charlemagne, he was a grandson of Charles Martel. While there was a gulf between an inner circle of royal Carolingians and the aristocracy – a gulf that remained un-crossed until 879 when Duke Boso made a bid for a crown and triggered the jealous wrath of the old royal dynasty – the border between the aristocracy and those members of the royal family who might be of high status but who were not legitimate sons of kings remained porous. As we have seen in the case of Theoderic, whose royal connections aroused resentment, the Carolingian status of such figures gave them a special place in the ranks of the aristocracy and played a role in political calculations and judgements. As a Carolingian, Wala worked for Charlemagne, the head of the royal house, in various theatres of the empire and his appearance at the head of the list of counts in his cousin's will testifies to his personal prominence, the high status of his Carolingian blood and also his subordinate position to Charles.[10]

Loyalty to the dynasty had brought these witnesses rewards. Count Audulf is probably the same Audulf who led an army against the Bretons in 786. But his fortune lay at the other end of the empire. In 799 he took charge of Bavaria, where he ruled as prefect till 818.[11] His move from north-west France to south-east Germany gives some idea of the scale of the great chessboard of opportunities created for this aristocracy by the conquests of the reign. We can also see the scale of the rewards available to Charlemagne for granting to his favoured courtiers. Unsurprisingly, Audulf was proud of this favour, or so we can assume from a charter drawn up after his death. This records a transaction involving his widow and son, and refers grandly to how 'Audulf was placed over the province of the Bavarians with power and honour by the pious emperor Charlemagne and then received the same power from Louis to guard, rule and govern that province'.[12] The fact that Audulf's widow Keyla appears in this document, proclaiming her late husband's status, shows something of how aristocratic women preserved and articulated family memories and identities.[13] Audulf's holding of the great command in the service of two Carolingian rulers was both a mark of his favour and status, and also a sign of that loyalty to the dynasty that was, as we have seen, a mark of the aristocracy's own identity and self-perception.

The final witness to be considered here, Count Stephen, was count of Paris – as his brothers were to be after him and as their father Gerard had been before them. Gerard had been among the followers of Pippin III before his coronation in 751, and he was connected to the new royal dynasty by marriage. One of his other sons, Bego, was to marry a daughter of Louis the Pious.[14] A family such as Stephen's was a partner of the royal house, not simply its servant. Its loyalty was bound up with its claim, surely seen by that family as a right, to hold the countship of Paris. Only through the holding of such offices, termed *honores* in contemporary sources, could aristocrats outstrip rivals from other families and from less highly placed branches of their own kin. Much of the political history of the period revolves around the struggle for *honores* and since kings could regulate access to them, royal favour was sought in fierce competition.[15]

Patronage over *honores* thus gave kings such as Charlemagne a useful lever of control over aristocrats, but competition within the royal family itself could heighten instability and competitiveness, as we shall see later. When the system worked smoothly, as it did in the case of Stephen's family for the period we are considering, the king gained loyal service and Stephen gained the county that his father had held. Stephen's very name reveals something of the horizon of opportunity opened up for members of the aristocracy by the rise of the new royal dynasty and what they made of them. Le Jan has pointed out that Stephen was named after Pope Stephen II who visited Francia in the winter of 753–54. The pope had come to anoint King Pippin and his sons Charlemagne and Carloman. But it was not only the royal family that benefited from the papal presence. The pope spent the winter at St-Denis, just north of Paris and it is probable that he baptised the son of Gerard, the count of Paris, and the son thus took the name Stephen.[16]

Some members of this aristocracy may have actually had wider horizons than their Carolingian masters. No Carolingian king ever visited Constantinople, but their magnates did so. Count Helmgaud travelled there as an envoy of Charlemagne in 802, as did Count Hugh of Tours in 811.[17] Such men, and the bishops who accompanied them, thus had experience of an imperial court other than Aachen. Even Charlemagne could not go everywhere. It does seem that Charlemagne had a gift for picking good agents, but his range of choices for tasks must often have been limited. In appointing Gerold to rule Bavaria after the elimination of the native ducal dynasty in 788, Charlemagne was keeping this high command in the family; Gerold was the brother of his late wife Hildegarde. Gerold, however, was related to the fallen Bavarian dynasty. His connections with this part of the empire made him acceptable there.[18] Charlemagne had to work with what he was given. This was not a weakness; it was simply a fact of political life. But it conditioned royal rule in this period and the power of king such as Charlemagne depended on the strength of the relationship between the royal court, as the conceptual centre of the realm, and the regions.[19]

Kings, through the twin forces of the lure of patronage and the threat of royal anger, had to win over local figures in order to govern and so we should not be surprised that regional and aristocratic self-interest survived within the Carolingian 'state'. The state could not otherwise have survived, let alone flourished as it did. Nor should we be surprised at bribery and greed for the profits of office. Bishop Theodulf of Orléans knew Charlemagne's court, and he served as a *missus* in the south of Gaul in 798. His vivid, poetic account of the bribes pressed on judges reveals the desirability of high office, but his own attack on the practice and royal legislation against it show that there was a strong contemporary sense that some of these fruits of office were unlawful.[20] To search for impersonal honesty among early medieval office-holders is to be disappointed. But it is equally naïve to make the reverse assumption that no standards of honesty existed for public office-holders and judges.

Warriors for God and profit

Those who governed in the name of Charlemagne were also warriors. Gerold fell in battle on the frontiers of the empire in 799, as did Eric, duke of Friuli. Both men were commemorated in poetic epitaphs that attest to their status in contemporary eyes as Christian warriors and governors.[21] But it was also remembered that they had fallen in Carolingian service. Einhard takes the details from the Royal Frankish Annals on the death of Eric and Gerold, and artfully places both deaths in a section dealing with Charlemagne's successful management of the war against the Avars. Towards the end of the ninth century, Notker, writing in the monastery of St-Gallen where Gerold was remembered, drew on the memory of his campaigns in order to write his account of Charlemagne's wars.[22] Thus the military activities of these men were subsumed into representations of Carolingian rule. This also reflected the historical situation. Eric assuredly profited from the campaigns against the Avars, but it was to Charlemagne in Aachen that he sent the captured treasure.[23]

That men such as Eric and Gerold were Christian warriors cannot be doubted. As we have seen, contemporaries represented them as such and the importance of this aspect of aristocratic identity should not be underestimated. In the late Carolingian period there is an example of one aristocrat, Gerald of Aurillac, who found that his Christian identity clashed directly with his secular aristocratic code and it was the latter that had to yield. Gerald may have been an extreme case, and that his *Life* presents him as a bit of a misfit may tell us more about Gerald's clerical biographer than about the historical Gerald. Nonetheless, Gerald's Christian conscience could have been real enough and the clerical authors who represented clashes between Christian values and the secular ethos of aristocratic warriors were themselves from the ranks of that aristocracy and knew that dilemma at first hand.[24] One of Charlemagne's companions, William of Gellone, retired to a monstery; another, Wido, a doughty warrior on the Breton march, received spiritual advice from Alcuin.[25]

Such men could fight Christian wars. Nelson has argued that there was more to the military activity of Charlemagne's aristocracy than the plunder and tribute highlighted by Reuter in an important article. Or rather, that there was *less* of plunder and tribute than we might think. Surveying the Saxon wars which dragged on for so long, she has found only one reference in the annals to gold and silver being taken out of Saxony by the Franks and concludes that we ought to take seriously what our sources say. We should give full weight to religious and ideological factors as motivating forces for Charlemagne's aristocracy: 'glory – heroic and heavenly'.[26] As we saw at the beginning of this chapter, glory was indeed a prize worth staking one's life on. Perhaps Saxony did not yield much plunder but there may be some reference to the plundering of Saxon *villae* in the annals, and the capitularies certainly reveal merchant activity and the expectation that the fines of Carolingian justice will be paid; and Saxony certainly yielded human resources, including high-status hostages.[27] Saxony was not a desert.[28]

If Reuter has underplayed the importance of ideological factors, Nelson's insights can be seen as adding to his model, rather than detracting from it. When Charlemagne captured the Lombard capital of Pavia in northern Italy in 774, he 'entered it with hymns and *laudes*, and the treasures of the kings which he found there he gave to his army'. Glory, pious thanks to a God who had favoured the righteous Franks, and the distribution of what must have been significant treasure all came together in the intoxicating cocktail of military victory.[29] Treasure could have more than a merely material significance. The treasure that Duke Eric of Friuli brought to Charlemagne in 796, as part of the spoils of the Avar campaigns, enhanced the great king's majesty and demonstrated his power, as Eric sent the treasure all the way from Avar Pannonia to the court. Some of that treasure probably stuck to Eric's fingers but this is hardly surprising; men such as Eric were not salaried civil servants. Charlemagne's decision to send on some of that treasure to the pope in Rome was probably seen by some contemporaries as restoring to the Church what was rightfully hers. Contemporary and later sources associate the Avar treasure with the despoiling of churches; its capture by the Franks with their beautifying.[30] In his *Life of Charlemagne*, Einhard gloats over the arrival of the Avar treasure and he can be taken here as representative of the voice of the secular aristocracy; but for that aristocracy and its rulers, treasure had an aura that went beyond its merely economic value.

Of course the economic value of treasure mattered hugely and treasure was welcome whether it came from pagans such as the Avars or from Christians such as the Lombards or the Bavarians. In the service of a successful king, Charlemagne's aristocrats enriched themselves and their own followers in turn. Treasure helped fuel an aristocratic way of life. It also helped maintain and develop bonds of loyalty and thus it had to circulate. Even a lavish patron such as Charlemagne could never assume that he had given his followers enough. The thirst of the aristocracy for treasure was insatiable. Royal service provided opportunities for acquiring it in war and government.[31] Only the molten gold poured down his throat by devils in hell could finally slake the avaricious thirst of Count Bego.[32] When his son Pippin ('the Hunchback') rebelled against him in 792 Charlemagne not only punished those members of the aristocracy who had backed the plot, but he also had to reward those who had taken no part in it with gold, silver and silks. Their loyalty could not be taken for granted.[33]

Less dramatic glimpses of the role of treasure in making fortunes and maintaining bonds of loyalty and empire can be seen in the case of one Johannes, a follower of Louis the Pious, in the 790s. He had served in campaigns against the infidels in Spain and had gained much booty, including horses and highly-prized military equipment. Some of this he had passed on to Louis the Pious, Charlemagne's son, who was king of Aquitaine and under whose aegis such campaigns were fought. In return, Louis had granted Johannes land. It is possible that Johannes and his followers were mercenaries who converted military victory into the means of landed settlement.[34]

Service to the Carolingian rulers could thus bring great rewards. But such service had its own problems. Who was the right Carolingian to serve and follow? Pippin III had two sons who succeeded him in 768: Charlemagne and Carloman. Both were legitimate kings and both looked like promising patrons. The death of Carloman in December 771 was a devastating blow for members of the aristocracy who had hitched their wagon to his star. They could not have known that he was destined to die so young. The division of the Frankish realms between Charlemagne and his brother in 768 had meant that the aristocracy faced the prospect of conflict and divided loyalties if the brothers did not get on. Some aristocrats hedged their bets. We have charters from Lorsch and from the Paris area that reveal, by the fact that they are dated by the regnal years of both brothers, that some people hoped to remain on good terms with both kings or that both might rule together in harmony.[35] It appears, however, that the brothers did not get on, and this meant that each brother would be bound to regard some of the other's followers with suspicion as being too committed to the one king to be able to serve the other.

Carloman's early death left such figures facing bleak prospects. We know that major figures from Carloman's kingdom rallied to Charles. They included the archbishop of Sens, the abbot of St-Denis and, from the ranks of the secular aristocracy, Count Warin of Alemannia together with Count Adalhard – who may well have been Charlemagne's cousin. Apart from Adalhard, who was young and at the beginning of a distinguished career, these men were experienced veterans who had served Charlemagne's father; even Adalhard had probably grown up at his court.[36] It is easy to see how their experience and political expertise would benefit Charlemagne, but it is equally easy to forget that these qualities had been deployed in the service of Carloman. In other words, Carloman was a contender, a perfectly credible Frankish ruler who had impressive personnel in his service and to whom ambitious magnates would have been happy to commit themselves.

Impact of dynastic rivalries

We can catch a glimpse of one of these ambitious magnates. When Carloman died, his widow and sons fled to the court of the Lombard king, Desiderius, in northern Italy. Desiderius was pleased to welcome them. Carloman's sons, one of whom bore the resonant royal name of Pippin, were potentially useful cards to play against that Charlemagne who had so recently seemed to desire an alliance with the Lombards.[37] An alternative Carolingian court in exile could now be set up, and it is no surprise to learn from papal sources that Desiderius tried to pressure the pope into anointing Carloman's sons as kings. The same sources make it clear that Desiderius was aided in all this by one Autchar, a Frankish magnate who had fled to Italy with Carloman's family. Autchar had been an important man in the service of Pippin III since 752, and the pope seems to have feared him as an agent of Desiderius.[38] He was a talented aristocrat who had profited from service to the new royal dynasty but who, on the death of his particular patron, was faced with ruin because he was so committed to that patron that he could not seek service with Charlemagne in 771. Instead he chose exile and the prospect of waiting for better times; the fact that his exile was at the court of a powerful rival of Charlemagne, a court now equipped with potential substitute Carolingian kings, shows how exile could be turned to aggression. Unfortunately for Autchar, Charlemagne moved against the Lombards in 774 and these better times never materialised.[39]

It is all too easy for us to forget men like Autchar, who backed the losing side in a Carolingian family struggle. But we will not understand the importance of these struggles for contemporaries unless we remember that, for Autchar, the end of these struggles was not a foregone conclusion. He had no idea that he was backing the losing side and his choice to follow Carloman's widow and sons into Italy in the winter of 771/72 was based on hope as much as on despair. For his part, Charlemagne could not count on the automatic loyalty of all of his brother's followers after Carloman's death. Our knowledge of the outcome of Carolingian history can mean that we fail to grasp how real some possibilities seemed to contemporaries. Choices such as those made by Autchar had to be made over and over again, even in Charlemagne's reign – as we shall see. The fate of men such as Autchar was widely known and, if not exactly celebrated, vividly recalled. Writing an account of Charlemagne's reign at the end of the ninth century, Notker of St-Gallen gives a vivid account of Autchar's terror as Charlemagne's mighty ironclad army marched on his Lombard refuge. Perhaps this account owes much to Notker's imagination and story-telling skills, but perhaps Notker was drawing on oral traditions, memories of the 'defeated' current among the aristocracy. Certainly Autchar was not forgotten in the Middle Ages, and we should not forget him either as he has much to teach us.[40]

Autchar had been forced to make choices, but there were aristocrats within the empire who did not simply wish to choose between rival Carolingians, but rather to reject wholesale the Carolingian dynasty. This is visible some thirty years after Charlemagne's father gained the kingship for himself and his sons; the Carolingian right to the throne was not taken for granted. It is important to remember this, not because it is desirable to cut Charlemagne down to size by envisaging him as a royal parvenu (though that is how some members of the aristocracy would surely have seen him), but rather because, if we bear in mind the resentments felt by some sections of the aristocracy towards Charlemagne's family and the tensions generated by the extension of strong royal rule, we can gain a better sense of the scale of Charlemagne's achievement in focusing aristo-cratic loyalties onto himself.[41]

Tensions and resentments rose to the surface in 785/86 when a serious conspiracy centring on Count Hardrad was formed against the king. The aristo-crats involved in it had connections stretching from Alsace up the Rhine to the great abbeys of Lorsch and Fulda.[42] Something of the conspirators' rancour speaks to us through the sources, and the fact that sources preserve this anti-Carolingian feeling suggests that there was sympathy for them in some quarters.[43] The plotters aimed to kill the king and they do not seem to have used a Carolingian prince or any other royal kinsman as their front man. Not simply Charlemagne but the whole Carolingian line would have been threatened. Charlemagne's oldest sons were only about sixteen and twelve at the time of the conspiracy. They could have fought for their inheritance but they would have had to fight very hard if the conspiracy had succeeded.

Paradoxically, this conspiracy highlights some of the means deployed by Charlemagne to cement his hold over the aristocracy and weld his kingdom together. One of the conspirators, described as a Thuringian, had refused to let his daughter contract a marriage alliance with a Frank, that is, a westerner. It was Charlemagne's demand that the Thuringian should hand over his daughter that triggered the eastern rising. Here the king's intervention had proved dangerous. The very fact of that intervention is, however, instructive. The king can here be seen as supervising and attempting to facilitate alliances by marriage across the kingdom in order to bind his elite together. Nor was Charlemagne merely a spectator. He had himself married an easterner, his Queen Fastrada, in 783; though the events of 785/86 demonstrate the potentially limited success of such alliances.[44] As things turned out, Charlemagne survived, the plotters were punished and the king learned from such conspiracies the importance of binding his followers to him in a web of solemn oaths.[45]

Charlemagne could win the aristocracy over to Carolingian kingship. The conspiracy of Hardrad was the last rising north of the Alps, against a Carolingian king and not led by a Carolingian prince or king, until that of Boso in 879. So, for nearly a century, conflict was kept in the family.[46] This, however, points to problems even Charlemagne could not solve. The inner tensions of the royal family were one of the key motors of politics in this period. We have already seen how choosing between the royal brothers Charlemagne and Carloman had been a headache for some members of the aristocracy in the late 760s. As the reign progressed, the problem of the succession cast its shadow. By the 790s, Charlemagne had slimmed down the throne-worthy members of the royal house to his own family: his brother's sons had vanished; his dangerous cousin, Duke Tassilo of Bavaria, had been turned into an un-person.[47] Aristocratic marriages may have been a way of binding the empire together, but none of Charlemagne's daughters married into the aristocracy and this must have been a deliberate policy to keep the shape of the royal family slim-line.[48]

Even Charlemagne, however, could not keep the royal family static and, if he managed to focus the aristocracy's loyalty on to his own family, that just brought trouble closer to home. The tensions within the royal family locked into the tensions within the aristocracy to produce a dangerous climate. Members of the aristocracy needed access to royal favour in order to guarantee their high status above their rivals, and that included less fortunate members of their own kin. As a result of this, shifts in the composition and balance of favour within the royal family itself were anxiously studied. If one son was seen to lose his father's favour, then not only he but also his followers began to feel fortune's wheel turning down under them. We have a series of anecdotes in the sources turning on such speculation among the aristocracy over the status of young princes in Charlemagne's favour, and on their rivalries with each other.[49]

It is therefore not surprising that the next conspiracy against Charlemagne was led by one of his own sons, and this set the pattern for much of the conflict of the next century. This was the conspiracy of Pippin the Hunchback in 792. Pippin was Charlemagne's eldest son, but he had gradually been marginalised within the royal family in favour of sons by the king's later wife, Hildegard. It is not clear whether Pippin was legitimate or not, and he may well have been, but the category of legitimate birth was not rigid at this period, and key points for the aristocracy scrutinising Pippin's potential would have been factors such as his indubitably royal name and his standing in his father's eyes. Charlemagne's preference for the sons of Hildegard muddied the political waters.[50] The acquisition of Bavaria by Charlemagne in 788 seems to have brought tensions among the royal sons to a head.

The conspiracy unfolded in Regensburg in Bavaria, and Charlemagne and the sons of Hildegard appear to have been the target. We have little hard information on the identity of Pippin's supporters so we cannot be certain that Pippin himself initiated the plot. He may have been a front man for those members of the aristocracy who felt that they were losing out under Charlemagne. The Frankish take-over of Bavaria had not been entirely smooth, and disenfranchised Bavarians are likely to have backed the plot.[51] Statements in the sources that Fastrada, Charlemagne's current queen, was resented by the plotters of 792 – as she had been by those of 785 – points to discontent in the eastern regions of the empire.[52] The conspiracy seems in fact to have to have stretched far into the heart of the empire. Charlemagne's cousin, the youthful Wala, probably joined it, though he later rose high in Charlemagne's favour.[53] The bishop of Verdun may also have been involved. He certainly had to regain the king's grace and have his reputation cleared (through trial by ordeal) of having plotted against Charlemagne.[54] This was in 794; only in 797 was Count Theudald, who seems to have had links with the abbey of St-Denis, permitted to regain property that he had lost through his involvement in the conspiracy of Pippin, 'on the devil's prompting'.[55] Theudald too had to re-establish his good name via the ordeal. Charlemagne balanced harsh punishments with the prospect of regaining the royal grace, as the examples of Wala, the bishop of Verdun and Theudald show. As we have seen, those who did not join it had to be rewarded for loyalty, whether active or passive.

Pippin's conspiracy was the last rising against Charlemagne and its suppression permitted the king to slim the royal family down further: only the sons of Hildegard were to inherit; Pippin was incarcerated in high-security confinement in the abbey of Prüm. But the problem of rivalry among the heirs apparent and their followers remained. Members of the aristocracy backed their patrons and awaited developments.[56] The ins and outs of politics need not concern us. What matters is the fact of tension among the ruling elite of the great empire, as that elite looked to a future without the old king and lined up behind one or other of the sons (or daughters).[57] Tensions may have been ratcheted up by the fact that the great days of profitable expansion of empire were drawing to a close.[58] Early medieval mortality rates simplified the picture to some extent. Three of Charlemagne's sons died between 806, when he drew up arrangements for the succession, and 811.

This left one legitimate son, Louis the Pious, as king in Aquitaine. But not all members of the aristocracy could feel safe at the prospect of his rule. A significant section of it had invested in his older brother, who had been king in Italy but whose influence stretched over the Alps into southern Germany. For such men, the son of this king, young Bernard, was a better bet than the king of faraway Aquitaine, who had his own followers to reward.[59] Charlemagne tried to hold the ring. He advanced his son but also his grandson, Bernard. He also seems to have pushed hard to create an atmosphere of peace to deaden future conflict. It has recently been argued that the language of legislation and Church councils from the last years of the reign is no conventional rhetoric but the echo of hard political negotiations designed to bring the young kings and their followers into harmonious concord.[60] That language fell on mostly deaf ears. This is not to say that Charlemagne had lost control of the aristocracy. Nor is it to suggest that his reign ended in 'failure' as some historians have thought.[61] If anything he had been too successful. The high aristocracy and the royal house were now indeed locked together in a close embrace and the consequences of that would stretch far beyond the reign of Charles the Great.

Notes

1 RFA *(Rev.)* 782; trans. King (1987), pp. 116–17. On Theoderic, Bullough (1985a), pp. 87–8, 90.
2 Collins (1998b), p. 51.
3 RFA *(Rev.)* 782; trans. King (1987), p. 117.
4 Wallace-Hadrill (1967), p. 95.
5 Reuter (1997), p. 183; Reuter, ed. (1979).
6 Einhard, *VK*, c. 33. On Charlemagne's will, see Brunner (1979), pp. 69–83, and Innes (1997b).
7 Brunner (1979), p. 72; on Lorsch, see Innes (2000a).
8 Brunner (1979), p. 74; Bullough, ch. 8 (pp. 136–50) in this volume.
9 Alberi (1998), pp. 9–10.
10 Brunner (1979), p. 78.
11 Brunner (1979), pp. 66, 79.
12 Bitterauf, ed. (1905), I, no. 397(c); Wolfram (1995a), p. 195.
13 Airlie (1995), pp. 442–3; van Houts (1999), pp. 65–92; van Houts, ed. (2001).
14 Le Jan (1995), pp. 255–6.
15 Airlie (1995), pp. 444–7.
16 Le Jan (1995), pp. 189–90.
17 RFA 811; trans. King (1987), p. 103.
18 Airlie (1999).
19 Innes (2000a); Airlie (2000).
20 Nees (1991), pp. 47–57, on the bribes offered to Theodulf as a *missus* on the king's business.
21 *Epitaph of Count Gerold*, MGH *PLAC* I, p. 114; *Verses on Duke Eric*, MGH *PLAC* I, pp. 131–3. See also Ross (1945).
22 RFA 799; trans. King (1987), p. 130; Einhard, *VK*, c. 13, trans. Dutton (1998), p. 24; Notker, *Gesta Karoli*, II, preface, MGH *SSRG* NS XII, p. 48, trans. Thorpe (1969), p. 134. On memories of Gerold's wars in Notker, see Innes (1998a), pp. 19, 23–4.
23 RFA 796; trans. King (1987), p. 89.
24 Airlie (1992).

25 On William, see Bullough (1985a), p. 90; on Wido, see Alcuin, *De virtutibus et vitiis, PL* 101, cols 613–38. See also Alcuin's letters of advice to Meginhar and Chrodgarius; Alcuin, *Ep.* no. 33, 224, trans. Allott (1974), no. 63, 117. In general, see McKitterick (1989), pp. 244–70.

26 Reuter (1985); Nelson (1996a), pp. xxviii–xxix.

27 RFA 786; trans. King (1987), p. 118. One hostage became bishop of Strasbourg: *Indiculus obsidum Saxonum Moguntiam deducendorum, MGH Capit.* I, no. 115. Borgolte (1983), pp. 25–6; Nelson (1998), p. 184, on recycled Saxon loot.

28 Stiegemann and Wemhoff, eds. (1999a).

29 McCormick (1986), p. 375.

30 For the poem on the defeat of the Avars by Pippin, see Godman (1985a), pp. 186–91; also, Notker, *Gesta Karoli*, II.1, MGH *SSRG* NS XII, p. 51, trans. Thorpe (1969), p. 137.

31 Godman (1985a), pp. 162–5; Hardt (1998), pp. 260–1; Reuter (2000), p. 15. Note also legislation against officials taking bribes, eg: trans. King (1987), p. 235.

32 Dutton (1994), pp. 68, 71–2.

33 *AL* 793; trans. King (1987), p. 140; Leyser (1979), p. 77.

34 Charlemagne's charter to Johannes (795), MGH *Dipl. Karol.* I, no. 179; Collins (1990), pp. 186–7; Reynolds (1994), pp. 108–10.

35 Innes (1998b), p. 309.

36 Collins (1998b), p. 41.

37 *Ibid.*, p. 60.

38 *LP*, 'Life of Hadrian', cc. 8–9, 25; trans. Davis (1992), pp. 126–7, 134.

39 Nelson (1998).

40 Notker, *Gesta Karoli*, II.17, MGH *SSRG* NS XII, pp. 82–4, trans. Thorpe (1969), pp. 162–4.

41 Wallace-Hadrill (1967), p. 95.

42 Innes (1998b), pp. 313–15; Innes (2000a), pp. 185–6.

43 *Annales Nazariani* 786; trans. King (1987), pp. 154–5.

44 Nelson (1997), p. 154.

45 Becher (1993), pp. 78–87; Innes, ch. 5 (pp. 71–89) in this volume.

46 For a parallel account of the Saxon aristocracy's involvement in Ottonian family conflicts, see Leyser (1979), pp. 9–47.

47 Airlie (1999).

48 Nelson (1993).

49 Brunner (1983), p. 5; Godman (1985b), pp. 263–4.

50 Nelson (1997), pp. 156–63; Collins (1998b), pp. 125–6.

51 Airlie (1999).

52 Nelson (1997).

53 Nelson (1991).

54 *Capitulary of Frankfurt* (794), c. 9, MGH *Capit.* I, no. 28, p. 75; trans. King (1987), p. 226.

55 Charlemagne's charter for Theudald (797), MGH *Dip. Karol.* I, no. 181.

56 Innes (1997b).

57 Nelson (1993), pp. 239–40.

58 Reuter (1990).

59 Werner (1990).

60 Fried (1998), pp. 77–83.

61 Ganshof (1971), pp. 240–60; Collins (1998b), pp. 171–4.

7

CHARLEMAGNE'S CHURCH

Mayke de Jong

A bishop reports to Charlemagne

Sometime between 809 and 812, Archbishop Leidrad of Lyon sent Charlemagne a report on all he had accomplished since the emperor had appointed him to the ancient see of Lyon in 797. It was a letter, from one elderly man to another, which takes us straight to the heart of the ideals and expectations shared by the emperor and the bishops with whom he governed.[1] Charlemagne had instructed Leidrad to rebuild a bishopric with an ancient and venerable past, which had fallen on bad times through the negligence of Leidrad's predecessors:

> In view of this you deigned to admonish me to exercise my office with great care, in order to remedy the sins of carelessness in the past, and to avoid those that might be perpetrated in the future. For at the time this church was destitute in many respects, internally as well as externally with regard to its buildings as well as its liturgical offices, and in other aspects of the ecclesiastical ministry.[2]

Leidrad's reforms were focused on two distinct but intricately connected domains, which he called the 'inside and outside': the cult of God and its material infrastructure. The divine office at his episcopal church was now performed according to 'the usage (*ritus*) of the sacred palace'; this was a lasting improvement. As the archbishop pointed out, 'I now have a school of cantors'.[3] These singers had been trained and would in turn instruct others; so too in Leidrad's school of 'lectors'. This he had filled with men who, apart from performing the readings in church, were capable of interpreting Scripture according to the principles of learned exegesis.

'With regard to the restoration of churches, I have incessantly worked to the best of my ability'. Leidrad's hectic building activities extended beyond Lyon's cathedral and other episcopal churches to a dazzling array of churches which

Leidrad restored or (re)founded within his episcopal *civitas*. These were mostly ancient religious communities (*monasteria*), for which the bishop provided the wherewithal, enabling monks and nuns to devote themselves to their central task: the cult of God. The regularity of this cult – the domain Leidrad had defined as 'the interior' – depended on having a steady income and a solid roof over one's head. Hoping for a visit from the emperor, Leidrad explained he had rebuilt a house near the episcopal residence, doubling its size and adding a sun-room or upper storey (*solarium*): 'I have had this work done because of you, so that if your majesty visits this diocese, you can be made welcome in these lodgings'.

What we encounter in Leidrad's report is Charlemagne's Church, from the perspective of a bishop acutely conscious of being one of the emperor's chosen representatives, serving as one of the many vital links between the palace and more distant regions. He had joined Charlemagne's court from Freising not long after 782, together with other talented men seeking Charles's patronage and the rewards of royal service. Leidrad had been hand-picked by Charles as a bishop for Lyon, which in 804 became an archbishopric. He remained close to the emperor, serving him on delicate diplomatic missions and responding to Charles's request for instruction on the nature of baptism; in 811, Leidrad was among those who witnessed Charles's will.[4]

To Leidrad, 'reform' (*emendatio*) meant ensuring that the cult of God (*cultus divinus*) was performed regularly, in a way that would please God, for it was on His benevolence that the good fortune of the Frankish realm depended. Effective armies of 'those who pray' were central to this endeavour, so a good bishop needed to ensure that the religious communities in their diocese prayed 'regularly', that is, in the proper way approved by both God and the palace. It was the ruler who initiated reform and instructed his bishops in their duties in this regard. Bishops, in turn, looked towards the palace for further instruction, counsel and approval, which was the yardstick of their accomplishments and success. This Church, of which Leidrad's see at Lyon was a part, revolved around what the archbishop called the 'sacred palace' (*sacrum palatium*) and the 'constant and sacred emperor' (*constans et sacer imperator*).[5]

In what follows, I shall take my cue from Leidrad's palace-orientated view of reform. This takes us as close as possible to Charlemagne's own ideals and expectations, but it should be remembered that it is not the only possible perspective. Using this as our vantage point runs the risk of also adopting the Carolingian palace's idiom of order, stability and regularity, while ignoring the inherent disorder over which the official documents and their authors tried to impose a measure of control. Control by means of the written word consisted of denying or simply ignoring the discordant voices, but at times these could not be silenced. The *Admonitio generalis* (789) not only projects a lofty vision of the Franks as God's people living according to God's law, and the king as the one responsible for its salvation, but it also condemned sorcerers, enchanters and weather-prophets, nuns who wrote and performed lewd songs, and men who roamed the countryside naked and in chains, claiming they were performing a penance, and 'pseudo-writings' (*pseudographia*) such as 'that most evil and most false letter which some, themselves in error and casting others into it, last year declared to have fallen from the sky ...'.[6] Such Letters from Heaven should be burned forthwith, the *Admonitio* said.

The palace's intense concern with heresy in the 790s also makes it clear that there was an undercurrent of disorderly religiosity, which is only partly hidden by the wave of capitularies, conciliar *acta* and treatises pitted against it. Yet this undercurrent of disorder was not disconnected from the palace and its bid for order, and neither were the palace and its ecclesiastical dependencies, especially monasteries, immune from occasionally fierce strife about the right way to go about 'correction' (*correctio*). Sharp criticism of inadequate reforms was expressed through the literary genre of the *visiones*, visions of kings and other powerful men punished for their failings in a limbo between Heaven and Hell, from which only the prayers of the living could free them.[7] Eschatological concerns surfaced in the writings of Alcuin and other palace intellectuals in the years around 800. According to the time reckoning established by Eusebius and Jerome, this was the *annus mundi* 6000 and it started on Christmas Day, when Charlemagne was crowned emperor. Some feared this date would herald the beginning of the seventh and final age of the world – the age of the Antichrist. These were dangerous times, in which men had to prepare themselves for the end, and the 'entire welfare of the churches' was placed in the new emperor's hands.[8]

It is hard to say how many outside this charmed circle worried about the *annus mundi*, but Charlemagne's efforts to involve his entire Christian people in collective acts of penance, fasting and litanies may have fallen on fertile ground precisely because there were men roaming the countryside naked and in chains, atoning for exceptional sins. 'Roaming' of any kind was not something Carolingian rulers looked favourably upon, but the need to atone for grievous sins which had offended God was something the palace and these vagabonds had in common. Did these pious vagabonds, and the admiration they inspired in ordinary folk, spur on the palace to penitential action of the more official kind? The constant stream of royal capitularies, letters and missives – insisting on order and correction to forge a polity that might be worthy of salvation – sprang from an awareness that these were indeed dangerous and disorderly times, as plenty of evidence showed – an awareness more strongly expressed as Charlemagne's reign progressed.

All this should be kept in mind while reading what follows, on Charlemagne's church. It has been written from the perspective of the 'sacred palace' and those who identified with it, and explores their visions and hopes for a terrestrial order which might live up to a biblical one, and in which the palace served as a half-way house between human failure and higher aspirations.

Ecclesia

Leidrad used the expression 'church' (*ecclesia*) with various inflections. At the most basic level, a church was a building with a roof invariably needing urgent repairs, but to the archbishop of Lyon 'the church' was above all his own bishopric at Lyon, the ancient and illustrious *ecclesia Lugdunensis*. This in turn was made up of a network of communities of prayer, monastic and otherwise, with the episcopal church and its own community of clerics at the centre. Yet the *ecclesia Lugdunensis* was also part of a more encompassing *ecclesia*, with boundaries which coincided with those of Charlemagne's empire – or, to put it differently, with those of an empire which was increasingly defined as an *ecclesia*.[9]

At the beginning of the twenty-first century, the expression 'Church' (with a capital C) has two basic connotations. It is either a separate and monolithic body of clerics, or a universal Christendom which includes all the faithful, transcending national boundaries. The separation of 'Church' and 'State' has been a central issue in Western culture from the late eleventh century onwards, and it remained so until well into the 1960s. Ganshof's vision of Charlemagne was one which relegated anything pertaining to religion safely to the domain of the 'ecclesiastical'.[10] This Charlemagne was above all a brilliant statesman, the enlightened creator of secular political institutions. This is a view to which contemporary specialists no longer subscribe, but it continues to surface in historical discourse and general textbooks on the Middle Ages, where Charles appears in two contradictory guises. On the one hand, he was a theocratic monarch who took it for granted that he ruled the church as well as his empire; on the other, he was a great conqueror who owed his real power to his military and political genius. Thus it has often been argued that ecclesiastical ritual and theory endowed Carolingian monarchs with the legitimacy of sacrality, enabling them to rise above their secular aristocracy – yet that this co-operation was a dangerous alliance. If bishops and popes created kings and emperors by anointing them, they might also claim the right to judge these rulers on their merits and depose them if need be. Could kings keep their bishops in hand?[11] The verdict has usually been that Charlemagne and his father Pippin managed to do so, but that things got out of hand once the great father was succeeded by his 'little son' Louis.

While his son Louis and grandson Charles the Bald have received a good deal of recent attention and reassessment,[12] Charlemagne himself has escaped such revisionist treatment until now. His two images – a theocrat and a secular empire-builder – remain strangely disconnected. This has a lot to do with Einhard's near-canonical *Life of Charlemagne*, which is still widely read as a 'muscular' and classicising testimony to an emperor who fought many wars, kept concubines and who was not impressed by a pope wanting to crown him emperor in 800.[13] Yet Einhard praised Charles's good care of many churches and churchmen – mainly in Rome and Aachen – when he portrayed the emperor governing his realm.

So what did Einhard and other Carolingian authors mean when they distinguished between the domains of the ecclesiastical and the secular? Such distinctions may seem familiar at first sight, but they in fact have little to do with later dichotomies between Church and State. During the last decade of Charles's reign the concept of 'ministry' (*ministerium*) became increasingly important. One gets a sense of an old man in a hurry to ensure that all office-holders, including the ruler himself, worked in unison for the salvation of the Christian people. Bishops and counts derived their ministry from that of the ruler; they were part of different but complementary 'orders', each with their own ministry, but counts were also held responsible for leading the Christian people to salvation. As four *missi dominici*, themselves counts, wrote to their colleagues in 806: 'Devote all your energy to everything pertaining to your ministry, [regardless] whether this concerns the cult of God, the service of our lord (the king) or the salvation and care of the Christian people'.[14]

Over the past decades, historians have once more become aware that the ideology of Christian kingship was not merely a matter of an alliance between rulers and a restricted group of clerics. A more positive appreciation of Carolingian levels of literacy – in this respect, Ganshof remained sceptical – has played a crucial role in this changing perspective.[15] Once one acknowledges that Charlemagne's Latin capitularies were the result of the ruler's serious deliberations with his magnates, lay and ecclesiastical, and were also accessible to literate laymen, such texts can no longer be treated as a mere exercise in ecclesiastical ideology.[16] These texts were once selectively mined for information on the pragmatic aspects of Charlemagne's rule, and neatly divided up in 'secular' and 'ecclesiastical' ones, with the so-called mixed ones as a residual category. Now they are read integrally and recognised as 'mixed' to begin with – that is, as documents with a profoundly religious perspective in which kings and their clerical and lay magnates all had a stake.[17] In fact, the closer one got to the corridors of power, the more important a good grasp of Latin texts became, for Latin was the language of power, secular and sacred.[18] Could one pray to God in any other language? This was a matter for debate, but there was no doubt that everyone spoke Latin instantly when communicating dreams and messages from the supernatural – even children and babes-in-arms.[19]

Furthermore, bishops or popes were not the only ones to bestow sacrality and legitimacy on rulers. Carolingian kings also owed their rise to power to the support of the lay aristocracy, the leadership of the *gens Francorum*. Such men participated in king-making rituals. According to Scripture, David was not anointed only by the prophet Samuel (1 *Samuel* 16:1–13), but also by the elders of Judah (1 *Chronicles* 11:1–9). Just as bishops identified with Samuel and other Old Testament prophets, Frankish lay aristocrats could find a fitting biblical precedent in Judah's powerful men. In other words, Frankish lay magnates were legitimate king-makers as much as the bishops. More often than not, the latter were their kinsmen; so how wide was the gulf that separated 'churchmen' from their brothers, cousins and nephews charged with a different kind of ministry?[20] As Nelson put it, the older historiography 'missed the involvement of a wider constituency than kings and clerics in the ideology of power'.[21]

'Ministry' (*ministerium*) became the key word for the powerful, lay and ecclesiastical, who shared the burden of leading the Christian people to salvation with their ruler. All those with a ministry operated within an *ecclesia* which at times assumed the meaning of a body politic: a 'Christian people' (*populus christianus*) governed by Charlemagne and defined by the correct cult of God.[22] This has led some historians to the conclusion that Carolingian theorists wrote of the realm as an *ecclesia* because they were incapable of thinking about the state in abstract terms. Apart from doing little justice to the sophistication of ninth-century intellectual reflection, this approach ignores a long tradition of late antique and early medieval rulers who had made liturgical correctness and catholic orthodoxy their business, for religious and political unity were two faces of the same coin.[23]

The participants' public platform was the synod. Here, rituals of unity were enacted, with correct Christianity defining the boundaries of the state. This held true of Constantine at Nicaea (AD 325), of King Oswy of Northumbria chairing the synod of Whitby (AD 664)[24] and of the Visigothic King Sisenand gathered with his bishops and magnates in Toledo (AD 633), declaring: 'Let there be no more diverse ecclesiastical custom among us, who are contained within one faith and one realm; for this is also what the ancient canons have decided: that one and the same province should keep to the same custom of singing the Psalms and celebrating the Office and Mass'.[25] The synod was the forum *par excellence* for such public affirmations of a political unity that was also a religious one, and its agenda far exceeded the affairs of 'the church' in any strict definition of the word. This also held true of two synods convened by the Merovingian King Chlotar II (d. 629). In 614 this king issued a decree 'for all the people united at the gathering of bishops during the synod of Paris'.[26] Clearly this was a meeting in which prominent laymen also played a part. The king was personally present in Paris, and he also dominated the deliberations in Clichy in 626/27. The bishops hailed Chlotar as a king who would not only turn the synod's decisions into royal precept, but who had also acted as a prophetic David during conciliar proceedings, 'anticipating what we should decide'.[27]

This tradition of royal synods becomes visible once more in the 740s, under the sponsorship of the mayors of the palace, Carloman and Pippin. Given his vociferous complaints about the Franks not having organised proper synods for 80 years, the Anglo-Saxon reformer Boniface usually gets all the credit for this revival, but this movement was not merely the work of one influential and articulate Englishman.[28] The decisions of these synods dealt primarily with the reform of the cult and the clergy; they have been preserved as precepts issued by the mayors of the palace. This has reinforced the impression, still held by some, of Frankish 'church law' suddenly invading the royal assemblies, which had remained largely secular while the Merovingians ruled.[29] With Chlotar's synods in mind, this supposed discontinuity seems to be less significant. Furthermore, one may well wonder whether the two issues which dominated the synods of the 740s – the purity of priests and clearly-delineated episcopal authority – were matters quite as purely ecclesiastical as they appear to be at first sight. These were both matters of state, for effective prayer and episcopal control could be formidable tools in the hands of able Christian rulers.

How does this reappraisal affect the traditional view that secular royal assemblies under the new dynasty were suddenly subject to the agenda of the Frankish church? In fact, an equally good or even better case can be made for the opposite development. Under Carolingian rule, episcopal synods served as a public forum for the business of the realm in the widest sense of the word, of which the reform of the cult and the clergy were an integral part. Carloman convened the so-called *Concilium Germanicum* (AD 742) together with 'bishops and magnates' (*episcopi et optimates*), calling for the 'recuperation of the Law of God (*Lex Dei*) and ecclesiastical discipline (*aecclesiastica religio*) which have fallen into ruin under past rulers of bygone days', and wondering 'how the Christian people can reach salvation and not perish due to false priests'.[30] These were issues which deeply troubled Boniface, but not exclusively so; nor were they merely ecclesiastical concerns since they reflected the ambitions of two rulers – Carloman and Pippin – who saw themselves as the guardians of the correct *religio* and the salvation of the Christian people.

This was the tradition Charlemagne grew up in.[31] We know little of the business of his own synods before the 780s, for these gatherings yielded only a few royal capitularies. Here we are confronted with the same problem already encountered for the period between 627 and 740. If there are no surviving records, should one conclude there was no synodal activity whatsoever? This is an *argumentum e silentio* of which to be wary, especially in view of the existence of some evidence hitherto unrecognised. A whole series of *synodi* of the 770s and 780s in the Royal Frankish Annals are usually interpreted by modern translators as secular 'royal assemblies' (or *Reichstage*), probably because these brief references contain no explicitly ecclesiastical connotations.[32] In the case of the *synodus magna* held in Frankfurt in 794, to which bishops from Gaul, Germany, Italy, Aquitaine and England flocked, translators opt for 'synod' or 'council', for this was (supposedly unequivocally) an ecclesiastical gathering – albeit one that was part of a more general assembly.[33]

Yet it should be noted that the contemporary terminology for synods and assemblies was fluid. The revised version of the Royal Frankish Annals uses different terminology for all these early *synodi*, including the one at Frankfurt, consequently designating these gatherings as *conventus generalis*, that is, a royal assembly. This new terminology most probably reflects a changed perception of the status of such meetings, but that does not mean that the early *synodi* of Charlemagne's reign should be automatically turned into royal assemblies, as opposed to 'proper' ecclesiastical synods such as the one gathered in Frankfurt. Any gathering convened by Charlemagne, whether called *synodus*, *placitum* or *conventus generalis/publicus* is likely to have had both bishops and lay magnates in attendance, and an agenda featuring a mixture of issues that may seem 'secular' or 'ecclesiastical' in present-day eyes, but not from an eighth-century perspective.

Likewise, the *aecclesiastica religio* as the ruler's central concern was not a new phenomenon of the 780s; it must have been an integral part of all these obscure *synodi* convened by Charlemagne and mentioned in passing in the Royal Frankish Annals. What was new in the 780s was the intensity and frequency of such meetings, the presence of a group of talented and articulate clerics at Charlemagne's court, and the production of the numerous capitularies still preserved.[34] These documents reflect a greater reliance on the written word for communicating ideas throughout the realm, but not necessarily a new emphasis on God's law and worship as an important issue on the agenda of a Frankish ruler and his magnates. This was a tradition well established since the early seventh century and visible again under Charlemagne's father and uncle in the mid-eighth century.

For Charlemagne, the 780s and 790s were decades of intensive reflection on his responsibility for the salvation of the Christian people. This was a burden Charlemagne shared with his ecclesiastical and secular magnates. In the course of his reign, capitularies increasingly stressed the need to distinguish between these various 'orders' (*ordines*), to make sure that the boundaries between their respective spheres of competence did not become blurred. In 811 Charlemagne rather impatiently demanded that bishops, abbots and counts would meet at the palace in separate groups, to discuss complaints about counts having trespassed on episcopal territory and vice versa.[35] This was inevitable in a world in which secular magnates were invested with religious responsibility and churchmen wielded extensive secular power. From time to time, the boundaries between these overlapping competencies needed to be redrawn, lest their identity and complementarity be lost.

Still, there was more at stake than a smooth division of labour between the king's *fideles*. Carolingian legislation used the expression *ecclesia* in an all-embracing as well as in a restricted sense. The *ecclesia* was the 'Christian people' led by Charlemagne and united by a correct worship of God, but at the same time, this cult and the clergy ministering to it should remain a sacred domain, separate and uncontaminated by the stain of secularity. This was the *ecclesia* in the restricted meaning of the word, namely, a well-ordered clergy able to retain its separateness and sacrality in order to mediate effectively between God and mankind. These two interconnected meanings of *ecclesia* also reverberated in Charlemagne's insistence on precise distinctions between various orders within the clergy. A detailed order should govern this *ecclesia* in the strict sense of the word: on no account should there be confusion between bishops, abbots, abbesses, monks, nuns, canons and canonesses, or their specific ways of life and duties.

A preoccupation with 'canonical' order and its precise ramifications is a persistent feature of Carolingian legislation. Superficially, it yields the impression of 'the church' pervading 'the state', to the extent that clerics appear to dominate the political scene. If one looks a bit closer, however, a different configuration becomes visible: that of a realm in which the king encouraged and maintained a clear-cut ordering of the *ecclesia*/clergy. This yielded clear channels of command, which in turn enabled the king to gain access to the resources of the sacred: prayer, gifts, land, and the military services of its tenants. Pippin's synod at Ver (AD 755) is all about a new king affirming his control of the sacred by creating clear hierarchical structures. The co-operation of bishops with well-established authority was crucial to this enterprise. Religious communities, male or female, were to 'lead a regular life, according to their order'. If they refused to do so, episcopal discipline would eventually be backed up by a 'public synod' – that is, by royal authority. Abbesses were forbidden to travel to the court unless the king invited them to do so; if they wished to bring him gifts, they should do so through messengers. Monks were not to go to Rome or other places of pilgrimage without their abbot's approval, or to change communities without that of their bishop. Nobody who had been tonsured or veiled should retain his or her property or live outside some structure of authority: such a person must either enter a 'regular' monastery of monks or nuns, or put himself or herself *sub manu episcopi* ('under the hand of a bishop'), that is, became a member of an episcopally approved community of canons or canonesses.[36]

'Everybody in his place, said the Red Queen'; but this was the world of Charlemagne, not of Alice in Wonderland. When in 794 Bishop Paulinus of Aquileia compared Charlemagne to a 'king and priest' (*rex et sacerdos*), appealing to the ruler to eradicate the heresy of Adoptionism, he did not mean that the priesthood and kingship were identical or indistinguishable. Yet Paulinus certainly ascribed episcopal qualities to the anointed ruler, for the most common meaning of *sacerdos* at the time was 'bishop'.[37] Two generations later, Archbishop Hincmar of Rheims thought differently, maintaining that only Christ himself was both king and priest.[38] Hincmar's view was in keeping with a long patristic tradition, and also reflected the claim of an articulate group of bishops in the 830s – albeit a minority – that they, not Louis the Pious, were the righteous vicars of Christ. Charlemagne's bishops had been less wary of a *sacerdos*-like ruler invested with the authority of a New Constantine. Under Charlemagne, clear distinctions between the various degrees of sacrality and the categories of clergy attached to such domains also mattered deeply, yet the ruler was acknowledged as the true guardian of the cult of God, and therefore transcended the ramifications of the order he imposed on it.

The uses of the past

In any traditional society good law is, by definition, ancient law. To those in the post-Roman kingdoms with direct or indirect access to written tradition, the Old Testament represented the most ancient and venerable law of all. The levying of tithes, the observance of Sunday, royal anointing, sexuality and marriage, the oblation of children, the purity of priests, fair weights and measures – in all these spheres the 'Old Law' (*Vetus Lex*) was a source of inspiration and regulation. Furthermore, the Old Testament contained the sacred history of God's 'people', a *gens* led by warriors, judges, kings, prophets and priests. Into this ancient past early-medieval authors inserted the histories of their own 'peoples' (*gentes*) and the formation of new kingdoms; Old Testament history thus helped to shape new political identities. This sacred past was not a distant one, for early-medieval *litterati* retained it at the back of their minds as an easily accessible 'imagined community',[39] an alternative and authoritative world with a history which helped to explain the puzzling events of the present. Last but not least, the Old Testament was also full of exciting stories of the kind which St Benedict forbade his monks to read just before bedtime, 'because it is not useful to those of feeble understanding'.[40] Benedict feared that the Heptateuch and books of Kings might fill monastic heads with tales of war and adultery; but these Old Testament texts may well have been among the 'deeds and histories of the ancients' read to Charlemagne at his dinner table.[41]

In Charlemagne's reign, the Old Testament 'was seen as having initiated and communicated a tradition. It provided evidence for God's first compact with a chosen people, it set down God's law. And it provided very concrete examples of kings and models of proper kingly behaviour'.[42] This is not to say that the Franks were reborn as God's chosen people overnight, as soon as the Carolingians had taken over. This was a gradual development to which non-Franks made crucial contributions.[43] Comparisons of the Frankish king with Moses, David and Solomon abound in papal letters to Pippin III, but they disappeared once Charlemagne succeeded his father. The English and Irish took over where the popes left off, notably Cathwulf, who in 775 addressed a letter of admonition to Charlemagne 'steeped in Old Testament thought about kingship, deliverance, fear of God and the law'.[44] Insular and Spanish pilgrims who became part of Charles's entourage in the 780s contributed to an intellectual climate in which Old Testament imagery dominated court poetry as well as official documents, a development that became even more pronounced in the 790s. Alcuin was central to this, but so too was the Spaniard, Theodulf. Between 790 and 793 he produced the *Libri Carolini*, an extensive refutation of Byzantine views on image worship, perceived as contrary to biblical and ecclesiastical tradition. This document was subject to close scrutiny and the topic of much discussion at the court, in which Charlemagne took an active part.[45]

Alcuin called the Franks a 'blessed people' (*beata gens*), which is as close as one gets to a reference to the Franks as the new Elect.[46] Historians have referred to the 'New Israel', but the expression *novus Israel* was never used.[47] This not surprising, for what one should expect is the 'true Israel' (*verus Israel*); in exegetical terms, *novus* had anagogical connotations, referring to the 'end of times' and a present in which mankind prepared for the Second Coming, rather than to an authoritative, historical Israel and its contemporary embodiment. Furthermore, Frankish authors who lived with the Old Testament on a daily basis rarely bothered to cite their sacred texts as literally as those looking nowadays for the 'New Israel of the Franks' might wish. Their references were implicit and allusive, meant for an informed audience which did not need to have everything spelled out or neatly defined. With increasing insistence, the Royal Frankish Annals of the 780s and 790s hammered home the point that the king acted together with the Franks, with God on their side. The message was that the Franks were a people (*gens*) defined by their special relationship with God, just as Israel had once been. This notion also pervades the triumphalist prologue to the revised version of the *Lex Salica* issued by Pippin in 763/4, which refers to the 'illustrious people of the Franks ... founded by God' (*gens Francorum inclita ... auctore Deo condita*).[48]

More importantly, the uses of a literal reading of biblical history were limited, for the historical Israel was seen as the 'earlier people' – a people which had forfeited its position as God's Elect, by failing to acknowledge Christ as its Saviour. Its history had meaning for the present only if it was read and understood within the context of the New Testament and patristic commentary. The books of Kings mattered deeply to Charlemagne, but such Old Testament histories were only one part of the 'sacred page' (*sacra pagina*). They remained a dead letter until they were brought alive by spiritual (or allegorical) exegesis, which elucidated their hidden meaning as a prefiguration of the history of Christ.[49] Typology played a crucial role in this allegorical translation of Old Testament history. David was seen not only as Christ's ancestor, but also as the *typus* of the Saviour, one whose life and deeds 'pre-figured' Christ's life, death and resurrection. Read allegorically, the deeper meaning of the history of David could be properly grasped; this was not merely about a king of the Old Israel, but about the salvation of God's people through Christ. Charlemagne was nicknamed David by his courtiers and, by implication, he was associated with the historical David and, possibly, although more indirectly, with Christ himself. In a famous passage, Notker of St-Gallen wrote of 'the most wise' (*sapientissimus*) Charlemagne inspecting progress in a monastic school, putting the lazy pupils on his left hand and the hard-working ones on his right, dispensing blame and praise 'in imitation of the Eternal Judge'.[50] This was a direct comparison but without the ruler being equated with the Saviour. Notker thought his hero capable of the highest level of *imitatio Christi*.

To his contemporaries, Charlemagne was a learned king (*rex doctus*) who took a keen interest in biblical scholarship; a later generation remembered him as a man who on his deathbed had assiduously corrected the text of the gospels. As Louis's biographer Thegan put it,

> ... after they [Charlemagne and Louis] had completed arrangements for succession, the emperor started nothing new, but devoted himself to prayer, almsgiving and correcting books. And last of all, on the day before his death he perfectly corrected the four Gospels of Christ, entitled Matthew, Mark, Luke and John, with the help of Greek and Aramaic texts.[51]

This is an image of the 'good death' of a ruler devoting the very end of his life to purely religious pursuits, either in the palace, as Charlemagne did, or in the monastery, like his grandson, the Emperor Lothar. Significantly, Thegan imagined Charlemagne preparing for death by correcting the gospels. This was based on Charlemagne's reputation, well established by 836, as a learned king who had surrounded himself with superb biblical scholars, such as Theodulf and Alcuin, and had commissioned a commentary on *Genesis* from the otherwise unknown cleric Wigbod.[52] These men worked within an authoritative mode of spiritual exegesis established by Augustine, Jerome, Ambrose, Gregory the Great and Bede; in turn, they created a lively Carolingian exegetical tradition which lasted for at least three generations.

Kings and queens were the main recipients of spiritual commentary on Old Testament books. They were the leaders of a Christian people which had transcended the 'earlier people', and should therefore on no account read Old Testament history in a literal-minded fashion. In other words, there was another and equally powerful ideal of the past, which joined forces with the sacred history of Israel: that of early Christianity as portrayed in the Acts of the Apostles, and the heroic and pristine church of the martyrs. The 763/64 prologue of the revised *Lex Salica* not only depicts the Franks as having been founded by God, but also as a valiant people which, after having shaken off the Roman yoke and received baptism, lavishly venerated the martyrs who had been burned, mutilated and thrown to the wild beasts by the Romans; it was the Franks' devotion to these martyrs which merited divine favour.[53] This widely disseminated text connected the theme of the Franks as God's people with that of Rome and the ancient church – the two most important strands in the 'imagined community' serving as a model for a Frankish kingdom on an increasingly formidable scale, and which in 800 became a new Western empire.

As Charlemagne's kingdom expanded, the notion of the Franks as a 'blessed people' gradually gave way to an image more suited to the realities of an ethnically diverse polity: that of St Paul's *ecclesia gentium*, not in Paul's sense of the 'Church of the gentiles' (non-Jews), but with the meaning of a church/empire comprising many peoples.[54] From the 820s onwards, men who were both biblical commentators and political theorists began to define the Carolingian empire as a 'holy church' (*sancta ecclesia*). In his commentaries on the Old Testament written for rulers, Alcuin's student Hraban Maur insisted that the 'prior' people had now been succeeded by the *ecclesia*, and its preachers enjoyed divine favour. This perspective was only fully developed under Louis the Pious, but the basic elements thereof are already present in some of Charlemagne's capitularies, including the *Admonitio generalis* of 789 in which Charlemagne presented himself as the '*rector* of the kingdom of the Franks and the devout defender and adjuvant of the holy church'.[55] The realm and the church were not perceived as identical, but the king's leading role in both domains pulled these two spheres together. The model of the *rector* derives from Gregory the Great's *Pastoral Care*, a treatise on the duties of bishops which became an early-medieval handbook for kings who saw themselves as the moral leaders of their people.[56]

The *Admonitio* was addressed to all those holding ecclesiastical or secular office, but in its preface the bishops were singled out as the 'pastors of Christ's churches, leaders of His flock and brightest luminaries of this world' who were to guide the 'Christian people' to the pastures of eternal life, leading errant sheep back inside the walls of the church. The most famous passage from the *Admonitio* deserves to be cited, for it is as good an example as any of how a powerful Old Testament model was transformed by an equally authoritative Christian tradition:

> For we read in the Books of Kings how the saintly Josiah, by visitation, correction and admonition, strove to recall the kingdom which God had given him to the worship of the true God. I say this not to compare myself with his holiness but because it is our duty, at all times and in all places, to follow the examples of the saints and necessary for us to gather together whomever we can to apply themselves to a good life in praise and glory of our Lord Jesus Christ.[57]

Josiah had been an exemplary king who purified Judah and Jerusalem from the veneration of idols, and ordered the restoration of the Temple. Among its ruins, the Book of Law was found and brought to the king. Josiah tore his clothes in a gesture of penance, for he fully realised his people had not followed the Law and therefore risked God's vengeance. God's rediscovered Law was read out throughout his kingdom, and he renewed the old covenant, reinstating worship according to God's written precepts.

Josiah was only one Old Testament embodiment of what became the most important ingredient of the ideology of early-medieval Christian kingship: the idea that rulers were accountable to God for the sins and salvation of their people. Josiah tore his clothes when he realised the people had not lived according to God's law. Implicitly, this theme surfaces early in the history of Carolingian reform, in the shape of the 'recuperation' of the *Lex Dei* ('God's law') mentioned in the *Concilium Germanicum* (742), and Carloman's prescriptions for a purification of the priesthood. These issues were also central to Charlemagne's *Admonitio generalis*, but there this theme was embedded in imagery deriving from a Christian tradition of spiritual exegesis.

115

According to the Old Testament, Josiah did all manner of things, except 'visiting, admonishing, and correcting in person'. These extra duties belonged to the king who was also a *rector* – or, put differently, a *rex et sacerdos* in the sense of a 'king and bishop'. What a *rector* did, above all, was preach to his people. In the *Admonitio generalis* – which could be translated as 'a sermon to all' – Charlemagne preached to his people, but above all to his preacher-bishops, reminding them of their pastoral duties. This was precisely Notker's point when he wrote Charle-magne's *Gesta* three generations later.[58] Bishops might be vain and crafty at times, but Charlemagne saw through them all, for he was capable of out-bishoping any of the men he had appointed.

Rome

From his father, Charlemagne inherited a bond which modern textbooks tend to call the 'Franco-Papal alliance', a co-operation usually analysed in terms of political expediency, in which the papacy gained a strong protector and the new rulers a papal stamp of legitimacy, followed in 800 by the imperial title. Charlemagne first encountered a bishop of Rome when he was still a boy. Reports on this event vary. According to the *Liber Pontificalis*, the series of papal biographies kept in Rome, in December 753 his father sent young Charles to ride for 100 miles to meet Pope Stephen II; when the party was 3 miles from the royal villa of Ponthion, Pippin himself 'dismounted his horse and prostrated himself on the ground in great humility, along with his wife, sons and chief men, and welcomed the holy pope'. In the early Spring of 754, Stephen proceeded to St-Denis, where he anointed Pippin and his two sons 'by the Christ's grace kings of the Franks'.[59] Such momentous meetings, and the question of who paid due respects to whom through a proper reception ceremony were the subject of much interpretation and image-making after the event. Hence, two generations after the author of the *Liber Pontificalis* wrote, his Frankish colleague in charge of the Chronicle of Moissac (shortly before 820) cast Pope Stephen in the role of the penitent suppli-cant, prostrating himself before Pippin.[60] Times had changed and the Franks had, meanwhile, gained considerable confidence as reflected in (and boosted by) a flourishing historiography.

For Charlemagne and his contemporaries, Rome was above all St Peter's city and a place of worship. He was the first Frankish ruler to visit the city, and did so four times, beginning at Easter 774, while the siege of Pavia was still continuing. Charles came to Rome first and foremost as a pilgrim, to pray 'at the threshold of the apostles'. He resided on the Vatican hill, along with other pilgrims visiting St Peter's tomb, and must have witnessed the liturgical prayer in the basilica on behalf of his family and his people, which had been performed there since 754 as part of the agreement between Pope Stephen II and his father.[61] Rome was a powerhouse of prayer, not unlike a large Carolingian royal monastery, except that its prayer was more efficacious than that of any other sacred site, for this was where apostles and martyrs had lived, died, and been buried.

The real co-operation between the papacy and Carolingian rulers started only in 781, when Pope Hadrian I and Charlemagne – king of the Lombards since 774 – began to work out what Frankish protection of Rome's sacred places and 'St Peter's Patrimony' actually meant. In Hadrian's eyes, this was usually something more than Charlemagne was prepared to deliver.[62] Hadrian's letters to the king demonstrate that he depended on his northern protector and called upon him to defend St Peter's Republic against its enemies in Ravenna, Benevento and Spoleto; they also reveal a king increasingly drawn into the affairs of what was only then becoming a truly papal city, courtesy of Frankish protection, admiration and support. This new 'Republic of St Peter' – a truly papal Rome which would last for the rest of the Middle Ages – was dominated by Hadrian's large-scale building activities, patronage of churches and conspicuous public celebrations.[63] But geographical distance tended to create misunderstandings and repeatedly the pope felt the need to clear himself from accusations of disloyalty to Charles, whom he addressed as 'your God-protected royal excellence'.[64] Yet for all its epistolary formality, their correspondence breathes a spirit of growing rapport and trust.[65]

In a letter of 796 to Hadrian's successor Leo III in which he lamented Hadrian's death, Charlemagne (and Alcuin) emphasised the complementary roles of himself and the pope. Whereas he, the king, had to defend Christ's holy church against pagans and infidels and strengthen it internally by knowledge of the catholic faith, it was the pope's duty to 'aid our struggle with hands raised to God, like Moses', ensuring victory by intercessory prayer.[66] From the north, Rome was perceived as the most efficacious channel to God's favour, to which the Frankish rulers had gained direct access in exchange for its protection. This potent source of prayer needed to be kept pure. Hence, when Pope Leo was in dire straits in 799, with his authority being severely threatened by Roman aristocrats, the Frankish ruler came to the rescue, not merely of Leo, but also of the sacred resources upon which he and his father relied for the 'stability' of their realm.[67]

Rome was not merely a source of powerful prayer, but also of canonical texts. The expression 'canonical' should be detached from its usual association with the clearly defined and well-organised canon law of the later middle ages. What mattered was that these texts were part of the authentic and uncontaminated Christianity with which the Franks associated Rome. In 747 Pope Zacharias had already supplied Pippin with a small collection of canon law, but this was extremely modest compared to the flood of authentic texts from Italy which started in the 770s.[68] At Easter 774, shortly before the fall of the Lombard kingdom, Pope Hadrian had presented Charlemagne with the revised version of the canon-law collection compiled by Dionysius Exiguus (d. before 556), the so-called *Dionysio-Hadriana*. This became the prime source of ecclesiastical legislation in the Frankish kingdom, gaining official status when large parts of it were promulgated in the *Admonitio generalis*. At the synod/assembly of Aachen in 802, parts of it were read aloud and commented upon.[69]

The Lombard scholar, Paul the Deacon, played an important role in transmitting authoritative texts to the north, having come to Charlemagne's court in 782 to plead for the release of his brother, held captive after a revolt in Friuli.[70] In 786 Charlemagne sent Paul's new homiliary, based on his thorough reading of 'the treatises and sermons of various catholic fathers' to all the 'lectors' subject to his rule. Following a direct request from Charlemagne, a copy of what was thought to be the Sacramentary of Gregory the Great (known in scholarly literature as the *Hadrianum*) reached Aachen between 786/7 and 791. (This request must have caused considerable embarrassment in Rome, for no authentic Gregorian sacramentary existed). In 787 Charles sent for an authentic copy of the Rule of St Benedict, for the benefit of the monasteries of his kingdom; all monks and nuns should now live by the rule of this 'Roman' abbot, according to a correct text to be disseminated from the palace.[71] For Charlemagne and his advisers, truth was to be found in the world once inhabited by St Peter, St Paul and St Benedict, and in the city once ruled by Christian emperors. What came from Rome was perceived as Roman by the Franks, but it should be kept in mind that much of the supposedly pure Roman liturgy, still venerated nowadays as such by modern liturgists, bore the imprint of the liturgical creativity of the post-Roman kingdoms, the Frankish one included.[72]

Charlemagne strove to correct the cult of God 'for the sake of unanimity with the apostolic see and the peaceful harmony of God's holy Church'.[73] This did not imply any full-scale and detailed Romanisation of the Frankish liturgy, however. If anything, the influx of 'authentic' texts from the south generated a new burst of liturgical creativity in the north, engendering an even greater diversity. Roman practices with regard to the kiss of peace, the recitation of the names of the dead during Mass, the correct mode of psalmody, and Roman usages for Lent and the Great Litany – a collective beseeching for God's mercy – were introduced in Francia through royal capitularies and conciliar texts, along with Paul's homiliary and the *Hadrianum*, thought to have been composed by 'St Gregory the Roman Pope'.[74] Yet the pontifical liturgy of Rome was ill-suited to Frankish needs. It needed to be adapted and expanded; hence, Benedict of Aniane was commissioned to write an extensive supplement to the *Hadrianum*.[75]

The fact that a given liturgy was called an *Ordo Romanus* did not necessarily mean that its contents derived from Rome. What matters is that it was perceived as Roman, and therefore as a text which connected God's people with its origins in the early, pristine church thought to be preserved and still present in Rome. But not all well-informed clerics took this view. When the *Hadrianum* came to Aachen, Alcuin grumbled that he saw no point in such innovations, for the sacramentaries at hand were good enough.[76] Leidrad's reform of chant has been invoked as evidence of a wholesale reform of the liturgy in his diocese, yet it should be kept in mind that Leidrad's letter dealt specifically with chant, not with the liturgy as a whole, and that he looked for guidance to Aachen and Metz, not to Rome. Lyon's chant was brought in line with 'the way we do things at the sacred palace', with chant as one of the top priorities, alongside a spiritual understanding of the *lectio* of Mass.[77] Apparently bishops such as Leidrad looked to Charlemagne rather than the papacy for authentic and authoritative versions of worship. The label 'Made in Rome' mattered, but Aachen served as a clearing-house, distinguishing false from true. After all, this was Charlemagne's church.

Cultus divinus

In Leidrad's report to Charlemagne, monasteries of one kind or another took pride of place. Local priests ministering to rural communities are passed by in silence. Leidrad's 'church of Lyon' was a network of religious communities filled with monks, nuns and clerics shouldering an intensive and integrated cult of God. The 'regularity' of such communities rendered their prayer efficacious. This was vital to the stability of the realm and therefore to the ruler, so Leidrad concentrated on his results in this prestigious domain.

Monasteria indeed harboured the elite of those who prayed, and therefore received a great deal of attention in Charlemagne's reform capitularies. Hailing predominantly from the upper strata of society and usually committed to religious life in childhood, monks, nuns, canons and canonesses lived a communal and ascetic life.[78] They guarded crucial channels to the sacred, for at the centre of any monastic community, there were invariably relics of powerful saints, or even better, of authentic Roman martyrs.[79] When ordering votive masses for themselves and their family members, kings and aristocrats turned to ascetic communities of monks or canons whose communal life and 'clean hands' turned them into effective mediators between God and mankind. By the late eighth century, mass had become a sacrificial gift to God, to be offered in order to secure the salvation of the soul, the victory of armies, the stability of the realm – and to ward off illness, infertility, crop failure and a whole host of other disasters.

Sexual activity was thought to contaminate the priest who offered this sacrifice and to render it ineffective; religious communities were the places where pure and efficacious prayer was to be found, empowered by the presence of the saints.[80] The ever-growing demand for votive masses turned male monasteries into communities in which most monks were ordained priests or were on the way to attaining the priesthood, rendering female convents at a disadvantage. This is not to say that nunneries were unimportant, however. The prayer of female communities also counted, and there were mighty convents closely connected with the court, such as Chelles, a nunnery that from Merovingian times onwards recruited abbesses from the royal family.[81] Charlemagne's learned sister Gisela

119

was its abbess, a woman of powerful words (*verbipotens*), as Alcuin called her, in charge of an equally learned community of women.[82]

This was the institutionalised clergy, in the sense of a cadre of religious personnel which included monks, nuns and clerics living a communal life. They were in command of precious resources, sacred and otherwise, which became the backbone of the Carolingian state: prayer; books; surplus land diverted to the *fideles* of monasteries, cathedrals and kings; and also a formidable pool of well-trained administrative talent ready to be harnessed to royal power. Merovingian rulers – notably Queen Balthild – had already tapped into these resources, granting immunities to their favoured monasteries, which guaranteed that no royal officials would have access to these 'sacred spaces' (*loci sancti*); they had also persuaded bishops to grant exemptions of various kinds, by which the bishop voluntarily gave up his right to interfere with the internal life in the monastic communities within his jurisdiction. By granting immunities and exemptions, kings and bishops created islands of sacrality that would remain undisturbed and therefore all the more effective in their prayer for the powerful that had guaranteed their special status.[83] This 'hands-off' policy also ensured that those who had granted these privileges retained an exclusive link with the monastery in question. The Carolingian rulers continued this practice, but the rules of the game were subtly changed; 'the Carolingians did not just favour and reform monasteries: they saw themselves as arising *from* monasteries and churches'.[84]

This also holds true for the way they rose to power. Control of monasteries had long been a mainstay of aristocratic power, but the Pippinids beat others at this game and gradually became major players in what had once been local and independent aristocratic networks. As Pippinid patronage became more valuable, members of local elites strengthened their bonds with the new rulers by placing their own monastic foundations under the protection of the mayors of the palace; once the latter had become kings, this became an even more frequent pattern.[85] Local aristocrats still jealously guarded their interests in monastic resources, but they increasingly did so with reference to the ruler.[86] A practice developed that was to remain crucial to the relation between the Carolingian rulers and 'their' monasteries: the ruler ensured that religious communities had sufficient property to carry out its duties of prayer, but he also had the right to harness surplus ecclesiastical wealth to the stability of the realm by handing it out as a 'benefice' to his military men.[87] Kings were not the only ones to build up a following in this manner. From the eighth century onwards abbots had conceded precarial grants in order to build a retinue, and they continued to do so in Charlemagne's age.

With monastic lands remaining subject to different and potentially conflict-ing claims, royal dominance of so-called royal monasteries was never complete; kings had to accommodate themselves to local interests. But if they managed to do so intelligently, these sacred places could serve royal authority in different and equally important ways. Louis the Pious had a list drawn up of the monastic and clerical communities that owed him prayer, gifts and/or troops, thereby formalising the kind of support upon which his father and grandfather had depended.[88] Occasionally, ambitious abbots put impossible burdens upon their communities in their attempts to maximise monastic wealth and its external manifestations. In Fulda, Abbot Ratger converted his community into an army of reluctant builders of a huge new church, an 'immense and superfluous building', as his detractors called it. No doubt Ratger saw himself as a faithful royal servant, but meanwhile his ambitious schemes caused hardship, and the time devoted to prayer was cut back. Worried monks from Fulda appealed to Charlemagne in 812, then to Louis the Pious in 816, demanding to be allowed once more to say their daily prayers for the king, his family and the 'Christian people', as well as for their benefactors and for the deceased members of the community. In their view, prayer was at the heart of royal service.[89]

Such large communities which went by the name of *monasteria* were not inhabited only by monks and nuns, but also by clerics leading a communal life. The first rule for these canons (*clerici canonici*) was drawn up by Bishop Chrodegang of Metz, appointed to this see by Pippin in 742. By turning the clergy attached to his cathedral into an effective army of prayer 'under the order of canons', he set a precedent for future bishops: this was the model Leidrad had in mind when he established a cloister (*claustrum*) for his own clergy, importing a cleric from Metz to teach them to sing the psalms according to the rites of the palace. Chrodegang also founded a 'proper' monastery at Gorze to which he extended liberties, which ensured continued episcopal control.[90]

The monastic network centred upon Metz was also sustained by the abbey of Lorsch, a foundation of Count Cancor and his mother Willeswind, Chrodegang's kinsmen. They staffed Lorsch with monks from Gorze, entrusting their fledgeling monastery to Chrodegang. He briefly became its abbot, before handing over this office to his brother Gundeland in 765. One of the earliest translations of Roman relics was initiated by Chrodegang: in 761 the sacred remains of the martyrs Gorgonius, Naborius and Nazarius found their way to Metz. Nazarius was triumphantly brought to Lorsch, where Count Cancor, the initial founder, led the cheering crowds.[91] In 772 Charlemagne extended his 'protection' (*mundeburdium vel defensionem nostram*) to Lorsch, and thus a promising family foundation became a part of the Carolingian corridors of power.

Increasingly, aristocratic founders of monasteries turned to royal *tuitio* and its benefits, for when it came to royal largesse and the honour of being a royal monastery, all other patronage paled into insignificance. In turn, such communities were Charlemagne's stepping-stones into the more distant regions of his realm. Lorsch and Fulda, two eighth-century monastic foundations, soon became regional centres in the Middle-Rhine area and two public domains where the powerful transacted their business. When the Carolingian rulers extended their *tuitio* over such centres, they found a ready-made nexus of regional contacts and alliances which might serve as an interface between regional and royal power. The incorporation of Lombard Italy into Charles's kingdom after 774 followed a similar pattern, with major religious communities enjoying royal *tuitio*, and serving as staunch bastions of Carolingian power: Farfa, Nonantola, San Salvatore in Brescia – and further south, in the still disputed territory of Benevento, Monte Cassino and San Vincenzo.[92]

The loyalty of abbots deeply mattered. For example, a scandal erupted in 781 around Abbot Poto of San Vincenzo. Frankish members of this community accused him of having left mass, refusing to chant the customary Psalm 54 for the Frankish king and his family. Reputedly, Poto had exclaimed: 'If it was not for my monastery and the Beneventan land, I would have treated him [i.e. Charlemagne] like a dog'.[93] At the slandered king's request, Pope Hadrian organised a trial, but the pope seems to have been remarkably sympathetic to Poto. The latter strenuously denied all accusations, backed up by 42 of his monks, and died in 784; a collective oath taken by San Vincenzo's monks put an end to the affair.[94] Whatever the many implications of this particular storm in the palatial tea-cup, it does indicate that Charles kept an eagle-eye on his abbots and their monasteries, and that royal monasteries, far and near, conducted in-house fighting with Charlemagne in mind.

Broadly speaking, the Carolingian priesthood was a more motley crowd, however; not all of those who misbehaved created an immediate scandal at the court. At the top of the heap, as we have seen, there were the powerful and wealthy religious communities, inhabited mostly by monks, nuns and canons with aristocratic or even royal family connections; at the bottom, there were humble rural priests involved in a daily struggle for survival. Charlemagne's *correctio* was also aimed at raising this rural priesthood to a level of chastity and literacy by which they would be worthy representatives of the *ecclesia*, rather than men whose lifestyle hardly distinguished them from the laity to whom they ministered. From the *Admonitio generalis* onwards, bishops were enjoined to examine their priests 'as to their doctrinal beliefs, baptisms and celebration of the mass'; they should understand the prayers of mass, sing the psalms according to the proper division in verses, know the Lord's prayer and preach it so all might understand, and sing the *Sanctus*, 'in a common voice with the Holy Angels and the people of God'.[95] In short, they were part of the vision of an entire earthly and heavenly kingdom worshipping in unison.

At the grassroots level, this programme was elaborated in the so-called *capitula episcoporum*, the written instructions issued by bishops to their diocesan clergy which began to appear shortly before 800, initially in well-established bishoprics such as Liège and Orléans. Both Ghaerbald of Liège and Theodulf of Orléans were closely connected to the palace, so one gets a sense of the initiative coming from Aachen. Like capitularies and conciliar acts, these episcopal statutes intended to set a norm, but they still allow us to glimpse some of the practical difficulties of Carolingian reform, at the level of bishops attempting to implement the high-minded directives from the palace. In these texts the issue of ritual purity looms large, and the standards were set – top-down – by the ascetic elite who inhabited court-connected *monasteria*. These places set the tone – hence, all priests were to refrain from familiarity with women, drinking and fighting, lest they touched the Body of the Lord with unclean hands and rendered mass inefficacious.

A measure of purity, albeit to a lesser degree, was also demanded of the laity whenever they approached the 'sacrosanct sacraments', as Theodulf of Orléans expressed it in his influential episcopal statutes.[96] Lay men and women should only attempt Communion after due purification – prayer and fasting – which in effect meant that the laity concentrated on Easter Communion and prepared for it by penance during Lent. Women were to be barred from the altar precincts and remain in their places well away from it where the priest would receive their oblations; the weakness of women – that is, their impurity because of menstruation and childbirth – turned any kind of ministering in church on their part into a dangerous affair.[97] But neither could lay men freely approach the altar with impunity. According to Theodulf, they risked the divine punishment inflicted on King Osias who, in defiance of the priesthood, had entered the Holiest of Holies to sacrifice on his own behalf.

Yet the *capitula episcoporum* are not to be read as the record of a staunch episcopal fight against a 'Wild West' of whoring and drunken rural priests, ministering to a near-pagan laity. These texts were aimed at a varied audience, ranging from priests who were local power-brokers to downtrodden men who lived like peasants, and from the sophisticated priesthood in an episcopal *civitas* to those operating in isolation in its rural reaches.[98] As Hraban Maur observed, it was easy to observe the canonical days for baptism – the Saturday before Easter and Pentecost – if one lived in a town (*civitas*) full of clerics, but what about those out there in the countryside (*pagus*), far away from churches and priests and under constant threat from pagans? Even if he, from the vantage point of Fulda and Mainz, envisaged more pagans than there actually were in far reaches of the country, he was aware that conditions could vary and argued for rural people who should be allowed to have their children baptised at the first opportunity.[99] Moreover, the lay people who needed to be reminded by Bishop Theodulf not to behave like Osias were probably inhabitants of Orléans and other towns abounding with clerics, men and women of high status, eager to be close to the sacred in view of all, instead of remaining humbly in the background. Bringing gifts to church articulated important social distinctions.

But who were the priests in a second set of episcopal statutes ascribed to Theodulf, who had noticed that the Old Testament priesthood had not been required to be celibate and who wished to follow suit? Surely these were not illiterate men urgently in need of basic instruction. Their bishop tried to convince them with references to papal decrees and an appeal to their understanding of history.[100] Whereas all priests of the Jews came from the tribe of Levi which therefore needed to procreate, nowadays the priesthood was recruited from all peoples (*gentes*). Jewish priests had only ministered in the temple occasionally, with amply time to purify themselves beforehand, while priests nowadays had to minister daily, dealing, moreover, with the immaculate body and blood of the Lord, instead of with sacrificial animals. 'Deacons and subdeacons should observe a similar chastity, because they also approach the altar as servants administering to such a great sacrament', said Theodulf. He was writing for educated men who knew their Scripture and could argue their case armed with biblical arrows. Clearly resistance to clerical celibacy included not only illiterate and perhaps also poverty-stricken priests in distant regions, who could not survive without the support of a life-companion and children, but also some of their well-read colleagues in the heart of Francia.

Did reform-minded bishops fight a war that was lost at the outset, or at best won only centuries later during the Counter-Reformation? This is too easy a question. The long history of clerical celibacy should not be written as a teleological story of failure and success, but in terms of a singularly powerful ideal of differentiation which defined the separateness of those who mediated between God and mankind. Carolingian *correctio* represents an important stage in the articulation of this ideal. By the ninth century, bishops, priests, deacons and subdeacons no longer had legitimate wives from whom they should abstain, as had been the case with their predecessors in late antiquity when married men became bishops and the bishop's wife (*episcopa*) was supposed to live chastely in the other end of the episcopal palace. During Charlemagne's reign, the focus of an ancient debate about priestly celibacy had narrowed to the issue of proximity of any women other than mothers or sisters. The episcopal statutes were above all concerned with priests getting too familiar with 'strange women' (*mulieres extraneae*); legitimately-married priests were no longer featured in the controversy.

Those who invoked the Old Testament in favour of clerical marriage there- fore seem to have been involved in a rearguard battle. Perhaps it is not so strange that these voices were raised in the heart of Francia, in Orléans, with its long- standing and diverse ecclesiastical traditions, where innovative reform was likely to clash with older norms and ideals. In response, Theodulf maintained that the Christian priesthood, deriving from all *gentes*, should reproduce itself by 'imitating good morals' (*imitatio morum*), not by procreation (*carnis successio*). This answer owes a lot to St Paul, but it is also typical of a bishop conscious of the needs of Charlemagne's realm and its many *gentes*. One of these was an ascetic priesthood capable of mediating between God and the 'Christian people' led by Charles. This priesthood should be uncontaminated by sexual activity, and remain apart from family or local interests which might involve them in networks of local solidarity and the inevitable competition for local power, which would sever these 'shepherds of the Lord' from the hierarchical body of the *ecclesia* – otherwise known as an empire.

Faithful courtiers such as Theodulf and Leidrad were rewarded with ecclesiastical offices. This inner circle was showered with royal favour, in a way which sometimes transcended the ecclesiastical order imposed by Charlemagne's legislation. Alcuin, a mere deacon, became part of the confraternity of prayer which embraced the bishops present at the synod of Frankfurt (AD 794), for he was a 'man learned in ecclesiastical doctrines'.[101] Charlemagne gave him a number of abbacies, including the prestigious monastery of St-Martin in Tours.[102] As abbot, Alcuin strenuously objected when in 802 Bishop Theodulf's strong-men abducted an escaped criminal who had sought asylum at the altar of St Martin. Theodulf himself was also the abbot of no fewer than five monasteries given to him by Charlemagne, but in this case he was a bishop coming down on the side of his own jurisdiction. Alcuin appealed to Charlemagne in a letter full of righteous indignation, but hastily retreated when the emperor sided with Theodulf. Ancient monastic liberties and the powers of the saints were all very well, as long as criminals were brought to justice and a bishop's local authority remained unchallenged.[103]

Both Alcuin and Theodulf were foreigners, which made them more dependent on their royal protector, and possibly also more dependable, from their patron's point of view. Yet this was not the only reason why they immediately appealed to Charlemagne. The control of sacred space was hotly contested, with bishops and abbots as the main contenders, but the ruler who had appointed these men remained the ultimate arbiter. Whenever insoluble conflict arose, those involved looked towards the palace for a solution, as was the case in 812 when Fulda's monks defied their abbot and sent a letter of supplication to Charlemagne.[104] Carolingian kings were the ones who initiated monastic reform and were therefore also the acknowledged guardians of sacred space – whenever it suited their own purposes.

A kingdom defined by prayer

The expansion of Carolingian territory meant the extension of the correct cult of God and the incorporation of new peoples into a kingdom conceptualised as 'the Christian people'. In other words, conquest was also a matter of conversion, a righteous cause for which missionaries such as Boniface had been martyred. But was there a correct conversion, just as there was a correct cult? And if baptism created one Christian people, would erroneous, hasty or forced baptismal rituals consequently undermine the unity of the state? The tenacious resistance of Saxony to Carolingian rule brought this issue to the fore. On the troublesome Saxon front, subduing rebellion had become tantamount to imposing Christianity by force, to the extent that public manifestations of paganism merited the death penalty.

At the court in Aachen, Alcuin reflected on the consequences of conquest in some remarkable letters written in 796, three to his friend Arn, bishop of Salzburg, and one to Charlemagne.[105] As Wood argues, 'Alcuin accepted the premise of the military subjugation of Saxons and Avars, but saw that as something to be built upon peacefully, and not by force'.[106] Baptism should be preceded by proper instruction in the Christian faith, Alcuin argued. To Arn, he wrote that 'faith, as St Augustine says, comes by will, not by compulsion'.[107] To Charlemagne, in a letter which was probably meant for the entire court, Alcuin explained that 'careful thought must be given to the right method of preaching and baptism, lest the washing of the body in baptism is made useless by the soul lacking in understanding of the faith'.[108]

This was a crucial issue in a world in which the polity was understood as 'the ecclesia'[109] and where ideological boundaries coincided with those of correct Christian practice. It should be kept in mind that Charlemagne's wars were not always fought against pure and pristine pagans, even if Carolingian authors did their utmost to get this view across. In the course of the long and arduous Carolingian conquest of Saxony (AD 772–804) indigenous paganism had hardened, becoming a badge of independence and resistance in the face of Frankish might. But Saxony had not remained entirely outside the orbit of Christianity before Charlemagne's conquests. Since the late seventh century, the region had been targeted by Anglo-Saxon missionaries; archaeological evidence, family connections and patterns of landholding all indicate that pre-conquest Saxony had become part of the Frankish world, to a much greater extent than Carolingian authors were prepared to admit.[110]

The Avars had an even more ancient Christian past; about the year 600, some pious Avars made a pilgrimage to the Holy Land. Christian communities continued to exist in the Avar empire throughout the seventh and eighth centuries, developing their own liturgical traditions.[111] When the Avar kaghanate fell in 796, Carolingian bishops did not only see it as their task to convert the heathens, but also to eradicate deviant forms of baptism dispensed by 'illiterate clerics' – that is, Avar priests pronouncing baptismal formulas which were incorrect in the eyes of the bishops who followed in the wake of Carolingian armies.[112]

During Charlemagne's reign, the Avars represented the other troublesome frontier.[113] As the Royal Frankish Annals for 791 expressed it, after having consulted the Franks, the Saxons and the Frisians, Charles set out to avenge the 'unbearable evil' committed by the Avars against the 'the Holy Church, otherwise known as the Christian people' (sancta ecclesia vel populus christianus).[114] When the Frankish troops arrived at the River Enns, where Avar territory began, they paused for three days for litanies and intensive celebrations of mass, and 'they asked God's support for the safety of the army and the aid of the Lord Jesus Christ with regard to the victory and vengeance against the Avars'. This represented no less than the crossing of a Great Frontier defined in terms of liturgical correctness, with the correct cultus divinus marking the transition from one world into another.

A similar drawing of liturgical boundaries is evident in 796, the year of the subjection of the Avar khagan, and of Alcuin's attempt to ensure that this new people coming into the fold would receive proper instruction in their new faith. A group of bishops met on the bank of the Danube, the new frontier between Avar and Frankish territory. It was a gathering attended by ecclesiastical luminaries, who must have gone through a lot of trouble to travel to this remote spot. The synod was chaired by Paulinus of Aquileia and attended by Arn of Salzburg. On its agenda were 'various ceremonies integral to the cult of God and the Christian religion', but it was baptism on which, predictably, the bishops spent most of their time, including the erroneous rituals conducted by Avar priests who used water but not the required Latin baptismal formulas; 'Water alone without the infusion of the Holy Spirit is worth nothing except that it washes off the dirt of a carnal or material nature', the bishops concluded.[115]

A proper and therefore efficacious baptismal ritual was one central item on the agenda; the other was effective preparation and instruction prior to baptism, the issue raised by Alcuin. Judging by his correspondence with Arn, Alcuin saw the conversion of the Avars as something of a test case, a new opportunity where the mistakes made in Saxony might be avoided. He anxiously followed the events in the East, repeatedly seeking information and reassurance from Arn ('what does Avaria do or believe?').[116] In both men's view, the stability of Frankish conquest depended on correct baptism and worship, for which bishops were responsible. As Alcuin despondently wrote to Arn, in the aftermath of an Avar revolt in 799: 'The loss of the Huns, as you said, has been caused by our negligence'.[117]

Such was weight of responsibility felt by Charlemagne's courtiers. In a realm defined by correct prayer and orthodox faith, one might indeed lose the Huns by one's own inability to transmit the true spirit of conversion, feeling sinful afterwards. And one might lose prominent and staunch members of the Christian people to heresy, thereby creating a 'scandal', which was the result of 'negligence'.[118] In 794, Charlemagne chaired the council of Frankfurt, sitting in judgment on Adoptionism. According to this heresy, Christ was the adoptive rather than the true son of God; its main protagonists were Elipand, bishop of Toledo, and Felix, bishop of Urgel.[119] The latter was called to account and subsequently condemned at synods in Regensburg (AD 792) and also in Frankfurt, but he was not present in person; it was Bishop Leidrad who had to watch over Felix when in 799 he was held in custody in Lyon.[120]

Felix had two formidable intellectual opponents: Alcuin of York and Paulinus of Aquileia. A lot of misunderstanding of the finer christological arguments was involved in the heated debates raging between 792 and 799, yet Adoptionism mattered deeply to the royal gathering in Frankfurt, for here was a natural concern for a regnum-ecclesia that measured its place in providential history by its orthodoxy and the rectitude of its liturgy. Bishops from Spain and Italy appealed to Charlemagne; it was in this context that Paulinus called the king rex et sacerdos. More than a whiff of empire was in the air, with Charlemagne assuming the role of Constantine presiding over a christological debate which helped to define the boundaries of an orthodox realm. In this sense, heretics were useful enemies, but they also inspired fear of the disintegration of a realm increasingly perceived as an *ecclesia*.

Yet such frontier battles needed to be supported from within, and most of all from the palace, the moral hub of the realm. Charlemagne gathered his synod/assembly of 794 in Frankfurt, for here his wife Fastrada lay dying.[121] The only extant letter that can be truly called his own was addressed to this queen. Einhard disliked her intensely and scathingly wrote of her 'great cruelty' – testimony perhaps to Fastrada's real power.[122] The letter to Fastrada was sent in 791 from the Avar front by 'Charles, by the grace of God king of the Franks and the Lombards and patrician of the Romans, to our beloved and loving Queen Fastrada', then in Regensburg.[123] Formal phrases abound, but Charlemagne's letter portrays Fastrada as a beloved wife and, above all, as a staunch ally to her husband. He sent her a report on the progress of the Avar campaign, including the momentous crossing of the Enns. The letter is much more detailed than the concise report of the Royal Frankish Annals. All present abstained from wine or meat prior to battle, or gave alms instead if infirmity made fasting impossible. All those in holy orders celebrated a votive mass, and all clerics who knew the Psalms were each to sing fifty, 'and they were to walk barefoot while performing these litanies. This was what our bishops decided, and we all agreed to it and with the Lord's aid fulfilled it'. Charlemagne urged his queen to organise similar litanies in Regensburg together with her entourage of *fideles*, leaving it to her discretion 'to decide what your infirmity permits'.

Such supplications at home helped to define the boundaries of Charlemagne's kingdom as much as demonstrations of the proper cult on the edges of territory inhabited by the Christian people. The years 791–93 saw victories, but also a major crisis in the revolt of Pippin the Hunchback in 792. More penitential action was needed. In the spring of 793 the kingdom was turned into one huge prayer machine, with all clerics of whatever ilk celebrating masses or singing psalters 'for the lord king, the army of the Franks, and the present tribulation'; detailed instructions were issued with regard to the laity and their assistance by means of alms and fasting, each according to his or her status.[124]

Such measures sprang from deep anxiety in the face of disaster: how have we offended God? The exceptionally bad weather, crop failure, and the ensuing famine and epidemic of 805 yielded a similar response: Charlemagne instituted an empire-wide, three-day fast, giving orders to make it clear in all baptismal churches and monasteries, if need be with the aid of interpreters, that fasts and penance were the only way to appease God's anger.[125] A capitulary issued in 806 at Thionville, the assembly which pondered arrangements for Charlemagne's succession, dealt with the eventuality of 'famine, mortality, pestilence, bad weather or any other tribulation, of whatever kind: that men are not to wait for our decree but are straightaway to pray for God's mercy'.[126] This language conveys a sense of time running out, and also an awareness of the limits of written communication, which might just be too slow in times of crisis. Also, the Christian people and its bishops had apparently become accustomed to a ruler who identified 'tribulations' and took the lead in any empire-wide intensification of prayer. Could one initiate fasts and litanies *without* having received proper instructions from the palace? This seems to have been a real issue, and it is a significant one.

Intensifying *correctio* was another way of trying to restore stability to the realm. In the summer of 813, towards the end of his life and with a sense of urgency, Charlemagne convened five large reform synods in Mainz, Rheims, Tours, Chalon and Arles; in the presence of the emperor, the records of the gatherings were collated in an official document and sent to Aachen, where in October another assembly discussed these decrees; they were also deposited in the palace archives for future reference.[127] The distant locations of these five synods may have had more than practical reasons. By 'celebrating councils' in places spanning 'all of Gaul', this core part of the empire was drawn together by hectic conciliar activity, which was subsequently focused on Aachen, the centre of the empire.

Correctio was everywhere – by virtue of the presence of vast groups of bishops deliberating on the purity of the cult of God, but also because such gatherings extended the public forum from the centre to the regions and back again. Synods were a way of organising the space of the realm and redefining it in terms of the reform of the *cultus divinus*. This held true of the meeting of bishops on the banks of the Danube, but also of the councils convened in 813. Louis's accession in 814 marked the beginning of a period in which the palace in Aachen was the main venue for reform activity. For years on end, Louis convened his synods/assemblies in Aachen, but when crisis hit in the winter of 828/29, he exchanged his palace-orientated strategy for one already employed by his father: penitential action throughout the empire, and five reform councils turning the realm into one interconnected space in which *correctio* reigned supreme.[128]

Sacrum palatium/the Sacred Palace

Charlemagne's state was an *ecclesia* held together by a network of sacred places – monasteries and bishoprics – many of which had ancient histories. From the 780s onwards, when it became a magnet to articulate and able men from distant places, his court became first a fixed place in the minds converging on it, and then, in the mid-790s, a geographical location: Aachen. Here Charlemagne built the celebrated chapel, following Solomon's example and the building of the Second Temple – or does this mean reading more Old Testament into early-medieval royal minds than is justified?[129] Aachen was a new place of power, to a large extent devoid of past meanings imposing themselves, and therefore all the more open to new interpretations derived from the authoritative past.[130] Even though bishops flocked there in droves, it was not an episcopal see; so, first and foremost, it was royal rituals that turned this new centre into the *sacrum palatium* that Leidrad had in mind. It was a place of resolutely male conviviality, where men met their king in the baths fed from Aachen's hot springs, and where Charlemagne dressed like a Frank, only donning foreign Greek outfits when the occasion absolutely demanded it, that is, when he was in Rome and needed to do as the Romans did.[131]

Aachen as portrayed by Einhard was a place of low-key rituals, which may have been all the more forceful because of it. A strict code for the conduct and dress of the clergy – and not them alone – was set by Charlemagne himself. As Alcuin wrote to the archbishop of Canterbury in 801 with regard to his imminent visit to the palace:

> If you come to my lord the King, warn your companions and particularly the clergy to conduct themselves respectfully in all religious observances, in dress and in church order, so that you always set a good example wherever you go. Do not let them wear gold ornaments or silk clothes in the king's sight; they should go humbly dressed as befits servants of God.[132]

This is reminiscent of Einhard's portrait of Charlemagne: a ruler who was moderate in dress, food and drink, who had Augustine's *City of God* read out to him during dinner, and rose four or five times per night to dispense justice.[133] Einhard's Charlemagne was also a king who made sure nothing 'sordid or indecent' contaminated his newly built church; he closely inspected the correctness of reading and psalmody, even if he himself did not venture to deliver the lessons in public and only sang the psalms softly.[134] These images have a distinctly monastic flavour, with humility, regularity and St Benedict's 'nothing in excess' (*ne quid nimis*) as key features. Charlemagne's moderation in food and drink and his reluctance to give large banquets (*convivia*) is a reference to monastic moderation as well, even if present-day students are amused by the notion that early medieval moderation meant three courses *and* a roast. This definition of 'moderation' is more understandable when we recall that Einhard was brought up in Fulda from childhood and became Charlemagne's *nutritus* ('nurseling') only in his late adolescence or early twenties.[135] This is not to say, however, that Einhard's famous *Life of Charles* was monastic, as opposed to secular. What is more interesting about this text is the ease with which Einhard fuses monastic and secular ideals of conduct. His Charlemagne was a secular ruler, at the heart of a palace which was a secular palace, but it was also a community with monastic traits. Einhard's Aachen was place of power precisely because it transcended the divide between religious and secular order. When Leidrad referred to the 'sacred palace', he knew very well that Aachen was not a monastery but, all the same, monastic models of conduct did contribute to the palace's reputation of sacredness.

Visiting monks felt at home in such a palace, and a monk such as Notker of St-

Gallen, recalling Charlemagne in the 880s, could easily write about Aachen in terms of his own monastic experience, casting him in the role of an abbot aware of everything going on in his community. The omniscient emperor could always see what his resident nobles were up to, Notker explained, from the vantage point of his private quarters (*solarium*) overlooking the court. Not even the servants escaped Charlemagne's eagle eye: 'All the dwellings of the magnates were situated on the second floor, so that underneath not only all their retainers and their servants, but anyone might find shelter from rain or snow, cold or heat, without ever being able to hide themselves from the eyes of the most acute Charles.'[136] This was a ruler who peered straight into the servants' quarters underneath the noble mansions; by implication, the aristocrats in their houses 'suspended in the air' were even more exposed to the royal gaze, and were acutely aware of it.

Einhard knew it too, as becomes clear from an anecdote he recorded in 828. The translation of St Marcellinus and St Peter from Rome, engineered and financed by Einhard for his private churches in Seligenstadt and Michaelstadt, had gone wrong, for the Archchaplain Hilduin had managed to divert part of these relics to his own church of St-Médard in Soissons. This was the delicate matter Einhard came to discuss with Hilduin, staying in the house (*mansio*) he still retained in Aachen.

> Quite a few days later after arriving at court, I went to the palace early one morning, since it was the habit of courtiers to rise very early. After entering, I found Hilduin there … . He was sitting before the doors of the royal bedchamber waiting for the ruler to come out. After greeting him in the usual way, I asked him to get up and come over to a certain window with me, from which one could look into the lower parts of the palace.[137]

The high window from which Einhard and Hilduin leaned, sorting out their differences, was also that from which Notker imagined Charlemagne inspecting all that went on in his court, like any good abbot or bishop in charge of a religious community.

The monastery that was a 'model for Empire' – as Noble expressed it with regard to Louis's reign – was already there when Charlemagne ruled, at least from the 790s onwards.[138] It was also a model for the palace at Aachen, in the sense that royal monasteries and palaces tended to be interconnected, with monastic and courtly models mutually reinforcing each other. As Notker's reminiscences reveal, the palace could also serve as a model for monastic life. The gallery in the sacred palace, evoked by Notker in the 880s and by Einhard in 828, also figures in Leidrad's report to Charlemagne draw up in 813, with which we began. Leidrad proudly told Charlemagne that he had built a *solarium*, so all was ready for a visit from his royal patron. Any house fit for an emperor needed a *solarium*, an upper storey with a window from which Charlemagne might see all of Lyon's clergy praying regularly, according to the 'rites' of the sacred palace.

Notes

I am grateful to the following benevolent readers and critics: David Ganz, Yitzhak Hen, Matthew Innes, Rosamond McKitterick, Jinty Nelson, Barbara Rosenwein, Irene van Renswoude, Jo Story and, above all, Philippe Buc. I did not always heed their good counsel; what follows is entirely my own responsibility.

1 Leidrad, *Epistola ad Carolum* (809x812), MGH *Epp.* V, pp. 542–4; Coville (1928), pp. 283–96.
2 Coville (1928), p. 283.
3 Coville (1928), p. 284.
4 Innes (1997b).
5 Coville (1928), p. 283.
6 *Admonitio generalis*, cc. 65, 79, MGH *Capit.* I, no. 22, pp. 58–61, trans. King (1987), pp. 215–18; *Duplex legationis edictum* (789), c. 19, MGH *Capit.* I, no. 23, p. 63; trans. King (1987), p. 221.
7 Dutton (1994).
8 Heil (2000); Fried (2001).
9 Staubach (1984), pp. 555–7; de Jong (2000), pp. 220–6.
10 Ganshof (1968, 1971).
11 For older views, see Nelson (1987b).
12 Noble (1976) and (1980); Godman and Collins, eds. (1990); de Jong (1992); for a traditional perspective, Boshof (1996).
13 Ganz, ch. 3 (pp. 38–51) in this volume.
14 *Capitula a missis dominicis*, MGH *Capit.* I, no. 85; trans. King (1987), pp. 258–9.
15 Nelson (1986a); Innes (1998a); McKitterick (1989); McKitterick, ed. (1990).
16 McKitterick (1989), pp. 23–75; Mordek, ed. (1986) and Mordek (1995); Wormald (1999), pp. 30–92; Innes, ch. 5 (pp. 71–89) in this volume.
17 McKitterick (1977).
18 Nelson (1990).
19 *Council of Frankfurt* (794), c. 52, MGH *Conc.* II, p. 171, where bishops rejected the idea that God could be addressed only in three languages (Hebrew, Greek and Latin). Also, *AF* 874, MGH *SSRG* 7, p. 82, trans. Reuter (1992), p. 74, and Einhard, *Translatio* III.14, MGH *SS* XV, p. 253, trans. Dutton (1998), pp. 103–4.
20 Nelson (1987b), pp. 137–80.
21 Nelson (1995), p. 423.
22 Staubach (1984), on the centrality of 'correct' worship to Carolingian *correctio* and *emendatio*.
23 Markus (1990); Brown (1996); Wood (2001); de Jong (2001a).
24 Bede, *HE* III.25, pp. 294–309.
25 *Fourth Council of Toledo*, c. 2, ed. Martínez Díez and Rodríguez (1992), pp. 183–4; Stocking (2001), pp. 156–60.
26 *Edictum Chlotarii II*, ed. de Clercq, CCSL 148A (1963), p. 283.
27 *Concilium Clippiacense*, ed. de Clercq, CCSL 148A (1963), p. 291.
28 Fouracre (2000), pp. 130–6.
29 For example, Collins (1998b), p. 104. Alternatively, see Depreux (1997).
30 *Concilium Germanicum*, prologue, MGH *Conc.* II.1, no. 1, p. 2.
31 Synods in which Charles may have participated before 768 include Ver (755), Verberie (756), Compiègne (757) and Gentilly (767); on which, see Hartmann (1989), pp. 68–82.

32 E.g. RFA, 771–72, 777, 779, 782, 788; translated as '(royal) assembly' by King (1987) and Scholz (1970), and as 'Reichstag' by Rau (1972).
33 RFA, 794, p. 95; trans. King (1987), p. 88; *Letter to Elipandus*, MGH *Conc.* II, pp. 159–60; On the 794 Frankfurt meeting, see Berndt, ed. (1997).
34 Bullough (1985b).
35 MGH *Capit.* I, no. 71, cc. 1, 5, p. 161; trans. King (1987), pp. 263–4; Nelson (2001c).
36 MGH *Capit.* I, no. 14, cc. 5, 6, 10, 13, pp. 34–6; de Jong (1996), pp. 250–1.
37 MGH *Conc.* II.1, no. 19D, p. 142; Angenendt (1997).
38 Hincmar, *De ordine palatii*, c. 1, p. 38.
39 Anderson (1991), pp. 6, 12–19.
40 *Regula Benedicti*, c. 42.4.
41 Einhard, *VK*, c. 24; Poeta Saxo, *De gestis Karoli magni*, lines 376–80, MGH *SS* I, p. 273.
42 Noble (1992), p. 63.
43 Garrison (2000a).
44 *Ibid.*, p. 145. Also, Garrison (1998a); Meens (1998); Story (1999).
45 Noble (1992), p. 61.
46 Alcuin, *Ep.*, no. 228, trans. Allott (1974), no. 91; Garrison (2000a), pp. 159–60.
47 Garrison (2000a).
48 *Ibid.*, pp. 129–36.
49 Chazelle (2001); de Jong (2001).
50 Notker, *Gesta Karoli* I.3.
51 Thegan, *Gesta Hludowici* c. 7; trans. Dutton (1993), p. 143.
52 Gorman (1982; 1997).
53 Nelson (1995), p. 424.
54 de Jong (2000), pp. 217–26.
55 On Alcuin's influence on the *Admonitio generalis*, see Cubitt (1995), pp. 160–75.
56 Markus (1968), (1991) and (1997).
57 *Admonitio generalis*, prologue, MGH *Capit.* I, no. 22, p. 54; trans. King (1987), p. 209.
58 Innes (1998a).
59 *LP*, 'Life of Stephen II', c. 25; trans. Davis (1992), p. 63.
60 *Chronicon Moissacense*, MGH *SS* I, pp. 292–3; Buc (2000), pp. 201–10.
61 Schieffer (2000).
62 Noble (1984), pp. 158–83.
63 Noble (1995) and (2001).
64 *CC* no. 77; trans. King (1987), p. 294.
65 Noble (1984), pp. 158–83.
66 Alcuin, *Ep.*, no. 93.
67 Fried (2001).
68 McKitterick (1985); Hen (2001), pp. 65–95.
69 *Ibid.*, pp. 65–68.
70 McKitterick (1999) and McKitterick (2004), pp. 60-83.
71 Theodemar, *Letter to Charlemagne*, ed. Hallinger and Wegener, CCM I (1963), pp. 157–75, at 159–60.
72 Hen (2000) and (2001), pp. 72–8.
73 *Admonitio generalis*, c. 80, MGH *Capit.* I, no. 22, p. 61; trans. King (1987), p. 218.
74 Hen (2001), pp. 75–6.
75 On Benedict of Aniane's authorship, see Hen (2001), pp. 77–8.
76 Alcuin, *Ep.*, no. 226; trans. Allott (1974), no. 19; Hen (2001), p. 79.

77 Coville (1928), p. 284. Also Charlemagne's *Letter to the Lectors*, MGH *Capit.* I, no. 30, pp. 80–1; trans. King (1987), p. 208. Hen (2001), pp. 72–3.

78 de Jong (1995) and (1996).

79 Smith (2000).

80 de Jong (1998).

81 Nelson (1986b); Fouracre and Gerberding (1996), pp. 97–118; Rosenwein (1999), pp. 74–81.

82 Nelson (1996b), p. 191.

83 Rosenwein (1999); Fouracre (1995a).

84 Rosenwein (1999), p. 99.

85 de Jong (1995); Le Jan (2001).

86 Innes (2000a), pp. 180–222.

87 Fouracre (2000), pp. 137–45; Rosenwein (1999), pp. 100–1.

88 *Notitia de servitio monasteriorum* (819), ed. Becker, CCM I (1963), pp. 493–9.

89 *Supplex libellus*, ed. Semmler, CCM I (1963), pp. 321–5; Patzold (2000).

90 Rosenwein (1999), pp. 101–14.

91 Innes (2000a), p. 19.

92 Bertelli and Brogiolo, eds. (2000), pp. 105–27; West (1999).

93 *CC*, no. 67.

94 West (1999), pp. 351–3.

95 *Admonitio generalis*, c. 70, MGH *Capit.* I, no. 22, p. 59; trans. King (1987), p. 216.

96 Theodulf, *Capitulare*, no. 1, cc. 36–43, MGH *Capit. Episc.* I, pp. 133–40. Payer (1984); de Jong (1998), pp. 49–55.

97 Meens (1999).

98 On the poverty of some Carolingian rural priests, see Nelson (1987a).

99 *Epistolarum Fuldensium fragmenta*, c. 16, MGH *Epp.* V, p. 522.

100 Theodulf, *Capitulare* no. 2, c. 8.4, MGH *Capit. Episc.* I, p. 170; de Jong (1998), pp. 49–51.

101 *Synod of Frankfurt* (794), c. 56, MGH *Conc.* II, p. 171; trans. King (1987), p. 230.

102 Chélini (1962), pp. 19–50.

103 Alcuin, *Ep.*, nos. 245, 247, 249; trans. Allott (1974), nos. 114–16.

104 *Supplex Libellus*, ed. Semmler, CCM I (1963), pp. 321–5.

105 Alcuin, *Ep.*, nos. 107, 110, 112–13; trans. Allott (1974), nos. 59, 56, 3, 137.

106 Wood (2001), pp. 85–6.

107 Alcuin, *Ep.*, no. 134; trans. Allott (1974), no. 131.

108 Alcuin, *Ep.*, no. 110; trans. Allott (1974), no. 56; Wood (2001), p. 86.

109 RFA 791; trans. King (1987), pp. 87–8.

110 Wood (2000).

111 Pohl (1988), pp. 203–5, on the 'Kezthely culture' which was the basis of Avar Christianity.

112 *Conventus episcoporum at ripas Danubii (a. 796)*, MGH *Conc.* II.1, no. 20.

113 Pohl (1988), pp. 308–31; Reimitz (2000b).

114 RFA 791.

115 *Conventus episcoporum*, MGH *Conc.* II, no. 20. On baptism, see Cramer (1993).

116 Alcuin, *Ep.*, no. 146; trans. Allott (1974), no. 138.

117 Alcuin, *Ep.*, no. 184; trans. Allott (1974), no. 65.

118 de Jong (1992).

119 Cavadini (1993).

120 *Ibid.*, p. 82.

121 Nelson (1997).

122 Einhard, *VK*, c. 20.

123 *Letter to Fastrada*, MGH *Epp.* IV, no. 20, pp. 528–9; trans. King (1987), pp. 309–10; McCormick (1984).

124 *Capitulare episcoporum*, MGH *Capit.* I, no. 21; trans. King (1987), pp. 223–4.

125 *Letter to Ghaerbald*, MGH *Capit.* I, no. 124; trans. King (1987), pp. 245–7; Meens (1998).

126 *Capitulare missorum*, c. 4, MGH *Capit.* I, no. 44, pp. 122–3; trans. King (187), p. 248.

127 RFA 813; trans. King (1987), p. 105. Also MGH *Conc.* II.1, nos. 34–8, pp. 245–306; Hartmann (1989), pp. 128–40.

128 *Epistola generalis*, MGH *Conc.* II.2, no. 50B, pp. 599–601.

129 Garrison (2000a), pp. 154–6.

130 Nelson (2001a).

131 Einhard, *VK* c. 23.

132 Alcuin, *Ep.*, no. 230; trans. Allott (1974), no. 51.

133 Einhard, *VK*, c. 24.

134 Einhard, *VK*, c. 26.

135 Smith (2003).

136 Notker, *Gesta Karoli*, I.30; Nelson (2001a).

137 Einhard, *Translatio*, II.2, MGH *SS* XV, p. 245; trans. Dutton (1998), p. 83.

138 Noble (1976).

8

CHARLEMAGNE'S
'MEN OF GOD'
ALCUIN, HILDEBALD AND ARN

Donald A. Bullough[†]

The term 'man of God' is one that belongs to the 'reformed religions' of the early modern period; but the Latin equivalent, *vir Dei,* is occasionally found in medieval texts to describe someone blessed with exceptional spiritual or intellectual qualities and, by extension, it is used of individuals who were exemplars and leaders in the society of their time. Carolingian-period sources intermittently use terms like *Deo servientes* ('servants to God') and *fideles Dei et regis* ('confidants of God and king') in similar ways. So I shall continue to use it, here, as a convenient piece of shorthand. It is possible, of course, to extend these collective plurals to all early-Carolingian bishops and abbots (as well as to learned clerics who were neither) and theoretically, therefore, to the many hundreds or even thousands of churchmen whose names are known to us from contemporary lists, but whose lives and deeds are otherwise undocumented.

From the adequately-documented minority, I have selected three men (no women, I am afraid) of notably different origins, whose careers in conjunction cover all but the first decade of Charlemagne's reign as king and emperor; whose separate lives none the less shared some common features and literally came together at several decisive moments of the reign; the evidence for whose careers draws on all the major contemporary source-genres; and none of whom, finally, was later commemorated as a saint.

Alcuin

The first, and the only one of the three certainly senior to Charlemagne in age, is the Englishman Alcuin. Born *c.*740 of a modest landowning family (*paterfamilias*) in southern Northumbria, he became at a very early age one of the *pueri* who constituted (as it were) the bottom rung in York cathedral's clerical, non-monastic community. He was to remain there for more than 40 years, at first with the simple clerical tonsure and eventually – but perhaps only from c.770 – as a deacon: for reasons unknown, he never proceeded to higher orders and, it seems, did not become a professed monk.

The *Vita Alcuini*, written more than two decades after his death in 804, reports a number of stories concerning Alcuin's early life; it claims that he and the other *pueri* had received part of their education in York from the archbishop (Ecgbert) personally, and that Alcuin had mastered the Psalms by the age of 11.[1] It goes on to describe Alcuin's precocious interest in Virgil (the most suspect of the stories) and how part of St John's Gospel had triggered a profound emotional response in him as a young man. The greatest single influence from these early years was the cathedral's daily liturgy, which provided a 'schooling', the content and impact of which it is very difficult for most of us now to comprehend.

Of course, the daily liturgy was just as influential for most of those with whom Alcuin was later to live and work, and for their pupils and successors; the difference is that, because of Alcuin's letters and other writings, we can construct a partial picture of the York liturgy for which there is (typically of the period) no direct evidence, such as the use of the psalter in the so-called 'Roman' and not the 'Gallican' version, the existence of mass-prayers and lections from non-Gregorian (perhaps not even Roman) books, with distinctive antiphons for both mass and office, and so on. At some stage he also became familiar with a repertoire of 'private prayers' to which he was later to make notable additions.

Away from the choir he developed a reverence for 'Bede the teacher' whom of course he knew only at second hand; but his own *magister* at York in his late teens and early twenties (*adolescentia*) was the future archbishop Ælberht, for whom his admiration was almost unbounded. His long poem on York, written probably in the early or mid-780s, includes an unusually full account of the latter's teaching programme, presented in terms of the Seven Liberal Arts as defined by sixth-century scholars.[2] In the early 760s, moreover, Ælberht took him to Rome: on their journey home they were visiting the Lombard 'capital' Pavia when a debate took place between a Jewish scholar and the Italian Peter of Pisa, whom Alcuin was to encounter later at the Frankish royal court.[3] But Alcuin does not claim that he was present at the debate and he certainly learnt nothing from it.

From the late 760s, in a Northumbria that was politically unstable and often violent, Alcuin was himself earning a reputation as a teacher of adolescents; and some small relics of his teaching may survive. In Ælberht's last years as bishop, Alcuin was (it was later reported) sent on a mission of unknown purpose to Charlemagne. This is the most likely, although not the certain, background of a lively 'letter–poem' which was dispatched, after his return, to some of the prominent clerics and courtiers whom he had met while travelling up the Rhine and at the court.[4] He was also working with a fellow-cleric, Eanbald – who was elected as Ælberht's successor during the old archbishop's life-time – on the construction of a splendid new church in York (on a site still unknown) with a highly unusual dedication to *Alma Sophia*, 'Beneficent Wisdom'.

In 780/81, Alcuin again journeyed to Rome to obtain the archiepiscopal pallium for Eanbald, and possibly taking with him a sister of a recently-deposed Northumbrian king.[5] Chapter 9 of the *Vita* records that it was at Parma on his way home that Alcuin again met Charlemagne, supposedly in March 781, and was invited to join his court. It has always been assumed that he departed for Francia almost immediately after this second encounter; almost every modern account of Carolingian court culture – and of royally-initiated policies in the 780s and 790s, and the part in them attributed to Alcuin – proceeds from that assumption. In fact, there are strong arguments for concluding that Alcuin was still at York when papal legates arrived in 786 and that he may have contributed to some of the reform-decrees which they promulgated there.[6] If so, it was probably in the legates' company that he travelled to Francia and, at the age of 45–plus, joined a still-itinerant royal court where the key figures had hitherto been Franks or Italians.

There is little doubt that he took with him from York his own collections of excerpts from texts he had read there and possibly some complete works. At the court, where he was to remain initially for about 3½ years, he would have found copies of grammatical and Patristic texts previously unknown to him and – in the light of evidence from a few years later – he began to seek out and re-publish short, predominantly late antique, works that had been neglected for centuries but had potential value as textbooks. He was now able to share literary and intellectual exchanges with men of different background and predominantly of higher social standing and clerical rank than himself. He now put his previously-acquired skills in Latin versification to distinctive use by composing, with others, virtuosic 'figured poems' designed to glorify his royal patron; less certainly in those years, he composed his first extant work of Biblical exegesis, the 'Questions and Answers on Genesis'.

What he almost certainly did not do was persuade the king to obtain a 'Gregorian sacramentary' from the Papal court, still less begin to assemble mass-sets from other books to make up for its serious deficiencies. On the other hand, his imprint on the Frankish king's great capitulary or General Admonition (*Admonitio generalis*) of March 789, a programme for the reform and better ordering of both the Frankish church and secular society, is apparent in both its content and language.[7] Evidence which it is customary to ignore, however, also shows that the involvement of this incomer aroused jealousy or irritation among the circle of those hitherto closely associated with the king and his favoured counsellors.

Early in 790, the fifty-year-old Alcuin returned to Northumbria. He had expected (he claims) that he would be sent to Britain to resolve a dispute between Charlemagne and Offa of Mercia; but its resolution was almost certainly the work of others. It was back at York that, highly unusually, he or anonymous amanuenses now began to keep texts of outgoing letters, which – together with the small number retained and copied by their recipients (mostly in fact by Arn of Salzburg) – ensured the preservation of about 275 letters from the last fourteen years of his life.[8] A very few of those written from Tours after 796 are strictly 'business' or adminstrative letters (surely an unrepresentative fraction of the whole). Letters to English kings, bishops, abbots, and laymen are overwhelmingly admonitory; letters to Charlemagne, to Arn and a few others are sometimes of considerable length, dealing with a topic or, more often, a number of topics of current interest or concern.

The repeated commonplaces and stylistic pretensions of many of them do not in fact exclude adaptation to the recipient and to the occasion. Their not-infrequent autobiographical references, paralleled in a small number of Alcuin's poems (which always circulated less widely), reveal him as uncertain of himself even when he was being most authoritative and assertive, sensitive to slights and to betrayal, especially by one-time pupils on whom he had lavished care and attention. They also reveal him as not merely acquisitive but, in the opinion of contemporaries, unacceptably avaricious – an accusation which he was correspondingly eager to deny. His letters to Arn and occasionally to some other correspondents often display an effusiveness of language – expressions of affection, of a longing to be with him once more (and enjoy a drink together or a joint fishing-expedition) and of his sense of deprivation that this almost never happened.

During his three years back in Northumbria (790–93), he evidently had little or no success in checking the chronic violence associated with the exercise of royal power there. Nevertheless, his advice was sought by both the Mercian and the Frankish kings. In response to the latter he seems to have contributed something on the topic of 'synodal authority' in matters of doctrine to the text commonly known as the *Libri Carolini* (but more properly as the *Opus Caroli regis*) that was being compiled at the Frankish court as a rebuttal to the Greek position on 'image worship'.[9] Before his final departure from his native *patria*, which he professed always to regret, it is likely that he was assembling a collection of Patristic texts demonstrating the falsity of the understanding of Christ's relationship with God the Father as was currently professed by Spanish and Pyrenean bishops, the 'Adoptionist heresy'.

When Northmen sacked Lindisfarne ('Cuthbert's Isle') on 8 June 793, Alcuin was already back in Francia, although not at the court, which was still in far-distant Regensburg (Bavaria). The event, which is not recorded in any Continental annals, provoked him to issue a series of letters in which he criticised the Northumbrian king and people, and southern as well as northern English clerics for the faithlessness and gross misconduct that had brought down the wrath of God.[10] It also inspired an even more pessimistic verse-lament addressed directly to the Lindisfarne community.[11] Having finally rejoined the court when it arrived at Frankfurt early in 794, Alcuin made a significant contribution to the proceedings of an unusually grand synod and national assembly: two letters addressed to the Spanish bishops, in the name respectively of the king and of the Frankish bishops, were clearly essentially his compositions; and it is apparent that he convinced himself and perhaps others that his series of citations from the Fathers and from the liturgy provided a definitive rebuttal of 'Adoptionism'. His reward was formal admission, although still only a deacon, to the bishops' *consortium* and confratern-ity of prayer.[12]

When the court finally established itself at the new Aachen palace (still some-thing of a building-site), Alcuin took up residence with noble-born counsellors, clerics of humbler origin, two generations of royal ladies and a cohort of scholar–poets, vividly characterised in verse exchanges – initially intended for reading aloud – to which he was party. But unlike many of his fellows, he remained there for less than two years; for many months Charles himself was absent on military campaigns, from which Alcuin always excused himself. With the exception of a passing reference in Einhard's *Life of Charlemagne* and another in one of his fellow-residents' poems on life at the court, almost all the evidence about Alcuin in this period is from his own writings: directly in his own poems and letters (mostly written after he had left the court), indirectly in his pedagogic writings.

The latter were partly composed while he was at Aachen and partly after his move to St-Martin at Tours, and I regard them as the definitive written versions of what had hitherto been oral teaching. Collectively they justify the modern image of Alcuin as a teacher to the king and his family, and to adolescents in court service, although hardly the supposed 'head of a Palace school' embracing men of his generation and comparable learning. In one area at least, namely the study of the physical heavens – stars, planets, the course of the sun – Alcuin seems to have been for some time the acknowledged leader. Moreover, none of Alcuin's fellow-scholars is known to have attempted anything like his little treatise titled in later copies *Of True Knowledge* which, drawing extensively on the re-discovered *De consolatione philosophiae* of Boethius, skilfully linked secular studies with the proper understanding of Scripture and the individual Christian's ascent to Heaven beyond the stars.

At the end of 795 Alcuin was apparently still hoping to return to York, possibly even as bishop. Some past misconduct, to which he alludes elsewhere, may have proved an insuperable barrier; and when in April 796 Æthelred was assassinated (the Northumbrian king to whom he had previously given his allegiance – but not without criticism), the last hope was dissipated. Sometime in the summer of that year he reluctantly accepted the abbacy of St-Martin at Tours, which had not latterly been closely associated with the Frankish court (and which is in fact almost as far from Aachen as is York!). The greatest number of his letters and the bulk of his writings belong to his eight years as abbot of St-Martin from 796 to 804.

Early letters from this phase show a particular concern that the mistakes made in the 'conversion' of the Saxons a decade previously should not be repeated

140

in the new missionary areas opened up by the defeat of the Avars: 'a man can be forced into baptism but not into belief', so potential adult converts must be persuaded of the truths of the Faith by good teaching.[13] Such letters are, however, outnumbered by critical missives to English recipients, until they also abruptly cease in 798. He had other preoccupations: raising the community of St-Martin, and probably other clergy and monks in the region, from what he perceived to be their 'rusticity'; and a more active management of the monastery's widely-distributed estates, without much sympathy for tenants and dependents. Nothing engaged him more than 'Adoptionism' which, since Frankfurt, had extended its 'infections' – he made much use over the years of medical metaphors.

To combat the heresy, Alcuin first wrote personal letters to its major exponents and then a succession of three treatises which, although each was directed to one or other of them personally, he clearly hoped would be widely circulated. In fact, in this he was disappointed and complained openly that he was not getting the royal backing which he felt should have been forthcoming. In the early summer of 799, however, he and the heretic-bishop Felix of Urgel were at the palace to 'dispute' the controversial doctrines in the presence of the king and other leading clergy; and once more he persuaded himself that he had secured his opponent's admission of error.[14]

He was on his way back to Tours when he was shocked to learn that a violent attack on the pope, Leo III, had caused to him to flee from Rome and seek out the Frankish royal court, then temporarily at Paderborn in Saxony. Alcuin wanted direct action against the miscreants, provided he wasn't expected to join the expedition because of his age and ill-health (possibly recurrent malaria as well as cataracts). But simultaneously he was complaining that he was not being kept informed about what was going on. Since 797 at the latest, he had referred in passing in letters to the king and to influential friends to a 'Christian authority' or a 'Christian empire' which the Frankish king exercised or ruled over. But he never attempts to explain what these terms mean to him (although modern scholars have speculated freely!): only in a poem of 799 or 800 does he speak of Charles's right and duty to restore 'the ruler of the church' to his position of lawful authority in Rome.[15]

In the late summer of 800 a royal expedition set out, without Alcuin but including several of his younger *discipuli*, to do just that. How it should be done and what should then ensue might have been discussed when the king visited St-Martin 'for the purpose of prayer' earlier in the year; yet the only reflection of that visit in Alcuin's writings is a distinctive funerary oration for 'the lady Liutgard', Charlemagne's fourth queen, who died there during the royal visit. His supposed initiative or leading voice in the events leading to Charles's coronation and acclamation as emperor at St-Peter's on 25 December 800 is much less clear than has often been claimed.

His subsequent enthusiastic approval for Charles's new dignity did not preclude an unexpectedly well-documented bitter conflict between them when the emperor aggressively supported the other side, in a dispute over a supposed violation of St-Martin's rights of sanctuary.[16] Yet Alcuin's final years were surprisingly productive: the completion of a great commentary on St John's Gospel which found readers in twelfth-century Cistercian houses; a three-book *De fide sanctae Trinitatis* which enjoyed an even longer after-life; a whole series of 'votive masses'; and a moral treatise, the *De vitiis et virtutum*, dedicated to the defender of the Breton frontier, Count Wido. Last but not least, if those manuscripts written in the earliest phases of the distinctive 'Tours minuscule script' – including complete Bibles and a rare Virgil commentary – really do belong to the years either side of 800, it is difficult not to accept Alcuin's personal influence not only on their orthography (sometimes misconceived!) but also on the stylish page-layout and distinctive 'hierarchy of scripts'.[17]

Alcuin died on 19 May 804, his last days being recorded in a largely conventional way in the *Vita*: but it also records a vision in Italy of his death and admission to Heaven as well as one closer at hand. A tomb was erected over his burial-place with an epitaph composed by himself: destroyed in Viking attacks in mid-century, the text of the epitaph is widely preserved in manuscript copies.[18] At least one of his disciples (possibly Candidus) included what seems to be a deliberately uncomplimentary reference to him in a sermon preached not long after his death. In general, however, Alcuin was held in high regard by those who had been taught by him or were pupils of his pupils; and only at the century's end are there signs that his reputation was diminishing.

Hildebald

Very different in both character and quantity is the evidence for our second 'man of God': Hildebald, bishop and courtier. From sometime before 788 until 818 he was bishop, then archbishop, of Cologne, which was at that time a quite small diocese which straddled the River Rhine and extended eastwards to the Saxon frontier. After the first few years he was also made head of the royal chapel and became, in the fullest sense, a courtier and royal/imperial counsellor, assuming guidance of the body of clerics responsible both for religious observances at the court and for the drafting and fair-copying of privileges (diplomas) and other documents in which the king or emperor expressed his will. As such, Hildebald is named several times in contemporary narrative and conciliar sources; more than thirty royal and non-royal documents from those three decades record Hildebald's name and office, although none of these records was initiated by him.

Indeed, not a single letter survives of which he is the 'author', although we do have one that was written to him by Alcuin when he was in trouble with the Emperor in 801/02.[19] Nor do we have any text that bears his name or can be plausibly attributed to him in any of the codices written at or for Cologne cathedral in his day. Unusually, however, no less than 12 manuscripts – all of them remarkably still held in Cologne only a few hundred metres from their medieval home – have or had a statement in capitals on their first page that it was written *SUB HILDEBALDO*, usually with the addition of *episcopo* or *archiepiscopo*.[20]

Because of the lack of 'personal' information, whether documentary or literary, we know nothing of Hildebald's place of origin, family connections or career before 787. The only clue, and it is a tenuous one, is his name. Although certainly not unknown elsewhere, in the eighth and ninth centuries it is particularly common in the middle-Rhine and middle-Main regions, and is clearly found in several different families. Moreover, in the early part of Charlemagne's reign, the recognised norm of canon law and the correspondingly common practice was still that a bishop should be chosen from among the clergy of the cathedral or, by extension, from those officiating in its dependent churches (although there were, of course, frequent exceptions in response to royal or other pressure). With Hildebald, the only certainties are firstly, that a predecessor (who is a mere name in the surviving sources) was bishop of Cologne in 779/80 when Alcuin met him and, secondly, that the earliest of ten documents relating to the collegiate church (*Stiftskirche*) of SS. Cassius and Florentius at Bonn which dates to 787/88, refers to Hildebald as both its superior or head and as bishop of Cologne. (A few years later the day-to-day responsibility for the *Stift* was in the hands of one of the brethren as *vicedominus*.)

The context of the first reference to Hildebald in a 'public' or royal record is specific and distinctive: according to the fifty-fifth and penultimate chapter of the 794 Frankfurt Council's surprisingly miscellaneous *acta*, the king recalled that he had previously had the permission of the pope to keep Archbishop Angilramn (of Metz) with him at the royal court *propter utilitates ecclesiae* ('for the service of the Church'); he was now asking the assembled bishops to agree that for the same reason permission should be sought for Hildebald likewise to reside there – which from 795 meant, most of the time, at the Aachen palace – and not in his diocese.[21] The reference to Angilramn, who had died *in Avaria* nearly three years previously, shows that Charlemagne had appointed or was about to appoint Hildebald as head of the chapel (although for many years to come his title – in documents that use it – was the simple *capellanus*, not *archicapellanus*).

In this capacity he was the subject of rather allusive vignettes in all three of the major poems written about the court and its personalities in 795/96. There is a brief but apparently complimentary reference in Alcuin's *Court Poem* to an unnamed individual who – we may assume – was Hildebald, from the preceding reference to the 'crowd of scribes'.[22] (Strictly speaking, though, it is only in 807, when the court was temporarily at Ingelheim, that there is explicit evidence of Hildebald's ultimate responsibility for the correct engrossing of imperial diplomas, so Alcuin's compliments could have been meant for another's ears.) Theodulf's verses note rather more explicitly Hildebald's piety and his duty both to give blessings at feasts and give effect to what the king has previously willed.[23] But Angilbert's lines are the most elaborate:

> you, the First Cleric of the Court,
> In you Aaron, once a great priest under Moses,
> Is now unexpectedly brought back to life in our palace.
> You wear the ephod, you carry the sacred fire to the altars,
> The chapel key in your hands and Heaven's key on your lips.
> With your prayers you constantly defend the people from the Enemy.[24]

By 798/99 Hildebald's standard designation, in documents and in other texts, was *archiepiscopus et (palacii) capellanus*: it is with that title that Hildebald is listed as the first among those who met Pope Leo III 'somewhere in Francia' in the summer of 799 and who conducted him into the Frankish king's presence at Paderborn. When, a year later, the pope made a triumphant return to Rome in advance of Charlemagne's arrival there, the first name in the list of Frankish royal *missi* included in his retinue is *Hildebaldus reverentissimus archiepiscopus*.[25] His dual title figures subsequently in a whole series of documents relating to the Bavarian (Austrian) monastery of Mondsee, which had been gifted to Hildebald in 799/800, presumably so that he could enjoy its resources. His archiepiscopal status is not entirely unambiguous: Angilramn, the previous head of the chapel, had had the title as a purely personal one, that is, without any metropolitan authority over other bishops. But by 798, metropolitan archbishoprics, including Rheims, Trier and Mainz, had existed for two decades and more: it is likely, therefore, that their common neighbour Cologne would have recently been given comparable status, although initially only with authority over Utrecht and Liège – the latter being the diocese in which Aachen lay.

If Hildebald was only rarely in his cathedral church and diocese – as was clearly the case – what did he contribute to them? The answer, rather surprisingly, is 'quite a lot', beginning with the books written in his time for the cathedral library and in some cases directly on his instructions. Two of the three oldest books in the collection – as recorded some twenty years after Hildebert's death – had been written elsewhere and subsequently acquired.[26] Rightly pre-eminent among his own commissions, perhaps when he was not yet archbishop, is the three-volume edition – more than 800 leaves – of Augustine's so-called *Enarrationes in Psalmos*, copied (as we now know) by the nuns of Chelles, a royal community near Paris.[27] In spite of its scale, it is arguable that if one is to have only one work of exegesis in an early-ninth-century library, this is it – an exposition of texts repeated in worship many times in the course of a year, and at the same time a guide to prayer in all its forms (but not, in fact, with much evidence of use!). Another of Hildebald's external commissions may be the closely contemporary copy of Jerome's letters written at Salzburg, although it has no inscription to prove that it was in Cologne in Hildebald's day.[28]

Why these external commissions? I think, because cathedral 'chapters' (including York) were, in general, small-scale bodies compared with major monasteries; and in the late-eighth century those of their members who were recognised *scribae* were probably fully occupied producing copies of books required for the celebration of the liturgy – of which none in fact survives, not even as fragments. (Even the earliest extant Cologne 'Gregorian' sacramentary, which was given a fortuitous importance in the history of the text because it was used by Pamelius for his 1571 edition is of the very end of the ninth century; and most of it was probably not written at Cologne anyway.)[29] But perhaps significantly, two manuscripts written at Cologne, the first probably while Hildebald was still a bishop, the second certainly at the very beginning of his archbishopric, are both 'computistic': Cologne, Dombibliothek cod. 103, the contents of which include both the *De natura rerum* (probably the oldest complete copy) and *De temporum ratione*; Cologne, Dombibliothek cod. 83.II, the first part dating to 798, the second to 805, but between them the work of almost 20 hands (perhaps the entire community?).[30] A few years later some of these scribes were, however, copying a range of Patristic and other texts, some of which had only very recently become available north of the Alps.

Hildebald's other great contribution to his see was the building of a new and massive cathedral to replace the quite modest pre-Carolingian bishop's church – or so many good scholars believe. But the evidence is not conclusive: the earliest written statement of Hildebald's involvement in this rebuilding project dates to the fifteenth century (although not impossibly copying an earlier text), and the remarkable excavations under the Gothic cathedral that were begun in the most unfavourable circumstances in 1946 have produced nothing that unequivocally establishes a date to Hildebald's time, *c.*780–820. However, a reasonable inference of Hildebald's involvement in the rebuilding of the cathedral at Cologne can be gleaned from evidence of very different kinds: two verse *tituli* composed by Alcuin for the new building and certain features of the earliest phases of the major rebuilding visible in the excavations, which have close parallels in other early Carolingian buildings.

Two final inferences about Hildebald's career and contributions to the Carolingian polity are more speculative (although I have to say that I have largely persuaded myself!). There is a strong possibility that Hildebald was responsible for the overall form and appearance of a beautiful and distinctive psalter with supplementary texts and original ivory book-covers intended for presentation to the pope in 795, commonly called 'the Dagulf Psalter' from the name of one of its two court scribes.[31] Additionally, a contemporary Cologne manuscript contains a note which dates it to 798 and refers to the notion of empire; *quando missi venerunt de Grecia ut traderent [Karoli Regis] imperium* ('when messengers came from Greece to hand over the empire [to King Charles]').[32]

This unique historical note reminds us of the prominent part accorded to

Hildebald in the *Liber Pontificalis* in its account of events of 799 and 800, and reminds us that, unlike Alcuin, he was regularly at the court in these critical years, raising questions – ultimately unanswerable – about Hildebald's part in preparations for Charles's imperial coronation. And even if the final initiative for the chanting at the Christmas mass 800 in St-Peter's, 'To the august Charles, crowned by God, the great and peaceful emperor of the Romans, *vita et victoria*' came from the papal side, who is more likely to have ensured that it was taken up by the Frankish court clergy than the head of the chapel?

Arn

The life and career of the third of my Carolingian 'men of God' – Arn, abbot of the northern monastery of St-Amand from 782, bishop (later archbishop) of the Bavarian see of Salzburg from 785 – is much more comprehensively documented than Hildebald's. Indeed, about some aspects of his life – notably his early life as a cleric – we are better informed than we are about Alcuin. But almost nothing of Arn's evidently once-extensive correspondence, and in particular that with Alcuin, has been preserved; and of the other writings attributable to him, with varying degrees of certainty, only one or perhaps two throw any real light on his learning and thought, although they certainly suggest the range that was perhaps expected from an early Carolingian bishop. The fullest picture of the man – through, one might say, other people's tinted spectacles – comes from Alcuin's letters to him over a fourteen-year period and in the tendentious, retrospective, later-ninth century account of the conversion of Bavaria's Danube valley and Alpine neighbours.

The documentary evidence that is lacking for both Alcuin and Hildebald allows us to say that Arn was born in the early to mid-740s (making him just a few years younger than Alcuin) into a south-east Bavarian family which would be reckoned as 'noble' on almost any definition of that social category. In 758, at a time when the dukes of Bavaria and the Frankish king (Pippin, then Charlemagne) were competing for the allegiance of churches and landowning families, a certain Haholt and his anonymous wife, in thanksgiving for the former's recovery from serious injuries, gave part of their family-land at Ausserbittlbach together with their young son Arn to the cathedral church of Freising. (Members of the same family, with the same name-sequence – Arn son of Haholt – were giving away other land in the same area three-quarters of a century later.)

If he is rightly identified with the deacon Arn who witnessed Freising charters from 765, he had almost certainly been ordained 'under the canonical age', although that would hardly have been exceptional. Between November 775 and August 776, Arn was advanced to the priesthood. Two years later, in unknown circumstances, he moved to the northern monastery of St-Amand but (like Alcuin) never professed as a monk; and indeed it is quite likely that it was only in 821 that the community accepted the Benedictine Rule. In 782 Arn became abbot of this community, although probably from the start a non-residential one, which suggests that he was a royal nominee. Three years later (785), without giving up his abbacy, he succeeded the Irishman Virgil as bishop of Salzburg, the eastern-frontier diocese between the Danube and the Alps.

Was his appointment to the see of Salzburg made on the initiative of its community (which may have been one of both monks and 'seculars'), of the Bavarian duke Tassilo, or of the Frankish king? The sources do not help us; but subsequent events, and notably an appeal to an apparently unsympathetic pope in 787, suggest that his appointment was intended to build a bridge between duke and king. If so, it failed: Tassilo was ousted and sent in exile to a monastery in 788. Some have claimed that Arn may briefly have lost royal favour, although the evidence for this very thin; if real, his disgrace was certainly short-lived. For more than two decades thereafter he was to be simultaneously a devoted and trusted royal/imperial servant, coming and going frequently between the court, his diocese and other parts of the wide-flung Frankish dominions, as a pastor and administrator of the Salzburg diocese, which became from 798 an extensive archdiocese.

Already by 790 an unusually detailed record was compiled of the properties and revenues owed to Arn, though this is preserved only in a much later copy, unfortunately. It may be no coincidence that 790 is also the date of the first letter from Alcuin to Arn to be preserved and later copied by one of Arn's secretaries at St-Amand or Salzburg.[33] This is just one aspect of Arn's renowned encouragement of a 'scribal culture' and the production of books which, to our eyes, are its most conspicuous consequence. An *elogium* written probably soon after his death in 821 (although again preserved only in a much later copy) records that 'among other innumerable and praiseworthy works he ordered the copying of more than 150 volumes'; and, on the evidence of what still survives (magisterially described by the late Bernhard Bischoff), this seems no exaggeration.[34] When, in 809, scholars at the Aachen court prepared what was evidently intended as a standard *computus* – revised a year later and subsequently expanded and revised – it was Arn's Salzburg scribes and artists who produced the finest copies of the 810 edition in the next decade. A recent commentator has seen in them something more than exemplary practical texts, noting 'the clear expression of an Imperial political ideology' influencing the illustrative schemes, and has even detected in one of the two some input from Hildebald of Cologne himself (which I confess I am unable to see).[35]

The defeat of the Avars in 795/96 brought the Franks not only an enormous accession of material wealth but also a huge new area for missionary endeavour, among the barely-Christianised 'Carantanians' and the Avars themselves. The extent and chronology of Arn's direct, personal involvement in the extension of Christian belief and ecclesiastical organisation to the newly annexed regions to the south and east of his own archdiocese is controversial but impossible to deny. His active encouragement of the work of subordinates is well documented, and

Alcuin's decision to write in confident terms to Arn on the proper conduct of missionary activity among the *rudi* – to avoid the premature imposition of tithe, for example – was founded in the sure knowledge of Arn's active involvement in these issues. Indeed, one short text on proper forms and stages of conversion may well be an adaptation by Arn of something drafted by Alcuin.

On a visit to Rome in April 798, to Alcuin's express delight, Arn was made metropolitan archbishop of the whole of the former duchy of Bavaria and the newly-acquired regions to the east – although it was left to imperial officials a decade later to define the southern boundary of his authority against the north-Italian patriarchate of Aquileia. Arn, however, seems to have formed a much more unfavourable view of Pope Leo's private behaviour than Alcuin was subsequently willing to believe; and there is evidence of exasperation in letters exchanged between the two friends when Leo fled to Francia in 799 (although we only have Alcuin's side of the discussion). When pope and king met at Paderborn in 799, Arn was among those present, while Alcuin was absent and complaining that no-one was telling him what was going on.

Whether or not he was eventually convinced of the pope's innocence, Arn's name follows Hildebald's in the record of those who conducted Leo back to Rome in triumph in November 799. Furthermore, Arn was almost certainly among the leading churchmen and laymen who, at Aachen in March 802, collaborated with the emperor to produce one of the reign's most substantial collection of legal and administrative decrees – the so-called Programmatic Capitulary.[36] He was certainly the most energetic, or at least the best documented, senior cleric to give effect to those decrees as imperial *missus* in his archdiocese and perhaps elsewhere over several years. He was no mere administrative bishop.

Whatever the differences between Arn and Alcuin at the political and even personal level, Arn had a real appreciation of Alcuin's qualities as a giver of spiritual advice and as a skilful composer of prayers for public and for private use. Arn was always ready to use the skills of Alcuin's young disciples in the Salzburg 'cathedral school', provided that they were good communicators in the vernacular as well as in Latin. The two men were still in correspondence in the spring of 803, when it was Arn's turn to complain about Alcuin's tardiness in letter-writing – caused by the distance between them and a shortage of messengers, Alcuin retorted.

I bid farewell to our three 'men of God' on the last occasion on which two of them and a disciple of the deceased Alcuin were provably together at a major gathering in the Aachen palace. In 811, as Einhard records, the emperor laid before his ecclesiastical and lay magnates the *constitutio atque ordinatio*, a document which we recognise as Charlemagne's last will and testament; the first and third names among the subscribing bishops who approved the emperor's will are Hilde-bald and Arn, while the first of the abbots is the English-born Fridugis of St-Martin, a favourite Alcuin disciple.

Notes

† This paper is substantially that delivered by Donald Bullough in February 2000. He was able to revise the text before his death in June 2002, but was not able to add the notes to the paper. Minimal notes have been supplied, referencing key works and editions; readers are directed to the detailed evidence as provided in Bullough, *Alcuin: Achievement and Reputation* (2004).

1 Anon., *Vita Alcuini*, pp. 182–97.

2 Alcuin, York Poem, lines 1432–49.

3 Alcuin, *Ep.*, no. 271 (to the monks of Murbach); no. 172 (to Charlemagne); trans. Allott, (1974), no. 75; Bullough (1995).

4 Alcuin, *Carmina*, no. 4; trans. Waddell (1976), pp. 150–5.

5 Adaltruda, daughter of Æthelwald Moll and thus sister of Æthelred I of Northumbria; Story (2003), p. 184.

6 George of Ostia, *Epistola ad Hadrianum* (Letter to Pope Hadrian), MGH *Epp.* IV, pp. 20–9; trans. Whitelock, *EHD* I, no. 191; Cubitt (1995), pp. 153–90; Story (2003), pp. 55–92.

7 *Admonitio generalis*, MGH *Capit.* I, no. 22; trans. King (1987), pp. 209–20.

8 MGH *Epp.* IV, pp. 18–481, many are translated by Allott (1974).

9 The arrival of a volume on this subject is recorded in contemporary Northumbrian annals, *Historia regum*, 792; trans. Whitelock, *EHD* I, London (1979), no. 3.

10 Alcuin, *Ep.*, nos. 16–22, 24; trans. Allott (1974), nos. 12, 13, 26–30, 48.

11 Alcuin, *Carmina*, no. 9; trans. Godman (1985a), no. 10, pp. 126–30 and Waddell (1976), pp. 160–75.

12 Bullough (1997).

13 For example, Alcuin, *Ep.*, nos. 99, 107, 110–11, 118–19; trans. Allott (1974), nos. 56–61.

14 Alcuin, *Ep.*, nos. 23, 41, 139, 148–9, 166, 172, 182, 193, 199, 200–2, 207; trans. Allott (1974), nos. 75, 79–80, 105–13, 143. See also Cavadini (1993).

15 Alcuin, *Carmina*, no. 45.

16 Alcuin, *Ep.*, nos. 245, 247, 249; trans. Allott (1974), nos. 114–16.

17 Rand (1929) and (1934).

18 Alcuin, *Carmina*, no. 123.

19 Alcuin, *Ep.*, no. 246.

20 Twelve Cologne manuscripts with contemporary inscriptions linking them to Hildebald are listed in Bischoff (1998): nos. 1884, 1888, 1890–1, 1897, 1900, 1907, 1910, 1916, 1925, 1938, 1946a. On Cologne books, see Jones (1932).

21 MGH *Capit.* I, no. 28; trans. King (1987), pp. 224–30.

22 Alcuin, *Carmina*, no. 26; trans. Godman (1985a), no. 7, pp. 118–21.

23 Theodulf, *Carmina*, no. 25, lines 125–30; trans. Godman (1985a), no. 15, pp. 150–63.

24 Angilbert, *Carmina*, no. 2, lines 56–61; trans. Godman (1985a), no. 6, pp. 112–19.

25 *LP*, 'Life of Leo III', cc.16, 20; trans. Davis (1992), pp. 187–9.

26 Cologne, Dombibliothek Cod. 63, 65, 67 (from Chelles) and Cod. 164 (from Western France); Bischoff (1998), nos. 1897 and 1937. A catalogue of the year 833 lists much of Hildebald's Cologne library; Bischoff (1994), pp. 59, 97.

27 Cologne, Dombibliothek Cod. 63, 63, 67 and 97; *CLA* 8.1152; Bischoff (1998), no. 1897; Bischoff (1957).

28 Cologne, Dombibliothek Cod. 35; *CLA* 8.1146; Bischoff (1998), no. 1881.

29 Cologne, Dombibliothek Cod. 137; Bischoff (1998), no. 1935.

30 Cologne, Dombibliothek Cod. 103; *CLA* 8.1158; Bischoff (1998), no. 1916. Cologne, Dombibliothek Cod. 83.II; *CLA*, 8.1154; Bischoff (1998), no. 1907.

31 Vienna, ÖNB Cod. 1861; *CLA*, 10.1504.

32 Cologne, Dombibliothek Cod. 83.II, fol. 14v; *CLA* 8.8.1154; Bischoff (1998), no. 1907; Mordek (1999), p. 49, pl. 2.

33 Alcuin, *Ep.*, no. 10; trans. Allott (1974), no. 135.

34 Bischoff (1980), pp. 52–83.

35 Borst (1993) and (1998).

36 MGH *Capit.* I, no. 33; trans. King (1987), pp. 233–42.

9

THE CAROLINGIAN
RENAISSANCE OF CULTURE
AND LEARNING

Rosamond McKitterick

The eighth century in western Europe was a time of new developments, an expansion of Christendom and fresh beginnings. It was a period of a remarkable efflorescence of culture, especially in the Frankish realm. This culture was based securely on the intellectual and cultural achievements of the preceding four centuries as well as the legacy of the Roman world. Yet, in the Frankish kingdom, very considerable impetus from the 780s onwards would appear to have been provided by the ruler, Charlemagne, himself.

Charlemagne's patronage of learning should be seen, first of all, in the context of the promotion and endowment of learning and culture by powerful and wealthy men and women in late antiquity and the early middle ages. The patrons of culture in this period were usually the rulers. Thus there was the encouragement of poetry in the time of the Roman emperor Augustus; the interests in learning cultivated by the Theodosian rulers in the Roman empire in the fourth century; the elaborate programme of public building and architecture conducted by the Byzantine emperor Justinian, Thrasamund, the Vandal king in North Africa, and Theoderic, the Ostrogothic ruler of Italy in the late fifth and sixth centuries; the cultural activities of the Merovingian rulers of Frankish Gaul such as Chilperic of Neustria and Dagobert I in the sixth and seventh centuries, as well as the achievements of the Lombard rulers Liutprand and Desiderius in the eighth century and the Byzantine emperor Theophilus; similarly, scholarship and the acquisition of books were promoted by such Anglo-Saxon rulers as Aldfrith of Northumbria, Offa of Mercia, Alfred of Wessex and Aethelstan of England.

All these instances indicate that it was clearly accepted, perhaps even expected, behaviour on the part of a ruler to evince an active interest in intellectual and cultural matters. Indeed, the patronage of learning could be regarded as one of the obligations of royalty. Yet Charlemagne's patronage of learning was combined with a legislative programme for reform and renewal within the Frankish church and society. In his reign we see an organised and determined assembly and deployment of resources to carry out specific aims.

The aim of learning

Charlemagne's own legislation, in conjunction with a story told by Notker Balbulus (The Stammerer) in his *Gesta Karoli*, helps us to identify what these aims were. Notker was from the monastery of St-Gallen in present-day Switzerland and was writing for the Emperor Charles the Fat (Charlemagne's great-great grandson) at the end of the ninth century:

> At the moment when Charlemagne had begun to reign as sole king in the western regions of the world, two Scots from Ireland happened to visit the coast of Gaul in the company of some British traders. These men were unrivalled in their knowledge of sacred and profane letters at a time when the pursuit of learning was almost forgotten throughout the length and breadth of Charlemagne's kingdom and the worship of the true God was at a very low ebb. They had nothing on display to sell, but every day they used to shout to the crowds who had collected together [in the market] to buy things: 'If anyone wants wisdom let him come to us and receive it; for it is wisdom which we have for sale.'
>
> They announced that they wanted to sell wisdom because they saw that the people were more interested in what had to be paid for than in anything given free. Either they really thought that they could persuade the crowd who were buying things to pay for wisdom too; or else, as subsequent events proved to be true, they hoped that by making their announcement they would become the sources of wonder and astonishment. They went on shouting their wares in public so long that in the end the news was carried by the onlookers, who certainly found them remarkable and maybe thought them wrong in the head, to the ears of King Charles the Great himself, who was always an admirer and great collector of wisdom.
>
> He ordered them to be summoned to his presence immediately and he asked them if it was true, as everyone was saying, that they had brought wisdom with them. They answered, 'Yes indeed we have it and in the name of God we are prepared to impart it to any worthy folk who seek it.' When Charlemagne asked them what payment they wanted for wisdom, they answered, 'We make no charge, O king. All we ask is a place suitable for us to teach in and talented minds to train; in addition of course, to food to eat and clothes to wear, for without these our mission cannot be accomplished.'
>
> Charlemagne was delighted to receive this answer. For a short time he kept them both with him. Later on, when he was obliged to set out on a series of military expeditions, he established one of the two, who was called Clement,[1] in Gaul itself. In his care he placed a great number of boys chosen not only from the noblest families but also from middle-class and poor homes; and he made sure

that food should be provided and accommodation suitable for study should be made available. Charlemagne sent the second man, Dungal,[2] to Italy and put him in charge of the monastery of St Augustine near the town of Padua so that all who wished might join him there and receive instruction from him.[3]

Notker associated learning with the worship of the true God, and stressed the role of teachers and students in the cultivation of learning. Charlemagne himself, in a letter (the *De litteris colendis*, 'On cultivating letters') sent *c.* 800 to the bishops and abbots of his vast empire, reinforced the association of learning and the Christian faith:

> We exhort you not only not to neglect the study of letters but also with most humble and God-pleasing application to learn zealously for a purpose, namely, that you may be able the more easily and the more correctly to penetrate the mysteries of divine scripture. And since figures of speech, tropes and such like are to be found embedded in the sacred pages, there is no doubt that the more fully anyone reading these is instructed beforehand in the mastery of letters, the more quickly he will gain spiritual understanding. But let such men be chosen for the work as have both the will and the ability to learn and the desire to instruct others. And let it be carried out with a zeal matching the devotion with which we order it.[4]

In an earlier decree, the *Admonitio generalis* (General Admonition) of 789, moreover, Charlemagne had insisted that 'schools should be established for teaching boys the psalms, *notas* (scholars dispute whether this means writing, shorthand, or musical notation), singing, computation, and grammar in every monastery and episcopal residence'.

The books were to be corrected properly 'for often, while people want to pray to God in proper fashion, they yet pray improperly because of the uncorrected books. And do not allow your boys to corrupt them, either in reading or copying: if there is a need to copy the Gospel, Psalter or Missal, let men of full age do the writing with all diligence'.[5] Not long after 786, Charlemagne had addressed a letter to the lectors or readers in the churches, pointing out how 'We long ago accurately corrected, God helping us in all things, all the books of the Old and New Testaments, corrupted by the ignorance of the copyists'.[6] Charlemagne, as a Christian ruler, was ensuring that the word of God in a proper and correct form was disseminated to all his leading monasteries and cathedrals. In the schools, correct language was to be taught by teachers – such as the two Irishmen in Notker's story – from correct texts, in order to achieve a correct and orthodox understanding of the Christian faith.

This extraordinary effort made by Charlemagne, his scholars and their pupils is the cultural and religious achievement that modern scholars have labelled the 'Carolingian Renaissance'. Nor was it an ephemeral achievement; this vibrant new culture of the late eighth and the ninth centuries provided the essential foundation for European culture thereafter. It must be stressed, though, that the Franks were Rome's heirs. They made Roman and Christian ideas and techniques of art and scholarship their own. The Christian church provided both the spiritual and moral framework, and the specific educational and liturgical needs which the Carolingians strove to fulfil. Yet the Franks in the Carolingian period were also intensely creative; they built on what they had inherited and made vigorous use of it to create something new and distinctively Carolingian that provided the bedrock for the subsequent development of medieval European culture.[7]

The most obvious symbol of cultural continuity with the Roman past is that the Franks used Latin as the language of government, education and worship, and thereby ensured the survival of Latin as a living, universal language in religion, government, law and scholarship in Europe throughout the middle ages and into the early modern period. In those areas under Carolingian rule which we now know as France and northern and central Italy, Latin was in any case the vernacular language of the Franks and the Lombards, although east of the Rhine Germanic dialects were current. In the Carolingian period, moreover, efforts were made to reform and correct written Latin in relation to the classical texts of Roman antiquity. This increasingly created a division between the spoken tongue and the written language; in the course of the later ninth and the tenth centuries, these modified spoken vernaculars developed their own written forms and emerged as French, Spanish and Italian.[8]

In the Carolingian period most of the extant books on all subjects are in Latin, but east of the Rhine a few glossaries, translations of religious texts and poetry, and some riddles and charms survive from the ninth century in various forms of Old High German. Writing and literacy, furthermore, were fully integrated into Frankish society – though there undoubtedly remained various levels of pragmatic literacy and scholarly accomplishment; and many, such as a freed slave, may have been able to do little more than grasp the importance of the written document that granted his or her freedom. Although Carolingian civilisation was largely dependent on the written word in Latin and German for its religion, government, learning, education and recording of the past, it was a society in which written and oral modes were fully interdependent. Thus texts could reach a wider audience by being read aloud or sung.[9]

Bibles and other books

It is with texts that any study of the Carolingian *renovatio* of learning and art has to be concerned; even the illustrations in Carolingian art spring primarily from interpretations and pictorial representations of texts, most notably that of the Bible.[10] The text of the Bible itself was corrected and edited in the early Carolingian period. As we have seen, the *Admonitio generalis* of 789, issued by Charlemagne, had identified a need to correct the texts used for the catholic religion. Many centres in the Frankish realms thereafter worked to produce a correct Bible text within the means at their disposal. That of the Anglo-Saxon scholar Alcuin at Tours was largely a matter of careful correction of the orthography and comprehensive attention to the layout and organisation of the text. The Visigothic scholar Theodulf of Orléans, on the other hand, produced a scholarly edition. These two Carolingian editions of the Bible are the most famous, but many more appear to have been produced, combining Old Latin versions of different books of the Bible with the Vulgate translations made by Jerome in the early fifth century.

Not only was the Bible corrected, but authoritative versions of other books were also prepared for use in the churches and monasteries, such as the liturgical books for the mass, the Homiliary or book of sermons, the Antiphonary, canon law and the Rule of St Benedict, as well as the secular laws, including Roman law and those of the peoples under Frankish rule. We are able to document from surviving manuscripts how these corrected texts – and those copied from exemplars regarded as authoritative – were produced and disseminated under the auspices of Charlemagne and his son and successor, Louis the Pious. In other words, it is clear that extraordinary and successful efforts were made to carry out the intentions of the rulers and their advisers with respect to the production of books to assist the reforms of education and the church.

The aim was to establish uniform religious observance throughout the Frankish realm, and the copies of the approved and authorised versions of liturgical and ecclesiastical texts were widely disseminated. Some centres even appear to have specialised in the production of particular categories of these books. Tours, for example, became famous for its magnificent large-format one-volume Bibles, though the Bible at this time was more commonly copied and distributed in separate books or small groups of books, such as the Heptateuch, the Prophets, the psalter, the gospels, the epistles of Paul or the Apocalypse / Book of Revelation. St-Amand produced sacramentaries or mass books on commission from many other centres. From a writing centre associated with the royal court came a number of law books. Despite these efforts to promote a standard religious observance, harmony rather than uniformity was achieved; a great diversity of practice prevailed and many local communities persisted in the use of versions of texts to which they had become accustomed.

The output of books from the scriptoria of the Carolingian realm was prodigious.[11] Even taking the problems of survival into account, the volume of book production was clearly far greater and more systematic than in the Merovingian period. These books served not only the needs of religious worship but also government and administration, spiritual discipline, intellectual endeavour, education and literary activity. In response to the need for texts, the distinctive caroline minuscule that had begun to evolve during the Merovingian period, based on Roman uncial, half-uncial and cursive letter forms, was refined and disseminated throughout the empire. In due course it was also introduced into Italy, England and Spain, along with many Carolingian texts. Many centres in

Carolingian Francia, Germany and Italy developed 'house styles' of script. Scribes were trained and scribal discipline was imposed to an unprecedented level.

Books were supplied for monastic and cathedral libraries, for both liturgical services in the churches and for individuals. The copying activities of the *ateliers* and the professional techniques developed for the efficient reproduction of texts were essential for the Carolingian achievement and the dissemination of ideas in Carolingian Europe. Every category of book was included, from sumptuous Gospel books, psalters, mass books and copies of the Church Fathers to canon and secular law, Carolingian royal capitularies, devotional texts, collections of saints' lives, martyrologies and manuals on all manner of practical subjects. Some new categories of book were created as well, such as *Libri memoriales* or confraternity books, cartularies containing copies of an institution's legal records organised geographically, episcopal handbooks which combined legal and devotional texts, history books comprising selections from more than one historical work and prayer books designed for particular individuals, the most famous of which is the Prayer Book of Charlemagne's grandson, Charles the Bald (840–77).[12]

Information also circulated, mostly in the form of library catalogues and lists, about what books the properly-educated should aim to possess, and where one might acquire exemplars in order to make copies of such texts. Thus Lupus of Ferrières referred to a list of Einhard's books that he had seen, and asked to borrow a copy of Cicero listed in it.[13] Books were lent to other centres for copying or reading. In *c*.800, for example, books were lent from Würzburg to Fulda and Holzkirchen and there are instances of connections in the form of books borrowed between St-Denis, St-Gallen, Rheims, St-Amand, Corvey, Corbie, Auxerre and Lorsch. Some centres simply acquired them from other scriptoria, but most copied and created their own books. Even the royal court had groups of scribes and artists associated with it. The work of two groups is attributed to the *Hofschule* ('Court school') of Charlemagne, producing art in very different styles from each other and writing the texts in uncial (a script used for Christian books in the late Roman period) and in the new caroline minuscule.[14]

Education

Both the *Admonitio generalis* of 789 and the *De litteris colendis* issued *c*.800 also placed great emphasis on schools and education. The latter stressed that bishoprics and monasteries should not only devote themselves to the practice of the religious life and the observance of monastic discipline, but should also cultivate learning and educate the monks and secular clergy so that they might achieve a better understanding of the Christian writings. Information about the physical location and organisation of Carolingian schools is sparse, but the monasteries and cathedrals certainly educated children in their schools and these included those who were not necessarily destined for the religious life or ecclesiastical careers. Some schools, such as those of Fulda, Tours, St-Gallen, Auxerre, Liège, Metz, Laon, Salzburg and Rheims, became particularly famous for their masters and for the teaching offered in such subjects as chant, music, philosophy, arithmetic or astronomy. These schools attracted many pupils who afterwards became prominent in public life and the secular church. Many centres became celebrated for the learned writings of certain scholars, such as Hadoard, Ratramnus and Paschasius at Corbie, Milo and Hucbald of St-Amand, Hraban Maur of Fulda, Martin of Laon, Heiric of Auxerre, Lupus of Ferrières or Walahfrid Strabo of Reichenau.

In the early Carolingian period not all these places had yet achieved prominence. A crucial role in the late eighth century was played by scholars from many countries who congregated briefly at the royal court and were thereafter established in various abbacies and bishoprics within the Frankish realms. These included the Franks Angilramn, Wigbod, Einhard and Angilbert; Alcuin the Northumbrian from York; Theodulf, a Visigoth from Septimania; Paul the Deacon, Paulinus of Aquileia and Peter of Pisa from the Lombard kingdom; Joseph and Dungal from Ireland; and many more. The court coterie is depicted in many of the poems written by these creative scholars.

Theodulf of Orléans in his poem on the court, for example, describes Charlemagne, the sight of whom 'is more brilliant than thrice-smelted gold', and his sons 'youthful and strong, of powerful build' and daughters 'lovelier than any other'. Many of the men at court are described, not always very kindly, and some are given evocative nicknames, though Theodulf's most vicious darts are reserved for the nameless 'Irishman': there is Wibod the brawny hero with the bloated belly, Eppinus the cupbearer, Flaccus (Alcuin), 'a stimulating teacher and a melodious poet', Riculf with his 'strong voice, alert intelligence, and polished speech', Ercambald taking notes on his tablets, Einhard, 'small as an ant' though 'greatness dwells in the caverns of his little heart'. The 'fine deacon Fridugis' is 'in company with Oswulf, both of them experts of Grammar and highly learned' and 'Menalcas' lays down the law 'as though at a synod'.[15]

The intellectual interests of the scholars at court embraced Christian theology as well as the metrical forms of classical antiquity. Major works such as the *Libri Carolini* by Theodulf of Orléans concerning the place of art in the Christian church and the issue of iconoclasm, or the varied responses to the Spanish heresy of Adoptionism, were the direct outcome of the intense theological and philosophical discussion at court, which involved the king himself. A dramatic expression of the theological preoccupations of the Carolingian court was the Council of Frankfurt convened in 794. It responded to the Second Council of Nicaea of 787 which had condemned iconoclasts and defined the veneration to be accorded images. However, due to the Franks' misunderstanding of the Greek arguments about images and the veneration that was due to them, the Acts of Nicaea II were condemned, along with the issue of iconoclasm. As well as the *Libri Carolini* on images, a dossier of treatises about Adoptionism was prepared.

Both compilations are impressive witnesses to the range of learning of early Carolingian scholars, the resources on which they were able to draw, in terms of earlier theological discussions and commentaries from the patristic period, and the independent views they were able to formulate.[16]

Many of the court scholars subsequently joined or set up monastic and cathedral schools and taught throughout the realm. Among these, Alcuin taught at Tours (having first acted as personal tutor to Charlemagne and his daughters) and numbered many leading scholars of the next generation among his pupils, not least Hraban Maur of Fulda. He also continued his theological and pastoral discussions with Charlemagne's daughters, by then established at the convent of Chelles, in a series of letters and biblical commentaries. Theodulf of Orléans' poem on the court suggests that Gisela, Charlemagne's sister and abbess of Chelles, sometimes came to court, and that should Charlemagne 'request that the ways of Scripture be revealed to her, may the king himself, taught by God, teach her'.[17] Alcuin's interaction with Gisela's nieces at Chelles and the letters he exchanged with them highlight not only the extended circle of royal patronage in which scholars continued to enjoy the favour of members of the royal family, but also the high level of attainment of the royal women themselves – far greater, from the evidence of Alcuin's letters, than the poem of Theodulf implies.[18]

We know nothing about Charlemagne's education as a boy, apart from a passing reference to Charlemagne's belief that 'his daughters and sons should be educated, first in the liberal arts, which he himself had studied'. Then the boys were trained 'to ride, fight and hunt'. Again this presumably is also what Charlemagne was taught to do.[19] Later, Einhard tells us that he was entertained while he was eating by listening to someone read the histories and deeds of the ancients, and that he was fond of the books written by St Augustine, particularly the *City of God*. As well as his native tongue he 'learned Latin so well that he spoke it as well as his own native language, but he was able to understand Greek better than he could speak it'. Einhard then adds this crucial comment on the king's own intellectual interests:

> He avidly pursued the liberal arts and greatly honoured those teachers whom he deeply respected. To learn grammar, he followed [the teaching of] Peter of Pisa, an aged deacon. For the other disciplines he took as his teacher Alcuin of Britain, also known as Albinus, who was a deacon as well, but from the Saxon people. He was the most learned man in the entire world. [Charles] invested a great deal of time and effort studying rhetoric, dialectic and particularly astronomy with him. He learned the art of calculation [arithmetic] and with deep purpose and great curiosity investigated the movement of the stars. He also attempted to [learn how to] write and for this reason used to place wax-tablets and notebooks under the pillows on his bed, so that, if he had any free time, he might accustom his hand to forming letters. But his effort came too late in life and [he] achieved little success.[20]

Thus Charlemagne himself received instruction from the gathering of scholars at court. Letters exchanged between the king and Alcuin, in particular, indicate that instruction and advice to the king continued even after Alcuin had retired to Tours and was teaching his pupils in the school there.

It is in the structure and emphases of the educational curriculum in Tours and other Carolingian schools that the revival and promotion of the classical heritage, as well as the enduring legacy of the Carolingians, may best be seen. The divisions of knowledge, for example, were those of late antiquity. The writer Martianus Capella – in his work *On the Marriage of Mercury and Philology*, written in the late fifth century – had established the categories known as the seven liberal arts. These comprised the *trivium* – grammar, rhetoric and dialectic – and the *quadrivium* – geometry, music, astronomy and arithmetic. The emphases of the Carolingian school curriculum, though similar to those of the schools of Merovingian Gaul and Anglo-Saxon England, were Christian. Basic arithmetical knowledge was taught by means of the *computus*, which gave instruction in understanding the calendar, calculating the phases of the moon (and thus the date of Easter and other feasts of the Christian year) and rules of simple arithmetic. Astronomy was related to this, for one could use it for calculating time and the seasons and it was also useful for navigation, agriculture and even medicine.

The first reading-matter for any school child was the psalter and probably almost everybody who went to school would know the psalter by heart by the time they had completed their education. Instruction in language was provided from the grammars of the late Roman grammarians, Donatus and Priscian, designed for those for whom Latin was a native language. With some knowledge of the psalter, grammar and arithmetic, a pupil might then proceed to study Christian didactic texts and manuals of the patristic writers, and also those written by Carolingian school masters, including those of Alcuin himself.

Education, therefore was designed to inculcate Christian learning and understanding. Although classical texts were drawn upon (especially those relating to language and its use), the Carolingian scholar would aim to perfect him- or herself in Christian learning and theology and would study the writings of the great Church fathers of late antiquity such as Augustine, Gregory, Jerome, Ambrose, Leo the Great and many more. These early Christian authors were as important a part of the Roman heritage as the pagan classical works of Cicero, Virgil, Tacitus and Suetonius, or the practical manuals concerning medicine, warfare, agriculture, surveying and the like. The Carolingians passed on an astoundingly rich collection of the learning of earlier centuries.

We should remember the processes by which such learning may have survived and been passed on. Before the Carolingian period there had no doubt been changes in taste so that a process of natural selection would have meant many texts going out of fashion and ceasing to be copied. In late antiquity, moreover, the official recognition of Christianity and its establishment as the religion of the

Roman Empire had had a marked impact on culture, with an increasingly Christian emphasis from the fifth century onwards. There were changes in the educational curriculum, and the fifth century saw the production of many epitomes or summaries of earlier works. Christianity was on the whole positive towards pagan culture and absorbed much of its emotional commitment and intellectual drive. Before the eighth century, moreover, many distinct contributions to learning had been made by such scholars as Boethius and Cassiodorus in Italy, and Isidore of Seville in Spain. Both Boethius and Cassiodorus had either themselves translated or commissioned translations of major Greek works. Isidore provided a compendium of antique knowledge known as the *Etymologiae* ('Etymologies') which was widely disseminated throughout early medieval Europe. Whereas learning in late antiquity was largely the province of secular schools and individual scholars, in the course of the early middle ages learning became increasingly the prerogative of monastic and episcopal centres and communities of scholars, teachers and pupils.

Classical texts

These same ecclesiastical centres did not jettison classical learning. On the contrary, it is to the Carolingians that we owe the survival of classical texts. From the years 550 to 750, we know of 264 books containing writings from classical antiquity that survive and only 26 of these are secular works, most of them of a technical kind embracing subjects such as Roman law, gromatic texts (used for surveying and land measurement), grammar, medicine and military matters. By the end of the ninth century, however, the major part of the Latin literature of classical antiquity, that is, the works of about seventy classical authors, including thirty-five works by Cicero, had been copied and were being circulated. Further, other texts translated from Greek into Latin – such as Aristotle's *Categories*, Plato's *Timaeus*, Galen on medicine, and many astronomical and mathematical treatises – preserved much of the wisdom of the Greeks in the west even though ever fewer people had the ability to read Greek. If one considers texts from classical antiquity, notably the literary and historical works, it should be remembered that the earliest manuscripts of nearly every known classical author are copies made in the Carolingian period; and two-thirds of these were written in the north Frankish, Rhineland and Alemannian monasteries of Corbie, Rheims, Tours, Fleury, Auxerre, Fulda, Lorsch, the Reichenau and St-Gallen. As far as we can determine from the evidence, indeed, the Carolingians made a determined effort to seek and salvage what they could of the classical heritage.[21]

As an explanation for the extraordinary concentration of classical text production in the Carolingian period, it has been surmised that Charlemagne himself may have sent out an appeal of some kind in about 780 asking for remarkable or rare books. There is also a famous list of arcane classical works associated with the royal court (Berlin, Preussische Kulturbesitz Diez B Sant.66). Bernhard Bischoff, the great palaeographer, conjectured as long ago as 1957 that the Berlin list, one of the oldest surviving book lists from the early middle ages, was a list of some of the books in Charlemagne's library, on the basis of the position that the Berlin manuscript occupies in the transmission of the Carolingian poetry composed at Charlemagne's court. The main grammatical texts in the book were written by a Frank and the additions, including the poems and the book list, by an Italian. Although Bischoff argued that this Italian was at Charlemagne's court,[22] a more recent argument has proposed that the list stems from northern Italy and possibly Verona.[23]

Whatever the outcome of this, as yet unresolved, debate, the list witnesses to a very wide range of texts from classical antiquity available in the early Carolingian period. It may also reflect the close links between the courts of Charlemagne and of Pippin of Italy, after the conquest of Lombard kingdom in 774 and the establishment of Pippin as sub-king of Italy in 781. Many of the classical texts no doubt were in Merovingian or North Italian libraries. All the same, only some copies of Virgil, Cicero and Livy, and scraps and fragments of a few other classical authors, survive from before the Carolingian Renaissance. Italian copies of classical works for the most part postdate the Carolingian conquest of the Lombard kingdom in 774, so that again it would appear to have been from the Frankish court that the stimulation of new interest came. If we consider the distribution of classical and patristic manuscripts in the Carolingian period and where particular types of text were concentrated, we might surmise that Tours and Lyons had been centres of patristic learning and Roman law, while classical texts were available at Corbie and Rheims and were copied for newer foundations such as Lorsch, Fulda, Reichenau and St-Gallen.

Early medieval writing

To a considerable extent we are observing, in the extant manuscript evidence of the eighth and early ninth centuries, the transmission and augmentation of existing knowledge. The manuscripts witness furthermore mastery of the technical skills of writing, book production and decoration. We can see how these skills of literacy were disseminated, how libraries were formed and how centres capable of copying books were established. The Franks appear to have been very conscious of their role in preserving their Roman heritage and moulding it for their own purposes. One crucial aspect of ninth-century culture, indeed, is the formation of a canon of knowledge, reflected above all in the extant library catalogues of the ninth century. The libraries and their inventories, together with the bibliographical guides produced in the ninth century, contributed substantially to the definition of a canon of knowledge and the organisation of this canon and its approved works and authors in relation to the perceived needs of the schools, the church and the administration.

The library catalogues in particular document the acquisition, whether from other centres or by copying in their own scriptorium, of all the texts perceived to be essential. The St-Gallen catalogue can be taken as representative: it lists biblical texts, the works of the fathers of the Church and important early medieval authors – with Gregory the Great, Jerome, Augustine, Ambrose, Prosper, Tichonius, Primasius, Isidore of Seville, Origen, Pelagius, Cassiodorus, Gregory of Tours, Bede and Alcuin predominating. There are also *florilegia* (collections of extracts from major authors organised under subject headings), monastic rules, lives of the fathers, and lives and passions of the saints and martyrs, conciliar decrees of the Church, expositions on the mass, canon law, secular law, history books, sermons, biblical exegesis and school books, which contain many classical literary texts.

The bulk of the surviving manuscripts dating from before 800 and those of the ninth century are in fact those of patristic, biblical and liturgical books, with Augustine, Jerome and Gregory the Great predominating among the patristic authors, and an increasing number of early medieval English, Italian and Frankish authors being introduced. These patristic and early medieval works are of real importance as far as the formation of European culture and the Carolingian *renovatio* are concerned. For one thing, the patristic authors were themselves well versed in the classics and passed on many of their cultural assumptions and allusions to succeeding generations. For another, their work in itself formed Christian life and thought, and – together with that of their scholarly successors from Anglo-Saxon England, Italy, Spain, Francia, Saxony, Alemannia and Bavaria – proved an enduring legacy.

It is of the utmost importance to appreciate not only what the Carolingians revived and passed on, but also their own achievements. Carolingian scholars wrote learned commentaries on the Bible, treatises on grammar, spelling, philosophy, rhetoric, poetry and theological doctrine. Alcuin, for example, dedicated his commentary on St John's Gospel to Gisela and Rotrud, Charlemagne's daughters; and his treatises on orthography, dialectic and rhetoric were used in the schools. Wigbod's commentary on *Genesis* and Alcuin's own commentaries were the precursors of the comprehensive exegesis of the Bible provided by Alcuin's pupil Hraban Maur later in the ninth century.

The Franks devised new genres of writing history, such as biography (of which Einhard's *Life of Charlemagne* is the most obvious example), annals and historical epics in verse, such as *Karolus magnus et Leo papa* (also known as 'The Paderborn Epic'). The Royal Frankish Annals in particular – first composed in the 780s and deploying the dating system according to the year of the Incarnation in order to structure the narrative – provided a distinctive and powerful affirmation of Frankish identity and of the success and greatness of the Carolingian rulers. They are as close to an official history as we can get. Unlike the many other annals (which witness to local history writing on an unprecedented scale within the Carolingian world to an extent still not fully appreciated), moreover, the Royal Frankish

Annals were widely disseminated throughout the Carolingian realm, from Brittany to eastern Bavaria and from Saxony to Italy. It was a dissemination in which the royal court itself played a role, as indicated by the evidence of a fragment of annals in the script of the scriptorium of Louis the Pious, now in Cologne. These diverse types of historical writing were continued and developed throughout the ninth century, as we can see in the biographies of Louis the Pious by Thegan and 'the Astronomer', Ermold the Black's epic poem in honour of Louis the Pious, and the extraordinarily rich narrative of the Annals of St-Bertin and Annals of Fulda.

Paul the Deacon from Italy appears to have been the first to take up the idea of the *Liber Pontificalis* or history of the popes and adapt it to provide a history of a Carolingian see, namely the history of the bishops of Metz; that bishopric was of fundamental importance to the Carolingian family itself, for it was there that their saintly ancestor Arnulf had been bishop. The new genre of *Gesta episcoporum* and *Gesta abbatum* became very popular and provided a vehicle for the inclusion of the documents relating to ownership of land by a see or a monastery, as well as for the narrative of the major events in an institution's past. Paul also wrote a *History of the Lombards* in the early 780s, which is a very skilful piece of image-making about the Lombards' past and identity. I have argued elsewhere that this history was written on behalf of the Lombards for the Franks, either in Francia itself or for the Franks and Lombards at the court of Pippin of Italy. It was designed to instruct the Franks about the Lombard past and provide some measure of legitimation for Carolingian rule in northern Italy.[24]

The Carolingian scholars, especially those at the court of Charlemagne from the 770s onwards, were highly versatile. They acted as advisers to the king, as ambassadors, teachers, theologians and experts on liturgy and biblical exegesis. Courtiers such as Alcuin, Paul the Deacon, Theodulf of Orléans, Angilbert of St-Riquier and Modoin composed poems in many different poetic forms. Some were adapted from classical metres, such as the complicated acrostic poems inspired by Porphyrius and the pastoral poetry modelled on Virgil's *Eclogues* and the later pastoralists Calpurnius and Nemesianus; other types, such as adonic verses, were adapted from fifth- and sixth-century writers, and still more types, such as rhythmic historical and riddle poems, were newly devised. Many of these poems evoke the Carolingian *renovatio* and revival of antiquity, and allocated classical nicknames to many members of the court as if to reflect their cultural aspirations. In the Paderborn Epic, for example, Aachen is called a new Rome, and Charlemagne himself is likened to Aeneas. The poetry gives us a strong sense of the personalities at court and their response to their historical situation.

Carolingian scholars also compiled compendia of knowledge on all manner of topics, such as mathematics, astronomy, geography and the computus. Dicuil's *De mensura orbis*, for example, provided a description of the world that relied on ancient works such as Pliny's *Historia naturalis*, only occasionally modernising his material by contemporary references.[25] One instance is his reference to the elephant sent as a present to Charlemagne by Harun-al-Rashid in 803 where he says that, contrary to the views of Solinus, the elephant can indeed lie down. A Cologne manuscript (Dombibiothek Cod. 83.II) preserves a tract on time first composed in about 737, subsequently extended, improved and added to the manual on time compiled by Hildebald, archbishop of Cologne in 805. A Carolingian 'Encyclopaedia' on time was also produced in about 793 and a revised version was compiled at Aachen in 809.[26]

Music

The Franks were creative musicians, though it is not until the later part of the ninth century that notated manuscripts and the new tropes and sequences enable us fully to appreciate what the Carolingians achieved in the musical sphere. Modern discussion has focused on the relationship between the existence and maintenance of Roman chant in Rome throughout the early middle ages and the development of Frankish and Carolingian chant in the Frankish kingdoms. There remains doubt about the extent of the 'Roman' contribution to the music and liturgy of the Franks in the early Carolingian period, though liturgy, music and chant were undoubtedly matters in which both Pippin III and his son Charles were closely concerned. Einhard tells us, for example, that Charlemagne was very interested in music and what was being sung in his chapel.[27] Whether musical notation (in the form of neumes as a way of graphically recording musical settings of texts) actually developed during Charlemagne's reign or later in the ninth century is still being debated. Whatever the chronological development of neumes, their existence is to be understood in relation to the Carolingian attitudes to the written word and to texts. Neumes document a musical performance practice of extraordinary subtlety; they articulate a reading of texts with dimensions of colour and rhythm, which enhance the impact of the words to far greater an extent than if it were merely spoken.[28]

Royal patronage

The capitularies and conciliar decrees, not least those of the Synod of Frankfurt in 794 or the reform councils of 813, make it clear that the king himself played a part in theological discussion and in the reform of the clergy, ecclesiastical organisation, and the liturgy. In whichever resplendent new palace it was temporarily based (at Frankfurt, Paderborn or Aachen) as the king moved on the royal itinerary round the kingdom, the central role of the court as a place where scholars could congregate is indicative of the crucial role of the ruler as a patron of culture. When we observe other powerful early medieval polities where the kings did not play such a role, our appreciation of the Carolingian rulers' achievements and intellectual energy is greatly enhanced. There is no evidence, for example, of the tenth-century Ottonian rulers' systematic patronage of particular centres, no group of schools associated with the court, no royal role in the dissemination of particular texts, no direction or impetus provided for the cultivation of contemporary scholarship, no court atelier for the production of fine books for use by the royal family, and little sign of even occasional sponsorship of individual scholars or craftsmen.

Charlemagne and his immediate successors, on the other hand, expended their wealth and exploited their superior position in order to serve their intellectual interests, enrich their libraries and enhance their pleasure. Yet Carolingian royal patronage (on the part of both the king and the queen, as well as other members of the royal house), as I have explained in this chapter, was not solely directed towards selfish ends. Close examination of the king's personal intervention and promotion of scholarship – and the particular texts and activities with which he can be associated – indicate that the patronage of learning was an obligation for the king. Royal patronage was not random aesthetic pleasure, but an organised and determined assembly and deployment of resources to carry out the specific aims articulated in the royal capitularies. The court school, for example, created a new edition of the gospels and disseminated it to major monasteries within the kingdom. Other corrected texts, as remarked above, were also disseminated from the court or under its auspices. Rather than acting as an occasional benefactor, the Carolingian ruler sustained groups of artists, scribes and craftsmen over a long period of time in order to create artefacts for his particular objectives. His patronage was designed to promote his royal power as a Christian king and to consolidate the Christian faith by disseminating the key texts on which that faith was based. Patronage is therefore inextricably bound up with *correctio* and *emendatio*, which were so fundamental a part of the Carolingian *renovatio*.

Notes

1 Clement the Scot was at Louis' court in *c*.817.
2 Dungal, monk at St-Denis 784–811, may have been teaching in Pavia in 825.
3 Notker, *Gesta Karoli*, cc.1, 2, ed. Rau (1960), pp. 322–3; trans. Thorpe (1969), pp. 93–4.
4 *De litteris colendis*, MGH *Capit.* I, no. 29; trans. King (1987), pp. 232–3. See de Jong, ch. 7 (pp. 103–35) in this volume.
5 *Admonitio generalis*, c. 72, MGH *Capit.* I, no. 22, pp. 59–60; trans. King (1987), p. 217.
6 *Epistola generalis*, MGH *Capit.* I, no. 30; trans. King (1987), p. 208.
7 McKitterick, ed. (1994).
8 Wright (1982); Wright, ed. (1991). See also Edwards (1994), on Germanic vernaculars.
9 Nelson (1990); McKitterick (1989).
10 Gameson, ed. (1994); Chazelle, ed. (1992); Kaczynski (1995).
11 Bischoff (1998) and Bischoff (2004). When complete, Bischoff's three-volume catalogue of extant ninth-century manuscripts will list more than 7,000 items.
12 Now Munich, Schatzkammer der Residenz, on which see Henderson (1994).

13 Lupus, *Epistolae*, ed. Marshall (1984) and Levillain (1927–35), no. 1; trans. Dutton (1998), pp. 166–8.

14 Köhler (1958); Braunfels, ed. (1965); Contreni (1992).

15 Theodulf, *Carmina*, MGH *PLAC* I, no. 25; trans. Godman (1985a), pp. 154–61. On nicknames at Charlemagne's court, see Garrison (1998b).

16 Theodulf, *Libri Carolini*, MGH *Conc.* II, Suppl. I, ed. Bastgen (1924) and Freeman (1998). On Adoptionism, see Alcuin, *Libellus contra haeresim Felicis*, ed. Blumenshine (1980) and Cavadini (1993). On the Frankfurt meeting, see Berndt, ed. (1997).

17 Theodulf, *Carmina*, MGH *PLAC* I, no. 25, lines 113–14, p. 486; trans. Godman (1985a), p. 157.

18 Alcuin, *Epistulae*; for translations of many of Alcuin's letters to the ladies of the Carolingian court, see Allott (1974).

19 Einhard, *VK*, c. 19.

20 Einhard, *VK*, c. 24, trans. Dutton (1998), p. 32.

21 Reynolds (1983); Reynolds and Wilson (1991); Nees (1991).

22 Bischoff (1965).

23 Villa (1995).

24 Paul the Deacon, *Gesta episcoporum Mettensium*, MGH *SS* II, pp. 260–8; *Historia Langobardorum*, MGH *SSRL*, pp. 45–187, trans. Foulke (1974); McKitterick (2004), p. 60-83.

25 Dicuil, *Liber de mensura orbis terrae*, ed. Tierney (1967); Dicuil, *Liber de astronomia*, ed. Esposito (1907); Stevens (1997).

26 Borst (1993) and (1998); Bullough, ch. 8 (pp. 136–50) in this volume.

27 Einhard, *VK*, c. 26.

28 Rankin (1994), pp. 292–300.

10

CHARLEMAGNE AND THE RENEWAL OF ROME

Neil Christie

Charlemagne's imperial coronation in Rome, on Christmas Day AD 800, has long been identified as a pivotal moment in the history of the early-medieval West. The details of the background to that event remain obscure, but it is clear that the involvement of the pope provided a crucial dimension to this extension of Carolingian power and authority.[1] Commentators such as Einhard presented the bonds between king and pope as a key factor in the development of Charlemagne's rule; the physical manifestations of these bonds, Einhard said, were the lavish gifts that Charles bestowed on the city of St Peter:

> He loved the church of St Peter the Apostle in Rome more than all the other sacred and venerable places and showered its altars with a great wealth of gold, silver, and even gems. He also sent a vast number of gifts to the popes. During his whole reign he regarded nothing as more important than to restore through his material help and labour the ancient glory of the city of Rome. Not only did he protect and defend the church of St Peter but with his own money he even embellished and enriched it above all other churches.[2]

Charlemagne's conspicuous generosity reflected his political and spiritual aspirations, as 'payment' for honours past and those yet to come, and a genuine piety which aimed to restore greatness to the Church of Rome through the physical renewal of its ecclesiastical buildings. Indeed, such prestige 'gift-giving' is regarded by some as a key stimulus for the Carolingian cultural renaissance that was witnessed in later eighth- and ninth-century Italy and across many parts of the 'new' West.[3] The surviving church fabric and art from Rome in this era is of outstanding quality, not least the mosaics and sculptural elements such as choir- and altar-screens. The extant art and architecture, in addition to contemporary commentators, thus reveal a brilliant phase of material expression in the Carolingian period.

The surviving textual and physical sources raise important questions about the links between Carolingian wealth and the renewal of Rome in the age of Charlemagne. For Rome itself, the sources imply that Charlemagne's personal patronage was significant. But the scale and depth of Carolingian contributions to the material fabric of the city needs close examination, in relation especially to the role of the popes as *de facto* rulers of Rome. The evidence of archaeology provides a vehicle by which to examine these issues and also to evaluate the extent to which Carolingian patronage percolated into the hinterland of Rome and to the towns and monasteries of northern Italy.

Charlemagne and the Lombard kingdom

We have seen elsewhere how Carolingian rule, articulated in no small part by the dynamics of warfare and territorial conquest, produced a society in which scholarly excellence and cultural achievement were highly valued. Charlemagne was able to harness the resources of a vast realm, and provide new wealth and stability in which to formulate and display his aims and desires. Italy was an essential component in this process.[4] Indeed, without the conquest of Lombard northern Italy in 774 and the extension of the Frankish territorial presence to the threshold of Rome, Charlemagne's aspirations might well have been much reduced.[5] As it was, by dint partly of his bonds with the pope in Rome, Charlemagne's personal power and influence extended well beyond his kingdom's physical borders.

It is important to stress that pre-Carolingian Italy was not a politically homogeneous unit and until the 750s there were two dominant secular powers within Italy: the Lombards (who ruled the bulk of the peninsula, with a northern kingdom and two semi-autonomous duchies in central and southern Italy based around Spoleto and Benevento), and the Greek-speaking Byzantine emperors who continued to claim governance of Italy through Ravenna in the north-east. The duchy of Rome formed a vital western bulwark in central Italy to these imperial territories, although the popes and its dukes often displayed unwilling allegiance to Constantinople.[6]

Lombards and Franks had been occasional allies in the seventh and eighth centuries, including a phase of co-operation in the 730s against the Arab threat. The Lombard king Liutprand had then expanded his northern territories, threatening Rome and the Byzantine lands in Italy; papal requests for protection from Byzantium went unheeded, as did calls to Francia. But a fundamental change came when the pope recognised the new Carolingian dynasty in 754; with papal anointing came a new title and a new bond, which made Pippin III 'patrician of the Romans'.[7] By this date, however, the Lombard king, Aistulf, had resumed the campaign to expand his kingdom, and demanded further lands from Rome. In response, Pippin invaded Italy in 754 and again in 756; and, subduing the Lombards, he won considerable prestige for himself.

This strengthened the papal position and temporarily weakened the Lombard threat; but in the early 770s the Lombards tried again under Desiderius to exploit discord in Rome and between the new Frankish rulers, Charles and Carloman. At his mother's insistence, Charles had married Desiderius' daughter in 770, but this bride was soon rejected and returned, dishonoured, to her father.[8] Soon afterwards, in December 771, Carloman died suddenly and Charlemagne rapidly annexed his brother's lands, forcing Carloman's widow and young sons to flee to the protection of Desiderius in Pavia. Thus the alliance that Charlemagne had forged with Desiderius through his marriage to the Lombard princess was comprehensively destroyed, since Desiderius was protecting not just his own daughter who had been rejected by Charlemagne, but also Charlemagne's nephews who had legitimate claims to land and influence in Francia. Prompted by this and by appeals from the pope, Charlemagne invaded the Lombard kingdom in 773. A brief campaign (albeit with longer resistance at Pavia) was won 'mightily', according to Notker the Stammerer, by Charlemagne's 'iron-clad warriors'.[9] But in contrast to earlier Frankish campaigns, Charlemagne's invasion of 773/74 had a dramatically different conclusion, resulting in the conquest and annexation of the Lombard kingdom and in Charlemagne's adoption, imperial-style, of the Lombard royal title.

Numerous dukes and officials duly flocked to pay homage to Charlemagne at the Lombard royal capital of Pavia. However, the new Frankish king of the Lombards did not remain in the region long enough to instil adequate fear or respect among some of these local elite, and rebellion soon flared up in the north-east of his new kingdom. However, this insurrection was short-lived, and swiftly extinguished by Charlemagne's army. Some of the Lombard elite fled south to Benevento and some were taken as hostages, but overt opposition to the Frankish takeover was limited. Accordingly, it is no surprise that many Lombard dukes and bishops remained in their positions, only being replaced piecemeal by Franks; the exception was in those areas which had rebelled and which required a swift introduction of loyal blood in military posts. Charlemagne saw no need for wholesale replacement of personnel. Indeed, it appears that there was no sizeable Frankish physical presence in Lombard territories in the 770s and 780s: the Lombard administrative machinery continued to function, effectively overseen by Frankish *missi*.

A different approach prevailed in central Italy: apart from the extended campaign in 786 to gain verbal submission (and noble hostages) from the Lombard principality of Benevento, Charlemagne largely resisted interfering in territories held or claimed by the pope. Instead he sought to extend influence through the powerful abbeys of Farfa, Montecassino and San Vincenzo al Volturno, confirming their lands and rights, offering them immunities, and providing or recommending abbots and new brethren. Extant sources indicate only partial success for Frankish benefactors since Lombard Benevento continued to be the major patron of both San Vincenzo and Montecassino. Farfa by contrast came within the Carolingian territorial orbit (although the abbots failed to get on well with the Frankish duke). But there is little sign of actual Frankish settlement in the Spoletan duchy until after 800, and – in monetary terms – the gold Lombard *tremissis* was replaced by the silver Carolingian *denarius* in Spoleto only in the last decade of the eighth century.[10]

The *Liber pontificalis* and the renewal of Rome

Our sources, Frankish and papal, project a paradoxical picture of papal autonomy yet papal dependence on Francia. On the one hand, Einhard and other Frankish sources glorify the deeds and piety of Charlemagne, talk of his desire to restore many churches, and make plain the substantial gifts and moneys sent to Rome to help revitalise the Church there. On the other hand, the papal sources play down Charlemagne's material contributions, all the while acknowledging his piety. Our key guide to the papal perspective is the *Liber pontificalis* or Book of the Popes (hereafter *LP*), a continuous series of papal biographies which, in the period examined, were composed contemporaneously with the lives they discuss.[11]

The *LP* is illuminating. The Life of Hadrian, for example, begins with a long narrative discussion (cc. 2–44) on the earliest years of Hadrian's pontificate and the events immediately preceding his election in 772.[12] Charlemagne was acclaimed as 'the God-appointed, kindly Charles the Great, king of the Franks and patrician of the Romans' (c. 37), but was directed and encouraged by the 'angelic and blessed' pope in all his important moves in Italy. The biographer was also at pains to stress how Hadrian entreated Charlemagne to confirm the extensive territories promised to the Rome Church in the 'Donation' of his father Pippin.[13] And yet there is nothing in Hadrian's Life to acknowledge the gifts of gold and silver coin and plate recorded by Einhard; in Hadrian's Life the works and precious items bestowed on the churches and hospices of Rome appear to derive purely from papal coffers.

There is certainly reference to Frankish treasures in the Life of Pope Leo III (795–816), especially following Charlemagne's imperial coronation (cc. 24–5); otherwise we hear of gifts from envoys, or gifts presented following Leo's own visit to the Frankish court in 799 when he was sent back to Rome 'with great honour as was fitting' (c. 18). Clearly this is not a complete picture: Frankish sources and copies of papal letters demonstrate Rome's reliance on Frankish resources, but papal biographers wrote as if papal wealth was independent. An example of this arose in 779. Hadrian's Life (c. 64) records the restoration of the roof of St-Peter's basilica:

> Also in the famous, world-renowned and venerable basilica of St Peter, Prince of the Apostles, as the beams there dated from ancient times, this distinguished pontiff took notice and sent Januarius his *vestiarius* [chamberlain], whom he

knew to be a suitable person, with a crowd of people, and replaced 14 beams there; and he freshly restored that basilica's whole roof and porticoes.[14]

Yet this was not solely a papal project: the *Codex Carolinus* preserves a letter from Hadrian to Charlemagne regarding the supply of timbers for this same project, a request for a master craftsman or *magister* to oversee the selection and cutting of the timbers (undertaken in the Spoleto district, since there was none suitable on Roman soil), and the provision of 200lb of lead.[15]

The truth often lies between the lines of the *LP*. We must infer regular movement between Francia and Rome of goods, people and money. But our problem is establishing the scale of this material input; after all, the timbers just noted were a significant but not substantial item, even if the logistics of cutting, transporting, and fitting them were. Yet, if we consider that in addition to the restoration of the roof of St-Peter's, Hadrian oversaw or laid claim to the restoration of fifty other churches, five monasteries and five *xenodochia* or pilgrim hostels (many of which needed new roofs because of their antiquity) then, cumulatively, Carolingian assistance to the restoration of Rome under Hadrian may have been extensive.

Careful scrutiny of the seventh- to late ninth-century entries in the *LP*, alongside examination of extant structures from the same period, has enabled scholars to chart building programmes and restoration efforts, and thus to assess the scale and nature of the late eighth- and ninth-century 'renewal' in Carolingian Rome, and to determine the source of this work.[16] The *LP* goes into minute details, weighing the generosity, devotion and piety of the various pontiffs by cataloguing carefully the items presented to various churches, their manufacture, and their weight and value. A count of the papal benefactions in the *LP* reveals 5,232 textiles (4,400 of which were silk), 4,480.4 lbs of gold and 45,867.51 lbs of silver.[17] Charlemagne's popes, Hadrian and Leo, donated 68 per cent of the gold recorded in the *LP* in this period; 48 per cent of the silver was given by Leo alone. In terms of building works, these two popes account for 56 per cent of the total number of projects recorded in the *LP* (147 out of 263) – and in practice they concerned themselves with some of the larger basilicas which, materially, were the most expensive.

Although literary references are rather crude data for assessing the scale of work, dependent as they are on the honesty and records of the biographers, we can nevertheless identify the ebb and flow of papal output in building, restoration and redecoration programmes. Delogu's analysis of this material suggests that a limited programme of work was pursued in the pre-Carolingian period from the seventh to the mid-eighth centuries, focusing on the restorations necessary to maintain at least some of the very numerous ancient churches of Rome. The city's population level was then perhaps as low as 50,000 inhabitants, and Church income was likewise restricted.[18] There was, in effect, little capacity for extensive display.

Population growth may be implied by the creation of new *diaconiae* ('deaconries') within Rome, linked perhaps to the improved productivity of papal lands and resources.[19] Indeed, in the 740s, Pope Zacharias had instigated a reorganisation of papal lands (primarily to the south of Rome), at a time before Frankish intervention and support.[20] We know little of the actual structures involved, but the texts at least confirm an ability to re-deploy lands. This created new workforces that were tied to the Church; we see these *militiae* again much later in the mid-ninth century assisting in the construction of the Leonine walls in Rome (AD 846).[21] A review of the evidence of the extant and lost churches of Rome between the seventh and tenth centuries has stressed that the traditional, rather bleak view of the Roman townscape for the period *c.*AD 650–775 is an inaccurate one. A significant phase of building and decoration is witnessed from the 730s – or rather *testified*, since structural survivals are much fewer than for the 'Carolingian' phase after 775. Even if this activity was small in scale, nonetheless it was more than the simple conversion of secular structures into churches. These efforts were papal-directed and they denoted, in part, a reaction against and release from the Byzantine east and its ban on figural representations in art (Iconoclasm).[22]

In the later eighth century, there was dramatic change to this pattern of building and restoration. Under Hadrian I there are references to a major series of (re)building and decorative campaigns: church, cemetery and monastery restoration, new or extended hostels and *diaconiae*, plus gifts and furnishings aplenty.[23] Intensive work continued well into the ninth century, with frequent mentions of repairs, rebuilding and new furnishings. Some of the interiors are specially notable for their major artistic programmes, as represented by the surviving apse and chapel mosaics of San Prassede, San Marco, and Santa Maria in Dominica. These mosaics are often resplendent for their use of gold leaf; they also often feature the figure of the dedicant pope, proudly displaying the model of the restored/new church and a square halo or nimbus to denote that he was still living to appreciate his work programme, and demonstrating his piety to the assembled audience by placing his own image (and often the papal monogram, or signature) alongside images of saints, the Virgin Mary or the Saviour himself.[24]

Such works projected papal power and pride; and provided employment, wages and confidence to the populus. One might even speculate a significant boost to the numbers of the urban flock. Certainly, papal provision of deaconries and food distribution centres, and the influx of pilgrims (some of status), are further indication of the increasing importance of the city as a Christian focus. Schieffer has argued that the creation of the hostel-hospice of the *schola Francorum* alongside the pre-existing Frisian, (Anglo-)Saxon and Lombard *scholae* was at Charlemagne's behest and reflected increased numbers of Franks visiting Rome.[25] The substantial ninth- and tenth-century hoards of Anglo-Saxon coins from Rome may similarly be linked to a much enlarged population of permanent residents and pilgrim visitors.[26] Notable here is the recognition of archaeological strata preserving domestic housing, dating from the later eighth century to the tenth century, in the central Forum zone and probably also in the Torre Argentina area of Rome. Although these buildings are not particularly opulent (they are two-storey structures with space for animals on the ground floor, built from the *spolia* of older classical-era buildings), they demonstrate a notable investment in private buildings in this period and are in striking contrast to the dearth of archaeological evidence for domestic housing in the period AD 550–800 elsewhere in the city. These 'Carolingian' buildings are a much-needed reminder that an apparent absence of evidence can be deceptive.[27]

The peak of documented work on churches and related structures in Rome coincides with the main periods of Carolingian influence during the pontificates of Hadrian I (772–95), Leo III (795–816) and (on paper at least) under Paschal I (817–24), before diminishing in the mid-ninth century alongside the dissipation of Carolingian unity during the 830s and 840s and the growing, twin threats of Viking attacks in the north and of Arab raids on the Italian coasts. In this later context we can observe a switch in papal resources to the repair of walls, and the creation of new defences, and even the building of new towns (Vatican City, Ostia, Centumcellae) which, as Noble has suggested, formed a special method of 'reassuring local populations that the papacy was still a functioning presence in Rome's *territorium*'.[28]

The chronological coincidence of the period of rebuilding and patronage in Rome, as seen in the *LP* and in the extant structures, and the zenith of Carolingian power in the later eighth and earlier ninth centuries seems to match a corresponding decline in both during the middle decades of the ninth century. But Pope Paschal's cool relationship with the Frankish emperor suggests that his largess stemmed from resources somewhat different from the patronage of Hadrian and Leo.

The main impact of Charlemagne's military conquests in Italy had been the removal of the Lombard threat in northern and central Italy, although the Lombard duchy of Benevento to the south of Rome remained independent and an irritant to Carolingian overlords. The Frankish conquest released Rome from sizeable military expenditure, and in the medium term created an environment for more secure papal patrimonies and even the extension of papal lands. A bigger agricultural base – with increased scope for generating income – is thus key to understanding enhanced papal wealth in the Carolingian era.

The evidence of both text and archaeology shows early signs of this new confidence.[29] The *LP* records Pope Hadrian's foundation of a set of six *domuscultae* – papal estates – around Rome, reminiscent of Pope Zacharias's reorganisation of papal lands earlier in the eighth century. Most prominent of these was Capracorum, 15 miles north of the City; its core was a family estate with various farms, and Hadrian expanded its lands 'by fair purchase'. The *domuscultae* collected and passed on produce from their lands for distribution to the poor of Rome and the Rome Church. A central church was constructed at *Capracorum* and dedicated in 780 and endowed with holy relics and the remains of no less than four pope-saints. The site became, instantly, a pilgrimage- and production-centre in one. Its open, undefended location suggests a general sense of security, its acquisition of land speaks of papal investment and its output tells of papal wealth. Yet excavations at Capracorum indicate that this was a relatively small building, typical of the contemporary city: the new, early medieval churches were generally much smaller than the older, bigger, early Christian models which, as the popes had long since found out, cost a fortune to maintain. Small buildings could be both beautiful and more manageable.[30]

Capracorum housed honoured relics; the *LP* reveals plainly (as do various Frankish texts) the attraction of such relics to the growing numbers of pilgrims and foreign visitors resident in the *scholae*, and the central role of the popes in promoting the cult of saints.[31] The close links with Francia had seen the export of numerous relics from Rome; but the search for more autonomy made the popes cling more tightly to the remaining relics – hence under Hadrian the outward flow was halted, while under Paschal I a vast mass of holy corpses was brought inside the walls from the extra-mural cemeteries and catacombs so that they could be better guarded (and exploited for the benefit of the Church within Rome).[32] According to an inscription copied into the *LP*, Paschal claimed to have translated no less than 2,300 holy relics/bodies of which 86 are named.[33]

It is impossible now to assess the scale of the income that pilgrimage and relic veneration generated; pilgrim tokens, badges, guides and gifts all translated into resources for the Church, but quite how it was gathered, stored and spent is not clear – remembering, of course, that much of it needed to be ploughed back into feeding and aiding the poor and pilgrims alike. But, as a result of the growth of the pilgrimage and relic 'industry', Paschal (and perhaps also Hadrian) did not need to depend entirely on Francia to fund ambitious building projects. The stimulus and the 'pump-priming' funds for all this *may* have come from Charlemagne, but circumstances subsequently permitted the popes a freer rein. Indeed, there is little tangibly 'Frankish' in Rome's ecclesiastical architecture bar the presence of a gate tower at SS. Quattro Coronati dating to about 845. However, ecclesiastical display and urban regeneration declined from the 840s, not because of any diminished input by Frankish rulers but rather because of the increased pressure on Rome's landed income through Arab incursions and the diversion of funds to defensive buildings (including new towns). The export of relics to Francia resumed in the period from the 820s to the 860s partly as a result of the comparative weakness of the papacy caused by these external pressures and internal political struggles.[34]

Beyond Rome: the Lombard north

Rome was not typical of all Italy, however, and although Charlemagne worked with Rome, he was not its master. Yet he had been directly responsible for the conquest and reorganisation of the Lombard kingdom of northern and central Italy, and presumably we should see at least some significant Frankish mark in these regions, given that this was an integral part of the empire. As noted above, the earliest Frankish phases in Lombard Italy were not destructive or divisive; compliant Lombards were not ousted from positions of authority, and Lombard bishops remained predominant in the ecclesiastical hierarchy. Indeed, under the Carolingian regime, Lombard bishops swiftly acquired much greater local prominence than they had enjoyed within the preceding administration. Military control was more firmly Frankish – similar to the pattern of Ostrogothic control three centuries earlier – as Lombard dukes were replaced by counts loyal to the Franks.[35]

A steady number of capitularies show Carolingian *missi* at work in Lombard territory and, in the Po valley, there is evidence for a relatively swift transition to Carolingian silver coinage (enforced at Pavia from August 781).[36] But the presence of Frankish personnel seems to have been minimal, a sign perhaps of a generally peaceful transfer in governance. Certainly Lombard hostages had been taken in the immediate aftermath of the conquest and others had been exiled. Some Lombard nobles had fled south to Benevento, but in doing so they left little scope for concerted resistance in the north where the absence of anti-Carolingian rebel leaders was underpinned by the knowledge that a powerful campaigning army could swiftly be summoned from across the Alps. Only in the 830s with Lothar's exile to Italy do we in fact see significant Frankish immigration into the north of Italy, in this case by displaced pro-Lothar Frankish nobility.

Although the volume of evidence is not great, archaeology, architecture and text again combine to reveal the Carolingian impact on a variety of northern Italian towns. Brescia, in the central sub-Alpine area, is a valuable guide. Having been a relatively ordinary Roman town, from the late sixth century it became the seat of a Lombard duke and, in the mid-eighth century, gained prominence through the patronage of the last Lombard king, Desiderius.[37] Most importantly, Brescia has been the subject of extensive, systematic and well published excavations between 1980 and 1992 in the eastern Santa Giulia district, revealing a fascinating sequence – more or less typical for north Italy. Primary in the building sequence was a fine Roman *domus* or town house, which underwent serious change in the fourth to fifth centuries when floors and mosaics were covered (or cut by postholes) and rooms partitioned. These structural changes signify a technological and material downturn, perhaps even denoting the billeting of soldiers. Extensive destruction levels across much of the city characterise the mid-sixth century layers and coincide with the Gothic-Byzantine war period. Occupation resumed only in the early seventh century, but with buildings timber-built, part sunken or partly reusing destroyed Roman buildings. The inhabitants of these buildings buried their dead close by; palaeo-pathological analysis indicates poor diets and significant levels of anaemia.[38]

Only in the second half of the seventh century do we see an upturn in the fortunes of the city with the construction of a church, reusing Roman materials, the first phase of the later San Salvatore. This building was maintained until the mid-eighth century, when it was replaced by a ducal monastery on royal land; traces survive of this second church, its frescoes and sculpture and of the attached monastic quarters. There is evidence in this phase for the creation of a system of piped water, the building of baths, churches and a palace complex, and the renovation of the town walls – in other words it was a town that was actively growing, with buildings on a monumental scale.[39] In contrast, the Carolingian takeover in the latter part of the eighth century is not demonstrable archaeologically. Documents in fact record new buildings only under the Frankish Bishop Rampert in the 830s – coincidental with the increase in Frankish numbers in north Italy under Lothar.[40] Tradition and street names attest suburban growth around Rampert's monastery of San Faustino, itself preserving scant traces of ninth-century build.

A similar picture emerges in other towns. At the old Lombard capital of Pavia, the foundation and renovation of church and monastic structures is apparent between the mid-seventh and mid-eighth century, denoting sizeable royal and episcopal patronage.[41] Sculptural and epigraphic survivals testify to high levels of technical skill, particularly during the reign of King Liutprand (712–44). Contemporary data from elsewhere in the Lombard north support this evidence for a substantial cultural revival, well before the renewal of Roman vitality under Pope Zacharias. Mitchell in fact claims that 'the artistic patronage of the Lombard courts and the Lombard elite in the century before the Carolingian annexation of northern Italy in 773/74 was one of the most sophisticated, ambitious, and refined in Europe'.[42] Further indication of this Lombard urban renewal might be the praise poem, the *Versus de Mediolano civitate*, dated *c.*AD 740, which recounts the ancient wonders of Milan, but with a main emphasis on its Christian edifices. Following the same vein of Lombard urban pride are the *Versus* for Verona, composed in the 'Carolingian' period towards the end of the eighth century.[43]

Two other northern Lombard centres with significant archaeological evidence from this period are Lucca and Cividale. Lucca, which contains an amphitheatre preserved through its colonisation by housing, offers a rich body of private charters for the eighth and ninth centuries which demonstrate the levels of local, aristocratic, episcopal and royal input within the townscape. A spate of monastic and *xenodochia* foundations in the town coincides, significantly, with the reign of Liutprand, followed by a further group of foundations in the 760s. After the Carolingian takeover, we wait until the 780s and 790s for new works (including crypt-building in the cathedral and at San Frediano). Subsequently, in the period 810–20, a final set of restorations and new structures is documented, linked largely to Bishop James. Noticeably, most of the Carolingian-period works are episcopal.[44]

Cividale, by contrast, has a wealth of archaeology, including tombs and finds of the later sixth and seventh centuries, plus church sculpture and art of the period c.AD 730–800.[45] Some of the key works, notably the exquisite Tempietto of Santa Maria in Valle, have been focal points in art-historical debates concerning chronology – whether masterpieces of this type are late Lombard or Carolingian in date and influence. But a wider understanding of Lombard court art and architecture from centres such as Pavia and Benevento has encouraged acceptance of a secure Lombard context for the creation of the Tempietto. Founded as part of a monastery attached to the royal gastald's palace, it conforms to Lombard notions of the display of power and investment. Artistic remains from the cathedral (such as the baptistery of Callixtus) and other churches further attest this aesthetic programme. As yet we have too little contemporary secular evidence for this important ducal capital (bar the high-status intramural burials), but documents and partial architectural survivals combine at least to pinpoint the early eighth-century palaces of the patriarch and gastald.

Finally, we should mention Ravenna. This had been the late Roman imperial seat, maintained by the Ostrogoths and thereafter by the Byzantine governor-general / exarch. Ravenna and its rulers always had a prickly relationship with Rome and the popes, exacerbated by the prominence attained by its archbishop under Byzantine rule; this rivalry persisted even after Byzantine control was lost in 751 with the (short-lived) Lombard takeover. Ravenna has justly famous fifth- and sixth-century architectural and artistic survivals; yet there is precious little to show renewal here in the eighth century. The archbishops of Ravenna were keen for recognition from the Frankish king, who sent *missi* to oversee elections. Charlemagne himself made few visits, but did not ignore the city, regarding it as a key source of architectural inspiration for his own building projects in Francia. Most prominently, he asked permission from Pope Hadrian to take away prized marbles and mosaics and other works from the palaces there (and from Rome, though the implication is that Ravenna was exploited most).[46] Charlemagne recognised the significance of the Ravennate Church and ordered in his will that it be included in the distribution of alms after his death to be shared with 19 other metropolitans across the Empire.[47] Interestingly, Charlemagne also bequeathed specific gifts to the bishops of Rome and Ravenna, namely fine tables: that to the pope featured an engraved image of Constantinople; that to Ravenna incorporated a map of Rome. How should these gifts be interpreted? Was the table for Ravenna a subtle indication of Charlemagne's favoured see? Brown instead sees it 'as an ironic reflection of Charles' exasperation at being called upon to decide between the claims of squabbling ecclesiastics'.[48]

The glory of Ravenna, however, was in the past. This city contrasts with the general revitalisation and evidence of new activity in both town and country (the latter expressed chiefly through monasteries) well under way in the Lombard north in the first decades of the eighth century, and even at the end of the seventh. This renewal was prompted by various factors: a general treaty of peace with Byzantium in Italy; economic and political stability; full Christianisation of the Lombards; and a desired demonstration of authority, as witnessed in the increased production of Lombard coinage. It is indicated by the proliferation of legal texts and private charters which show, for example, increased levels of property transactions. Lombard Italy was then much stronger than Byzantine Italy, which looked in vain for assistance and attention from the eastern Mediterranean; Rome and Byzantium still faced the Mediterranean and the Arabs, whereas the Lombards could look to a more interactive north and west. The 'renaissances' under Liutprand and Aistulf denote expressions of strength, stability and identity, inspired by Roman, Frankish, Byzantine and Lombard cultural legacies.

Thus, when Charlemagne took over the Lombard north, he acquired a kingdom with considerable cultural vitality in terms of building, art and learning; some of its contributors fled south to Benevento, but Charlemagne was able to harness much of what was left (in terms of scholars, artists, architects and their designs).[49] Some monuments *may* belong to the transition phase, such as the Tempietto at Cividale, but Frankish artisans and patrons do not need to be put into the equation here: rather, this was a persistence of local Italo-Lombard culture. Carolingian rule made no major physical impact in the north of Italy, though bishops began to take a more prominent role, if at the expense of wider civic input. The most significant cultural impact of the Carolingian conquest of the Lombards should rather be sought in Francia itself, where Lombard scholars, such as Peter of Pisa and Paul the Deacon, added significantly to the cultural vibrancy of the Carolingian court.

Conclusion

Charlemagne's renaissance did not embrace all of Italy. Despite his conquest of the Lombard kingdom, Charlemagne's interests predominantly lay with the papal city and, to a degree, also with the independent monasteries of central Italy. Why so? As we have seen, Charlemagne sought recognition from the popes and inspiration from the Roman past, and his promotion of cultural and religious renewal were key ingredients in this. In the case of Rome, he undoubtedly gave funding and gifts aplenty (not just on his four visits to Rome), and these fed into the papal treasury. Schieffer argues that Charlemagne sought to secure a Frankish presence (a palace, a hospice for Frankish pilgrims) near St-Peter's, but he was careful not to intrude physically beyond this sphere.[50]

Hadrian must consciously have been guided by Charlemagne's wishes – no doubt largely matching his own – for the restoration of the ecclesiastical heritage of Rome, both spiritual and physical. Einhard stresses that Charlemagne desired above all that St-Peter's 'be more richly adorned and endowed than any other church' – and so, accordingly, many of the resources were thus directed. But many other churches were also essential components of papal Rome, and their maintenance and restoration could not be neglected. We should perhaps not expect Charlemagne to have directed the distribution of his moneys and gifts, but Hadrian's distribution of chalices, candelabra, patens, altar cloths, silk hangings and so on were advertised to the king via correspondence and the *LP* (which circulated extensively in Francia). Such items and the large-scale restoration projects must have consumed vast resources. The problem is, as noted, that our Roman sources are not explicit on funding sources: the contribution of Charlemagne and later Frankish rulers is ignored, at least in the context of buildings, and so we cannot be certain what funds and gifts flowed into Rome. Perhaps this wealth, once in Church hands, was no longer deemed 'Frankish' – hence the *LP* omits mention of Charlemagne as its source – and so Hadrian, as later Leo III, had a relatively 'free hand' to dispose of this booty.

On the one hand we could view Charlemagne as the great 'provider', whose prestige and authority were enhanced through piety and generous financial backing of restoration works to the city's ecclesiastical heritage. These acts also would have portrayed him as a good emperor, pious and strong like Constantine long before him, or benevolent like the Ostrogothic king, Theoderic, who in the early sixth century courted popularity and sought to be 'imperial' and 'Roman'.[51] On the other hand, Charlemagne can be seen as a 'facilitator' for papal ambition: as Noble has argued, the popes had, since the earlier eighth century, begun to mould their own dominant ideology in art and architecture; Charlemagne freed them from powerful external threats and gave opportunity for greater expression. Charlemagne was strong and he may have in part led this expression, but after him the popes seem to have been largely able to choose their own direction.

Charlemagne did much to increase pilgrim traffic to the City: Frankish bishops, Anglo-Saxon abbots, Frisian monks, as well as laymen and women, all came to venerate the holy martyrs, to search for relics and sometimes to die 'at the threshold of the apostles'. Major works of urban renewal were undertaken to accommodate these visitors – improved roads, new welfare centres and deaconries, better water supply, renovated accesses to the catacomb churches and then, later, a careful translation of relics inside the town walls to improve their display and protection, but also to better direct and exploit the pilgrims who came to view them.[52] The pilgrim traffic, the peace created by Frankish expansion into Italy, the new security of papal lands and the stimulation of better trade markets all contributed to an increased income for the Church. This in turn provided increased prestige and power for the popes – reflected by the mid-ninth century in more substantial palaces and lodgings, and their creation of defended towns or suburbs bearing their own names: Gregoriopolis, Leopolis.[53] Rome then indeed became 'a papal city'.[54]

The art and architecture of ninth-century Rome certainly belonged, in part, to a wider 'renaissance' that was nurtured by Charlemagne's cultural ambitions. But, as we have seen, Rome was already showing signs of urban upturn; Charlemagne helped facilitate a more splendid renewal both through material input and by creating conditions of increased political stability conducive to the creation of wealth and cultural expression. The Lombard kings and dukes had already sponsored a revitalisation in both the north and the south from the early eighth century, with a renewal of the urban fabric, the building of churches and the reorganisation of land holdings through monastic foundations. As Mitchell has argued, we should be seeking to recognise far more the ways in which Lombard cultural strategies and influences impacted on Rome and, most particularly, on Charlemagne.[55]

The wealth and architectural display exhibited in the Lombard palaces and monasteries were, most probably, far more developed than in Francia, and Charlemagne seems to have wished to transplant various of these Lombard ideas beyond the Alps. Arguably, Charlemagne deflated this northern boom through conquest of the Lombard kingdom; but one might equally claim that centres like Brescia, Cividale and Pavia simply continued their strong cultural trajectories, needing no encouragement from Charlemagne. But his contribution to the revitalisation of Rome was the stronger, and there he helped to embellish an influential ally. The popes benefited fully, during his reign, and the Carolingian alliance contributed to the restoration and redirection of Rome's early Christian heritage; it also laid the foundations for a more expansive Renaissance in the eleventh and twelfth centuries, characterised by bigger churches, bigger mosaics and even bigger papal ambitions.

Notes

1 Collins (1998b), pp. 141–59, and ch. 4 (pp. 52–70) in this volume; McKitterick (2000).

2 Einhard, *VK*, c. 27; trans. Dutton (1998), p. 33.

3 For example, Conant (1979), pp. 31–2.

4 Delogu (1995) and (2000); Noble (1995) and (2000); Schieffer (2000); Smith (2000).

5 On Paul the Deacon, see McKitterick (1999) and McKitterick (2004), pp. 60–83.

6 Christie (1995), pp. 73–108; Wickham (1981), pp. 28–47; Collins (1998b) pp. 58–64; Gasparri (2000); Zanini (1998).

7 *LP*, 'Life of Stephen II', cc. 27–30; trans. Davis (1995), pp. 64–5; Noble (1984), pp. 87, 277–91; McKitterick (2000).

8 Nelson (1998); Noble (1984), pp. 122–9.

9 Notker, *Gesta Karoli*, c. 16.

10 West (1999); Day (1997); Balzaretti (1999); Hodges, ed. (1995), pp. 153–75 on the input of the Beneventan court.

11 *LP*, ed. Duchesne (1886–92); trans. Davis (1989), (1992) and (1995).

12 *LP*, 'Life of Hadrian', cc. 2–44; trans. Davis (1992), pp. 107–72.
13 *LP*, 'Life of Hadrian', cc. 26, 41–3; trans. Davis (1992), pp. 108–11, 134–5, 140–2; Noble (1984), pp. 138–83.
14 *LP*, 'Life of Hadrian', c. 64; trans. Davis (1992), p. 155.
15 *CC*, no. 65; Noble (2000).
16 Delogu (1988).
17 Noble (2001). On textiles, see Delogu (1998) and Noble (2000), both discerning busy trade and patronage systems.
18 Gatto (1998); lower figures of 40,000 and only 5,000 were suggested, respectively, by Krautheimer (1980), pp. 291–2 and Hodges (2000), pp. 55–6.
19 Marazzi (1993), pp. 278–81. Lombard territorial expansion had required rethinking of the food supply to Rome: Noble (2000) and Llewellyn (1993), pp. 137–40, 199–207.
20 Marazzi (1993).
21 Gibson and Ward-Perkins (1983), p. 237.
22 Coates-Stephens (1997). High-quality frescoes in S. Maria Antiqua reveal the ability of eighth-century artists: Romanelli and Nordhagen (1964); Osborne (1987).
23 Spera (1997), p. 237.
24 Noble (2001).
25 Bianchi (2000); Schieffer (2000), pp. 291–3; Spera (1997).
26 Rovelli (2000a), p. 97.
27 Santangeli Valenzani (2000).
28 Gibson and Ward-Perkins (1983); Nardi (1992); Paroli (1993).
29 Christie, ed. (1991).
30 On the fine foundation-period marble and its Lombard influences, see Paroli (1998), pp. 93–122.
31 Bianchi (2000).
32 Smith (2000); Geary (1990); Caroli (2000), pp. 259–74.
33 *LP*, 'Life of Paschal', c. 9; trans. Davis (1995), pp. 10–11.
34 Smith (2000), pp. 323–4.
35 On social changes in northern Italy in this period see Gasparri (2000).
36 Day (1997), p. 27.
37 Brogiolo (1989) and (1993); Brogiolo, ed. (1999); Bertelli and Brogiolo, eds. (2000).
38 Brogiolo (1993), pp. 90–6.
39 *Ibid.*, pp. 97–110.
40 *Ibid.*, pp. 111–13.
41 Hudson (1981), pp. 24–9, 62–5; Blake, ed. (1995); Mitchell (1999), pp. 95–108.
42 Mitchell (2000a) and (2000b).
43 Hyde (1966), pp. 311–15; Ward-Perkins (1984), pp. 224–8.
44 *Ibid.*, pp. 245–9.
45 Christie (1995), pp. 144–61; Brogiolo (2001); Jäggi (2001); Mitchell (2000a), pp. 350–1; Cantino Wataghin (2000, 2001).
46 Einhard, *VK*, c. 26; *CC*, no. 92; Peacock (1997).
47 Einhard, *VK*, c. 33.
48 Brown (1990).
49 Mitchell (2000b), pp. 176, 179–80, briefly reviews the Lombard south, again stressing a vibrant eighth-century court culture.
50 Schieffer (2000), pp. 293–4.
51 Christie and Kipling (2000), pp. 30–2.

52 For example, *LP*, 'Life of Hadrian', cc. 72, 79–81; trans. Davis (1992), pp. 159–70, 164–6; 'Life of Paschal', c. 9; trans. Davis (1995), pp. 10–11. See also Milella (2000); Romana Strassola (2000); Nelson (2000a). Crypt-building was part of this process.
53 For example, *LP*, 'Life of Gregory IV', cc. 38–42; trans. Davies (1995), pp. 67–9.
54 Noble (2001).
55 Mitchell (2000b), pp. 182–3.

11

CHARLEMAGNE
AND THE WORLD
BEYOND THE RHINE

*Timothy Reuter**

For the Carolingians, the Rhine was a significant boundary.[1] Except when campaigning, neither Pippin III nor Charlemagne, nor Louis the Pious spent much time beyond it. There were royal resources which enabled them to extend their normal itinerary east of the Rhine, but these were not normally used in this way except for campaigning, either to subdue 'German' regions such as Saxony or Bavaria, or to carry out plundering and retaliatory raiding against Slavs, Avars and Northmen.[2] The major eastern palaces and assembly-points lay either west of the Rhine, like Ingelheim, or (more or less) on it, like Frankfurt. Palaces like Regensburg and Paderborn were visited on occasions, and were something more than mere assembly-points for armies, but such occasions remained occasional.

The Rhine in effect marked the eastern limits of the Frankish heartland. What lay beyond it occupied much of the Frankish rulers' attention, but it was not, even from a Frankish perspective, a homogeneous region, and the attention it received was very varied. We can divide it up into four regions, defined largely in ethnic terms. Immediately east of the Rhine lay a number of German *gentes* ('peoples') that had long been subject to Frankish hegemony, though the campaigns by Charles Martel, Pippin and Charlemagne brought them fully within the Frankish fold (or in some cases back within the Frankish fold). To the north of these *gentes* were the Northmen, only really emerging fully into view towards the end of Charlemagne's reign; to the east and south-east were a number of Slav *gentes*; beyond the Slavs in the south-east lay the Avar empire. As we shall see, there is more to be said about the world immediately beyond the Rhine than there is about these more distant worlds, but it is nevertheless convenient to begin with the latter.

The Northman and the Avars

The Northmen do not seem to have featured in Frankish consciousness until the late eighth century. Ambassadors of the Northmen appeared at a Frankish assembly in 782, and it has been conjectured that these contacts had something to do with support from the Northmen for Saxon resistance.[3] But real contact did not begin until after the peace of Selz in 803 and the resettlement of Saxony beyond the Elbe in the years which followed. By 808 at the latest border conflicts were apparent, and in 810 Charlemagne had to mobilise a substantial army against the threat of an invasion by the Danish king, Gottfried.[4] The immediate threat was lifted by Gottfried's murder in the same year, following which the Franks pursued a Byzantine-style policy of supporting rival claimants to the Danish throne; their success in doing this contributed, paradoxically, to the growth of Viking raiding parties in the ninth century, many of them led by permanently or temporarily dispossessed members of the Danish royal house. Though Frankish sources present the issue as one of Danish aggression, the Danes clearly felt insecure against the Franks (or possibly the Saxons) as well, since the great earthwork known as the *Danewerk* appears to have been erected across the bottom of the Danish peninsula in the course of the eighth century, with more work done on it in 808, according to the Royal Frankish Annals.[5]

The Avars had also not figured greatly in Frankish consciousness before Charlemagne's time, at least not for many years. The Avars were a nomadic people who had come into existence in the course of the fifth and sixth centuries.[6] Their empire, ruled jointly by a priestly high king and a more secular warrior figure, was based on tribute-taking; mainly and most continuously from the Slav peoples of eastern Europe, but initially also from the Byzantine empire, and on occasions in the sixth and seventh centuries from Franks, Bavarians and Lombards too. It was the absorption of the Lombard kingdom into the Frankish realms and the defeat of the Agilolfing duke Tassilo III of Bavaria that brought the Franks up against the Avars. Tassilo had appealed to the Avars for assistance in his final struggle against Frankish domination in 787–88, or at least the Franks claimed that he had done so.[7] Certainly Charles's lengthy stay in Bavaria to establish the post-Agilolfing settlement was followed by first negotiating with and then campaigning against the Avars. The largest campaign was that of 791, in which three separate armies were directed against the Avars; but it was the campaigns of 795 and 796 which destroyed the Avar kingdom. The *hring*, a fortified centre which held the accumulated royal treasure, was captured and cartloads of moveable wealth (mostly gold and silver) were brought back to Francia and distributed as largesse amongst churches, military followers and neighbouring rulers.[8]

There was further campaigning (with occasional casualties) in the next ten years, but by the end of Charlemagne's reign the Avars had more or less ceased to exist as a people – the name survived to be used erroneously for the Magyars in the late ninth and tenth centuries, but the destruction of the Avar political leadership led to a process of ethnic disintegration. As the Russian *Tale of Bygone Years* put it three centuries later: 'they vanished away like the Avars', a form of ethnogenesis in reverse which left no more than a proverb behind; the biological descendants of the Avars were presumably absorbed into local Slav, Magyar and Bulgarian populations. The immediate consequence of this was the emergence of new predatory empires in the Balkans: the Bulgarians (a threat and a problem to the Byzantine empire, but to the Franks the object of only very intermittent diplomatic contacts and attempts at mission), the Moravians (not clearly visible until two generations after Charlemagne's death) and, from the end of the ninth century, the Magyars.[9]

The Slavs

Northmen and Avars were – by the standards of 800 – polities of some substance, with central leaders capable of mustering considerable forces. Along the eastern frontiers of direct Frankish rule, between the Northmen and the Avars, lay in Charlemagne's time a whole number of Slav ethnic groupings, descendants of peoples who had moved into east central Europe between the fifth and seventh centuries. Frankish narrative sources make intermittent references to these, and we have more detailed information from sources like the mid-ninth-century 'Bavarian Geographer' or the late-ninth-century *Conversion of the Bavarians and Carinthians*.[10] It is not easy, and indeed probably not entirely feasible, to make coherent sense of these references. The ethnic groupings mentioned in the narrative sources cannot easily or fully be made to correspond with the archaeological evidence. Partly this is because of the well-known general problem that areas of common material culture do not necessarily correspond with areas of common ethnic consciousness. Partly it is because the writers were writing for their own audiences and not for us; sometimes they were probably not very well-informed themselves, but did not feel that they needed to be, while sometimes they were probably so well-informed that they did not bother to spell out things which were clear to them but cannot now be deduced.

We are easily tempted to see in each named reference to an ethnic grouping a delineation of a separate 'people'; but some at least of the names we find in late-eighth- and ninth-century sources are not of this type. 'Wends' and 'Slavs' are generic names without ethnic specificity; other names, as for example the *Lanai* and *Bethanzr* mentioned by the Moissac Chronicle in its report for 811, are almost certainly references to sub-groupings within larger ethnicities.[11] In Charlemagne's time we can make out the following major groupings running along the frontier from north-west to south-east: Abodrites, Sorbs (often called 'Wends', though as noted above this can be a more generic term), Bohemians (mentioned in 805–6, but not clearly visible as a significant group until the time of Louis the German) and Carinthians, separated from the others until the end of the eighth century by the western outposts of Avar domination.

Of these groupings, the most important for the Franks were the Abodrites and Carinthians. The Abodrites, who – unlike some Slav ethnic groupings – had a royal/ducal house not unlike those found in Bavaria and, earlier, in Alemannia, were often though not invariably allies of the Franks against both Saxons and, later, Danes, being referred to as 'our Slavs' by the Lorsch Annals in 798.[12] The Carinthians had already been the object of both conquest and mission by the Bavarians in the period before 788. Alone among the Slav frontier peoples, they were coming to be fully absorbed within the Frankish empire by the time of Charlemagne's death. Other peoples remained in a state of tributary subjection to Frankish hegemony, punctuated by occasional rent-strikes and uprisings. The Franks raided them, partly to quell them, partly for slave-taking (though the word slave and its cognates in other west European languages, etymologically related to 'Slav', had not yet replaced the classical *servus*). They also traded with them, though they were careful to try to prevent the export of military technology to the Slavs beyond the eastern frontier, not always successfully. The capitulary of Thionville/Diedenhofen in 806 specifically forbade the export of swords and mail-shirts (byrnies) to the Slavs, and established customs-posts along the frontier in order to put this prohibition into force.[13]

In Charlemagne's time, neither Northmen nor Slavs, nor Avars, were central to Frankish consciousness. They were not yet the objects of Christian mission: the limited ninth-century efforts at converting the Northmen did not begin until well after Charlemagne's death, while missionary work among the Slavs began even later, in the 840s and 850s but without Carolingian involvement. There were some limited attempts at conversion of the Avars following the defeats of the 790s, but the ethnic disintegration prevented any serious conversion: the top-down methods characteristic of early medieval mission required a top to work down from.[14] Missionary work, even had it been undertaken, would necessarily have been limited in scope. (As we shall see, the introduction and consolidation of Christianity within the 'Germanic' regions immediately east of the Rhine over-stretched the resources of the Frankish church as it was.) Conquest of these more distant regions was also not envisaged. These were regions which presented a threat to the core area of Frankish hegemony, a threat which was to be contained by very traditional methods: punitive raiding; controlled trade; and diplomacy, including the harbouring of pretenders and the fostering of potential successors in regions where there was a sufficiently monarchic constitution, as with the Danes, Abodrites and Avars. Acceptance of the Frankish mission statement and business plan was not required.

The eastern borderlands

It is the nature of the Frankish response, above all, which distinguishes the regions beyond the eastern frontier from the regions immediately beyond the Rhine. In areas just east of the Rhine, the Frankish rulers were dealing with a number of ethnic groupings which had long been under Frankish hegemony and whose elites were often linked by marriage and common descent both with each other and with the Frankish elite (that 'imperial aristocracy' first identified by the 'Freiburg School' – Gerd Tellenbach and his pupils – of German medieval historians).[15] There were five of these ethnic groupings. To the north of the limits of early eighth-century direct Frankish rule lay the Saxons and the Frisians; to the south lay the duchies of Bavaria and Alemannia (with associated territories in Carinthia and Rhaetia respectively); to the east lay an area of mixed settlement – partly Frankish, partly smaller, separate ethnic groupings including the Hessians and the Thuringians. By the end of Charlemagne's reign all these regions were fully part of the broader Frankish empire, both politically and ecclesiastically, and a good deal of Frankish effort in the period 768–814 had been devoted to making this so.

The Frisians had been ostensibly conquered by the Franks in campaigns in 695, 719 and 734 (though the parts bordering the Saxons were probably not finally subjugated until the Saxon campaigns of the 790s), and in the eighth century they were the objects of missionary activity directed from the newly-established bishopric at Utrecht.[16] They do not figure greatly in Frankish sources in Charlemagne's time, cropping up occasionally as allies both of the Saxons and of the Franks in Charlemagne's campaigns. The written codification of their law also dates from Charlemagne's time; but although monasteries and bishoprics outside Frisia held lands there, the region retained a somewhat anomalous status, part of the empire and yet not part of it. It is significant that ninth-century rulers were willing to entrust it to Viking leaders on occasions – it was felt, somehow, to be a border region with a degree of autonomy (rather like Brittany, though in other respects it did not at all resemble Brittany).

Relations with the Saxons, a warrior confederation visible in the sources from the third century onwards, were quite different. Merovingian rulers had campaigned against the Saxons on occasion, as had Pippin II, Charles Martel and Pippin III. Relations were rarely cordial, but they had been marked primarily by raids from both sides and what Frankish sources depict as a state of normality defined by Saxon tribute-paying. Boniface and other Anglo-Saxons had wanted to convert their continental cousins to Christianity, but there is little sign that this desire was shared by Frankish leaders.[17] Under Charlemagne the Frankish strategy changed – according to Einhard, because of increased border disputes. There were repeated campaigns directed against Saxon fortified centres and sacred places in the 770s and early 780s: the attacks on shrines marked the beginning of a policy of eliminating Saxon paganism. These culminated in a kind of peace around 785, with the submission of the Saxon leader Widukind and the issuing of a very harsh capitulary by Charlemagne which in effect defined the terms of Frankish occupation.[18] Hostilities broke out again and continued intermittently until the early 800s, with a mitigation of the terms of the first Saxon capitulary in 797 and a formal peace treaty in 803, followed by a final settlement of the status of the lands beyond the Elbe in the period 804–10. The codification of Saxon law probably dates to this final period as well.

The Franks found it difficult to deal with the Saxons, who did not have a monarchic constitution and could rally round a literally militant paganism in defence of their independence. Consequently they took up an agenda of conversion from the 780s onwards, and by the end of Charlemagne's reign had been largely successful. There was a brief pagan reaction in the *Stellinga* uprising of 841–43, but this was not on anything like the scale of the otherwise comparable pagan reactions in Poland and Hungary in the early to mid-eleventh century, following the conversion of those regions. Confiscation, hostage-taking and deportation broke Saxon resistance – both to political incorporation and to conversion – in the end. But so also did intermarriage between the Frankish elite and the Saxon nobility, and the preservation (and indeed consolidation) of most of the privileges of the Saxon nobility, once they had submitted to Frankish rule: the *Stellinga* revolt was directed as much against these as against Christianity.[19]

Alemannia and central Germany had already been largely absorbed into the Frankish empire by the beginning of Charlemagne's reign, and the major changes this had entailed were essentially complete. The Alemannic ducal family, which was closely related to the Agilolfing rulers of Bavaria, had ceased to rule, though it had not ceased to be influential: Charlemagne's wife Hildegard, for example, was a member, as was her brother Gerold, Charlemagne's first deputy in Bavaria following the deposition of Tassilo III. Though it was a duchy with its own Merovingian-inspired law-code, it had never been a unified area (the Black Forest cut through the areas of Alemannic settlement, and it was itself not settled substantially until the high middle ages), and it was not a core region of Frankish concern in Charlemagne's time: the major players were the bishopric of Constance and the monasteries at the Reichenau and St-Gallen, along with Frankish aristocratic families from the middle Rhine area who had established themselves there prior to and following the conquest and submission of Alemannia in the mid-eighth century.

A similar pattern is found in central Germany, where the Hedenid dukes of the late seventh and early eighth centuries had ceased to rule by Charlemagne's time and the major players were, again, ecclesiastical: the archbishop of Mainz and the bishop of Würzburg, together with the monasteries of Weißenburg, Lorsch and Fulda. A revolt – which included some Thuringian aristocrats – in 786 may hint at a greater degree of opposition to incorporation on the ground than is otherwise visible for this part of the world, but the details of the revolt and what lay behind it are hazy, though an aborted marriage alliance between them and Frankish aristocrats apparently played a part.[20]

Bavaria was rather different. It too had an ethnic law-code and a native ducal family, the Agilolfings, possibly (though not certainly) of Frankish origin – but undoubtedly one which had come to power with Merovingian backing and had retained strong links with the Frankish elite even in times of tension. Nominal acceptance of Frankish overlordship and hegemony had not troubled the ducal family much before the 740s; the Agilolfings had supported missionary work amongst the Carinthians, and established diocesan organisation with Boniface's assistance, apparently without reference to Frankish rulers or churchmen in either case. They ran Bavaria as a quasi-kingdom of their own (even on occasions dividing it, as the Merovingians had done for the Frankish kingdom), a 'kingdom' which by eighth-century standards was fairly tightly organised and commanded substantial resources in land and power.

As Airlie explains, it was Bavarian backing for Grifo against his half-brothers Pippin III and Carloman, and the marriage between the Agilolfing duke Odilo and Charles Martel's daughter Hiltrude, which brought the new Carolingian dynasty into conflict with the old Agilolfing one: Tassilo III, a cousin of Charlemagne and Carloman, had been forced to acknowledge Frankish overlordship publicly in 757, soon after he came of age.[21] He had also been left increasingly isolated by Frankish expansion into Lombardy: the Agilolfing dukes and the Lombard royal house formed in effect a large-scale family grouping, and whereas Charlemagne had repudiated his Lombard wife in 771 or 772, Tassilo had retained his.[22] Frankish sources hint at her support for Tassilo's oppositionalism, all the more dangerous as the Hrodgaud revolt of 776 showed that the Frankish hold on Lombardy could not be taken for granted even after the exiling of its royal family, and there is a hint at a possible attack by the Bavarians on Lombardy in 784. Direct incorporation of Bavaria was pursued systematically from the late 780s: Tassilo was brought by the threat of military force to accept judgment, and deposed; Charlemagne spent three years in Bavaria reorganising the duchy (which meant in particular taking over the ducal fisc); finally, in 794, Tassilo was forced once more to confirm in public his and all his family's complete renunciation to his cousin of their claims to the duchy and its fiscal lands and rights.[23]

The regions beyond the Rhine were too disparate for the application of a consistent or uniform Frankish strategy to their subjugation, but we can nevertheless make out a number of common features. Most important was the elimination of the position of ethnic leaders of the kind whom Merovingian sources would have described as dukes (and who might often have thought of themselves, or been seen by their own followers, as kings). The powerful men who replaced them were often of Frankish origin or had marriage ties to Frankish aristocratic families; but they were powerful by landholding rather than through office, and the offices they did hold they held from the king. Alongside the disappearance of ethnic leaders went the Frankicisation of local institutions and at the same time the written codification of ethnic legal practice, itself a form of Frankicisation, since it meant that ethnic law was now defined and potentially modifiable by Frankish royal authority.[24] Important in all regions was the endowment of churches and major monasteries with at least some of the spoils of incorporation: local elites were largely left in possession, even in Saxony, but there were inevitably forfeitures (Tassilo's being the most spectacular example) and not all the profits from these were retained in the ruler's hands.

Charlemagne completed the process of incorporation, but he did not begin it, and he was not working to a new agenda. The Carolingians had campaigned extensively in this region from the time of Pippin II onwards. Taken overall, they spent more time campaigning here than anywhere else in the period 687–814, more even than on Aquitaine and southern Gaul. It could be argued that they were proceeding with an even older agenda. Seen in a longer perspective, the trans-Rhenan policy and actions of Clothar II and Dagobert I share many features with those of their Carolingian successors. These later Merovingian rulers had encouraged missionaries (Columbanus, Gallus) and helped to establish new bishoprics at Augsburg and Constance. They had seen to the codification of ethnic law: early versions of Bavarian, Alemannic and Ribuarian Frankish law go back to this period. And they had campaigned extensively – like Charlemagne, they had taken their campaigning not only to the Germanic world, but also to the Slavs and Avars beyond the frontier.

Charlemagne did not so much change the plan as change the methods used to implement it. A loose dependence, marked by family ties and the payment of tribute, was no longer felt to be sufficient: the incorporation was now to be full and systematic. Einhard thought that the incorporation of Saxony had been so complete that they and the Franks had now 'come to make up one people'.[25] It is not clear, incidentally, that the Saxons agreed: Widukind of Corvey, writing a century and a half later, glossed Einhard's phrase by saying that it was 'as if they had come to make up one people', and though ninth- and tenth-century writers do on occasions speak of 'Francia and Saxony' as if it were a single unit, tenth-century Saxon writers often also showed considerable hostility to the Franks.[26] But incorporation was the intention, here and elsewhere in the German-speaking lands. We shall see shortly that in many aspects it was surface rather than structural, but that does not alter our assessment of the policy.

One empire, many folk

It is worth noting here that, whatever may have lain behind this policy, it was not some kind of pan-Germanic sentiment. There was an awareness among intellectuals of the common roots of the various Germanic languages and dialects spoken in eighth- and ninth-century Europe, but that did not produce the kind of linguistic 'imagined community' dear to many manifestations of nineteenth-century nationalism.[27] Carolingian writers knew perfectly well that language did not make peoples, still less membership of linguistic families – Einhard speaks of the Slavs as a single linguistic group with wide variation in custom and political formation. The various versions of 'German' around in Charlemagne's time – Frankish, insular and continental Saxon, Frisian, Alemannic and Bavarian, to list only the major groupings – were *probably* mutually comprehensible to those who spoke them, though it is by no means clear how fully this was true.

But this basic North Sea/Rhine valley/Upper Danube valley Germanic language-zone did not make for a 'sense of us-ness' (to translate the useful German term *Wirgefühl*). The terminology used to describe it and those who spoke it came from outside: words like *theudisc* ('language of the folk/people'), *Teutonici* ('Teutons', thought mistakenly to be a classical variant of this, and used especially in Italy) and the Slav *nemci*, were either purely linguistic or else were used by outsiders to refer to broad groups whose members differentiated themselves much more finely in their own dealings with each other. The ethnic groupings of the world beyond the Rhine remained separate in their consciousness, even after full incorporation into the Frankish empire, a separateness which long survived that transient political arrangement and survives to some extent even at the present day.

If incorporation did not mean the surrender of ethnicity, what did it mean? Principally, it meant the adoption of Frankish institutions, as these had evolved and been defined by Charlemagne. As in the regions west of the Rhine, the trans-Rhenan regions had groups of royal estates, often serving palaces, found in sub-regional concentrations rather than spread evenly across the countryside, notably around the mid-Rhine valley and along the Main to Würzburg, in the southern Black Forest, and in the region around Regensburg. Formally, at least, local government was the responsibility of counts with comital territories (counties), though areas of forest and royal fisc were only imperfectly incorporated into these arrangements. As elsewhere, the counts were subject, especially in Charlemagne's later years, to the supervision of travelling royal representatives (*missi dominici*); as elsewhere, they held regular court meetings for the free men of their counties; and other Frankish judicial institutions – such as *scabini* (in effect, permanent jurors) and the use of charters to record land transactions – were also introduced throughout the trans-Rhenan world. Counts raised military contingents from these regions for the later campaigns under Charlemagne. Frankish writers did not always rate their fighting-capacity highly, but they did see the unconditional willingness to serve as an important signal, both for incorporated regions and for the territories beyond: for Einhard, acceptance of Frankish rule or overlordship meant 'doing what you were told' (*imperata facere*), especially in military matters.

Perhaps most importantly, it was Charlemagne's reign which saw the completion and reshaping of the diocesan network east of the Rhine.[28] The Bavarian church, already established by Boniface in 739, became a full province in 798 with its own archbishopric at Salzburg; the anomalous bishopric at Neuburg – unlike the other Bavarian bishoprics, probably not as such a royal/ducal foundation – seems to have disappeared at about the same time. There were no new foundations in Alemannia, but the huge diocese of Constance was at least put on a secure footing. In central Germany much of the Bonifatian settlement was dismantled: the Bonifatian bishoprics at Erfurt and *Büraberg* disappeared (or became the 'sees' of chorbishops), leaving Mainz and Würzburg in possession of the field. In the north, most of the Saxon bishoprics were founded during Charlemagne's time: Minden, Münster, Paderborn, Verden and Bremen certainly existed by 814, and only the eastern bishoprics at Hildesheim and Halberstadt were to be added under Louis the Pious. Not all the 'German' bishoprics were initially rich, and some were still struggling two centuries later. Vestiges of pre-diocesan organisation remained, for example in the extensive tithe rights of the 'missionary' monasteries at Fulda, Hersfeld, Corvey and Herford. Nevertheless, the level of diocesan organisation was at least comparable with that in contemporary Anglo-Saxon England.

Some aspects of incorporation were more superficial than real: the lasting confusion about the nature of comital authority east of the Rhine (a confusion found in ninth- and tenth-century sources and compounded by nineteenth- and twentieth-century constitutional historians) was almost certainly the result of the practice of applying the *term* count to existing local holders of authority rather than restructuring the nature of that authority. Yet, by and large, incorporation was a success. However much grief the German ethnic groups may have given the earlier Carolingians, by the time of Louis the Pious they were not only a full part of the kingdom but were to give Louis substantial support in the troubles of the 830s. Incorporation meant a good deal more than mere political support and loyalty, however. Christianity was not only firmly established but also capable of developing autonomously. There was still quite a lot to do by way of 'inner mission' at the point of Charlemagne's death, but it was now 'inner mission', where half a century earlier much of the trans-Rhenan regions had been genuinely missionary territory, with few or no established churches, and bishops, where they existed at all, without fixed sees. Slowly – probably more slowly than an older generation of historians thought – the 'classical' bipartite organisation of great estates spread east of the Rhine in the course of the ninth century. The powerful aristocratic families of Bavarian, Alemannic and even Saxon origin merged with the Frankish aristocracy to form a ruling elite that transcended borders (as witness their presence in large numbers in positions of power in ninth-century Italy).

Last but not least: it was in the regions east of the Rhine that the posthumous legend and reputation of Charlemagne were first developed. Einhard, Charles's first biographer, had studied at Fulda before rising to hold estates by royal gift near the mouth of the Rhine and in central Germany.[29] Not only was the early dissemination of his work at least as great in the regions east of the Rhine as west of it; his version of the legitimacy of the transfer of power from the Merovingians to the Carolingians was propagated also by two other east Frankish works: the so-called Annals of Fulda, which for the earlier Carolingians offer what is admittedly a compilation but one not found elsewhere; and the 'Small Lorsch Frankish chronicle'.[30] Later ninth-century writers continued this tradition – notably the *Poeta Saxo*, who retold the conquest and conversion of Saxony by Charlemagne from a Saxon (but nevertheless admiring) perspective, and Notker the Stammerer, who not only developed the mythologising of Charlemagne but used his picture to underpin the legitimacy of what was now the east Frankish kingdom as the true heirs of Charlemagne's legendary achievements.[31]

Incorporation meant that the east Frankish kingdom which emerged in the decades either side of the treaty of Verdun remained a Frankish kingdom, one which sought and achieved hegemony within the pan-Frankish world stretching from the Baltic and the Channel down to the Pyrenees and the Abruzzi. For the east Frankish rulers and their Ottonian and Salian successors, the 'local hegemony' of dominance over the Slav peoples to the east was always less important than the 'European hegemony' of dominance over France, Burgundy and Italy. For most of the period from the late ninth to the early eleventh century, they achieved such a hegemony, politically and culturally at least, in spite of residual economic underdevelopment. To the pan-Frankish world whose construction Charlemagne's reign had completed they were what America has been to Europe for most of the last century: former colonies which had evolved to become the dominant partners, 'more Frankish than the Franks'.

Notes

† This paper was written by Tim Reuter a short while before his death in October 2002. The editor is very grateful to Simon MacLean and Jinty Nelson for their assistance in bringing this paper to publication.

1 Reuter (1991); Smith (1995a).

2 Reuter (1985).

3 RFA, 782; trans. King (1987), pp. 81–2; Jankuhn (1965).

4 RFA, 810; trans. King (1987), pp. 102–3.

5 RFA, 808; trans. King (1987), pp. 99–100; Hellmuth Andersen et al. (1976); Jankuhn (1986), pp. 56–65.

6 Pohl (1988).

7 RFA, 787–88; trans. King (1987), pp. 84–7.

8 Pohl (2001), pp. 439–66; Bowlus (1995).

9 Urbanczyk, ed. (1997).

10 Bavarian Geographer, *Descriptio civitatum et regionum ad septentrionalem plagam Danubii*, ed. Bartonková (1969), III, pp. 285–91. On the *Conversio*, see Lošek (1997);

Wolfram (1995b); Airlie (2001).

11 Moissac Chronicle, 811; trans. King (1987), p. 148.

12 *Ibid*; *AL*, 798; trans. King (1987), pp. 142–3.

13 Double Capitulary of Thionville (806), c. 23.7, MGH *Capit.* I, nos. 43–4, p. 123; trans. King (1987), p. 248.

14 On Alcuin's letters to Arn, see Bullough, ch. 8 (pp. 136–50) in this volume.

15 Reuter, ed. (1979); Reuter (1997).

16 Levison (1946), pp. 45–69; McKitterick (1995), pp. 66–70.

17 Levison (1946), pp. 70–93; McKitterick (1991); Reuter, ed. (1980).

18 First Saxon Capitulary, MGH *Capit.* I, no. 26; trans. King (1987), pp. 205–8. King (1987), p. 25, dated this to 782, but Halphen (1921) and Ganshof (1959), p. 110, dated it to 785.

19 On the *Stellinga* revolt, see the *AX*, 841, p. 12; *AF*, 842, pp. 33–4, trans. Reuter (1992), p. 21; *AB*, 841, pp. 38–9; trans. Nelson (1991), p. 51; Nithard, *Hist.* 4.2, 4.4, 4.6, pp. 41–2, 44–6, 48–9; trans. Dutton (1993), pp. 358, 360, 362. For commentary, see Goldberg (1995).

20 Airlie, ch. 6 (pp. 90–102) in this volume.

21 Airlie (1999).

22 Nelson (1998).

23 Capitulary of Frankfurt (794), c. 3, MGH *Capit.* I, no. 28, p. 74; trans. King (1987), pp. 224–5.

24 Nelson (1995), p. 412; Wormald (1999), pp. 31–53.

25 Einhard, *VK*, c. 7; trans. Dutton (1998), pp. 20–1.

26 Widukind, *Gest. Sax.*, I.15; ed. Bauer and Rau, *AQ*, VIII, p. 44.

27 Geary (2002); Edwards (1994).

28 Wallace Hadrill (1983); de Jong, ch. 7 (pp. 103–35) in this volume.

29 Dutton (1998), pp. 50–2; Ganz, ch. 3 (pp. 38–51) in this volume.

30 Reuter (1992), pp. 1–12.

31 Poeta Saxo, *Ann.*, MGH *PLAC* IV, pp. 17, 42–3. On Notker and Einhard, see Ganz (1989). On Notker and east Frankish legitimacy see Nelson (2001a), pp. 234–6.

12

CHARLEMAGNE
AND THE
ANGLO-SAXONS

Joanna Story

When Wilhelm Levison wrote his seminal study on *England and the Continent in the Eighth Century* in the early 1940s, his primary focus was the contribution which the Anglo-Saxons had made to the cultural and political evolution of Charlemagne's realm. Levison's insights were informed by an unsurpassed knowledge of the manuscript sources, he having spent a lifetime in the archives and libraries of Europe. But his analysis of the cultural dynamics of the eighth century was coloured by his experiences in his final years as a Jewish exile from the Nazi regime of his homeland in Germany. He came to England as a refugee in 1939 and there, in the dark days of world war, told the story of the eighth century in terms of the essential contribution which the ancestors of the English had made to the precursors of Germany and France; he talked (with resolute optimism) of his hope that his work would 'contribute to join again broken links, when the works of peace have resumed their place lost on the turmoil of war'.[1] Many scholars since Levison have taken up his theme, and have furthered our understanding of the contribution of Anglo-Saxon monasteries such as Fulda and scholars such as Alcuin to Charlemagne's Europe and the Carolingian Renaissance. But we have also come to realise that the influence was not just one-way, and that Charlemagne's Francia also had a considerable impact on Anglo-Saxon England.

Chronicles and connections

News of the rout of Charlemagne's army in 782 by Widukind and his Saxon rebels reached Anglo-Saxon England and was recorded by one of the sources of the Old English *Anglo-Saxon Chronicle*.[2] The entry for 780 in the earliest copy of that text records that, 'In this year the Old Saxons and the Franks fought'. The entry is very brief and, like all other annals in that section of the *Chronicle*, it suffers from a systematic dislocation of the chronology by two or three years, and so may properly be read as an event of the year 782.[3] Despite its brevity, the entry is important, not least because it is one of only two contemporary Old English entries in the *Anglo-Saxon Chronicle* relating to Charlemagne.[4] The other records the date of his death (again misplaced by two years, *s.a.* 812) and notes that he had reigned in Francia for forty-five winters, thereby demonstrating knowledge of the date of his accession.

On the basis of these two sparse entries in the *Chronicle*, we might be forgiven for thinking that Charlemagne and the activities of the Franks across the sea did not matter much to the Anglo-Saxons, at least not enough to impinge on the priorities of the record-keepers. Even the reference to Charlemagne's death is best regarded as part of a short, tightly-focused package of information about foreign affairs inserted into an otherwise empty portion of the *Chronicle*. Four consecutive annals, those for the years 814, 815, 816 and 817, stand out because their primary focus is not England (or Francia for that matter) but Rome: as well as the death of Charlemagne in 814, these annals record the death of Pope Leo III and the succession of Pope Stephen IV in 816; the death of Pope Stephen and the succession of Paschal I a year later (817); the burning down of the English quarter near St-Peter's in Rome (817); the journey to Rome of Archbishop Wulfred of Canterbury and Bishop Wigberht of the West Saxons in 814; and Wulfred's return to Canterbury with papal blessing in 815. The only element in this group not directly linked to events on the continent is a reference to the invasion of Cornwall by Ecgberht of Wessex in 815.

The comparative lack of interest shown in continental affairs by the compilers of the eighth- and early ninth-century part of the *Chronicle* is matched by the contemporary contributors to the Royal Frankish Annals, who did not note events concerning Anglo-Saxon England. The exception is the episode relating to the exile and restoration of King Eardwulf of Northumbria (808), followed by the kidnap and ransom of the papal envoy who had accompanied Eardwulf, and his safe return to Francia. However, these events are included primarily as an illustration of the extent of Charlemagne's imperial authority and, in that respect, their English subject-matter is incidental.

However, in their mutual lack of interest, the major sets of annals of Anglo-Saxon England and Carolingian Francia are deceptive. Other types of evidence, particularly contemporary letters, reveal the existence of a dynamic political and cultural relationship between the Anglo-Saxon kingdoms and Charlemagne's Francia.

The brief entry in the *Chronicle* for 780 opens the door on a world where contact between 'peoples' (*gentes*) was commonplace. The Old English name for the adversaries of the Franks was carefully selected by the Chronicler; they are *aldseaxe*, the 'Old Saxons'. By defining them thus, the Anglo-Saxon Chronicler implicitly distinguishes the 'Old' Saxons across the sea from the 'New' Saxons who were his audience at home. The *Chronicle* is not alone in its use of this terminology; the term *aldseaxe* (or *antiqui saxones*, to give it its Latin equivalent) was a familiar one, first attested by Bede, and used by other eighth-century Anglo-Saxon writers to identify the continental Saxons.[5] The eighth-century source which lies behind the Latin chronicle known as the *Historia regum* (often attributed to its twelfth-century editor, Symeon of Durham) noted the return to York in 767 of an Anglo-Saxon missionary called Aluberht in order that that he could be consecrated bishop of the Old Saxons.[6] Similarly, in a letter dated to 790, Alcuin, writing from Francia, sent to his Irish friend Colcu news of Charlemagne's victorious campaigns against the *antiqui saxones*.[7]

Notions of consanguinity are inherent in this label, and it implies a widespread familiarity with the origin myths of the Anglo-Saxons. By Bede's day in the early eighth century, the belief that the Anglo-Saxons were linked by blood and a common heritage to the Saxons across the sea had become a central motivation for Christian missionaries who travelled from England to evangelise the still-pagan tribes of the continental homelands. The most famous of these missionaries, Boniface, wrote home in 738 to remind the Anglo-Saxon bishops that 'they (the Saxons) themselves are saying that "We are of one blood and bone with you"'. At Boniface's prompting, Pope Gregory III wrote a letter to 'all the people of the Old Saxons' urging them to embrace salvation through conversion; in another contemporary letter, Bishop Torthelm of Leicester wrote enthusiastically to Boniface: 'Who would not exult and be glad at such accomplishments, whereby people of our own race [*gens nostra*] are coming to believe in Christ the Almighty God?'[8]

The Frankish sources also recognise the essential sameness of Saxons who lived on either side of the Channel, but their terminology reflects a Frankish ethnic geography;[9] both groups are generic *Saxones* but the Anglo-Saxons are defined as 'Saxons from the island of Britain' (*de Brittania insula*). Thus Aldulf, the papal legate who was sent by Pope Leo III to England in 808 to restore Eardwulf to Northumbria, came (according to the RFA) 'from Britain, from the nation of the Saxons', and Eardwulf was king of the Northumbrians 'from the island of Britain'. Alcuin too (in Einhard's eyes) was 'a man from Britain, of Saxon stock'.[10] This geographical determinism thus distinguished the Saxons in Britain from both the 'perfidious' *Saxones* who lived to the east of the Frankish homeland and from the 'troublesome' *Britannii* or Bretons whose homelands were *in Brittania cismarina* – that is, 'in Britain-on-this-side-of-the-sea', bordering the Ocean in the marchlands to the north-west of the Franks. The Frankish naming-patterns thus locate their neighbours in relationship to their own perceived central geographical location. But by using the shared naming elements, *Saxones* and *Brittanii*, the Frankish sources also recalled the quasi-historical cross-Channel connections that linked the Anglo-Saxon migrants and native British refugees of the fifth and sixth centuries with 'Old' Saxony and Brittany in the eighth century.

This naming pattern preferred by the Frankish writers contrasted with the terminology current in Rome. Following the practice established by Pope Gregory the Great in the late sixth century, papal sources invariably referred to the Anglo-Saxons as the *gens Anglorum* (the 'Anglian' or 'English' people). Gregory's preferred terminology was popularised by the success of Augustine's mission to Britain and the consequent spread of Gregory's cult among the Anglo-Saxons. This, in combination with Bede's admiration for Gregory and the extensive use which both he and Boniface made of Gregory's letters, was sufficient to ensure that the *gens Anglorum* was the label used most often by papal writers to describe the Germanic inhabitants of Britain, even in letters to Frankish recipients.[11] It is interesting then that that the term 'Anglo-Saxon', a mixture of Frankish and Papal terminology, is first recorded in the formal address of a report to Pope Hadrian I by a bishop who held sees in Francia and in Rome. Bishop George of Ostia and Amiens chaired a series of synods in 786 in 'English Saxony' (*Anglorum Sax[o]nia*) in order, as the Chroniclers recalled, to 'renew the bonds of friendship which Pope Gregory taught us through the blessed Augustine'.[12] Thereafter, until it was taken up in the late ninth century by Alfred in Wessex, the 'Anglo-Saxon' label is used sporadically in Carolingian sources, often by foreign scholars working at the Frankish court, such as Paul the Deacon (a Lombard from Italy) in his 'History of the Lombards', or the Spanish Visigoth, Galindo, who received promotion at the court of Louis the Pious under the name of Prudentius and later became bishop of Troyes, and who was author of the entries for *c.* 835–861 in the important west Frankish chronicle, the Annals of St-Bertin.[13]

The bonds of myth and memory that linked the Anglo-Saxons of Britain with the continental 'homelands' were thus powerfully reinforced in the eighth century through the Anglo-Saxon mission to convert the continental Saxons, and other pagan tribes living east of the Rhine. The 'imagined community' of the past became a contemporary reality in the interlocking networks of personal friendships, kin groups and political ties that linked the Anglo-Saxon missionary monasteries in eastern Francia and beyond the Rhine with men and women in Kent, Wessex, Mercia and Northumbria.[14] Furthermore, the eastern focus of the mission brought the Anglo-Saxon missionary leaders into direct contact with the nascent Carolingian dynasty who were *de facto* rulers – but not yet kings – of the eastern Frankish kingdom of Austrasia. It also provided the motivation and mechanism by which Anglo-Saxon men and women could journey to Rome, to the threshold of the apostles and the fount of their faith. The Anglo-Saxon mission therefore provides both the context and backdrop for the political and cultural connections which characterise the cross-Channel contacts of the age of Charlemagne when (contrary to the impression given by the chronicles) Rome and the court of the Carolingians lay securely within the purview of the secular and ecclesiastical rulers of the Anglo-Saxon kingdoms.[15]

Pax et amicitia: peace and friendship

The web of connections facilitated through the Anglo-Saxon mission is well illustrated by a letter written in 773 for Alhred, King of Northumbria (765–74) and his wife Osgifu to Bishop Lul, Boniface's successor at Mainz.[16] Alhred thanked Lul for the letters and presents which he had sent with his messengers, and in return the king sent gifts, twelve cloaks and a large gold ring. These gifts prefigured the exchange of something much more precious, the gift of mutual prayer. Alhred and Osgifu asked Lul 'to devote care and prayers for our welfare', and promised the same in return for him and his companions abroad. This exchange is made tangible and permanent through the medium of the written word; Alhred had ordered that the list of names sent by Lul be committed in 'the everlasting memorial of writing ... [in] all the monasteries subject to our authority', and he and his queen asked Lul that the same be done in return with the list of names of their friends and relatives which they had appended to their letter (though the list does not survive).

In this way, though separated by great distance, selected members of the Northumbrian nobility and the clergy of Lul's network in Germany were brought into daily contact through the routine of monastic prayer and the celebrations of the mass.[17] Alhred and Osgifu also sent envoys to Charlemagne, and asked Lul to assist them in order that the bond of *pax et amicitia* might be strengthened between the Frankish and Northumbrian kings. This call for 'peace and friendship' was made perhaps more pressing by the 'disturbances in our churches and people' which Alhred had earlier reported to Lul. Indeed, barely a year after his letter to Lul was written, Alhred was deposed in York at Easter 774 and was sent into exile.[18] He went north, first to the fortress at Bamburgh and thence into Pictland, accompanied by only a few loyal companions – men whose names, unknown to us now, may yet have been recorded beneath that of their lord in the confraternity book of some distant German monastery.

The context for this exchange of letters is not known for certain, but it was certainly not unique. In 773 a pallium was sent by Pope Hadrian to Archbishop Ælberht of York, and perhaps the letters and messengers from Lul were associated with that event.[19] We know from other sources that earlier in his reign Alhred had commissioned the Northumbrian Willihad as a missionary to the Frisians and Old Saxons. It was during Alhred's reign too, that the Anglo-Saxon Aluberht and his Frisian followers, Sigibod and Liudger, came to York to be consecrated as bishop of the Old Saxons, priest and deacon, respectively. After their ordinations, Liudger decided to return to York to continue his education with Alcuin who was then master of the archbishop's school. The *Life of Liudger* also tells us that a community of Frisian traders was based in York in the early 770s, until they were forced to leave after one of their number killed the son of a Northumbrian nobleman in a brawl.[20] Lul also wrote to Ælberht requesting copies of books from the York library; he wanted some of Bede's biblical commentaries, as well as works which would explain the workings of the Earth, the tides and the heavens.[21]

Alhred's letter is found uniquely in a collection of the correspondence of Boniface, between two other letters from an otherwise unknown Anglo-Saxon abbot called Eanwulf, one to Lul and the other addressed to Charlemagne himself. Eanwulf's letters were also written in 773, and may have been sent simultaneously with that from the Northumbrian king.[22] Eanwulf's letter to Lul offered confraternal prayers; that to Charlemagne offered eulogies of praise for his victories against the pagans and alluded to the destruction of the Saxons' pagan sanctuary in 772. Eanwulf assured Charlemagne that prayers would be offered incessantly for him and his people and, echoing Alhred's request for 'peace and friendship', begged in return for the king's friendship and intercession, that 'we may have you as a protector and patron'.

The extant letters and saints' Lives indicate the depth and complexity of the networks that linked lay and ecclesiastical communities in Northumbria and the Rhineland in the early years of Charlemagne's reign. The connections were cultural and mercantile as well as political and spiritual; they involved the movement of books and letters, items traded by merchants, textiles and metalwork exchanged as diplomatic gifts between kings and bishops, as well as the movement of individuals and the establishment of confraternities of prayer which linked distant communities. They also reveal that within the first few years of his reign Charlemagne had made a considerable impression on kings and clergy in Anglo-Saxon England, who desired affiliation and friendship, and who recognised the value of a distant Frankish 'patron'.

Fidelitas: fidelity

This picture from the 770s can be paralleled by sources from the period of Charlemagne's prime, enabling us to trace the development of an increasingly complex relationship between Charlemagne and the Anglo-Saxon kingdoms. The distribution of the spoils from the war against the Avars is a case in point. In 795 / 96 two Frankish armies marched into Pannonia where, exploiting factional divisions among the Avars, they captured the Khagan's residence known as 'the Ring' and with it an immense treasure.[23] Convoys of loot were sent to Charlemagne in Aachen; he sent some to Rome to the new pope, Leo III, and the remainder he distributed among 'his leading men [*optimates*] both clergy and laymen, and upon his other faithful men [*fideles*]'.[24] The Lorsch Annals confirm this, adding that 'giving thanks to the almighty King, he distributed the treasure among the churches and bishops, abbots and counts, and also rewarded all his *fideles* from it in wondrous fashion'.[25]

Some of these *fideles*, it seems, were in Anglo-Saxon England. In a famous letter written for Charlemagne to Offa of Mercia early in 796, we hear of the distribution of parts of this treasure to English recipients, 'we have sent something to each of the metropolitan cities, and also to your love ... we have sent a sword-belt, and an Avar sword and two lengths of silk'.[26] In societies where one of the essential qualities of good lordship was generosity, the redistribution of parts of the Avar treasure to Offa and the English archbishoprics was loaded with the overtones of *fidelitas* that are explicit in the Frankish annals. The gifts were double-edged (literally perhaps); their origin and value honoured the donor but, at the same time, military trophies from a conquered tribe were a pointed reminder – for a Mercian king who had made his own reputation through the ruthless suppression of rivals – of the fate of Charlemagne's enemies.

It is doubtful whether Offa, from his standpoint as lord of a greatly expanded Mercian kingdom, would have concurred with the viewpoint of the Frankish annalists and thought of himself as a *fidelis* of the Carolingian king. But another letter from Alcuin on the same topic would have left Offa in little doubt of the Frankish opinion of his neighbours in Northumbria. Gifts from the Avar treasure had also been sent to Northumbria, to King Æthelred and his bishops. But, when these gifts and letters had been put into hands of the envoys, news came through of the murder of Æthelred. Charlemagne reacted with fury, and Alcuin says that he 'withdrew his generous gifts, and was greatly enraged against that people, "a perfidious and perverse race" as he called them "who murder their own lords", for he thought them worse than pagans'. It was only Alcuin's intercession which prevented the king from depriving the Northumbrians 'of every benefit and doing them every harm he could'.[27] Even though we see this crisis through the eyes of Alcuin, himself a Northumbrian deeply distressed by the turmoil of recent Viking raids and civil unrest in his own country, there is an echo in Alcuin's account of Charlemagne's furious revenge against the Saxon rebels in 782. Charlemagne's indignation was the attitude of a lord who considered treachery against another Christian king to whom he had shown his favour as a direct affront to his own dignity.

Soon after the capture of the Avar treasure, came news of the death of Pope Hadrian I, who had died on 26 December 795. News of Hadrian's death is prominent in the English and Frankish sources. Indeed, the entry in the *Anglo-Saxon Chronicle* is the first record of a pope's death in that source since the entry concerning the death of Gregory the Great in 604. A number of letters written in Francia suggest that, perhaps for the first time, co-ordinated efforts were made outside Rome to commemorate the passing of a pope.[28] The contemporary Lorsch Annals say that Charlemagne 'asked that prayers be said for [Hadrian] throughout the whole Christian people within his boundaries and sent an abundance of alms for him'.[29] Again, it seems that Anglo-Saxon England was included within this instruction; Alcuin wrote a letter to all the bishops of Britain saying that, 'Our Lord King Charles greatly desires your prayers for himself and the stability of his kingdom, and the spread of Christianity, and also for the soul of our blessed father Pope Hadrian, for loyal friendship towards a deceased friend is always highly regarded'. Alcuin's letter was carried to England 'with some small gifts in order to further this request' and he asked the English bishops 'to accept what [Charlemagne] has sent gratefully and to do faithfully what he asks'.[30]

It is possible that these emissaries also carried the Avar treasure-gifts to Offa and the English sees. Charlemagne's letter to Offa on that subject reiterated the edict concerning the commemoration of Pope Hadrian, adding that 'we have sent each of the sees in your kingdom and in King Æthelred's [Northumbria] a present of dalmatics and palls on behalf of our father and your friend Pope Hadrian, praying you to order intercession for his soul'. The incorporation of the English bishoprics and kingdoms in this instruction for co-ordinated mourning for the pope is revealing, and indicates (once again) that, from the Frankish perspective, the Anglo-Saxons lay within the boundaries of Charlemagne's authority when it came to the proper performance of Christian duties. The systematic organisation of prayer for the 'stability of his kingdom and the spread of Christianity' mirrors other instructions from the king to galvanise the power of prayer through the co-ordination of ceremonial litanies and fasts. In this way, the army of 'those who pray' could aid 'those who fight' with a battery of spiritual weapons.[31] Coming as it does with news of the successes against the pagan Avars, these instructions are effectively orders for the Anglo-Saxon bishops to organise prayers in support of the Christian Frankish army.

These incidents may lie behind Charlemagne's appearance in another rich Northumbrian source. A mid ninth-century manuscript, known commonly as the Durham *Liber Vitae* (Book of Life), contains lists of several hundred names sumptuously copied in alternate lines of burnished gold and silver leaf, organised according to social rank. This Northumbrian Book of Life is a rare Anglo-Saxon survival of a type of document much better attested on the continent. But, as the letter from Alhred to Lul discussed above demonstrates, confraternity lists of this type were being complied in monasteries in northern England in the 770s.[32] Their purpose was to record the names of people for whom the community had promised prayers and confraternity. The lists might thus include the names of members of the community to which the book belonged as well as outside benefactors who had earned its gratitude. The original portion of the Northumbrian book was copied *c.* 840 but the text was evidently a fair copy of much older lists, with names stretching back to the later seventh century.

Charlemagne's name, *Karolus,* is recorded on folio 15v of the Book of Life, within the list of 'Kings and Dukes'. Two places above is the name of another Carolingian nobleman, Mægenfrith. He had been a close friend of Alcuin, a military commander in the campaign against the Avars and *camerarius* or chamberlain to the king.[33] The *camerarius* was probably the official responsible for the distribution of the Avar treasure hoard captured in 795. The distribution of gifts to foreign legations is listed as one of his duties in the tract 'On the organisation of the palace', written in 882 but based on an earlier treatise by Charlemagne's courtier Adalhard of Corbie.[34] Gifts to commemorate the soul of Pope Hadrian and the redistribution of parts of the Avar treasure to the royal and ecclesiastical courts of Anglo-Saxon England provides a plausible context for the inclusion of the names of Charlemagne and his treasurer in the Northumbrian Book of Life.

Exiles and King Offa

The relationship between Charlemagne and his Anglo-Saxon counterparts is best known through the sources which reveal contacts with Offa, King of the Mercians (757–96).[35] Indeed, Carolingian connections with the other Anglo-Saxon kingdoms were conditioned by the state of Frankish diplomacy with Mercia, especially over the handling of exiles who had fled from England to Charlemagne's protection in Francia.

The Carolingian messengers to Offa's court in the spring of 796 arrived there only a few months before Offa's death in July that year. They or another group of envoys had also been to *Scottia* and brought back the news of the assassination of Æthelred in Northumbria on 18 April, which had prompted Charlemagne to recall his gifts to the *optimates* of that kingdom and caused Alcuin to write despairingly to Offa. Mercian mediation in the connections between Francia and the *Scottii* is confirmed by another letter from Charlemagne to Offa, his 'brother and friend', concerning the return of an errant priest to Ireland from the diocese of Cologne.[36] This priest had been accused of eating meat during Lent and, for fear of discrediting the authority of the church 'among the ignorant people' where he was working, Charlemagne asked Offa to ensure that the priest was returned to his homeland. This letter may have been drafted by Alcuin in the summer following the Synod of Frankfurt in June 794.[37] The synod was attended by all the bishops of the Franks, and Italy, Aquitaine and Provence.[38] The first two actions of the collected dignitaries of the Frankish church had been to pass judgment on the heresy of Adoptionism that was current in the Spanish church, and the Iconodule (pro-image worship) stance of the Seventh Ecumenical Council called by the Byzantine Empress Irene in 787. The errors of the Irish priest were modest in comparison, but Charlemagne's decision to repatriate the priest demonstrates his concern to safeguard the reputation of the Church and his assumption that this remit stretched to Christians everywhere – that is, not just within Francia but in Ireland too.

Alcuin attended the Frankfurt synod and other churchmen from Britain may also have contributed; certainly Charlemagne expected their compliance in the important matters of faith discussed at the synod.[39] Alcuin drafted a letter to the heretical Spanish bishops on the king's behalf informing them of the recent synod and of Charlemagne's decision to summon not only the holy fathers from 'all the churches under our rule', but also 'some men of ecclesiastical discipline from the regions of *Brittania* so that the Catholic faith might be investigated by the diligent consideration of many'.[40] Additionally, he says, the king had ordered statements of orthodoxy to be gathered from the pope, from the bishops of Italy, Germany, Gaul, Aquitaine and Britain. In order to emphasise the aberration and theological isolation of the Spanish heretics, it was useful and necessary to present the bishops of Britain as part of orthodox opinion, alongside the collected episcopacy of Francia and Italy.

This display of theological unity was partly also a response to the council called by the Byzantine Empress Irene in 787 to discuss the variant theologies of iconoclasm and image worship. Frankish opinion was not sought at that synod and, offended at their exclusion and in receipt of only a rather poor Latin translation of the Greek discussion in favour of the veneration of images, Charlemagne and his advisers felt it necessary to offer a robust response. Northumbrian opinion was also sought; in 792, prior to the Frankfurt gathering, Charlemagne had forwarded to Alcuin 'a synodal book, sent to him from Constantinople, in which (sad to say) were found many things improper and contrary to the true faith, especially ... that images ought to be adored, which the Church of God utterly abhors'. This book had reached Alcuin while he was on an extended visit to Northumbria; it provided Alcuin with the excuse to return to Francia, but not before he had written a treatise in response to it which he presented to Charlemagne 'in the name our [Northumbrian] bishops and nobles'.[41]

Another letter from Charlemagne written about this time reveals an even wider range of personal contacts between the king and Anglo-Saxon churchmen. In a letter to Æthelheard, archbishop of Canterbury, and Ceolwulf, the bishop of Lindsey, composed between 793 and July 796, Charlemagne reminds the English bishops of 'that friendship which once, when we were together, we established in loyal words'.[42] There is no other record of this meeting although Æthelheard travelled through Francia a few years later in 801 to argue the case for the abolition of the third English archbishopric at Lichfield. He and his companions – Cyneberht, the bishop of Wessex, another unnamed bishop, the Northumbrian *dux*, Tortcmund (who had avenged the murder of Æthelred) and the Mercian thegn, Ceolmund – were introduced at Charlemagne's court. Alcuin provided transport for them and wrote letters of introduction, advising them to be modest in their dress and behaviour in Charlemagne's presence.[43]

Æthelheard had been to Rome before: the long letter from Charlemagne to Offa discussed earlier says he was there early in 796, and it may be that Charlemagne's letter to him refers to a meeting during that journey. Charlemagne's letter to Offa had referred to the case of an exiled priest named Odberht, an enemy of Offa, who had fled from England to Francia. This priest – along with other exiles, who 'in fear of death have taken refuge under the wings of our protection' – Charlemagne had sent to Rome 'so that in the presence of the apostolic lord and your archbishop [Æthelheard] ... their cause may be heard and judged'. There had been some disagreement about the status of the exiles – Offa thought that they were clerics but, as Charlemagne said, 'the opinion of others is different' and he evidently thought it prudent to allow the pope to decide the case. But the tone of Charlemagne's letter leaves little room for doubt where his own sympathies lay in this matter.

Charlemagne's letter to Æthelheard also discussed exiles from England, specifically the followers of a man called Hringstan who had also fallen foul of Offa and had fled abroad 'to shun the danger of death'. Charlemagne clearly approved of the selfless loyalty of Hringstan's men, who had followed him into exile, and was impressed by Hringstan's readiness to pledge himself under oath that he had always been loyal to his lord. But Hringstan had died in Francia and his loyal followers were stranded, freed from their obligation to Hringstan but too fearful to return home. Charlemagne asked Æthelheard to intercede for the men with Offa, 'so that they may be allowed to return to their native land, and without unjust oppression of any kind, to serve anyone whatever'.

We do not know where Hringstan was from in Britain, nor the ultimate fate of his men. They could have been the group mentioned alongside the priest Odberht in the letter to Offa or they may have been entirely unconnected with that episode and represent another group of Anglo-Saxon exiles at the Carolingian court. But their case and that of Odberht makes it clear that, when opposition to Offa made life in England too hot to handle, influential Anglo-Saxons were finding with Charlemagne not only refuge but also an eloquent advocate on their behalf, who was prepared to support their cases both in Rome and against Offa in Mercia. Recalling Abbot Eanwulf's eulogistic request from twenty years before, 'that we may have you as our protector and patron', these Anglo-Saxons found the Frankish king true to his word.

More is known about the fate of the priest Odberht. His name is the Frankish version of the English name Eadberht, and should be identified with the man of that name who is surnamed 'Præn' in the *Anglo-Saxon Chronicle*, 'the Priest'. Events moved fast in 796. Pope Leo's judgment on Odberht/Eadberht's dispute with Offa and the archbishop is lost but, when news came of Offa's death on 26 July, Eadberht's pious desire 'to remain abroad for the love of God' was quickly forgotten. Eadberht seized the Kentish throne on his return from exile in Francia in defiance of his clerical status, suggesting perhaps that the earlier controversy may have arisen as a result of forced, involuntary tonsuring in an attempt to disqualify him from secular office (a technique for removing difficult opponents favoured by Anglo-Saxons and Franks alike). Eadberht's *coup* was entirely successful; he returned to Kent and was able to rule it for two years, producing coins in his own name at Canterbury, using moneyers who had previously minted coins for Offa.

Alcuin was deeply critical; he wrote to Archbishop Æthelheard who, as Offa's creature and spokesman against Eadberht in Rome, had himself been forced into exile when Eadberht established himself in Kent. Alcuin scolded Æthelberht for deserting his see and berated him 'as a hireling who flees in panic from the ravening wolf'.[44] He wrote also to the men of Kent, urging them to review their actions and to recall their archbishop, reminding them that they could not ordain anyone else in his place.[45] Pope Leo too was critical and, in a comment that may provide an indication of his earlier judgment in the case (though Leo was nothing if not an opportunist), he demanded the renewed expulsion of Eadberht Praen, 'that apostate cleric who has mounted the throne'.[46] Eadberht's clerical status, whether voluntary or not, sealed his fate. In 798, Mercian armies 'ravaged the people of Kent and (Romney) Marsh, ... seized Præn their king and brought him in fetters to Mercia'. There his eyes were poked out and his hands cut off, but since he was deemed to be a priest, his life was preserved.[47]

Mercian attempts to control Kent may also have lain behind Frankish involvement with another royal Anglo-Saxon exile. Offa's daughter had been married in 789 to Beorhtric, the king of Wessex, and this had forced a young man called Ecgberht to go into exile in Francia.[48] Ecgberht was the son of Ealhmund, who had ruled east Kent in the 780s during a previous insurrection against Mercian overlordship there. But Ecgberht also had claims to the West Saxon throne, and was thus a threat to Offa's interests across the south of England. Ecgberht cannot have been much outside his early teens by 789 – he was actively campaigning against the Vikings in the 830s and died only in 839 – so the threat he posed in England was as much to the hoped-for heirs of Offa's daughter, newly married to her father's ally, as to Beorhtric himself.

The *Chronicle* says that Ecgberht spent three years in Francia, presumably 789/90–792/93. We do not know whether he was received by Charlemagne but, by analogy with the better attested cases of Hringstan and Eadberht, it seems probable that he was. This is rendered the more likely by what else we know of Franco-Mercian relations in these years. This is exactly the period when a variety of sources record a serious collapse in relations between Offa and Charlemagne. It may have been no coincidence either that the dispute arose ostensibly from a breakdown in negotiations for a marriage alliance between the two kingdoms. Charlemagne had been seeking the hand of another of Offa's daughters for his eldest son Charles and had commissioned Abbot Gervold to negotiate the match. Gervold was abbot of the monastery of St-Wandrille near Rouen, and had 'for many years served as superintendent of the kingdom's trade, collecting the taxes and tolls in the various ports and cities, especially in Quentovic'.[49] He was well known to Offa too and had 'on many occasions' served Charlemagne as an envoy to his court.

This was a marriage-match of real significance and one which conferred considerable prestige on the father of the bride. But, as the author of The Deeds of St-Wandrille makes clear, Offa knew the rules of this particular game and demanded a reverse match, asking for the hand of Charlemagne's daughter

Bertha for his own son, Ecgfrith. Charlemagne was 'not a little angered' by this and 'gave the command that no-one from the island of Britain or the people of the Angles was to set foot on the shores of Gaul for the purposes of trade'. Letters from Alcuin confirm that the quarrel had escalated, 'fuel has been devilishly heaped upon the fire so that on both sides traders are forbidden to sail'.[50] Writing from Northumbria late in 790 to his friend Adalhard back in Francia, Alcuin asked for Adalhard's angle on the quarrel and how it might be resolved.[51]

The imposition of trade sanctions suggests that Offa could show that he too was 'not a little angered' and had mechanisms equivalent to Charlemagne's for imposing an embargo on Frankish merchants in his territory. But this was more than a clash of royal egos and damaged pride – for Offa the stakes were high. His request for a bride for his son was very specific – the princess he required was Bertha. There could have been little more powerful expression of Offa's acquisitive intentions towards Kent and ambitions for his own dynasty than to secure for his son a Frankish bride by the name of Bertha. To any eighth-century audience of Bede's *Ecclesiastical History*, Charlemagne and Offa among them, talk of the marriage of a Frankish princess named Bertha to an Anglo-Saxon prince must have recalled the historic union between a Merovingian princess of that name and King Æthelberht of Kent in the late sixth century – a union which precipitated the advent of Christianity within Anglo-Saxon England and aided Æthelberht's rise to become the most powerful king among the Anglo-Saxons in Britain.[52] Under these circumstances the bitterness of the dispute becomes understandable, all the more so if Charlemagne was also providing refuge for the exiled *ætheling*, Ecgberht.

The most explicit example of Charlemagne's intervention on behalf of an Anglo-Saxon exile is also the most compelling. The RFA record in 808 the arrival of the exiled king of Northumbria at the palace of Nijmegen. Eardwulf was received by Charlemagne and, when he had discussed with him the reasons for his journey, he then travelled on to Rome. On his return, the annalist continues, Eardwulf 'was escorted by envoys of the Roman pontiff and of the lord Emperor back into his kingdom'. The two Carolingian legates who accompanied him, Hruotfrid, abbot of St-Amand and Natharius, abbot of St-Omer, returned home safely the next year, but the papal envoy Aldulf was captured by pirates and had to be ransomed by one of Coenwulf's men before he could resume his return journey to Rome.[53] The evidence of the annals is unambiguous; an exiled Anglo-Saxon king was able to appeal to the emperor and pope, and – with their active intervention – to return to his own kingdom.

The story is amplified by three remarkable letters from Pope Leo III to Charlemagne, which discussed Eardwulf's problems alongside a variety of other issues that the pope wished to draw to Charlemagne's attention.[54] These reveal that Eardwulf's troubles had been the subject of extensive correspondence between Rome, Francia and various interested parties in England; Leo says that he had received conflicting letters and envoys on the subject from the archbishop of York and the Mercian king, as well as from Eardwulf. But, Leo assured Charlemagne, he knew well that Eardwulf had always been 'your faithful man' (*vester fidelis*) and thus, when news came through that Charlemagne had secured Eardwulf's safe passage to Francia, talk of 'your imperial defence resounds everywhere in many ways'. Leo (or his secretary) was a master in the art of diplomatic flattery, but his language here is nevertheless astonishing. From Leo's perspective, Frankish intervention on behalf of Eardwulf sprang from the Northumbrian king's loyal fidelity to Charlemagne, and as such it was quite right and proper that the authority of the emperor should reach far beyond the borders of the Frankish kingdom, even to the distant land of the Northumbrians.

Leo's other two letters continue in this vein, though he had to apologise for his envoy: Aldulf had committed a grave error of etiquette by failing to attend Charlemagne's palace on his return journey from England, where he had been sent by Leo to collect the archbishop's representative. Aldulf had been warmly entertained on his outward journey and clearly Charlemagne expected that the envoy would return via the court in order to debrief him on developments in the case. But Aldulf kept Charlemagne waiting and instead hurried to Rome (presumably with the archbishop's envoy in tow); Leo had some sharp explaining to do before he could appease the emperor's irritation at having been bypassed. Having become involved in the case, Charlemagne clearly expected all future communications between England and Rome to be channelled via his own court, and Eardwulf's subsequent return to Northumbria in the company of two Carolingian abbots (and the hapless Aldulf) should be seen in that light.

After 800, the language of imperial power comes naturally enough to papal and Frankish writers. As the sources on Eardwulf's exile and return to Northumbria are exclusively continental, we cannot know how Anglo-Saxon writers would have described the episode, since English sources for early ninth-century history are almost non-existent. Nevertheless, even if Leo's language were to be considered hyperbolic and treated with suspicion, his letters demonstrate the readiness of Anglo-Saxon kings and clergymen to seek the opinions of foreign powers in order to prosecute their differences. In fact, the evidence is very much stronger than that, since it illustrates Charlemagne's expectation that he would have the pivotal role in communications between Anglo-Saxons and Rome; the road from England to Rome very definitely led via Aachen. Eardwulf's case is extraordinary because of the quality of the evidence which survives and because that evidence leaves little room for doubt about the reality of Carolingian intervention in the politics of Anglo-Saxon England.

Notes

1 Levison (1946), p. vi.
2 RFA *(Rev.)*, 782; Airlie, ch. 6 (pp. 90–102) in this volume.
3 *ASC*, 754–845; Bately, ed. (1986), pp. xcvii, 39.
4 Latin annals were much later interpolated into *ASC* (E).
5 Bede, *HE*, I.15; V.9; V.10; V.11.
6 *Historia Regum (York Annals)*, 767; trans. *EHD* 1, no. 3.
7 Alcuin, *Ep.*, no. 7; trans. Allot (1974), no. 31.
8 Boniface, *Epistulae*, MGH *Epp. Sel.* I, nos. 46, 21, 47, 73; trans. Emerton (1940), nos. 36, 13, 37, 57.
9 Pohl and Reimitz, eds. (1998).
10 RFA, 808, 809; Einhard, *VK*, c. 25.
11 *CC*, no. 92, MGH *Epp.* III; Leo III to Charlemagne, MGH *Epp.* V, no. 3, p. 90; Brooks (1999).
12 *ASC* 786; *Historia Regum (York Annals)*, 786; George of Ostia, *Epistola ad Hadrianum*; trans. *EHD* I, nos. 1, 3 and 191. Levison (1946), pp. 127–30; Cubitt (1995), pp. 153–90; Story (2003), pp. 55–92, fig. 3.1.
13 Paul the Deacon, *Historia Langobardorum*, IV.22, AB, 844, 855, 860; trans. Nelson (1991), pp. 55, 80, 92. Levison (1946), p. 92; Keynes (1998), pp. 25–6.
14 McKitterick (1991); Geary (2002).
15 Story (2003), pp. 19–54.
16 Boniface, *Epistulae*, MGH *Epp. Sel.* I, no. 121; trans. *EHD* I, no. 187.
17 On confraternity books, see below, n.32.
18 *Historia Regum (York Annals)*, 774; trans. Whitelock, *EHD* 1, no. 3.
19 *Historia Regum (York Annals)*, 773; trans. Whitelock, *EHD* 1, no. 3.
20 *Vita Liudgeri*, c. 11, MGH *SS* II, pp. 403–19; partial trans. *EHD* I, no. 160.
21 Boniface, *Epistulae*, MGH *Epp. Sel.* I, nos. 116, 124–7.
22 Vienna, ÖNB Cod. 751; Eanwulf to Charlemagne, MGH *Epp. Sel.* I, no. 120; trans. *EHD* 1 no. 186.
23 Pohl (1988) and (2001); Reuter (1985).
24 RFA 796; RFA *(Rev.)*, 796; trans. King (1987), pp. 89–90, 127.
25 *AL* 795; trans. King (1987), pp. 141–2; Collins, ch. 4 (pp. 52–70) in this volume.
26 Charlemagne to Offa, MGH *Epp.* IV, no. 100; trans. *EHD* I, no. 197, Allott (1974), no. 40.
27 Alcuin, *Ep.*, no. 101; trans. *EHD* I, no. 198, Allott (1974), no. 41.
28 Story (2003), pp. 104–10.
29 *AL* 795; trans. King (1987), pp. 141–2.
30 Alcuin, *Ep.*, no. 104; Allott (1974), no. 25.
31 McCormick (1984).
32 London, British Library, Cotton Domitian A.viii. Keynes. ed. (1996) and Keynes (1997); Gerchow (1988); Geuenich et al., eds. (2000)
33 Alcuin, *Ep.*, nos. 111, 211; trans. Allott (1974), nos. 57, 64. Story (2003), p. 103.
34 Hincmar, *De ordine palatii*, MGH *Fontes NS* IV (1980), pp. 72–5; trans. Dutton (1993), no. 72.
35 Wallace-Hadrill (1965) and (1971), pp. 98–123.
36 Charlemagne to Offa, MGH *Epp.* IV, no. 87; Nelson (2001b), pp. 140–2. On Irish links to Francia, see also Einhard, *VK*, c. 16.

37 Nelson (2002a).

38 MGH *Capit.* I, no. 28; trans. King (1987), pp. 224–30. On the Frankfurt meeting, see Berndt, ed. (1997).

39 MGH *Capit.* I, no. 28, c. 56; trans. King (1987), p. 30; Bullough, ch. 8 (pp. 103–35) in this volume.

40 Charlemagne to Elipand, MGH *Concilia* II.i, pp. 158–60. On Adoptionism, see Cavadini (1993).

41 *Historia Regum (York Annals)* 792; Bullough, ch. 8 (pp. 103–35) in this volume.

42 Charlemagne to Æthelheard, MGH *Epp.* IV, no. 85; trans. *EHD* I, no. 196.

43 Alcuin, *Ep.*, nos. 104, 230–1, 255; Allott (1974), nos. 25, 51–3.

44 Alcuin, *Ep.*, no. 128; trans. Allott (1974), no. 49.

45 Alcuin, *Ep.*, no. 129; trans. Allott (1974), no. 50.

46 Leo III to Coenwulf, MGH *Epp.* IV, no. 127; trans. EHD 1, no. 205.

47 *ASC* 798 (*recte* 796); Brooks (1984), pp. 124–5.

48 *ASC* 839; Story (2003), pp. 214–24.

49 *Deeds of the Abbots of St-Wandrille*, c. XII.2; trans. King (1987), p. 334.

50 Alcuin *Ep.*, no. 7; trans. Allott (1974), no. 31.

51 Alcuin *Ep.*, no. 9; trans. Allott (1974), no. 10.

52 Bede, *HE*, 1.25; Wood (1994), pp. 176–9; Story (2003), p. 186.

53 RFA, 808, 809.

54 Leo III to Charlemagne, MGH *Epp.* V, *Epistolae Leonis III Papae*, nos. 2–4, pp. 89–94; Wallace-Hadrill (1965); Nelson (2002a); Story (2003), pp. 148, 202.

13

CHARLEMAGNE'S COINAGE: IDEOLOGY AND ECONOMY

Simon Coupland

Introduction

Was Charles the Great – Charlemagne – really great? On the basis of the numismatic evidence, the answer is resoundingly positive. True, the transformation of the Frankish currency had already begun: the gold coinage of the Merovingian era had already been replaced by silver coins in Francia, and the pound had already been divided into 240 of these silver 'deniers' (*denarii*). Charlemagne brought Italy into this system, in effect creating a single European currency. He gave the medieval penny its familiar form, enlarging the size of the *denarius* from *c.* 16mm to *c.* 20mm and increasing its weight from *c.*1.3g to 1.7g. He also standardised the appearance of the Carolingian *denarius*, creating a single coinage type which flowed freely across this vast territory, from the Spanish march to Frisia and from Brittany to Germany. He centralised minting processes, bringing monastic and comital mints under closer royal control and ensuring that all coins henceforth carried only the king's name. Last but by no means least, his portrait coinage sent an impressive and influential message of imperial status and power throughout the Frankish world – and beyond, as shown by the examples that have turned up in Viking-age graves in Norway and Sweden.

For those unused to dealing with numismatic evidence, this brief survey underlines how valuable coins can be for the historian. The choice of designs and inscriptions ('legends') on the front ('obverse') and back ('reverse') of the coins not only often enables us to attribute coins to specific rulers and mints, but it can also, as we shall see, convey an ideological message. The fact that each coin was struck from a pair of hand-carved stamps ('dies') permits us to look for pairs of coins from the same dies, and dies for different mints cut by the same craftsman. The number and location of finds, both coin hoards and stray finds, give an indication of the circulation of coinage and the volume of output from the various mints, while the number and location of the mints reflect the level and purpose of royal control. Further evidence of this comes from the effectiveness of the periodic recoinages, when the existing coin stock was completely replaced by a new design, and from the amount of foreign coinage in circulation. In addition, the weight and 'fineness' (silver content) of the coins can be a useful indication of economic prosperity. In all these respects, the coinage produced in Francia during Charlemagne's reign reflects the latter's strong and increasingly centralised control over the economy, despite the vast size of his territory. The coins are thus a very important source for understanding Charlemagne's impact and legacy.

Apart from the general surveys of Carolingian coinage,[1] Charlemagne's coinage has been the subject of a number of important studies. These include Grierson's magisterial survey, Völckers' corpus of finds of the pre-reform and monogram types, and Lafaurie's study of the portrait coinage, a subject to which Kluge has recently returned.[2] Compared with other aspects of Carolingian numismatics, this is an embarrassment of riches, all the more valuable because of the deeply flawed nature of standard reference works such as those by Morrison and Grunthal [MG] or Depeyrot.[3]

As a result of these studies, there is little doubt about the broad outlines of Charlemagne's coinage, even if significant details remain uncertain. Three basic coinage types were minted, of which the first – the small 'pre-reform' *denarius* – can be further subdivided into an earlier phase, when the mints reproduced the king's name as they saw fit, and a slightly later one, when a standardised form was used throughout. Minting began in 768, the year of Charlemagne's accession, and Grierson has suggested that the standardisation took place three years later in 771, when Charlemagne became sole ruler on the death of his brother and co-ruler Carloman.

In 793/94 this coinage was replaced by the larger, heavier coins bearing on one face the monogram of *KAROLVS* and on the other a cross. This coinage was struck throughout the empire with only minor variations, a uniform type manufactured at a reduced number of mints. It was replaced towards the end of Charlemagne's reign by the third and final coinage type, bearing the imperial portrait. The small number of finds of this third type implies a date significantly later than the imperial coronation of 800, later even than Grierson's original suggestion of 806. He has subsequently accepted Lafaurie's proposal that the coins were minted from 812, when Charlemagne was recognised as emperor in the West by the Byzantine emperor in the East.[4]

References in contemporary texts reveal that large and small transactions alike involved silver, and suggest that coins were in everyday use for many people. For example, at about this time one *denarius* could buy a dozen two-pound loaves, two *denarii* a *modius* of oats, and four *denarii* a sheep or a pig, while a cobbler received seven *denarii* for two pairs of shoes with new soles.[5] Nor were large sums of cash owned only by merchants: in the early ninth century, a priest in Brittany paid *XXX solidos argenti* ('30 *solidi* in silver', i.e. 360 *denarii*) for some land.[6] Even the poorest might have a coin or two in their purse: Corbie Abbey gave more than 1500 *denarii* per year to the travellers who spent the night within its precincts.[7]

Pre-reform coinage: 768–793/94 (Figure 7a, 7.1–7.8)

The general pattern of these small coins, weighing about 1.3g, was an obverse bearing the royal name, *CARO–LVS*, in two lines (with the A and R ligatured), and the name of the mint on the reverse. If this was the general rule, there were exceptions. The earliest coins, perhaps minted until 771, were less regular, with a variety of obverse legends, such as *CAR–LVS* (Figure 7.1), *CA–ROL'–REX*, *RF* (for *Rex Francorum*) with *CA* (for *CArolus*) inserted, or *CARLO*, the latter coins having been mistakenly attributed to Carloman, Charlemagne's brother (*MG* 83, 85).[8] Thereafter, however, there was a remarkable degree of uniformity everywhere except Italy, indicating that the king must have laid down a design, such as we know happened in 864 under Charles the Bald.[9] The reverse occasionally bears an image rather than an inscription, generally following a Merovingian model: a standing figure on coins minted at Chartres, for example (*MG* 152) or an anchored cross with pendants, resembling a large barred *m*, at the Paris mint (*MG* 229).

Several mints included the name of a magnate instead of a mint-name, among them the celebrated Roland, count of the Breton march (*MG* 276). Other named individuals were Autramnus (*MG* 234), Gervasius (*MG* 257), Leutbrand (*MG* 85, 'Carloman'), Mauringus (*MG* 266), Odalricus (*MG* 272) and Walacrius (*MG* 300), unless this is from the island of Walcheren. Although most of these individuals remain to be identified, the names Leutbrand (Liutprand) and Mauringus are both associated with Italy, the former with the line of the Lombard kings and dukes of Benevento, the latter with the dukedom of Brescia. Another well-known magnate whose name appears on contemporary coinage is Count Milo of Narbonne, although on these coins Milo's name takes the place of the king's in a clear assertion of comital power.[10]

On the vast majority of coins, however, the mint-name is on the reverse. Unfortunately, a combination of the small flans, the poor skills of the die-cutters and the contemporary predilection for abbreviations and ligatures means that the interpretation of the legends is often far from obvious. Even so, many of Morrison and Grunthal's huge list of 'Indeterminate Mints' can now be attributed with a degree of confidence. In 1965 Grierson referred to fifty known mints. Now we can list at least eighty, and possibly as many as one hundred, given those which remain to be identified. They stretch right across the empire, from Dorestad to Narbonne and Rennes to Treviso. A significant number are at ecclesiastical foundations, including St-Bavo in Ghent (*MG* 241), Ste-Croix in Poitiers (*MG* 285),[11] St-Denis (*MG* 253), St-Firmin in Amiens (*MG* 125–6), St-Maixent (*MG* 267), Ste-Marie in Rheims (*MG* 136–8), St-Martin and St-Maurice in Tours (*MG* 148–51,

7a Pre-reform coinage of Charlemagne

1 Chartres (*CARNOTIS*) – Fitzwilliam, *MEC* (as n.1) 1.721
2 Louis the Pious (*hLU-DUIh*), Clermont (ARVR+NIS) – Étienne Page sale, 4.x.1989, 129 (Breuvery hoard)
3 Dorestad (*DOR-STAD*) – KPK (as n. 25), M.545 (found at Domburg)
4 Melle (*MEDOLVS*) – Fitzwilliam, *MEC* 1.727
5 Mainz (+*D-MAG-CS*) – KPK, M 550 (found at Domburg)
6 *CLS* – KPK, M 536 (found at Domburg)
7 *RF* – KPK, van Rede 21207a

288), St-Peter in Trier (*MG* 294) and St-Trond (*MG* 290), along with various others whose location is as yet unclear. Many mints are known from only one or two specimens, but others were evidently much more prolific. To gauge their relative importance, we need to consider the evidence of the finds.

Völckers laid a superb foundation in his 1965 survey of hoards and single finds, though further discoveries have since come to light. I know of four additional pre-reform hoards: from Breuvery, Dijon, Dorestad (III) and Larino,[12] and over forty further single finds, too many to list here. The hoard finds fall into two rough groups, and it is surprising to note that there are great swathes of the Frankish heartlands where none has yet been reported. The first group lies north of the Rhine: one hoard, Prerow-Darss, actually comes from beyond the borders of the empire (two coins of Charlemagne alongside sixty-seven Arab dirhems), another,

Krinkberg, from just inside (thirty-five plus eighteen imitations).[13] The other four hoards in this northern group are Dorestad III (seventeen), 'Gelderland' (eighteen), Jelsum (ten) and Zetel (four). The second group of hoards runs south-eastwards from eastern France down through Switzerland and into Italy. The French hoards are Breuvery (eleven), Chézy (three), Dijon (four), Imphy (thirty-two) and 'Jura' (seven); two are from Switzerland: Bel-Air (ten) and Ilanz (thirty-eight pre-reform and one post-reform), and three from Italy: Larino (one, but see below), Sarzana (thirteen) and Vercelli (twenty-five to thirty). This pattern of finds should certainly not be equated with a pattern of monetarisation, as is clear from both the wider distribution of the single finds and the circulation pattern which emerges from analysis of the finds (see below). What it does remind us, however, is that the discovery of a hoard in, say, Neustria or Aquitaine might add significantly to our understanding of the pre-reform coinage.

A good illustration of this is provided by the most important – and surprising – fact to emerge from the hoards which were unknown to Völckers, namely the scale of the coinage minted in the name of Louis the Pious by Charlemagne on his son's coronation as sub-king of Aquitaine in 781.[14] Only two such coins were listed by Völckers, one of Limoges (III.15) and one of St-Stephen, Bourges (XXV.88), but since then three have been found in the Breuvery hoard and nineteen more at Larino. These twenty-two coins were struck at five mints: one at Clermont (Figure 7.2), one at an unknown ecclesiastical mint (Lafaurie has proposed St-Romain de Blaye) and three in Bourges: the city itself, the cathedral of St-Stephen and the abbey of St-Sulpice. Significantly, only two of the twenty-five known coins were struck from the same dies, namely a coin of Bourges and one of St-Stephen. The use of several dies per mint implies that this was more than just a token coinage and must have formed part of the everyday currency of the empire, albeit for a short time.

The hoards and single finds alike emphasise the outstanding importance of two mints in Charlemagne's realm, Dorestad (Figure 7.3) and Melle (Figure 7.4). This comes as no surprise: Dorestad was the largest emporium in northern Europe, and its coinage was so familiar in the north that contemporary imitations were produced by Frisians or, less probably, Scandinavians.[15] Evidence of Dorestad's widespread influence is provided by the discovery of its coins in Austria (Carnuntum) and England (St-Albans), as well as at Kregme in Denmark and in the Slav hoard at Prerow-Darss, not to mention the finds at Breuvery (two), Domburg (fifteen stray finds), 'Gelderland' (eleven), Ilanz, Jelsum (three), Krinkberg (thirty-one, and eighteen imitations), Mainz, Sarzana, Schouwen, Worms and Zetel (two).[16] In addition to this are the finds from Dorestad itself: the 1972 hoard mentioned earlier, which included nine local issues, and seventeen stray finds, of which three were minted locally.[17]

The second major mint was located at the silver mine of Melle in Poitou, whose coins have been discovered at Breuvery (two, plus one imitation),

Chalonnes-sur-Loire, Fontenay-le-Comte, Imphy (two), Melle itself, Neuville-en-Poitou, St-Cyr, Vercelli (two) and two other uncertain findspots in Vendée. There are also finds further afield: Dorestad, Krinkberg (three) and Speyer, as well as Carnuntum (two) and Southampton.[18] The significance of Melle is further demonstrated by the fact that silver from the mine was used to produce not only the pre-reform coins of Melle itself, but also those of Rennes.[19]

After Dorestad and Melle, the finds suggest that the next most significant mints were Mainz (Figure 7.5) and two uncertain sites, whose coins bore the legends *CLS* and *RF* (Figure 7.6–7). Next in importance came Chartres, Dinant, Milan and St-Martin in Tours. Mainz was a major urban centre and archbishopric, but what was the location of the ateliers which produced the *CLS* and *RF* coinages? The distribution of finds of the *CLS* coinage points to a northern mint: Cologne, Mons and a lost toll port near Bruges, *Clusas*, have all been suggested.[20] Mons is too insignificant for the scale of the coinage, and although Cologne initially seems attractive, the scarcity of its post-reform issues (and similarly those of Louis the Pious and Lothar I) indicate that it was not a prolific mint, nor is there a plausible explanation for the letter S in the legend. Yet the lost port also suffers from a major difficulty, namely that charters continued to refer to tolls at *Clusas* long after the *CLS* mint had ceased operation in the 790s. Nor were these toll points necessarily major mints: although Dorestad was, just one find of a pre-reform coin of Quentovic has been recorded (at Krinkberg), a situation paralleled in the post-reform finds (three coins of the monogram type), and indeed under Louis the Pious and Charles the Bald. This cumulative evidence should incidentally cause historians to question the long-held assumption, based on written sources, that Quentovic was a wealthy mercantile site in the late eighth and early ninth centuries. It does not appear to have been in the same league as any of the mints listed above, let alone Dorestad.[21] As for the source of the *CLS* coinage, regrettably, it remains unknown.

Before considering the identity of the mint that produced coinage with *RF* – for *Rex Francorum* – on the reverse, we must briefly review the situation in Italy, where coins with the same reverse legend were also produced. When Charlemagne took power in Italy in 773/74 he allowed Italian mints to continue manufacturing gold *tremisses* in his name: forty of them were present in the Ilanz hoard. Although other gold coins or medallions were struck in Charlemagne's name in other parts of the empire, such as Dorestad (*MG* 643, wrongly 'Charles the Bald'), Uzès (*MEC* 1.734), *Aurodis* and Arles,[22] none of these was intended for general circulation, unlike the Italian gold coinage. In 781 it was withdrawn from circulation, when the Capitulary of Mantua laid down: 'After August 1 no-one shall dare to give or receive those coins which we can be seen to be using now'.[23] In its place the king introduced the silver *denarius*, bearing the standard *CARO-LVS* obverse as seen elsewhere in Francia, but distinctive in three ways (Figure 7.8): the flans were larger than those of the rest of the empire, the lettering was sprawling and spiky, and the *RF* legend on the reverse was accompanied by a letter or group of letters indicating the mint. The most common of these was *ME* (ligatured) for Milan; other mints included Bergamo, Pavia, Piacenza, and perhaps Cremona and Verona (or Vercelli). Later in the reign, possibly in 787 when Charlemagne was again in Italy, these coins were replaced at some if not all mints by a more standard form, on smaller flans bearing the mint-name.[24]

Having described the Italian coinage, we can return to the quite different, and more common, group of coins bearing the reverse legend *RF*. These are on standard flans, have no abbreviated mint-name, and were minted outside Italy. The find distribution suggests a mint somewhere in modern France, ruling out the possibility of the palace at Aachen, but we cannot at present locate the mint more precisely.

The hoards and single finds reveal not only which were the most important mints at this time, but also something of the pattern of circulation of the coinage, although we must bear in mind the absence of hoards in the west. Finds naturally tend to be concentrated close to their place of origin, as is illustrated by the cluster of finds around Melle listed earlier. Nonetheless, as we have seen, other coins from Melle found their way to the northern and eastern borders of the empire and across the Channel. Similarly, a coin from Angers was found in the Great St-Bernard pass in the Alps; one from Avignon at Minnertsga in Friesland. Coins from Bingen on the Rhine have turned up at Middelstum in northern Holland and Vercelli in Italy; a coin from Condé was found at Bel-Air in Switzerland and one from Parma at Domburg.[25] Many other similar examples could be cited, all of them showing that there was regular long-distance movement of coins across this vast empire, surely due in part, if not indeed in the main, to trade. This marks a significant change from the end of the Merovingian era, when coins circulated within local currency pools close to their place of origin.[26]

Finally, what was the fineness of these pre-reform coins? Several coins include more than 90 per cent silver,[27] though the coins in the 1987 Dijon hoard all contained less than two-thirds silver.[28] Among the first group, it is not surprising that two coins from Melle had a high silver content, 93 per cent and 93.4 per cent, but a coin of Mainz was even finer, with 94.52 per cent silver. A coin of Lyon contained 92.39 per cent, and a coin from Dorestad 90 per cent. Among the coins of the Dijon hoard, however, the finest was one of St-Martin in Tours, at 65 per cent; next came a coin from Paris, at 61 per cent, then one from an uncertain ecclesiastical mint, *SCISEPHF* (St-Stephen?), containing just 50 per cent silver. Yet even this surpassed a coin from Troyes, with a mere 38 per cent. It is hard to account for the discrepancy between these two sets of figures, but if they are accurate, they demonstrate the need for a reform to bring a consistent standard to coinage which was freely circulating and mingling, good alongside poor, across the empire.

Monogram coinage 793/94–812 (Figure 7b, 7.9–7.16)

In 794 Charlemagne issued a capitulary at the Synod of Frankfurt declaring that 'these new *denarii* shall be legal tender in every village, town and market, and shall be acceptable to everyone'.[29] These were the broader, thinner, heavier deniers, struck to the new weight standard of 1.7g which, as the capitulary stated, bore 'the monogram of our name', the stamp of royal authority: *KRLS* around a lozenge. It is unclear from the text whether or not they were already in circulation; Lafaurie has suggested that the recoinage took place at Martinmas, 11 November 793, since that was the date chosen for coinage reforms in 825 and 864.[30]

In the nineteenth century there were heated debates over which coins bearing the name 'Charles' should be attributed to Charlemagne and which to his grandson Charles the Bald, but hoard evidence now enables us to resolve virtually all the issues. There are unfortunately fewer recorded finds than of the preceding type and, astonishingly, again none from the west – in this instance, not even single finds. There are two hoards from the south of France: Château Roussillon (six coins of Charlemagne) and Limoux (145–160 coins),[31] but nothing else from modern France or Switzerland. From Italy there is just one hoard, Bondeno (only five mints recorded from a large find).[32] Most of the rest of the hoards lie close to the Rhine: Biebrich (only forty-eight coins were recorded from a large hoard, forty-four of them of Charlemagne), Ibersheim (fifteen, all of Charlemagne), Leer (just two) and Dorestad I (twenty-one monogram coins out of forty-eight in total).[33] One hoard has also been found in the eastern Netherlands (Borne: fifteen monogram coins and one pre-reform).[34]

Certain of these hoards are indisputably from Charlemagne's time, and demonstrate the general uniformity of the coinage, as well as the minor variations. Usually the mint-name surrounded the cross on one side, and the king's title – *CARLVSREXFR*(*ancorum*) – encircled the monogram on the other, though the mint-name could encircle the monogram, and the title the cross. Occasionally there were points around the cross, as for example at Dorestad (*MG* 103–4) or Laon (*MG* 130), and sometimes more unusual marks: crescents at Bourges (*MEC* 1.740), wedges at Dorestad (Figure 7.9), semicircles at Cologne (*MG* Plate IV, 106), circles at the mint producing the '*Ex metallo novo*' coinage (Figure 7.11). At Mainz the die-cutters sometimes put the cross with points on the obverse, sometimes without points on the reverse, and at other times put the cross on steps or replaced it with a large letter P (Figure 7.12–13). On most coins the mint-name is the locality without any further designation, though some coins from Agen bear the title *AGINCIVITAS* (*MG* 1088, 'Charles the Bald', but present at Biebrich). These characteristics allow us to attribute to Charlemagne similar coins from Chelles (*MG* 856, present in the Dorestad I hoard), Orléans (*MG* 946, single find at Dorestad), Paris (*MG* 828–9), Quentovic (*MG* 1371, a single find at Domburg and two single finds at Dorestad), Sens (*MG* 983, not present at Zelzate) and *TVNNIS*

7b Monogram coinage of Charlemagne
  9 Dorestad – KPK, 1978-336
  10 Dorestad obole – KPK, van Rede 21211b
  11 *Ex metallo novo* – KPK, 17647
  12 Mainz – Fitzwilliam, *MEC* 1.742
  13 Mainz – KPK, 17487 (found at Dorestad)
  14 Toulouse – KPK, 17620 (found at Dorestad)
  15 Pavia – Fitzwilliam, *MEC* 1.745
  16 Milan – Fitzwilliam, Blunt 1-2844-1990

(*MG* 1373–4, single find at Dorestad).

Unfortunately, an identical type was struck by Charles the Bald in the south-west of his kingdom over fifty years later, with the result that for some mints it is now impossible to attribute individual coins to one or other ruler without a context. This is the case at Bourges and Melle, where hoard evidence shows that identical issues were produced under the two rulers, but as we shall see, not at Toulouse, where a distinction can be made. Nor is it the case at Clermont, which is only known to have struck monogram coinage after 864. With regard to the mints at Agen (*MG* 177–9, 1087–9), Arles (*MG* 192–7, 1110), Béziers (*MG* 183), Dax (*MG* 180, 1090–4), Lyon (*MG* 166, 1037) and Vienne (*MG* 191), hoard evidence at present shows only that they were active under Charlemagne. As for Ampurias

(MG 186), Barcelona (MG 188–9), Gerona (MG 187), Marseille (MG 202–3) and Roda (not in MG),[35] single finds at Dorestad or comparison with the other mints listed here suggest that they, too, are more likely to have been in operation under Charlemagne than in the time of Charles the Bald. However, we should note the example of Narbonne, whose issues are known only from stray finds and a hoard of Charlemagne (Château Roussillon), but which was explicitly named in the Edict of Pîtres as one of Charles the Bald's mints.[36]

Several of Charlemagne's mints also struck monogram 'oboles', or half-deniers. In the past, these have all been attributed to Charles the Bald, in part due to the misconception that minting of oboles only began under Louis the Pious.[37] It is often difficult to recognise oboles in the pre-reform period because of weight variations among the *denarii* and the small size of the flans, but following the reform of 793/94 the oboles are distinctive, being not only smaller in size and half the weight of the *denarii*, but also bearing the monogram filling the field on one face and usually the mint-name around a cross on the other. That they are coins of Charlemagne and not just Charles the Bald is clear from their manufacture at, for instance, Dorestad (Figure 7.10), where Charles the Bald never minted, since he never ruled there.[38] The oboles listed by Morrison and Grunthal under Charles the Bald's name should consequently be restored to Charlemagne (MG 914, 1037, 1060, 1089, 1106–7, 1110 and probably also 1131 and 1152), although as we have seen, some of these were minted under both rulers.

The clarification of this misconception makes it plain that the five deniers and one obole of the Château Roussillon hoard, sometimes attributed to Charles the Bald, are actually of Charlemagne, as is confirmed by the presence of monogram coins from Dorestad and Pavia. A coin in the same hoard minted at Toulouse bears the short reverse legend *TOLVSA*, supporting the thesis that all such coins can be attributed to Charlemagne, while those with the longer mint-name, *TOLVSACIVI(tas)* (or variant) should be ascribed to Charles the Bald.[39] This is also borne out by the Biebrich, Borne and Ibersheim hoards and the eight single finds from Dorestad, all of which have the short title (Figure 7.14), and by the coin from the Roermond hoard of c. 850, which reads *TOLVSACIVI*.[40] This in turn indicates that we should also attribute to Charlemagne the Limoux hoard, which contained 120–130 deniers and 25–30 oboles, all from Toulouse and all bearing the short title.

The hoards demonstrate the effectiveness of the recoinage which accompanied the reform of 793/94. Only two included both pre-reform and post-reform issues together, Borne and Ilanz, and they contained just one of the old coinage type and one of the new *denarii* respectively. Was there a similar recoinage in 768, when Charlemagne's pre-reform type was introduced? Although two hoards, Imphy and Ilanz, contained Pippin's coinage alongside Charlemagne's, none of the others did so. (Dorestad III, which also included a parcel of Louis the Pious's Class 2 coinage, is presumably a so-called 'savings hoard', in which a group of coins has been added to an existing deposit.) It therefore seems possible that there was a recoinage at the beginning of Charlemagne's reign, which the coins at Ilanz and Imphy somehow escaped. The hoards also reveal how effectively foreign coin was excluded from circulation, with only two containing foreign issues: Ilanz, with three Anglo-Saxon pennies and two Arab 'dirhems' from North Africa, and Biebrich, with a single North African dirhem.

Where did the silver for this recoinage come from? One new mine had evidently opened, as is indicated by the existence of coins reading *Ex metallo novo* (*MG* 309–12, Figure 7.11). However, the small number of surviving specimens (including one in the Ibersheim hoard and stray finds at Dorestad and Tournai) suggests that this mine, whose location remains unknown, was not particularly large. There is very little evidence of large-scale importation of Arab silver at this time. Military conquest may have brought in plunder and tribute,[41] but the question as stated earlier may reflect a false assumption. In 864, when Charles the Bald reformed the West Frankish coinage, increasing its purity and restoring the weight standard,[42] the kingdom was apparently losing silver in large quantities to Viking raiders. Seventy years earlier, Charlemagne's reform was primarily a reform of weights and measures,[43] designed at the same time to increase royal control over the currency and bolster confidence in its use. As long as the exchange rate of old coins for new was judged to be fair (a point on which contemporary sources are silent) the reforms may not have required a significant injection of extra silver.

Hoards and single finds also shed light on the operation of the mints producing the monogram type. There were significantly fewer – around forty – and this was evidently part of a concerted effort to bring coin production under stricter control. A capitulary of 808 stated: 'Let coinage be struck nowhere other than at court (*ad curtem*); and these palace coins shall be traded and circulate everywhere'.[44] This cannot mean that production was restricted to a single palace mint, with the coins transported to their places of emission: the distances involved are too great, the coins too numerous.[45] A more likely interpretation is that the mint was to be located at a royal site, or *curtis*, in each place.[46] This is consistent with a fragmentary capitulary issued by Louis the Pious, which laid down, 'Let the town mint be under the protection of the count on behalf of the state ... These moneyers shall not presume to [coin] money on behalf of the state elsewhere, nor anywhere inside or outside the town apart from the appointed place'.[47] It is thus significant that there were fewer ecclesiastical or monastic mints after the reform: the only known examples are St-Denis (*MG* 139a) and Ste-Marie in Laon (*MG* 131–2). Moreover, Charlemagne's name was now the only one to appear on the coinage.

A few mints cannot be identified with any certainty (the new mine or *metallum novum* mentioned earlier, *DVNNOS*, *SENNES* and *TVNNIS*), but none of these seems to have been particularly prolific. Melle was again among the most important, though it now shared this honour not with Dorestad, but with Pavia and Milan (Figure 7.15–16). Nor is this because of a large number of Italian finds: there

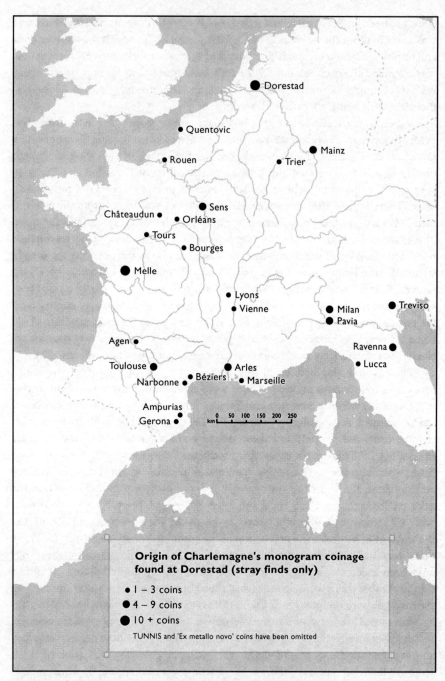

8 Origin of Charlemagne's monogram coinage found at Dorestad

is only one hoard, Bondeno, as well as a few single finds.[48] Rather, it is because large numbers of Italian coins were finding their way northwards and westwards:[49] for example, at Dorestad eight Pavian coins have been found (two in a hoard and six single finds) and nine coins from Milan (one in a hoard and eight single finds). This trend continued under Louis the Pious, although by then Venice had evidently overtaken Milan.[50]

Other prolific mints at this time, though not apparently as significant as these three, were Dorestad and Mainz, as in the pre-reform period, but also Agen and Toulouse. This is all the more remarkable given the absence of hoards and single finds from the south-west. True, the hoards from Limoux and Château Roussillon both contained Toulousan issues, but the mint's importance is also attested by other finds: Biebrich (five), Borne, Dorestad I and Ibersheim, as well as eight single finds at Dorestad, two at Schouwen and one apiece from De Houw and Münster. Agen is similarly represented at Biebrich (two), Dorestad I (four) and Ibersheim, and in single finds from Bolsward, Dorestad (two deniers and one obole) and Jutland.[51]

Taken together, these finds again indicate that coinage was flowing freely across this enormous empire, with the finds at Dorestad in particular coming from virtually all parts of the Carolingian world (Figure 8). The monogram coinage is especially common at Dorestad, second only to the *Christiana religio* issues of Louis the Pious. This is significantly different from nearby Domburg, where just eight monogram issues have been found, compared with twenty-seven pre-reform coins and twenty-three of Pippin III. The early ninth century thus appears to have been a period of intense economic activity at Dorestad, the beginning of a boom which reached its peak in the 820s.[52]

Finally, as yet only two monogram coins have been analysed to determine their silver content: one from Pavia and one from Milan.[53] They contained 97.5 per cent and 98 per cent silver respectively, both exceptionally high figures, higher than any of the pre-reform deniers. This is, however, too small a sample to draw any conclusions about the coinage as a whole.

Portrait coinage 812–814 (Figure 9, 1–11)

Charlemagne's third coinage type, bearing the imperial portrait, is arguably the least economically significant of the three, but ideologically the most important. Its purpose was undoubtedly to convey an image of imperial power and prestige, depicting Charlemagne as successor to the Roman emperors on whose coinage this type was modelled.[54]

The coinage's lack of economic importance is apparent from the very small number of finds: one in the Dorestad I hoard and one in the much later Achlum hoard represent the sum total of hoard finds. As for single finds, six have turned up at Dorestad (Figure 9.2), three elsewhere in the Netherlands – at Minnertsga

(Figure 9.5), Oosterbierum and Tiel – two at Trier, one at Market Weighton in Yorkshire (Figure 9.6), and two in Scandinavia, at Moksnes and Birka. Indeed, only about forty coins are known in total.[55] This undoubtedly reflects the fact that they were minted for only a short period, probably from Charlemagne's recognition as emperor by Constantinople in 812 until his death in January 814.[56]

The great majority of the coins are anonymous, bearing the reverse inscription *Christiana religio*, or more accurately, *Xpictiana religio*. This legend surrounds a temple, which may represent the palace chapel at Aachen or perhaps the 'Christian Church' more broadly. Some have a letter beneath the obverse bust: *C*, *F*, *M*, *V* and perhaps *B* (Figure 9.3–6). The first four have been identified as Cologne, Frankfurt, Mainz and Worms, and the fifth – if correctly read – presumably represents either Bingen or Bonn, both of which struck pre-reform coinage and are situated, like the other mints, on the Rhine. Other coins bear mint-names on the reverse: Arles, Dorestad (Figure 9.8), Lyon, Quentovic (Figure 9.9), Rouen,[57] Trier and *METALLGERMAN* (Figure 9.2), the latter almost certainly signifying the mine at Melle, bearing in mind its economic importance (i.e. *germanum*, meaning 'genuine', not *Germanicum*, 'German').

The *Christiana religio* issues bear three different obverse inscriptions. Some have a long title, *DNKARLVSIMPAVGRFETL*, for *D(ominus) N(oster) KARLVS IMP(erator) AVG(ustus) R(ex) F(rancorum) ET L(angobardorum)* ('Our Lord Charles, Emperor Augustus, King of the Franks and Lombards'), the latter title suggesting an Italian connection (Figure 9.1). Others bear the legend *KAROLVSIMPAVG* (Figure 9.3–6), while a third group read *KARLVS IMP AVG* (Figure 9.7). Within each of these groups there are also stylistic affinities, suggesting that each die-cutter consistently used the same title. There is also at least one distinctive feature on the reverse of the portrait coins which parallels to an extent those on the obverse: the coins reading *KARLVSIMPAVG* and some of those with the longer Italianate title include small flame-like darts on the horizontal roof line, but these are not found on any of the known coins reading *KAROLVSIMPAVG*. Putting this evidence together, it would seem that the dies for the coins reading *KAROLVSIMPAVG* were

---

9 Portrait coinage

    1 *DNKARLVS Christiana religio* – Courtauld collection, University of Zimbabwe. Photo courtesy of Graham Pollard

    2 *DNKARLVS* Melle – ROB 7335 (found at Dorestad)

  3–4 *KAROLVS Christiana religio* 'M' (Mainz) – Paris, Prou (as n. 10) 981

    5 *KAROLVS Christiana religio* 'B'? – KPK, 1995-1005 (found at Minnertsga)

    6 *KAROLVS Christiana religio* 'M'? (found at Market Weighton)

    7 *KARLVS Christiana religio* – Paris, Prou 983

    8 Dorestad – Brussels, de Jonghe 34

    9 Quentovic – Fitzwilliam, *MEC* 1.749

   10 Louis the Pious Class 1, Dorestad – Brussels, no inv. no.

   11 Louis the Pious Class 1, Quentovic – Paris, Prou 187

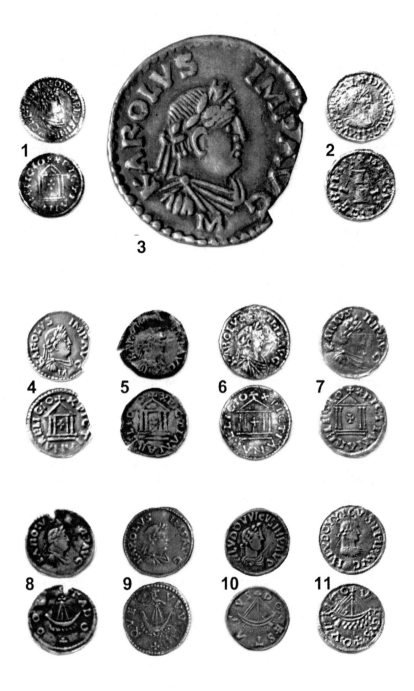

produced at a different location from those bearing the other titles; whether the latter were produced together is less clear.

Among the mint-signed coins, those from Dorestad, Lyon, Quentovic, Rouen and Trier read *KAROLVSIMPAVG*, as do some from Arles. Some of these are unquestionably the work of the same die-cutter, notably the coins from Dorestad and Quentovic (Figure 9.8–9). Indeed, the same hand evidently produced both these dies and those for the *Christiana religio* issues with the same title: the coin from Mainz illustrated here is a good example (Figure 9.3–4). The portraits and lettering of the coins from Arles, Lyon and Rouen are also of a comparable style, though not the single specimen from Trier. The dies for these mints were consequently cut at a single location although, as was said earlier, it is unlikely that the coins themselves were produced centrally. This is particularly obvious in the case of Dorestad and Quentovic, where imported coin and silver were surely turned into coin on site. The portrait coinage produced by Louis the Pious at the two *emporia* reveals a significant change: the ships illustrated on the reverse not only differ in style from those on the coins struck locally by Charlemagne, but now those at Dorestad also differ from those at Quentovic (Figure 9.10–11). The implication is that after 814 both ports went back to cutting their own dies. As for the possible location of Charlemagne's die-cutting centre, the most likely place to have produced dies for Arles, Bonn or Bingen, Cologne, Frankfurt, Dorestad, Lyon, Quentovic, Mainz, Rouen and Worms was undoubtedly the palace at Aachen. The high standard of the portrait on the coins is consistent with this.

By contrast, the anonymous coins with the title *DNKARLVSIMPAVGRFETL* were presumably produced in Italy, most likely at Milan or Pavia, even though coins with the same obverse legend are also known from Arles and Melle. In the case of the coins from Arles, there are clear stylistic differences distinguishing these from the coins with the title *KAROLVSIMPAVG* (the gold 'solidus' belongs to the Italianate group).[58] Those with the longer title have points in the mint-name; those with the shorter title do not. On those with the shorter title the city gate on the reverse is comparable to that on coins from Lyon and Rouen; on the Italianate coins it is quite different. On the latter, the mint-name begins above the gate; on the former, below. Since it is unlikely that Arles' coinage was struck in two different places, presumably the source of its dies changed from one die-cutting centre, in Italy, to the other, at Aachen.

Finally, at Melle the picture is different again, with the reverses of the single known coin with the Italianate title (Figure 9.2) and the one surviving specimen of the two known coins reading *KARLVSIMPAVG* appearing virtually identical, if not indeed from the same die. Yet the bust on the latter is nothing like the bust on the *Christiana religio* issues with the same legend, but of a unique style. Perhaps Melle was initially supplied with dies from Italy, but subsequently began manufacturing its own dies. The place of origin of the anonymous coins reading *KARLVSIMPAVG* remains unclear.

To summarise, towards the end of Charlemagne's reign the centralisation of coin production was taken yet further, with a very few centres producing dies for a handful of mints. The fact that Louis the Pious evidently abandoned this practice two years later, as the evidence from Dorestad and Quentovic shows, might suggest that it was not viable, or might simply mean that Louis was able to train additional skilled die-cutters. Whichever was the case, Louis' choice of a portrait coinage as his first type implies that this imperial coinage was perceived as having achieved the desired ideological impact.

Summary: ideology and economy

As we look back over the forty-six years of Charlemagne's reign, the coinage bears clear and impressive testimony to the emperor's control and development of the economy. The evidence includes not only the transformation of the size, weight and possibly fineness of the *denarius*, but also the exclusion of foreign coinage, the move from gold to silver in Italy, the standardisation of the coinage types and the tighter control over die and coin production. It is equally plain that these changes would have had a powerful ideological impact, as they were undoubtedly intended to do.

Thus, at the start of Charlemagne's reign, a Frankish merchant with a bag full of silver might have had in his purse coins bearing the names of Pippin, Carloman, Charlemagne and Milo of Narbonne. By the time of the emperor's death, all his coins would have borne Charlemagne's name, and some would also have displayed his portrait, as grand as his Roman predecessors'. Even the illiterate would have noticed the changes, for contemporary texts reveal that many common people were using coin. The bigger, heavier coins must have been impressive, their uniformity would have made clearer which coins were legal tender, and the portrait coins were a source of wonder, as the specimens retained as jewellery bear witness. In short, in putting his stamp so firmly on the Frankish coinage, Charlemagne's people, rich and poor alike, cannot but have been impressed by the emperor's power and prestige.

Notes

Many thanks to all who kindly permitted me to photograph coins in their collections, particularly the Koninklijk Penningkabinet, Leiden (KPK) and Mark Blackburn at the Fitzwilliam Museum, Cambridge.

1 The best general survey of Carolingian coins is Grierson and Blackburn (1986), pp. 205–10.
2 Grierson (1965); Völckers (1965); Lafaurie (1978); Kluge (1999) and (2002).
3 Morrison and Grunthal (1967); Depeyrot (1993). See *Numismatic Chronicle* (1969), pp. 346–50; *RN* 6.9 (1967), pp. 291–5; *RN* 6.36 (1994), pp. 352–6.

4 Grierson and Blackburn (1986), p. 209.

5 *Synodus Franconofurtensis* (794), c. 4, *Capitulare missorum Niumagae datum* (806), c. 17; MGH *Capit.* I, no. 28 and 46, pp. 74, 132; *Polyptyque de l'abbé Irminon*, cc.42, 35, ed. Guérard (1845), II, pp. 5, 74, 308–9 (*Statutes of Adalhard of Corbie*, I c. 3).

6 De Courson, ed. (1863), p. 129.

7 Duby (1962), p. 301.

8 Lafaurie (1974), pp. 39–40.

9 Coupland (1985).

10 Prou (1892), no. 834; Grierson and Blackburn (1986), no. 1497.

11 *RN* 4.35 (1932), pp. xxxi–xxxii.

12 Breuvery, Marne: *Numismatic Circular* 76 (1968), pp. 150–4; Dijon, Côte d'Or: *BSFN* 44 (1989), pp. 577–81; Dorestad, Utrecht: van Es and Verwers (1980), pp. 215--21; Larino, Molise: *RN* 153 (1998), pp. 217–43.

13 Hatz (1985), pp. 125–32.

14 Coupland (1990), pp. 24–5.

15 Malmer (1966).

16 Finds not included in Völckers (1965) or n.12 above are Carnuntum: *MOnG* 21 (1979), pp. 33–4, 57–8; *MOnG* 24 (1984), pp. 12–13; *MOnG* 27 (1987), p. 84; St-Albans: Blackburn, ed. (1986), p. 129; Kregme: pers. comm. C. Moesgaard; Mainz: Wamers (1994), p. 178.

17 Coupland (2002).

18 Finds not included in Völckers (1965) or nn.12 and 16 above are Southampton: Blackburn, ed. (1986), p. 129, and a number listed in Jeanne-Rose (1996).

19 Barrandon and Dumas (1990).

20 Grierson and Blackburn (1986), p. 635.

21 Coupland (2002).

22 Martin (1997).

23 *Capitulare Mantuanum* (?781), c. 9, MGH *Capit.* I, no. 90, p. 191; trans. Loyn and Percival (1975), pp. 49–51.

24 Lafaurie (1972).

25 Finds not in Völckers (1965) or nn.16 and 18 above are Great St-Bernard: *BSFN* 42 (1987), p. 155; Minnertsga: KPK, 1991–07–03.

26 Lafaurie (1974), p. 34.

27 Metcalf and Merrick (1967), p. 179; Metcalf and Northover (1989), p. 106.

28 Depeyrot (1993), pp. 122, 202, 244, 248.

29 *Synodus Franconofurtensis* (794), c. 5, MGH *Capit.* I, p. 74; trans. King (1987), p. 225.

30 *Admonitio ad omnes regni ordines* (825), c. 20, MGH *Capit.* I, no. 150, p. 306; *Edictum Pistense* (864), c. 10: MGH *Capit.* II, no. 273, p. 315.

31 Haertle (1997), nos. 21 and 48.

32 Morrison and Grunthal (1967), Find 12.

33 *Revue Belge de Numismatique* (1857), pp. 34–6; Haertle (1997), no. 7. The coins were mistakenly listed by Völckers (1965) among the single finds: III.20, 29, 35 (*recte* six coins), 44, 48, 69, 72, 78–9, 86 (but not 85).

34 *Overijsselse Historische Bijdragen* 105 (1990), pp. 147–51.

35 Crusafont i Sabater (1983).

36 *Edictum Pistense* (864), c. 12, MGH *Capit.* II, no. 273, p. 315.

37 Grierson and Blackburn (1986), pp. 206, 213; Grierson (1965), p. 518; Coupland (1990), p. 26.

38 Coupland (1988).
39 Pierfitte (1933).
40 *JMP* 72 (1985), p. 44.
41 Reuter (1985).
42 Coupland (1991), pp. 152–5.
43 Grierson (1965), pp. 528–30.
44 *Capitula cum primis constituta* (808), c. 7: MGH *Capit.* I, no. 52, p. 140.
45 Lafaurie (1976), pp. 66–9.
46 Coupland (1986).
47 *Capitulare de moneta* (c.820), cc.1–2, MGH *Capit.* I, no. 147, p. 299.
48 Rovelli (2000b), p. 216.
49 Metcalf (1988).
50 Coupland (1990), p. 32.
51 Finds not in Völckers (1965) or nn. 3–4 above are De Houw: KPK 02–04–1998; Münster: Stiegemann and Wemhoff, eds. (1999a), p. 389; Bolsward: Haertle (1997), no. 528/ 001; Jutland: Bendixen (1988), p. 38.
52 Coupland (2002).
53 Metcalf, Merrick and Hamblin (1968), p. 57.
54 Kluge (1999), pp. 82–3.
55 Coins not in Kluge (2002) are Dorestad: van der Chijs (1866), p. 132 (pl. XII.36, 37); Trier: Gilles (1985), p. 46; Market Weighton and Courtauld Collection, University of Zimbabwe (Figure 9.1 and 9.6), unpublished.
56 Lafaurie (1976), p. 67.
57 Delaporte (1989).
58 Martin (1997).

14

RURAL SETTLEMENT HIERARCHY IN THE AGE OF CHARLEMAGNE

Christopher Loveluck

Archaeological analysis of a range of settlement remains from the Carolingian period has enhanced our view of the nature of settlement patterns in the diverse regions ruled by Pippin III and his successors. This paper reviews the archaeological evidence from a range of defined settlement types within a selected region under Carolingian control. Through a synthetic analysis of the structural character of settlements and their patterns of production and consumption, we can investigate how the material remains reflect the hierarchy of Carolingian settlements and how social and economic functions interacted. The geographical focus will be mainly on the north of Charlemagne's realm (see Figure 2): namely, northern France from the Seine, to Belgium, the southern Netherlands and the northern extremity of the German Rhineland. In the terminology of the early Carolingian period, this area corresponds to the eastern part of the kingdom of Neustria and western part of Austrasia.[1] Some additional comparative evidence is drawn from the regions of Burgundy, Bavaria and the Saxon-Danish border region.

The chronological range of the study, AD 700–1000, encapsulates the period of Carolingian dynastic hegemony, but also looks beyond it. The reason for this broad timescale is twofold. Primarily, it relates to the nature of archaeological remains as a particular form of evidence distinct from textual sources. Textual evidence tends to refer to specific people, places, actions or events, within a particular context and (usually) a limited time-frame. In contrast, the circumstances of archaeological site-formation and the creation of settlement deposits usually make it impossible to focus on events within the short time-spans preferred by many historians.

Settlement deposits regularly comprise re-worked refuse material derived from a collection of actions from different dates; therefore, it is inappropriate to focus on very tight chronological periods. It is rarely possible to date such deposits to within a century without significant quantities of datable artefacts – or dendro-chronological and radio-carbon dates – analysed alongside evidence of deposit disturbance and movement. Furthermore, in most areas west of the Rhine, unfurnished inhumation had become the norm in cemeteries by the eighth century. Dating of unfurnished burial practices often requires the assignation of broad chronological ranges, derived from radiocarbon error-margins or stylistic dating of mortuary structures and sarcophagi. Hence, the complexities of dating settlement deposits, in combination with the wide dating margins for unfurnished graves, make a broad timescale more appropriate for purposes of analysis.

A broad chronological framework that spans the Carolingian period also capitalises on the wide perspective that archaeological evidence is well suited to provide: demonstrating settlement trends of long duration and providing evidence for aspects of everyday life, often less apparent in contemporary written records. Continuation of the survey to include later ninth- and tenth-century remains also enables evaluation of the legacy of Charlemagne and his successors on new settlement forms and hierarchies, which led to the widespread growth of towns as focal points within society.[2]

The nature of urban settlements and their evolution between the eighth and tenth centuries are subjects for special attention in their own right; perhaps less familiar are the developments in rural settlement. The range of 'rural' settlement types discussed here includes farmsteads; hamlets; nucleated and fortified settlements; estate centres (when they can be identified); monasteries; and settlements with several components – known to archaeologists as 'polyfocal settlements'. To differentiate between the more complex 'rural' settlements and their 'urban' counterparts is not a simple matter, whether in terms of physical character, provisioning, or patterns of production and exchange. Indeed, many polyfocal settlements, which originally consisted of several 'rural' foci, acted as the immediate precursors of the towns that emerged during the course of the ninth and tenth centuries. The point at which these complex rural settlements became urban depends largely on individually-held definitions of a 'town'.

Elements of rural settlement: farmsteads, hamlets, and nucleated settlements

In the seventh century, significant changes in elements of the settlement pattern occurred across the region under study. A recent review of the early medieval evidence in northern France noted that new settlement agglomerations were being established from the end of the sixth century and through the seventh century. Unlike their Merovingian forebears, these new settlements were not in close proximity to the row-grave cemeteries of earlier centuries. Lorren and Périn see these new settlement agglomerations as evidence for the infilling of the landscape between existing settlement foci. They are more circumspect, how-ever, in suggesting the reason for their creation, putting forward 'economic' and demographic growth as possibilities, as well as territorial reorganisation.[3]

The character of smaller settlements, whether single farmsteads or small hamlets, is much less clear during the Carolingian period. It is not currently possible to tell whether those that have been identified, primarily from scatters of pottery in field-walking or during the course of development projects, show signs of abandonment or relocation contemporary with the changes witnessed for larger settlements, due to the lack of comprehensively excavated examples in northern France. Similarly in Flanders, constraints on the extent of excavations imposed by limitations of land use and the modern urban environment, also make it difficult to know whether the recently discovered Merovingian- and Carolingian-period settlements are parts of small hamlets or larger settlement agglomerations.[4]

Counterbalancing the ambiguous evidence from Flanders and northern France, excavations in the sand regions of the southern Netherlands have yielded useful information on the nature of smaller settlements and their development in the seventh century and beyond. Theuws has suggested that the settlement pattern of the Kempen region was characterised by small, dispersed settlements of farmsteads until the mid-seventh century, on the basis of excavations at Reusel-De Mierden and Geldrop. Subsequently, from the mid-seventh to mid-eighth centuries some farmsteads such as Geldrop developed into larger hamlet agglo-merations of up to five farm units, each with a focal earth-fast building, ancillary structures and some fences.[5] A similar sequence of development is also becoming apparent at Venray-'t Brukske, in the Limburg area of the Meuse valley, where there was a significant shift from the fifth- to seventh-century settlement site to the eighth- to twelfth-century hamlet.[6]

In other instances in the Kempen region, for example at Dommelen and at Hulsel, completely new settlements were founded during the second half of the seventh century and the course of the eighth century. Like Geldrop, the settle-ment at Dommelen also developed into a significant hamlet with a series of farm units at the turn of the eighth century.[7] A similar pattern of settlement founda-tion, shift or expansion in the seventh century is also evident in the Rhine delta area. Chronological zonation within the settlement at Valkenburg De Woerd (see Figure 2) suggests that the northern area of the hamlet was inhabited between the seventh and tenth centuries, prior to shift southwards in the eleventh century.[8]

At Geldrop and Dommelen, the expansion of the newly founded or existing hamlets was accompanied by a change in burial custom. Small numbers of rela-tively wealthy, furnished male and female graves were located close by the farmsteads, rather than in the earlier communal cemeteries in the area.[9] A similar phenomenon has also been observed at the contemporary site of Laucheim 'Mittelhofen', on a tributary of the middle Rhine in Baden-Württemberg.[10]

232

Interestingly, Theuws notes that the male graves at Geldrop and Dommelen also contained belt sets most closely paralleled in the Mosel and middle Rhine regions. He has linked the foundation of new settlements and the expansion of existing hamlets with both population growth and territorial reorganisation, associated with the formation of larger estates and the emergence of a new elite, elements of which may not have been local to the region.[11] None of the hamlets excavated in the Kempen region (Geldrop, Dommelen and Hulsel) yielded evidence of a church during the Carolingian period. At Valkenburg, in the Rhine delta, however, traces of a ninth-century stone church were discovered, overlying traces of an earlier wooden church and a late seventh- to eighth-century male grave with weapons.[12] This possibly reflected a higher status for this settlement in comparison with sites like Geldrop and Dommelen, within a hierarchical framework provided by complex composite landholdings.

The picture for larger settlement agglomerations is also complex.[13] Some of the sixth-century settlements in northern France appear to have been abandoned in the course of the seventh and eighth centuries; for example, Goudelancourt-les-Pierrepont (Aisne), and Brebières (Pas-de-Calais).[14] In contrast, other settlements with sixth-century phases of activity were occupied into the Carolingian period: for example, Mondeville (Calvados) and Villiers-le-Bacle (Essonne).[15] A similar picture of a long-lived settlement is evident at Rijnsburg, in the Rhine delta, with occupation stretching from the sixth to the twelfth centuries.[16] However, the apparent abandonment of certain settlements may be a reflection of limited-area excavations which miss small-scale, localised shifts of the communities. Other sites also remind us that the foundation of new settlements or reorganisation of existing foci also occurred in the late sixth and seventh centuries, for example, at Grentheville (Calvados); 'Portjoie'-Tournedos-sur-Seine (Eure); Rigny-Ussé (Indre-et-Loire); and Saleux-les-Coutures (Somme), in northern France; and at Valkenburg and Dommelen, in the Netherlands.[17]

In terms of morphology, many elements of settlement layout remained the same between the sixth/seventh and tenth centuries. They comprised farmstead agglomerations made up of individual units of rectangular buildings with earth-fast, or more rarely stone-sill foundations; ancillary buildings and other structures, such as sunken-feature buildings (*Grubenhäuser*), granaries, wells and ovens.[18] South of our area, a similar picture can be observed in settlements occupied from the sixth to ninth centuries: for example, at Develier-Courtételle (Jura), where farming and artisan units, primarily for iron-working, retained the same general layout throughout the occupation sequence.[19] Long-term use of existing settlement zones is also suggested by the few partially excavated settlements in Flanders, despite significant alterations during the seventh and eighth century in the character and size of certain buildings.[20]

In the mid- to late-seventh century, newly founded settlements were often located in close proximity to small groups of graves, which subsequently became the focus for larger cemeteries and churches. This phenomenon can be seen at Saleux (Somme) and at Valkenburg in the Rhine delta.[21] A similar re-organisation of burial within and around newly constructed churches can also be seen on pre-existing Merovingian settlements at Mondeville (Calvados), 'Portjoie'-Tournedos-sur-Seine (Eure) and Serris (Seine-et-Marne).[22] In these cases, however, the churches are regarded as the foci around which the cemeteries developed and not *vice versa*. The same can be said for the cemetery which developed around the seventh-century church at Rigny-Ussé (Indre-et-Loire).[23]

The site at Saleux-les-Coutures provides a useful case-study for assessing the character of one of these new settlements; the excavations were extensive (4 hectares / 10 acres) and the site had excellent preservation conditions, including a waterlogged area.[24] This settlement, which incorporated a cemetery of 1,500 individuals, was to the south of Amiens on the bank of the River Selle, a navigable tributary of the Somme (see Figure 2). The excavations indicated that settlement first developed along the bank of the river during the course of the seventh century, and consisted of farm units defined by ditched enclosures. Each farm unit contained the remains of rectangular buildings in the form of post-holes, as well as ancillary sunken-feature buildings, and storage or refuse pits. A cemetery was also established to the south-west of the habitation area, and developed around a single grave that was distinguished by interment in a stone sarcophagus and enclosed within a wooden mortuary structure. These signs of social differentiation, marking out the special status of this individual, may reflect the veneration of a 'founder' of the settlement, either as a member of an emerging local aristocracy or as the head of an extended family group.

During the eighth or ninth centuries, a church in the form of a large rectangular building of post-hole construction, possibly with an annex at its eastern end, was built over the mortuary edifice of the founder-grave. The church and its environs then formed the focus for further unfurnished burials, and a ditched enclosure was dug around the church and cemetery later in the ninth or tenth century. A watermill was constructed during the eighth or ninth centuries, fed by a leat from the Selle, and the overall settlement expanded to the north, south and west of the church, making the church the focal point of the habitation area. A new church was constructed on chalk-sill foundations at the end of the tenth century, and it continued to act as the focus of the settlement into the eleventh century.

The evolution of the settlement into a 'nucleated' focus during the Carolingian period is reflected by its reorganisation around the nodal points of the church and watermill. This could imply that the religious and grain-processing foci were facilities that the community held in common. The construction of both might instead reflect the patronage of a local aristocratic family which consolidated its position in the community by acting as the channel through which lesser families gained access both to 'bread and salvation'. However, the excavations did not identify the residence of such a leading family, if it existed; there was no significant difference in the character or size of buildings in the excavated farmsteads.

The quality of the excavated evidence from Saleux also enables observations about patterns of agricultural production, manufacturing and exchange. It is possible to define the resources that the population consumed from various habitats within their contemporary environment. The pollen evidence from the waterlogged part of the site, near the River Selle, indicates that the surrounding landscape was one of open pasture and cereal cultivation, with intermittent woodland, and a wetland zone along the river. The remains of a range of cereals, vegetables and wild fruits have been recovered, including wheat, rye, barley, oats, pulses and locally available wild berries.

Among the remains of the main domesticated animals, cattle predominated, followed by sheep, with smaller numbers of pigs and horses. The predominance of cattle, the presence of horses and the maturity of these animals suggests that their primary role was as traction animals, for use in ploughing or overland transport. Cattle were probably the main source of meat given the small proportion of pig bones amongst the main domestic livestock; the cull pattern of the sheep also suggests husbandry for wool and milk rather than meat.[25] The small number of pigs consumed could reflect a lack of woodland pannage, although the botanical remains may suggest otherwise. Alternatively, the lack of pigs could reflect their role as a form of taxation-in-kind rendered for consumption at higher-order settlements.[26] Wild mammals do not appear to have been a significant food source, and this trend has been noted of other contemporary rural settlements in northern France, which are deemed neither 'seigneurial' nor religious in character.[27] Overall, the picture emerging suggests that the inhabitants of a settlement like Saleux were supported primarily by cereal and pulse cultivation, with meat consumption subordinated to the needs of producing crops, wool and dairy products.

Very similar patterns of animal exploitation to those at Saleux are evident amongst the larger settlements in the Meuse–Rhine delta area of the southern Netherlands. At Rijnsburg and Valkenburg almost all bones came from domesticated animals. At Valkenburg, bones from cattle predominate, although the proportion of sheep on the site rose through the Carolingian period; pigs made up just over 10 per cent of the main domestic livestock. The recovery of wild game remains on excavated settlements in the southern Netherlands has so far been very low. Only about 1 per cent of animals consumed at Rijnsburg and Valkenburg were wild species (boar, deer and fowl); it is likely that much of the evidence for deer reflects importation of antler for craft-working.[28]

Material indications of craft activities are encountered on a widespread basis on settlements, whether defined as agglomerations of farmsteads or nucleated foci. The quantity and quality of evidence for craft-working, however, often have a direct correlation with the occurrence, survival and size of refuse deposits. With these filters on the evidence, we must exercise restraint when commenting on the scale of specialist artisan activity. Nevertheless, it is possible to explore the range of craft activities practised. At Saleux, there was evidence of textile production (in the form of spindle whorls, loom-weights, pin beaters and glass slick stones), bone- and antler-working, and slag from iron-working.[29] Yet there is nothing to suggest surplus production, beyond the level of the settlement's needs. A similar array of activities is apparent on settlements in the southern Netherlands. Evidence for textile manufacture and iron-working is widespread, although indications of non-ferrous metalworking are much rarer and, when found, the scale of production seems to have been small.[30]

In contrast to settlements such as Saleux, Valkenburg and Rijnsburg, which seem to have provided for the needs of families primarily involved in agricultural production, there are also indications of hamlets supported by more specialist artisan activity. At the site of Develier-Courtételle, in northern Switzerland, approximately six plots of buildings yielded evidence for iron-smelting and smithing in all areas, comprising three to four tonnes of slag and hammer-scale (from hammering iron on an anvil); non-ferrous metalworking is also attested by several small crucibles with traces of bronze.[31] The other main attribute of this site, dating from the sixth to ninth centuries, was a collection of buildings and structures interpreted as relating to storage of crops and penning livestock.[32] It is possible to interpret this hamlet as a settlement of specialist metalworkers whose inhabitants provided their skills in exchange for agricultural produce and livestock, or were cared for within a wider estate framework. Other specialist communities, such as the eighth- and ninth-century pottery manufacturers of the Rhenish Vorgebirge region, may also have been sustained in a similar fashion, at least as seasonal craft-specialists, supported to a significant degree by commodities from beyond their settlements.[33]

The existence of communities of craft specialists presupposes a network of exchange between settlements, at least at a local and regional level. Indeed, all the settlements discussed above have produced evidence of products acquired from distant regions. The character of imported goods recovered, and the distances they travelled, depended partly on proximity to arterial communications routes (such as distance from coastal seaways or major river systems); although the character of particular communities and their place in the social hierarchy must also have influenced access to imports. For example, part of the iron-working community at Develier-Courtételle had access to pottery imported from the middle Rhine region or Alsace, as well as glass vessels; presumably transported via the Saône and Rhône in exchange for iron objects or iron-working skills.[34]

Proximity and linkage to the exchange routes of the North Sea and Channel coasts, via *emporia* such as Dorestad, Quentovic and Rouen, and possible beach trading sites like De Panne, could also account for the presence of imported glass vessels and early eighth-century *sceatta* coinage at the hamlets on the landward edge of the former coastal marshes in Flanders.[35] Further inland, at settlements such as Saleux, luxuries such as glass vessels are absent, although imported pottery, glass slick-stones and imported raw materials, such as iron, were certainly in evidence. In the settlements of the Meuse and Rhine river systems, imported pottery and other commodities are consistently present, reflecting exchange to and from the delta areas.[36] Consequently, all the settlements reflect different degrees of integration within regional or longer-distance exchange networks, and none can be viewed as self-sufficient in either the support of everyday life or social relations.

Estate centres, palaces and fortified sites

Despite new expressions of social ranking in hamlets and nucleated settlements during the early eighth century, distinctive settlement zones which correspond to the residences of the social elite have rarely been identified. For example, at Saleux and Valkenburg signs of a hierarchical society are reflected by founder-graves in cemeteries and the construction of churches over them, rather than by residential complexes. Yet in the later seventh and eighth centuries, new forms of elite settlement did develop. These new elite nuclei augmented others like the residences of kings, bishops and counts, which had evolved from the fifth century onwards and were located within the fortified *enceintes* of former Late Roman towns, at *castra* or at monastic centres. The monastic and episcopal (and possibly comital) foci in Tours provide excellent examples, as do the episcopal, royal and extra-mural church foci known from archaeological and historical sources at Tournai.[37] Between the eighth and tenth centuries, both the old and new elite settlements witnessed an increased investment in stone structures as a medium of display, with the juxtaposition of palace and churches, or hall (*aula*) and church, as key features. From the late ninth century, substantial defences also became integral to the layout of these settlements.

Two non-royal, elite settlement foci have been found in the Schelde and Meuse valleys, at Petegem in Flanders and Thier d'Olne, in Wallonnie (see Figure 2). At Petegem, a residential focus – of wooden buildings, a church and a cemetery – was constructed in the eighth century. Sometime during the ninth century, a large rectangular stone hall (*aula* or *sala*), with a tiled roof and ancillary buildings, replaced the earlier residential complex. The church was also rebuilt in stone, with a rectangular nave and square apsidal end, and both the hall and church were constructed in stone brought from Tournai. This transformation was associated with the digging of ditches 7 m (23 ft) wide around the hall and church, forming a figure-of-eight plan.[38] This settlement has been likened to the description of a 'typical' *curtis* estate centre, described in the *Brevium Exempla* of *c*.800.[39] The importance of Petegem is implicit in the record of a meeting there between the Count of Laon and the Bishop of Noyon-Tournai, in 854 or 859/60, and by the ratification of a charter at *Pettingehem villa* by Charles the Bald in October 864, soon after the assembly of Pîtres.[40] There is nothing, however, to suggest that Petegem was a Carolingian royal vill, although it was located on the strategic boundary of West Francia and Lotharingia, defined in the Treaty of Verdun.

At Thier d'Olne, Engis, on the opposite bank of the Meuse from Amay, a settlement was founded on an isolated hill overlooking the river, in the seventh or early eighth century. It initially consisted of a mortuary chapel, built on stone-sill foundations, enclosing two 'founder graves' in trapezoidal stone sarcophagi and a further thirty graves thought to represent the leading family of the settlement. The mortuary chapel was associated with rectangular buildings made of wood and wattle-and-daub, and the complex was enclosed in a wooden palisade. This focus was replaced by a further chapel and associated buildings in the second half of the eighth century, prior to a major transformation of the high-status nucleus during the ninth century when the chapel was replaced by a stone church (20 × 6 m / 65 × 20 ft), and a large stone hall was built 20 m (65 ft) away, measuring 27 × 18 m (about 90 × 60 ft), with an external wooden staircase to the entrance, and painted plaster on the interior walls.[41] This high-status hall and church has been equated with the estate centre of the *villa Alnith*, mentioned in a charter of Charles the Fat in 885.[42]

Both Petegem and Thier d'Olne are assumed to have possessed subservient settlements nearby, perhaps equating to some of the nucleated settlements and hamlets of the type discussed above. Indeed, both sites continued to act as high-status settlement foci throughout the periods of Carolingian and Ottonian dominance. Thier d'Olne was abandoned in favour of a new location in the early eleventh century, and the Petegem *curtis* developed into a castle, before abandonment in the late thirteenth century. But other estate centres in northern France and Belgium developed differently, and the picture is complex. For example, in contrast to the ninth-century 'church-and-hall' complexes at the centres of secular aristocrats, like Petegem and Thier d'Olne, the estate centre (*colonia/villa*) belonging to the monastery of St-Martin of Tours, at Rigny-Ussé (Indre-et-Loire), possessed a focal core of stone church accompanied by large stone storage and residential buildings from the late seventh century; there is no sign that the settlement was ever monastic. It was one of numerous settlements, with associated territory and population, which contributed provisions to a major monastic institution, and had a continuous occupation history from the seventh century until the post-medieval period.[43]

In many respects the royal residences of the Carolingians at their vills and palaces are simply grander, more impressive reflections of the hall-and-church complexes seen at Petegem and Thier d'Olne. Many of these royal palaces, with their large stone halls, churches, ancillary buildings and enclosure structures, were constructed during the eighth century and enlarged in the age of Charlemagne and his immediate successors. As such, the palace–church complexes, such as Aachen, Ingelheim and Paderborn, and palace–monastery complexes such as at

St-Denis, provided new fashions of status display as 'theatres of kingship'. The royal model of stone hall and church at the heart of a high-status settlement was copied by the nobility during the course of the ninth century, becoming a physical manifestation of lordly rank. Much has already been written about Charlemagne's palace complexes at Paderborn, Aachen and Ingelheim,[44] but it is essential to give some attention to the transformations in physical character of some of the royal palace complexes and estate-centres through the later Carolingian period.

In an analysis of the physical reflections of a Carolingian royal itinerary in the Aisne valley, in northern France, Renoux has demonstrated that the royal estate-centres, with their halls, churches and ancillary buildings, were surrounded by substantial defensive enclosures from the mid- to late-ninth century. Documentary evidence shows that such changes were instigated by Charles the Bald at Com-piègne, and possibly also at Quierzy.[45] Others were constructed at Corbeny and Laon, where a tower was also added before the mid-tenth century.[46] This also occurred in the Rhineland: for example, at Soest on the River Lippe, in West-phalia, where a rectangular stone rampart was built around a palace complex of the Archbishop of Cologne about AD 900.[47]

This is not to say, however, that fortifications were absent in earlier phases. An eighth-century mortared stone rampart has been excavated at the fort at Karlburg, on the River Main, where the defences were subsequently refurbished and enlarged during the Ottonian and Salian periods. This fortification was associated with a Carolingian royal vill in the mid-eighth century, and was donated to the newly founded bishopric of Würzburg by Pippin III.[48] Other larger fortifications, often comprising combinations of earth and stone ramparts on hilltops, were much more common further east. This was especially the case in the eighth- and ninth-century marchlands of Westphalia–Saxony, and in the eastern marches of Ottonian Saxony, during the tenth century.[49] The strategic planning behind the latter fortifications seems to have been largely offensive; they acted as bases for military campaigns, and as foci for the administration of newly subjugated areas.[50]

West of the Rhine, stone halls at palace sites were also converted into large defensive towers, or *donjons*, during the course of the late tenth and early eleventh centuries. This was achieved by constructing an additional stone storey onto the halls, and the lower levels were then encased within a mound or motte. This happened at a royal palace at Mellier in Belgium, which had belonged to Pippin III, and at Doué-La-Fontaine (Maine-et-Loire) in France.[51] At Doué the converted stone hall probably belonged to the counts of Blois, although Louis the Pious had previously had a palace there.[52] Recent excavations of a tenth-century stone hall with a tower at Mayenne, can probably be viewed as part of the same pheno-menon. The hall focus was transformed into a fortified stronghold by the con-struction of a stone enclosure wall, and was buried and encased in further stone castle defences during the twelfth and thirteenth centuries.[53] A similar sequence of 'enmottification' of a tenth-century wooden hall can be seen at Douai (Nord). The hall was enclosed within a mortared stone rampart, probably built by the penultimate Carolingian king of West Francia, Lothar (AD 954–86). Subsequently, the hall was encased within an earth mound and some of its beams were used to support a small tower or *donjon*, probably in the last decades of the tenth century.[54]

These defensive developments on palace sites were accompanied by the construction of ring-forts along the Channel/North Sea coast during the late ninth century, and by the emergence of smaller, fortified strongholds, often termed a *castellum* or *turris* from the mid-tenth century.[55] The ring-work forts at places such as Veurne and Oostburg in Flanders, and Oost-Souburg in the Netherlands, have traditionally been viewed as *vluchtburgen* or 'refuge forts' against Viking attacks on the coastal plain.[56] At Oost-Souburg, in Zeeland, the initial phase of temporary occupation was soon followed by permanent habitation from the early tenth century, as indicated by both the structural evidence and material culture.[57] The permanent role of these ring-forts within their coastal landscapes is unclear. By the eleventh century, however, the fort at Veurne had become a residence and estate-centre of the count of Flanders, incorporating a motte and church within the earlier rampart.[58]

The smaller fortified strongholds or 'embryonic castles' – like those excavated at Montfélix-Chavot (Marne) and Sugny in the Walloon Ardennes – cannot be interpreted as either large estate centres or shelter fortifications for surrounding populations.[59] Instead, Montfélix and Sugny, founded in the late ninth century and tenth century respectively, can be viewed as strategic defended points sited between the major estates and nascent urban settlements of the emerging principalities and seigneuries of the tenth and eleventh centuries. The former Late Roman and Merovingian site at Montfélix was refurbished at the end of the ninth or early tenth century. It overlooks Épernay, which was then an estate centre of the archbishop of Rheims, and the fortification was linked to the counts of Vermandois – later the counts of Champagne – by the mid-tenth century.[60] Sugny is also likely to have been a comital foundation, on the part of the newly emerged counts of Bouillon.[61] During the tenth century, both these small fortified settlements were defended primarily by virtue of their natural location on promontories, enhanced by rock-cut ditches; Montfélix consisted of a group of buildings with post-hole and sunken-feature foundations, and was situated on a rocky spur, defended by a ditch on one side.[62]

When evidence is available, patterns of consumption of animal resources and other commodities show some common traits among high-status settlement nuclei, as well as signs of differentiation. Discussion of trends in animal consumption is of necessity biased towards sites with significant bone assemblages, although wider comparison is possible through artefact profiles. The remains from the palace at Paderborn provide an excellent case-study of patterns of consumption at such a royal centre. The proportion of pig bones was very high within the remains of the main domesticated animals (cattle, pigs and sheep), comprising over half the bones recovered.[63] The unusually high proportion of pigs at Paderborn probably reflects significant provisioning of the palace by 'renders' of these animals, as a medium of taxation or tribute.[64] The culling pattern of the main domesticates also indicates a preference for the slaughter of relatively young animals at the optimum age for eating; pigs were slaughtered at two years and lambs were also consumed.[65] This pattern contrasts very sharply with settlements primarily involved in agricultural production, like Saleux. The royal/episcopal fortification of the vill of Karlburg on the River Main likewise displays a pattern of animal consumption which contrasts sharply with the habits of its attendant valley settlement. During the eighth and ninth centuries, the domestic animals consumed at the defended site were all under three years old when killed. In contrast, the animals consumed in the attendant valley settlement were significantly older.[66] Hence, a pattern is emerging of the slaughter of young animals, at the optimum age for consumption of their meat, on the sites of highest status. Among communities involved in agricultural production, however, older animals were consumed, perhaps after use for traction activities.

Animal bone assemblages from estate centres at Soest and Höxter, in Westphalia, exhibit the more commonly-found dominance of cattle over pigs among domesticated animals, and they were older than those killed at Paderborn.[67] Nevertheless, these sites certainly possessed high-status foci; Höxter had been a royal vill of Louis the Pious, prior to its acquisition by the monastery of Corvey, and Soest was an important estate for the archbishops of Cologne.[68] Cattle bones also predominated at the ring-fort of Oost-Souburg, although the slaughter of younger animals demonstrates some similarities with Paderborn and Karlburg. This preference for cattle consumption, over sheep and pigs, is slightly surprising given the large number of references from the tenth century onwards to grazing sheep on the Flanders and Zeeland coastal plain.[69] At the *castellum* of Sugny, pigs again significantly outnumbered the other domesticated animals, as at Paderborn. In this instance, however, the location of the site in the Ardennes Forest, the ideal environment for keeping pigs, may account for this pattern of consumption.[70] Like Paderborn and Karlburg, the bones of the domesticated animals at Sugny were also killed at a young age, again reflecting consumption when the meat was at its best.

In addition to the domesticated animal evidence, the remains of wild animals from Paderborn, Karlburg, the Westphalian estate-centres and Sugny also hint at the high status of some of their inhabitants. The identification of numerous wild-boar bones and the claws of a brown bear at Paderborn attests to the hunting pursuits undertaken at the palace (although it is possible that the bear claws could have come from an imported bearskin).[71] The importance of hunting and the consumption of wild game at high-status settlements is also reflected at Karlburg. Within the fortified settlement, over 10 per cent of the animals consumed were wild (mostly red deer) whereas in the attendant valley settlement and monastery less than 1 per cent of animals were wild.[72] At Soest, bones from a large hawk perhaps reflect the elite pastime of falconry, and at Sugny a high proportion of wild animals also suggests hunting for pleasure, rather than necessity.[73] General surveys of material, primarily from northern France, also emphasise the exploitation of wild resources as a consequence of hunting at high-status secular settlements during the early middle ages, in particular the high consumption of wild birds, boar and red deer.[74]

The artefact remains from Paderborn, and the vill centres of Karlburg, Soest and Höxter, again provide useful examples of the patterns of exchange and artisan activity that can be expected at high-status centres. At the Paderborn palace, interregional exchange contacts are reflected in the use of significant quantities of pottery imported from the Rhineland, in the form of Walberberg and Badorf finewares, relief-band amphorae and Tating ware jugs.[75] The recovery of 340 fragments of glass vessels also probably reflects supply from the Rhineland, although not all were necessarily imported, since evidence of the production of glass vessels and tesserae was found at the palace, along with over 1,600 pieces of window glass.[76] Most of the glass vessels were cone or funnel beakers used for drinking. Considered alongside the animal bone evidence from the excavations, the luxury utensils suggest exchange or provisioning in support of feasting.

Imported architectural materials were also incorporated into the palace buildings, in the form of porphyry and marble decorative tiles. These commodities, originally quarried in Egypt and Turkey, were probably derived from Roman imperial buildings in Italy, or possibly from imperial or major public buildings in former Roman provinces north of the Alps.[77] Imported porphyry and marble tiles for *opus sectile* decoration have also recovered at the palaces at Compiègne, Aachen and Ingelheim.[78] At these sites, the imported tiles augmented the much more ostentatious use of Roman porphyry, granite, marble and limestone columns in the main hall–church complexes.[79] The long-distance movement of both the luxury utensils and the exotic architectural materials reflects the support of Carolingian royal display and imperial aspirations, through rituals associated with food consumption and through architectural features linking the Carolingian emperors with their Roman antecedents.

The palace enclosure at Paderborn also seems to have possessed an artisan quarter, primarily engaged in iron-working but also glass-working and fine metalworking. The glass-working evidence included a furnace, melt and slag, and crucible fragments demonstrated fine metalworking.[80] Literacy was also a key element behind the organisation of the provisioning and commodity-producing aspects of the palace, at least at the level of estate management and possibly tuition – represented archaeologically by styli.[81]

The estate centres of Karlburg, Soest and Höxter also reflect the specialist production and inter-regional integration, which can be regarded as a feature of high-status settlements, although they do not present evidence of the scale or range of commodity movement apparent at palace complexes. Karlburg and Soest were classic polyfocal settlements. At Karlburg, evidence of inter-regional contact within the Rhineland was manifested mainly within the fortified part of the settlement, while a zone of workshops relating to iron-working and other crafts was situated in part of the attendant valley settlement of the vill.[82] At Soest, there were separate artisan zones for salt production, iron-working and fine metalworking, and finds of Badorf-ware pottery reflect exchange contacts along the Rhine waterways.[83] Likewise, Höxter has yielded evidence for significant non-ferrous metalworking, iron-working and some textile manufacture; the settlement's role in exchange is also reflected by its recorded market and the recovery of Rhenish pottery.[84]

Like the estate centres incorporating fortified *enceintes*, the finds from the larger fortification at Oost-Souburg also reflect extensive exchange contacts along the Rhine, Meuse and North Sea coast from the turn of the tenth century. Indeed, the majority of the material culture within the settlement seems to have been procured as a result of exchange or possibly provision by render.[85]

Monasteries

Monastic centres are the final type of settlement to be considered, both small foundations and large establishments. In order to reflect the archaeological variety of sites labelled as 'monasteries', three examples act as a basis for discussion. These comprise the royal palace–monastery of St-Denis (Paris), the Carolingian Benedictine foundation of Corvey, east of the Rhine, and the recently excavated settlement of Hamage (Nord), between Valenciennes and Douai (see Figure 2).

The exceptional vertical stratigraphic sequence at Hamage demonstrates the diversity of forms that a single settlement could take through its occupational history, as a 'monastic' and also possibly as an elite 'secular' focus. A saint's Life (the *Vita Rictrudis*) of the early tenth century notes the foundation of a monastery at Hamage in the 630s, but the only reliable indication that the settlement housed a monastery comes from a charter of Charles the Bald, dating from July 877, which describes the need to provide for the 'brothers and sisters serving God' there.[86]

Between the mid-seventh and mid-eighth century, two churches were founded at Hamage, presumably in wood. The church of St-Pierre was associated with a major burial focus; the other – St-Eusébie (now Ste-Marie) – to the south, was housed within a roughly square ditched enclosure, approximately 50 m (165 ft) square. To the south of this church within the enclosure, a large rectangular building was constructed (18.5 × 10.5 m / 60 × 34 ft) on an approximate east–west alignment. This building, with indications of a continuous wooden-sill foundation, was divided into a dozen small compartments or 'cells', and most had internal hearths.[87] A structure interpreted as a latrine was located outside the southern long wall, with a domestic oven nearby. Vast ash-rich refuse deposits had been dumped against the northern wall of the building and the enclosure ditch was also used for refuse disposal. Due to the high water-table, remains in the ditch were waterlogged, ensuring the survival of wooden planks, and possibly a bridge abutment.

Some of the ditch deposits may pre-date the rectangular building. Notable among the finds were fine ceramic goblets of the first half of the seventh century with scratched graffiti – one with the female name *Aughilde* – together with dress accessories, fragments of glass vessels, and crucibles with glass-working debris. Small silver coins (*sceattas*) and the glass vessels probably reflect exchange contacts along the Scarpe and into the Schelde river system. Finds from the ash dumps included ceramic bowls (one with the scratched name *Bertrane*) and pitchers, animal bones, textile-working debris and dress accessories. This has led the excavator to suggest that this building acted as the domestic quarters for female members of a religious community.

During the course of the eighth century, three buildings replaced the earlier rectangular structure, constructed with earth-fast and drystone interrupted-sill foundations. A refuse dump in the enclosure ditch, adjacent to one of the buildings, provided further evidence of the settlement's integration within inter-regional networks in the form of two silver coins – deniers of Pippin III and Charlemagne. In the ninth century, these buildings were in turn replaced. The church of St-Eusébie was rebuilt in stone or on a stone footing, graves were placed in a corridor outside the nave, and a series of large rectangular or trapez-oidal buildings were constructed around a cloister. These changes are dated to the ninth century on the basis of the ceramics and brooches, and a denier of Louis the Pious, found in one of the buildings. This introduction of the cloister plan has been attributed to the influence of the monastic reforms of Louis the Pious, in 816–17.[88] The area around the cloister appears to have been abandoned in the course of the tenth or eleventh century, although it is unclear whether the church and cemetery of St-Pierre went out of use in the same period.

The occupation sequence at Hamage provides an exceptional but tantalising glimpse of the radical changes in structural organisation of a settlement which housed a monastic element, certainly in the ninth century and probably earlier. The excavations have illustrated the structural evolution within an enclosure linked to one of the ecclesiastical foci on the site, but the nature of the wider settlement or agglomeration of other foci is unclear. The church of St-Pierre may have formed a burial focus for the recorded male element of the ninth-century religious community, while also serving the burial and religious needs of the wider population of the estate or locality. The possibility of a lay abbot at Hamage has also been considered.[89]

Outside the religious *enceinte*, the archaeological remains might be indistin-guishable from those of a secular estate centre. In this sense, a scratched graffito on a seventh-century pottery goblet saying *Mitte Plino* – 'refill' – need not be seen in anything other than a secular light, nor should such evidence of literacy be seen as out of place amongst the seventh-century secular elite.[90] Indeed, all other aspects of the material culture of the site reflect traits common to secular estate-centres, such as evidence for craft-specialisation, conspicuous consumption of imported luxuries and use of silver coinage as a medium of exchange.

The royal monastery–palace of St-Denis – on a tributary of the River Seine, 9 km (5½ miles) north of the Île de la Cité in Paris – provides a considerable contrast in terms of its origins and patronage network which are reflected in its physical character. Like many royal estate-centres and monasteries, it was located on a navigable river system and had more than one ecclesiastical focus. The nucleus of the settlement, which by the Carolingian period comprised at least three churches, a palace, monastic buildings and an associated settlement agglomeration, had developed over the martyrial grave of St Denis, within a late Roman cemetery. Following earlier excavations, over 13 hectares (32 acres) have been excavated within the monastery–palace complex since 1973. This long period of research has allowed the identification of a sequence of churches, residential buildings, cemeteries, engineering features and defences.

About AD 475, a basilica to commemorate the saint was built on the site of two earlier mausolea. The cult site became closely associated with the Merovingian dynasty, and the main monastic church was refurbished by Dagobert I in the early decades of the seventh century. The archaeological evidence for the Merovingian basilica comprises the foundations of a rectangular building made with Roman *spolia*, foundations from the enlargement of the structure in the seventh century and highly decorated architectural fragments, both underneath and incorporated within its Carolingian and later medieval successors.[91] Two stone mortuary chapels (St-Pierre and St-Barthélemy) were built to the north of the basilica in the sixth or seventh century, and another, external cemetery was founded between the mortuary foci provided by the churches.[92]

Central to the development of St-Denis, however, was the patronage of the Carolingian family and the choice of the basilica as the burial place of key members of the dynasty, namely Charles Martel, Pippin III and Charles the Bald. During the course of the eighth century, a large stone building was constructed to the west of the mortuary chapels. It has been identified with the Carolingian palace–hall, known from contemporary texts. At its full extent, the building was 50 × 14 m (165 × 46 ft). in size, comprising a large hall, several smaller rooms and possibly also a tower.[93] The walls of the building were bonded with extremely hard mortar and the interior faces of the building were covered in painted plaster. Imported marble tiles from *opus sectile* mosaic paving also covered at least some of the floors. To the north of this building, a water supply system was constructed with a limestone water-leat which fed three stone-lined pools, accessed by stone steps 1.5 m (5 ft) below ground level.[94] The leat probably ran from a distant spring up to 700 m (765 yd) away. After use during the second half of the eighth century, it was filled with architectural fragments and other refuse.

Around 870, the palace-monastery was fortified by Charles the Bald; the excavations have identified elements of a stone and wooden rampart and an encircling moat, fed by a water channel 7 km (4 miles) in length. The area enclosed was approximately 400 × 500 m (440 × 550 yd). with a circular street 20 m (66 ft) inside the ring-work defences, which enclosed the lay settlement associated with the monastic and palace complex.[95] This large ring-work fortification bears some similarity to the ring-forts constructed along the Channel-North Sea coast, also built in the late ninth century.[96] The excavated material culture provides evidence for the character of occupation within the palace–monastery zone of the settlement. As at the royal palace complex at Paderborn, luxury utensils were recovered in the form of Tating-ware jugs from the Rhineland, alongside glass drinking vessels and glass bowls with applied reticella trails.[97] Vessels with similar decoration have been found on contemporary sites around the North Sea, on both rural settlements with high-status elements and at *emporia*.[98] It is often supposed that they originated from the Rhineland like the Tating-ware, and this may indeed be the case, although their distribution along the Rhine is currently very sparse. A lead trial-piece for striking coins, from the reign of Pippin III, was also recovered from the water leat, reflecting the presence of a mint at St-Denis.

The skeletal remains hint at changing patterns in the disposal of the dead at the site, which may reflect other changes in the settlement. Wyss noted patterns of zoning in burial practice and burial location of seventh- and eighth-century graves; a greater proportion of burials within the main basilica used imported stone sarcophagi than the graves in the mortuary chapels and cemeteries, which may reflect the interment of non-local individuals at the cult focus.[99] Additionally, interment in the basilica (and proximity to the graves of Frankish royalty) indicates significant social status. Men outnumbered women throughout the excavated burial sequence outside the basilica (71 men, 29 women), and it has been suggested that this zone may have been used by the monastic canons. This is supported in one case by an inscription on the interior of a sarcophagus describing the deceased as a monk.[100] From the ninth century onwards, however, the demographic complement of men and women was more equal, which may reflect a change in the function of the cemetery in line with its use by a broader spectrum of the inhabitants of the settlement or locality.

As a final illustration of the diversity of monastic sites, the Benedictine abbey of Corvey serves as an example of a major religious house founded and patronised by the Carolingian dynasty, particularly by Louis the Pious. The monastery of Corvey, on the east bank of the River Weser, just within Saxony, has produced a combination of structural features, contemporary images and archaeological evidence hinting at the character of life in the vicinity of the main cult focus. In this sense, conclusions on the nature of the settlement as a whole are limited.

However, the concentration of research on the abbey church zone and the buildings to its north, allows for some comparison with excavated areas of Hamage, St-Denis and the 'display-building' zones of palaces.

The monastery at Corvey was founded in 822, taking its name and its first abbot (Adalhard) from its mother establishment at Corbie (Somme), in northern France.[101] It is uncertain whether the new foundation was located within, or in the immediate vicinity, of an existing settlement. The best-known physical aspects of the Corvey monastery are the main abbey church, particularly its western façade, and the manuscripts produced in its scriptorium.[102] Excavations in the abbey church have illustrated aspects of the architectural sequence. The abbey church was built in two phases, with its first phase thought to date between 822 and 844. This comprised a single nave and apsidal end, 34.5 m (113 ft) in length, overlying a crypt with plastered walls and painted ceiling with red, yellow and blue designs, thought to have housed the remains of St Vitus, brought from St-Denis in 836.[103] Also found in the debris from this phase was a glass tile from the decorated walls and a golden inset letter, originally set into a stone inscription.[104] The church was subsequently enlarged with the addition of the western façade, between 873 and 885, and its interior was decorated with painted plaster frescoes, including the classical motif of Odysseus facing the sea monster Scylla and a Siren.[105]

As at the royal palaces of Aachen, Compiègne, Ingelheim and Paderborn, and the palace–monastery of St-Denis, the main basilica was embellished with imported tiles fashioned in porphyry and marble for an *opus sectile* floor, many of which may have originated as *spolia* from earlier Roman buildings. The excavations north of the church also yielded evidence of specialist artisan activity, non-ferrous metalworking and glass-working, especially slag and mould and crucible fragments; these are interpreted as evidence of workshops, run by lay or monastic craftsmen.[106]

Overall, the archaeological remains from these very different monastic settlements reveal a range of similarities and some distinct differences, which relate ultimately to the status of settlements and the patronage-networks which supported them. One factor linking all the sites is the excavation strategies, which have targeted the cult buildings, that is, the churches and their adjacent structures. This has resulted in a significant body of knowledge about the core church buildings, but we lack a commensurate understanding of the peripheral zones of monasteries and their attendant settlements. The cult buildings were all foci for graves or the remains of saints, but the buildings were constructed in different media and on a different scale.

All the monastic settlements, however, demonstrate integration within interregional and long-distance exchange networks; and all display the conspicuous consumption of luxuries that marked out the high social status of elements of their populations, whether permanently or temporarily resident. Specialist production of certain commodities is also reflected, sometimes strictly controlled.

For example, textile production was undertaken at Hamage and non-ferrous metalworking at Corvey, in addition to glass-working at both. Evidence for the minting of coin at St-Denis also reflects the importance of that centre. Nevertheless, the evidence for specialist production at these settlements cannot be viewed as peculiar to monasteries. Indeed, with the exception of the structural evidence, imagery and funerary foci provided by the cult buildings and adjacent cemeteries, the artefact profiles of monastic settlements are very similar to their contemporary 'secular' counterparts of equivalent social rank.

A difference might become apparent in the future, especially with more sophisticated analysis of the faunal remains from these sites, but this depends on the availability, sampling and retrieval of animal bones. The organisation of refuse disposal within settlements in the past is also a fundamentally important factor; if rubbish from both the lay and religious elements of the monastic communities was combined in middens, the totality of that evidence would produce profiles relating to the whole population of the settlement, rather than individual elements which might otherwise have displayed a distinctive material culture. At Karlburg, differences have emerged between the excavated areas of the fortified, attendant and monastic elements of that settlement. There, over 10 per cent of animals consumed on the fortified site were wild, whereas less than 1 per cent were wild on sites within the attendant valley settlement and 'Marienkloster' monastic focus.[107] In another key aspect, major monasteries like Corvey were also distinctive in their production of books.[108] Bearing in mind that monastic animal husbandry regimes needed to produce vellum in quantities, it is conceivable that a high proportion of juvenile and neo-natal cattle bones might reflect a major monastery with a scriptorium. Recovery of such evidence, however, would depend on finding detritus from the processing of carcases, and this refuse was probably dumped away from high-status cult foci. Hence, if a broader appreciation of the nature and variety of monastic settlements is to be achieved, peripheral zones of sites must be excavated to locate refuse dumps.

Interpreting settlement hierarchy in the Carolingian period

This review has examined a range of settlement types which developed in the region between the Seine and eastern Rhine tributaries between the mid-seventh and tenth centuries. They have been defined by structural character and material-culture profiles, in conjunction with contemporary labels attributed to them in the Carolingian period. This approach is not perfect because the case studies may be unrepresentative, but this is a problem faced in all archaeological sampling, given the variable size of excavations, different recording and retrieval strategies, and the targeting of different settlement zones for investigation. Nevertheless, comparative information from similar settlements or similar zones of excavated sites permits some assessment of their representativity.

The range of settlements discussed exhibit a series of archaeological traits which reflect some aspects of their character and their relationships with other sites in contemporary settlement hierarchies. Analysis of the archaeological reflections of documented settlements (or certain parts of them) highlights the complexity and diversity of traits hidden behind the textual 'snapshots'. Furthermore, the archaeological patterns of commodity consumption and means of social display also provide indications of hierarchical relationships, which articulate points of difference and similarity other than those derived from documentary sources. The discussion which follows outlines some synthetic approaches that can be applied to the settlements discussed in order to draw out archaeological traits relating to settlement character, and the hierarchical social relations which supported them.

The character and use of stone-built 'display buildings', and the activities associated with them, provide a starting point for general discussion, and also an abundant source of data due to excavators' preference for 'hall-and-church' complexes and monastic cult foci. The palatial 'hall-and-church' complexes, constructed in the second half of the eighth and the early ninth centuries, demonstrated royal prestige through their monumentality and the 'conspicuous consumption' of human and material resources in their construction. These extravagant stone structures contrasted with vernacular buildings made of wood or, more rarely, stone-sill-based construction, and reflected the aspirations of Charlemagne and his successors as heirs of the Roman empire.

The Carolingians re-worked Roman and Byzantine media of display in their buildings by reusing rare stone and *spolia* from antique structures, in the form of columns and tiles made of porphyry, marble, and granite.[109] In so doing, they created new symbols of imperial aspirations in western and central Europe during the later eighth and ninth centuries. The re-use of antique Roman columns as imperial symbolism continued under the Ottonian emperors in the second half of the tenth century, in conjunction with a greater use of explicitly imperial motifs and images derived from contemporary Italy and Byzantium. Roman black and purple porphyry columns from a major Ottonian building at Magdeburg were re-incorporated into the city's thirteenth-century cathedral, along with a porphyry font.[110] The ability to control the movement of bulk commodities, such as stone columns, over considerable distances is also a mark of power. The construction of a limestone aqueduct with cisterns at St-Denis, although short-lived in use, can also be interpreted as a reflection of the aspirations of the Carolingians as successors to Roman power. The imagery of the painted frescoes and monumental inscriptions at Corvey likewise reflects these goals, especially within the west façade. Consequently, despite differences in the function of the display buildings supported by the Carolingians, whether cult and burial foci, palace halls or churches, common mechanisms were used to express a new imperial identity.

On those settlements or settlement zones which probably equate to aristocratic estate centres and smaller monastic foundations, an investment in stone buildings was seen during the ninth century and beyond, probably emulating royal centres but on a smaller scale. At Petegem and Thier d'Olne, the wooden buildings and sill-based churches were replaced by large halls and churches in stone during the course of the ninth century. Like the royal centres, the interiors of these buildings were plastered, but less extravagantly decorated – and marble and porphyry were absent. Nevertheless, the ability to move bulk commodities around the landscape is reflected in the importation of Tournai stone to Petegem. At Hamage, which may have been an aristocratic centre with both 'secular' and 'monastic' elements, a stone-based church was built in the ninth century; likewise at Valkenburg, in the Rhine delta area. On nucleated settlements like Saleux-les-Coutures, some of which may have been subordinate to linked estate centres, the churches constructed with wooden superstructures were replaced with stone-sill-based constructions over a longer period. The late seventh-century stone buildings at Rigny-Ussé, however, imply that this model may be regionally specific, and thus less applicable in the Loire valley and areas further south in Gaul.

The structural remains of fortifications also reflect social hierarchy and modes of display. From the mid- to late-ninth century through to the eleventh century, existing settlements were progressively fortified. For example, Charles the Bald fortified the palace of Compiègne and the palace–monastery of St-Denis, the latter on a grand scale. Social control and royal power was demonstrated as much by the ability to build such defences as by their actual strength. Indeed, as a defensive barrier the moat at St-Denis could have been slighted without difficulty by cutting or filling its supply channel, so its use as a display feature may have far exceeded its defensive value. Like the St-Denis defences, the building of the coastal ring-forts reflect a large-scale mobilisation of resources, in terms of people, skills and the provisioning of a workforce during construction. All can be viewed as actions reflecting the initiative and power of leaders in society, who wielded power at the levels of kings and regional potentates.

The fortification of the Petegem estate centre, with ditches and an earthen rampart, can also be considered an expression of social display as well as defence. The ring-works encircled only the high-status elements, rather than the settlement as a whole, and in this sense it may have differed from the St-Denis fortification. Nevertheless, the defensive value of the ring-works for all the inhabitants of the Petegem settlement was probably secondary to its demonstration of social differentiation, in terms of who and what was worth defending. The same can be said for a similar ninth-century settlement, identified as a *curtis* at Poortugaal, in the Rhine delta of the Netherlands, which had a defended enclosure and attendant external settlement.[111] A series of earth and timber ring-work fortifications were also constructed on the North Sea coast, east of the Rhine, between the ninth and mid-tenth centuries. For example, the large ring-work of the *Hammaburg* became the focus for the development of Hamburg, and some smaller ring-forts, possibly housing aristocratic families, were also built along the coastal sand belt of Schleswig-Holstein at the Stellerburg, Bökelnburg and Kuden, overlooking the inhabited marshes.[112]

In the tenth century, other settlements such as the palaces and estate centres of Quierzy, Laon and Corbeny gained fortified enclosures, as did some east of the Rhine, such as Soest.[113] By AD 1000, standing palace halls were being converted into towers (donjons), at Doué-la-Fontaine, Mellier, Mayenne and Douai. Thus, Carolingian and comital 'theatres' for public ritual and conspicuous consumption were transformed into fortified strong-points (castella), focused on a tower as the new expression of local power and social rank.[114] This pattern is reflected in northern France and the Ardennes, at Montfélix-Chavot, Sugny, Warcq and Chanteraine; in coastal Flanders, at Veurne and Gent; and in Rhineland Germany.[115]

Patterns in the consumption and production of commodities on different types of settlement also reflect hierarchical social relations, augmenting those seen in 'display buildings' and other structural features. Conspicuous consumption of resources, seen in the animal remains and imported luxuries, is a consistent feature of the 'display-building' zones of palaces, probably reflecting the important secular display ritual of feasting. At Paderborn, the large quantities of glass beakers for drinking, and the slaughter of young animals to ensure tender meat, can be viewed as a reflection of such high-status eating and drinking.[116] The consumption of young animals also seems to be the predominant pattern in the high-status zone at Karlburg.[117] The high proportion of pigs at Paderborn, in comparison to vill centres at Höxter and Soest, suggests provisioning and payment of tax renders in pigs, demonstrating the centrifugal pull of certain animal resources to settlements at the top of their regional settlement hierarchies.

The hunting of wild animals as a pastime rather than as a provisioning necessity is also reflected at elite settlements, from palaces like Paderborn to villa centres, such as Karlburg and Soest, and castella, like Sugny. All these settlements produced significant quantities of wild animal bones, especially wild boar and deer, in addition to possible indications of falconry at Soest.[118] The occurrence of horse fittings and spurs on sites from royal and comital centres, such as tenth-century Douai, or the small, late ninth- and tenth-century castellum of Montfélix-Chavot also reflects the presence of inhabitants with the ability to move about the landscape quickly on horseback, for hunting, travel or warfare.[119]

The artefact remains from a settlement like Hamage, which has a reliably documented monastic component at least from AD 877, are all but indistinguishable from the material-culture profiles of palace and vill estate centres. The differences between palaces, leading monasteries and their smaller aristocratic counterparts relate more to the scale of consumption, reflected archaeologically particularly in exploitation patterns of faunal remains and in the quantity of luxuries discarded in the course of everyday life. However, this picture of similarity in the structural and material culture profiles on elite settlements is due partly to the targeted excavation of display buildings and cult foci, rather than peripheral settlement areas; and excavation of attendant settlement components and refuse dumps might yield greater indications of the true complexity of these settlements which provided the means for high-status display among a social minority. In this context, it is important to note that elements of just such a supporting settlement have been sampled recently by excavation, on the periphery of the monastery of St-Bertin, at St-Omer (Pas-de-Calais). The excavations have begun to provide a more comprehensive picture of settlement development in St-Omer, which developed from the vill estate centre of *Sithiu*, documented in AD 651, to the abbey of St-Bertin with its associated attendant settlements in the Carolingian period.[120]

Patterns of specialist production – at royal palaces, vill centres and both major and minor monastic settlements – were again very similar. At the royal palace of Paderborn, evidence for significant levels of iron-working, non-ferrous metalworking and glass-working was uncovered. Similarly, at the Benedictine house of Corvey indications of 'workshops' for glass-working and non-ferrous metalworking were also found. Likewise, large numbers of crucible fragments and furnace evidence were recovered at the royal vill centre at Höxter, which later belonged to Corvey, and both Karlburg and Soest possessed specialised craft-working zones. Soest had separate settlement elements for iron-working, non-ferrous metalworking and the saltern zones. Overall, the evidence reflects the ability of leading members of society to control specialist skills and the access to them. This is also reflected in recorded obligations of certain centres to maintain ranges of tools and skills, and to supply specialist products as renders to the king, whether from vill *caput* settlements or monasteries.[121] Even at the smaller centres like Hamage, glass-working, metalworking and textile manufacture are visible archaeologically, alongside discarded tools. This ability to discard valuable artefacts, such as tools, also marks out the affluence of some inhabitants of estate centres.

A potentially important reflection of the organisation of production and consumption at both royal and aristocratic centres was the presence of literate elements in their populations. At Paderborn, literacy was represented in the form of styli, which could relate either to estate administration or tuition delivered by clerics. At St-Denis and Corvey, literacy is reflected through inscriptions, and at Hamage by graffitti on ceramic goblets. Book production, and its economic support, however, probably sets the major monasteries apart from other literate elements on settlements.

On nucleated settlements and smaller agglomerations, such as Saleux-les-Coutures, Valkenburg, Geldrop, Dommelen, Venray and Develier-Courtételle, the archaeological trends convey the impression of communities with characteristics different to those in settlements further up the hierarchy. Some, like those at Saleux, were involved in agricultural production, supported by small-scale craft-working for domestic needs. Others were involved in specialist commodity production, as in the case of Develier, whose inhabitants seem to have been specialist iron and non-ferrous metalworkers. They were involved either in significant exchange transactions, or were provisioned within an estate framework in order to compensate them for their degree of craft-specialisation. A common feature of these settlements was the absence of evidence for the conspicuous consumption of luxuries, as well as the lack of an identifiable high-status settlement nucleus. This is not to say, however, that all their inhabitants were of a low status, and internally-ranked communities of extended families can be envisaged.

At Develier, the presence and use of imported luxuries could reflect social differentiation between or within families. But communities which relied on the exchange of specialist products for their sustenance, as suggested at Develier, may have possessed luxuries which need not necessarily have reflected their social status in every case. At Saleux, located on the navigable Somme river system, luxuries were not in evidence, suggesting that here levels of access were conditioned by the lower status of the inhabitants. Yet, the layout of the cemetery at Saleux shows signs of social differentiation during the seventh and eighth centuries; this may not be consistent with the conclusion that all the inhabitants were lowly individuals. The limited access to luxuries at Saleux is a distinct contrast with the hamlets in the delta areas of the Rhine and Meuse, all of which had access to valuable commodities from the Middle Rhine, such as Vorgebirge pottery. These sites cannot be regarded as high-status foci or settlements of artisans, and their advantageous location on arterial riverine routeways seems to have enhanced their access to imported commodities, rather than reflect higher social rank.

The archaeological evidence from nucleated settlements and hamlets reflects a complex range of social relations influenced by the activities which supported the inhabitants, by their social status, and by geography. Overall, however, the archaeological remains do not exhibit the imagery, conspicuous consumption and means of social display in buildings that were the hallmark of the nuclei of royal palaces, monasteries and aristocratic centres. The provisional results of the analysis of the faunal remains from Saleux and the Karlburg attendant settlement provide perhaps the most telling contrast to these high-status sites. The predominance of mature cattle reflects above all their use for traction in preference to meat; likewise the bones of sheep reflect their husbandry for wool prior to mutton consumption.[122] This contrasts completely with the slaughter of animals at a young age for the tenderest meat at Paderborn or the Karlburg fortress – a fundamental reflection of preferential and hierarchical access to food.

Polyfocal settlements

In conclusion, the phenomenon of 'polyfocal' settlements must be examined. The archaeological characteristics of the range of settlements considered so far have been examined as if the different types existed independently. In reality, settlement foci of different types were often located in very close proximity to each other, forming larger agglomerations of distinct settlement elements. In the course of the ninth and tenth centuries, some of these juxtapositions of different types of 'rural' settlements gradually emerged as towns. This transformation – involving the coalescence of administrative, ecclesiastical, craft-working and market functions within single urban settlements – was fundamental to the emergence of High Medieval settlement patterns in north-western Europe. Here, it is necessary to summarise the nature of some polyfocal 'rural' settlements, in order to appreciate their trajectories of 'urban' development.

The subject of the emergence of towns in north-western Europe has recently been reviewed by both the archaeologist Richard Hodges and the historian Adriaan Verhulst. Both highlight the growth of new urban settlements in the course of the ninth and tenth centuries, emerging from existing administrative and ecclesiastical settlement foci. For Hodges, this transformation represented a usurpation of the roles in specialist production, regional trade and toll collection, previously held by major *emporia* like Dorestad and Quentovic. This change in the control and promotion of craft-specialisation and trade is considered to be a reflection of the regional dispersion and active acquisition of these roles by major monasteries and estate centres, to some extent in response to Viking disruption.[123] Verhulst, in contrast, has laid less emphasis on taking over the functions of the *emporia*. Instead, he views the transformation of important palace, vill and monastic centres into towns as a more organic process stemming from their own internal dynamism. He put particular emphasis on the change from production and movement of commodities linked to high-status nuclei, to wider production and trade for profit.[124]

The archaeological reflections of both these theories would look the same in the ground, and the change from agglomerations of rural settlement foci to towns may have been gradual and largely imperceptible to their inhabitants. The exact time at which some polyfocal rural settlements became towns is debatable, and depends to a large degree on the individually-held definition of an urban settlement.[125] Yet, both the archaeological and textual sources are beginning to provide hints of the nature of these juxtaposed rural foci, composed of different combinations of the settlement types defined in this study, often alongside a craft-working and trading zone, described as a portus. The addition of a portus element seems to be the key distinction between polyfocal rural settlements and those that would become towns.

From the historical and archaeological work on Gent and Ename in Flanders, it is possible to describe some of these polyfocal elements. They possessed separate palace and fortified zones, and later *donjons*, together with multiple ecclesiastical foci, in the form of churches and monasteries, and *portus* nuclei.[126] Similar polyfocal elements, which subsequently coalesced to become urban over the tenth and eleventh centuries, are also suggested in textual sources at Valenciennes, and by a combination of historical and archaeological evidence at Tournai and Douai.[127]

In contrast, other vill centres with multiple settlement elements such as Soest and Karlburg seem not to have possessed significant trading zones.[128] These settlements seem to have coalesced into urban entities in the twelfth and thirteenth centuries. Similarly, Liège – a vill and the seat of the bishops of Tongeren-Maastricht-Liège from the eighth century –possessed an attendant settlement, but its growth with the addition of new abbeys and further foci took place gradually from the eleventh century onwards.[129] Consequently, the composite historical and archaeological picture beginning to emerge from these most complex of rural settlements is that they gained 'central' functions at different rates, relating to specific political, religious and economic contexts, before collective impetus resulted in their evolution into towns.

To conclude, therefore, this survey – of rural settlements that existed between the late seventh and early eleventh centuries – has pointed towards a series of traits and approaches that can be used to characterise settlements and to examine aspects of the hierarchical social relationships that supported them. In some respects, it has provided as many questions as answers, in the sense that our current sample of excavated and published settlement evidence forces reliance on optimum sets of data. This is a feature of both historical and archaeological research, and future analyses may disprove these observations. Yet the identification of the media of social display, and of patterns of consumption and production, can generate preliminary hypotheses on the characteristics of settlements as a whole and on the activities of different settlement zones.

Nevertheless, numerous tantalising questions for further investigation remain. The attendant settlement zones, away from the high-status nuclei of palaces, estate centres or monasteries, desperately need archaeological attention in order to assess their role in relation to the high-status foci that they supported. Similarly, our published sample of nucleated settlements and hamlets is dangerously small for purposes of comparison, although synthetic summaries of the extent of research are beginning to appear. Add to these research avenues the dimension of regional differences and the complexities of the transformation of polyfocal settlements into towns, and it becomes apparent that we still have much to add to our understanding of rural settlement in Carolingian Europe.

Notes

1 McKitterick (1983), p. 370.
2 Verhulst (1999), pp. 68–9; Hodges (2000), pp. 100–6; Verhaeghe, ch. 15 (pp. 259–84) in this volume.
3 Lorren and Périn (1997), p. 109.
4 Ervynck et al. (1999), pp. 115–16.
5 Theuws (1999), pp. 340–2.
6 Proos (1997), pp. 151–2.
7 Theuws (1990), pp. 60–3 and (1991), pp. 368–9.

8 Bult and Hallewas (1990), p. 80.
9 Theuws (1990), p. 60 and (1991), pp. 367–8.
10 Stork (1993); Damminger (1998), pp. 62–4.
11 Theuws (1999), p. 343–5.
12 Bult and Hallewas (1990), p. 86.
13 Zadora-Rio (1995), pp. 146–8.
14 Nice (1988) and (1994); Demolon (1972).
15 Lorren and Périn (1997), pp. 104–7.
16 Sarfatij (1977).
17 Hanusse (1999), p. 89; Carré (1996); Zadora-Rio and Galinié, eds. (2001), pp. 238–9; Catteddu (1997); Bult and Hallewas (1990), p. 80; Theuws (1990), p. 60.
18 Lorren and Périn (1997), p. 107.
19 Federici-Schenardi and Fellner (1997).
20 Hamerow et al. (1995).
21 Catteddu (1997), p. 143; Bult and Hallewas (1990), p. 86.
22 Zadora-Rio (1995), pp. 146–8; Carré (1996).
23 Zadora-Rio and Galinié, eds. (2001).
24 Catteddu (1997).
25 *Ibid.*, p. 144.
26 Ervynck (1992), pp. 154–5; Doll (1999).
27 Lepetz et al. (1995), pp. 178–9.
28 Bult and Hallewas (1990), p. 87.
29 Catteddu (1997), pp. 143–4.
30 Bult and Hallewas (1990), p. 87.
31 Federici-Schenardi and Fellner (1997), pp. 125–8.
32 *Ibid.*, p. 125.
33 Hodges (2000), p. 97.
34 Federici-Schenardi and Fellner (1997), p. 128.
35 Lebecq (1997), pp. 75–7; Hamerow et al. (1995), p. 6; Scheers (1991), pp. 32–42.
36 Theuws (1999); Proos (1997), p. 155.
37 Galinié (1999), pp. 103–4; Verslype (1999), pp. 147–50.
38 Callebaut (1994), pp. 95–7.
39 Loyn and Percival (1975), pp. 98–105.
40 Tessier et al. (1952), no. 274; Callebaut (1994), p. 93; Nelson (1992), p. 207.
41 Witvrouw (1999), pp. 105–8.
42 MGH *Dip. Germ.* II, no. 130.
43 Zadora-Rio and Galinié (2001), pp. 223–36.
44 On Paderborn. see Mecke (1999) and Gai (1999a); on Aachen, see Nelson (2001a); on Ingelheim, see Rauch and Jacobi (1976) and Grewe (1999).
45 Nelson (1992), pp. 230–1.
46 Renoux (1999), pp. 134–6.
47 Melzer (1999), p. 367.
48 Ettel (1998), pp. 75–8.
49 Best et al. (1999).
50 Reuter (1991), p. 166.
51 de Meulemeester (1983), p. 207; de Meulemeester et al. (1997), pp. 143–4; De Boüard (1974).

52 Renoux (1999), p. 130.
53 Early (2001), pp. 276–83.
54 Demolon and Louis (1994), p. 55.
55 Bur (1999), p. 33.
56 de Meulemeester (1983), p. 203; Henderikx (1995), p. 94.
57 van Heeringen et al. (1995), pp. 232–4.
58 de Meulemeester (1983), p. 203; Ervynck (1992), p. 153.
59 Ervynck (1992); Matthys (1991), pp. 213–14.
60 Renoux (1997), pp. 124–5.
61 Matthys (1991), p. 214.
62 Renoux (1997), p. 124.
63 Doll (1999), p. 445.
64 Reuter (1985), p. 75.
65 Doll (1999).
66 Ettel (1998), p. 83.
67 Doll (1999), p. 446.
68 On Höxter, see Grothe and König (1999), p. 374; on Soest, see Melzer (1999), p. 367.
69 Lauwerier (1995); Tys (1997), p. 157; Ervynck et al. (1999), p. 116.
70 Ervynck (1992), pp. 154–5.
71 Doll (1999), p. 448; Wigh (1998), pp. 85–6.
72 Ettel (1998), p. 83.
73 Ervynck (1992), p. 153.
74 Yvinec (1993), pp. 492–6; Lepetz et al. (1995), p. 179.
75 Grothe (1999), p. 209.
76 Gai (1999b).
77 Peacock (1997), pp. 710–11; Stiegemann and Wemhoff (1999a), 1, no. III.5.
78 Stiegemann and Wemhoff (1999a), 1, no. II.57; Grewe (1999), p. 105.
79 Peacock (1997), pp. 710–12; Rauch and Jacobi (1976), p. 112.
80 Mecke (1999), p. 181; Stiegemann and Wemhoff (1999a), 1, no. III.59–60.
81 Stiegemann and Wemhoff (1999a), 1, no. VI.11; McKitterick (1989), pp. 222–7; Nelson (1990), pp. 14–15.
82 Ettel (1998), pp. 78–80.
83 Melzer (1999), pp. 369–72.
84 Grothe and König (1999), pp. 375–9.
85 Van Heeringen et al. (1995), pp. 234–5.
86 Tessier et al. (1952), no. 435; Louis (1997), pp. 55–6.
87 Louis (1997), pp. 59–60.
88 *Ibid.*, pp. 61–2.
89 *Ibid.*, pp. 56–9.
90 *Ibid.*, p. 58; McKitterick (1989), pp. 213–16.
91 Crosby (1987), pp. 15–50.
92 Wyss (1997), p. 112.
93 *Ibid.*, p. 114.
94 Wyss (1999), p. 140.
95 Wyss (2001), p. 195–6.
96 Henderikx (1995), pp. 96–9.
97 Wyss (1999), p. 141, and (2001), p. 195.
98 Steuer (1999), p. 411.

99 Wyss (1997), p. 112.
100 *Ibid.*, p. 114.
101 McKitterick (1983), p. 118.
102 Conant (1979), pp. 63–5; Ganz (1990).
103 Stiegemann and Wemhoff (1999a), 2, nos. VIII.43–4.
104 *Ibid.*, nos. VIII.45, VIII.51–3.
105 *Ibid.*, nos. VIII.61.
106 Stephan (1994), pp. 207–16.
107 Ettel (1998), p. 83.
108 McKitterick (1989), pp. 139–41.
109 Peacock (1997), p. 712.
110 Peacock (1997), p. 713; Ludowici (2001), pp. 74–7.
111 Hoek (1986), p. 116.
112 Busch (1995); Hoffmann et al. (1997), pp. 243–56.
113 Renoux (1999), pp. 135–36; Melzer (1999), pp. 367–8.
114 Duby (1991), pp. 59–61.
115 Bur (1999), p. 33; de Meulemeester (1983), pp. 200–3; Callebaut (1994), pp. 103–7.
116 Doll (1999).
117 Ettel (1998), p. 83.
118 Doll (1999), p. 449.
119 Demolon and Louis (1994), p. 55; Renoux (1997), p. 124.
120 Barbé et al. (1998), pp. 9–40.
121 Loyn and Percival (1975), p. 70; Reuter (1985), pp. 85–6; Steuer (1999), pp. 413–14.
122 Catteddu (1997), p. 144; Ettel (1998), p. 83.
123 Hodges (2000), pp. 100–1.
124 Verhulst (1999), pp. 66–9.
125 Verhaeghe, next chapter in this volume.
126 Callebaut (1994), pp. 98–103; Verhulst (1999), pp. 74–9, 100–2.
127 On Valenciennes, see Verhulst (1999), p. 95; on Tournai, see Verslype (1999), pp. 148–58; on Douai, see Demolon and Louis (1994), pp. 54–6.
128 On Soest, see Melzer (1999), p. 366; on Karlburg, see Ettel (1998), pp. 75–80.
129 Verhulst (1999), pp. 70–2.

15

URBAN DEVELOPMENTS
IN THE AGE
OF CHARLEMAGNE

Frans Verhaeghe
with Christopher Loveluck and Joanna Story

Over recent decades, our understanding of the early medieval urban world has changed dramatically. Historians and archaeologists have long debated the demise of Roman towns and the emergence of the medieval cities; Merovingian and Carolingian economic developments and the role of Frankish rulers have always been at the core of the debate. Documentary evidence is scant and does not readily permit straightforward interpretations, but with the development of urban archaeology since the 1960s much has changed. Archaeological data also have their limitations but have led to new insights, making it obvious that the urban world of Charlemagne's Europe was far more complex than we have appreciated hitherto.

This chapter examines the present state of understanding of urban developments in the age of Charlemagne, surveying the major evidence as well as the main interpretative models and the research questions still open. It looks also at the possible role of the Carolingians as agents of urban developments, and at contemporary perceptions of towns. Our geographical focus is the heartland of the Carolingian realm and empire, that is, north-west Europe; chronologically we must also examine aspects of the urban phenomenon in pre- and post-Carolingian times because the Carolingian situation and developments cannot be assessed in isolation. For the same reason, the evidence for the Anglo-Saxon and Scandinavian urban worlds also comes into view.

Towns: problems of definition

The definition of a town has been long (and often hotly) debated, and the problem remains unsolved. As a rule of thumb, however, towns can be characterised as agglomerated settlements with multiple functions, mainly – but not necessarily exclusively – in the secondary and tertiary sectors of socio-economic life (crafts, trade, administration, services, religion and so on). These functions are reflected in the physical appearance and the spatial organisation of the settlement, which will often have specific types of buildings and other infrastructure components such as harbours and structured plot or street systems.[1]

Furthermore, towns are inextricably linked to the society of which they are a part, though without necessarily being faithful reflections of that society.[2] They can also be seen as ideological statements about how a society sees itself and not solely as the result of economic factors.[3] In other words, they can be created, re-created or changed by the interaction of social, economic, political and cultural developments affecting that society. In this sense, towns can have 'life trajectories' that are not static: they can emerge, disappear and change through time and space. This is particularly important because from late Roman times to the tenth century, towns – just like society – went through fundamental transformations. Any discussion of towns in the Carolingian era, therefore, has to take into account the earlier and later manifestations of the urban world as well as the socio-economic, cultural and regional contexts of the period.

Our discussion of towns relies, in part, on what has been termed a *Kriterien-bundel* ('criteria-bundle').[4] However, a measure of overlap may persist between urban sites on the one hand and some rural settlements – whether monastic or seigneurial – on the other. For pre-Viking England, the problems related to the ranking of 'urban' sites and a range of elite ones (including so-called 'productive' sites) illustrate the point.[5] But the use of a more generalised version of a *Kriterien-bundel* does have a few practical advantages. First of all, it allows us to avoid the use of specific legalistic or morphological criteria like charters, fortifications, planned spatial organisation or harbours, which are often selected as definitive urban markers but which can also be applied to rural settlements, and which are often of little real significance in Merovingian or Carolingian towns. Similarly, questions of size and population are problematic; a town can be any size depend-ing on its setting, and the lack of precise data makes it difficult to define 'large' and 'small' towns.[6] This characterisation of towns does not exclude the presence of rural elements within an urban settlement nor does it ignore those cases where some specialised craft activities were rooted in an obviously rural setting.[7]

Because the early medieval urban world was in constant flux, scholars have tried to categorise settlements by using more-or-less contemporary terms like *emporium*, *wic*, *portus* or *civitas*. These contemporary terms seem to denote specific types of 'towns' and change of use through time.[8] But any perusal of the literature shows that these terms are not used consistently by present-day scholars. Furthermore, their current use tends to 'create' specific categories of towns; these then become the focus of attempts to characterise *emporia*, *civitates*, *portus*, or *wics* as specific and different types of urban settlement. However, this modern typology of town-types was not necessarily the same as early medieval perceptions of towns, and the differences between the many types of settlements with these urban features or functions are not clear-cut in the contemporary evidence. These terms will thus be avoided except when referring to their specific use by some scholars; here, urban settlements of all varieties will simply be called 'towns'.

Other modern terms that are used include 'proto-town', 'proto-urban settlements' and 'primary towns'. These labels denote settlements not yet fully urban but which already possessed a few urban features, and which developed eventually into 'classic' medieval towns. Galinié has argued that such terms tend to obscure the issues since the concept of a town is not constant over time and inhabitants of towns do not act in a teleological way towards a specified urban form.[9] These terms are thus preferably avoided, and there is good reason to accept Hodges' point that 'a site is either urban or it is not', even if the adjective 'proto-urban' makes some sense when considering the development of the economy.[10]

The study of early towns often reflects a strong bias towards economic issues and trade, which are used as the basis for the explanation of urban development and for typologies of later, medieval towns.[11] But however important, economy and trade are not the only factors involved, given the complex nature of an urban settlement and its multiple and intricate relationships to the local, regional and broader social context.[12] Towns are indeed social – in the broadest sense of the word – as well as economic phenomena and cannot be seen as purely functional and utilitarian economic constructs. It is equally important to realise that the inhabitants of each phase in a town did not necessarily see their urban space as a functional whole under their total control. Apart perhaps from very early phases of new urban settlements, the inhabitants' and/or builders' view of the future evolution of the settlement must have been limited. Once it existed, the settlement influenced the socio-economic and cultural contexts as well as the behaviour of its inhabitants. In other words, the inhabitants' and/or builders' actions had consequences which they could not necessarily predict. This is perhaps all too often forgotten by archaeologists, and at least part of the evidence is then – again – readily interpreted in terms of pre-existing models of long-term development. For these reasons, it may be appropriate for archaeology to focus on urban space as both an agency and a social construct within a limited time-scope.[13]

Major issues

Notwithstanding the significant progress made in the study of early medieval towns, many problems still remain; new information and interpretations have led to new questions while earlier ones have to be reassessed in new ways.

One major debate concerns the issue of continuity or discontinuity between the Roman and early medieval urban worlds. Ward-Perkins has characterised this as a debate between optimists and pessimists, the former adhering to the notion of continuity, the latter to that of the demise of the Roman town.[14] Others have suggested that the question is no longer relevant, or questioned whether it can be answered even by archaeological research.[15] Hodges – ranked among the pessimists by Ward-Perkins – has restated this view: 'Archaeologists and historians now share a measure of certitude about the discontinuity in urban life that, with the special exception of Rome, characterised Latin Christendom'.[16] In view of the very different natures, functions and contexts of Roman and Carolingian towns, as well as their vastly dissimilar morphological appearance, one can only concur with this view. By Carolingian times it appears that the link with the Roman past was not a driving force in urban development.

But the notions of continuity and discontinuity are complex ones; however important the differences, there were still a number of links between the Roman and the Carolingian towns. Perhaps the 'dark earth' on top of so many late-Roman urban sites hides more than is generally believed (see below). Until archaeology learns to 'read' these 'dark earth' deposits in some detail, final judgement on its significance is best reserved. Important also is the observation that in most formerly Romanised regions of the Carolingian Empire, the number of Roman towns which became the sites of early medieval ones far outweighs that of deserted Roman towns which were never re-occupied: 'Most towns persisted, even if much of the Roman heritage did not'.[17]

Also it is clear that, in the old Roman regions, most if not all of the later towns were located on or immediately next to Roman sites, most of which had left visible remains. Dorestad lies next to a Roman *castellum*; Domburg had important Roman predecessors. Rouen, Tours, Paris, Trier, Cologne and a host of others complement the list. The same is true in the case of most towns along the Meuse (Maastricht, Namur and possibly also Huy) and Scheldt valleys (Tournai, Cambrai, Valenciennes). For Ghent and Antwerp, the situation is less clear but Roman and Merovingian rural habitation has been archaeologically attested.[18] This may simply result from suitable topographical and geographical conditions, but it may also mean that old Roman sites had some meaning. Notions of power and prestige, together with administration, could have been perpetuated as a 'desired link with a Roman past'. In Merovingian and Carolingian times – and notably through the role of the Church – Rome was still an example. As successors to the emperors of the old Roman West, the Carolingian rulers had an interest in Rome itself and were impressed by it, and thus may well have seen towns not only as an economic tool but also partly as a political means of enhancing their prestige.[19]

So, some kind of symbolic, political continuity between Roman, Merovingian and Carolingian towns did exist – though we need more research to prove theories of a physical link between Roman buildings of power (like the *basilica* and *praetoria*) and later churches as seats of power. But this continuity with the past took different forms for different towns: topographical continuity for some, continuity of function for others, and a continuation of political focus elsewhere.

This means that the situation has to be assessed for each town individually, while simultaneously taking into account the broader supra-regional socio-economic and socio-political framework. For the many early medieval towns that lay beyond the borders of the Roman empire, the situation was different, and here there is no evidence, physical or otherwise, of deliberate attempts to refer to a Roman past.

The physical appearance of early medieval towns is another important area of research since the visual 'experience' of the town may have influenced the perception and behaviour of contemporaries towards their urban environments. This is difficult to do, and more data is needed on the sizes and layout of Carolingian towns; future excavation priorities should go to sites of a fair size, covering wherever possible several house plots, in order to gain a better insight into spatial organisation. A closely related question concerns Carolingian 'urban material culture', whether the inhabitants of these settlements possessed a range of commodities different from that normally found on elite sites, estate centres or other contemporary components of the rural world; if so, how and why was such 'urban material culture' different? This issue poses a range of detailed questions relating to specific categories of commodities, from pottery and foodstuffs to toilet implements, jewellery and clothing, each of which require systematic analysis and comparison with the relevant finds from rural sites.

Lines of development

At the dawn of the Carolingian age, the urban world of western Europe was fairly complex, characterised by the presence of different traditions and by near-constant processes of change. Generally speaking, towns had been absent from the non-Romanised regions of Europe until the seventh or eighth century. The only settlements in these areas with some 'urban' characteristics were some of the 'Type A' or seasonal *emporia* as defined by Hodges (see below). Later, in the age of Charlemagne, other towns appeared in the Baltic world and, subsequent to that, a number of settlements linked with early strongholds.

Things were of course different in western and southern Europe, where towns had been a normal feature of Roman society. On the whole, the Roman urban network had been a political and administrative tool rather than an economic one; Roman towns have been characterised as 'consumer cities', even as parasitic units in economic terms – a view which has been attacked by some and modified by others.[20] In the later Roman period, towns started to change; public investment seems to have regressed significantly and, even though it was becoming relatively more important, so did private investment. The upkeep of public buildings and infrastructure declined, and many were wholly or partly demolished to provide raw materials for other, less prestigious ones.[21] Additionally, from the third century onwards, much public investment went into the construction of defences. There are regional differences, and in some cases the changes were marked but did not necessarily reflect a 'decline' – as for example with some towns in Gaul.[22] In other cases, as in Roman Britain, the third-century crisis was followed by a temporary revival while the towns moved into a 'state-directed, command economy, wholly subordinated to the demands of war'.[23]

The situation changed again in the fifth and sixth centuries. There are sufficient indications that not all towns were totally deserted, far from it, but they dwindled dramatically. Were these diminished settlements truly urban in nature? The sites yield fragmented information; some have scant remains of rubbish pits and a few wooden buildings, and many show Roman occupation horizons to be covered with deposits of dark soil, commonly known as 'dark earth'. Such layers are generally taken as an indication of abandonment and dereliction.[24] But they also seem to be thoroughly and repeatedly re-worked soils with a significant organic content, which suggests that the site was in use and had not been deserted. This 'dark earth' remains largely 'unreadable' archaeologically and may conceal more than is often suspected.[25] Nor should we forget that traces of smaller wooden buildings are ephemeral and that only a small sample of the relevant urban sites has so far been excavated (let alone published). In addition, apart from being reduced, the focus settlement may also have shifted (sometimes only slightly) away from the old Roman core – as indeed happened at Metz and perhaps also at Lyon.[26] Therefore, the 'dark earth' should not be taken as proof of desertion.

On the issue of urban population, the consensus is one of a severe decline in the fifth and sixth centuries. But it has also been argued that a drastic reduction in population size does not necessarily result in an extremely small population, nor even in a loss of urban function. Furthermore, serious doubts have been raised regarding towns supposedly depopulated where, nevertheless, bishoprics were established, palaces built, tolls exacted and churches founded.[27]

Still, the evidence for dramatic change is incontrovertible, particularly the drastic reduction in size and altered appearance characterised by material degradation. Some Roman towns were thus deserted and eventually vanished. In Italy, for instance, it has been estimated that 116 of the 372 documented Roman towns disappeared.[28] But throughout southern and western Europe, many did not disappear and – given the complexities of interpreting the 'dark earth' – some kind of occupation may have been maintained into the sixth century. In many cases (Trier and Cologne, for example) Roman buildings survived and were re-used. It is a moot point whether the occupants of such settlements perceived their environment to be urban, that is, as something different from the normal rural sites of the period. Therefore, at the level of contemporary perception, the debate over urban continuity or discontinuity between Roman and later towns needs to be redefined. To use Galinié's characterisation of early medieval Tours, these settlements may well have been 'towns without urban life', at least urban life as *we* normally understand it.[29]

By the sixth and early seventh centuries, towns were again prominent in large areas of the former Roman Empire. One needs only to read Gregory of Tours' *Libri historiarum X* ('Ten Books of Histories'), compiled in the late sixth century, to see a Gallic world where towns were a normal part of landscape and society. Gregory focused on the Church, the *civitas* (both as a city and as an urban centre in its territory) and the regions under Frankish rule. This reflects his own background, interests and agendas, and he offers a few direct observations of economic phenomena, buildings and other physical features such as urban decay. Nevertheless, his towns were engaged in trade and production, many had imposing town-walls and – apparently at least– a substantial population. Gregory's towns, 'continued to perform a range of administrative, social, economic and military functions which could not (or not all) be found elsewhere'.[30]

The exact appearance of such towns remains extremely difficult to assess, given the fragmentary nature of the historical and archaeological evidence. It would, however, appear that a number of Roman buildings still dotted the urban landscape, both within and outside the walls, and that a number of towns still had Roman defences. In some cases, the walls were still effective – with gates and towers around Dijon – but elsewhere they had decayed or were no longer of any practical value (as in the case of the huge wall around Trier). Gregory's description in his 'History' (III.19) of the walls around Dijon is a well-known example. Inside the wall-circuit, however, the occupation may not have been very dense; the same may apply to other parts of the 'town', as shown at Tours. Here, the Roman town had shrunk to a fortified *castrum* (housing a group of episcopal buildings) and an emerging external *vicus christianorum* ('quarter of the Christians') around the monastery of St-Martin, 800 m (half a mile) to the west. The latter is also referred to as a *suburbium* ('suburb'); it was separated from the *castrum* by a largely open space which had once been part of the Roman urban townscape. Similar open spaces also occur in the area around the funerary basilica at St-Martin. Judging from the sixth- and seventh-century texts for Gaul, groupings of episcopal buildings (including palace, church and so on) dominated the urban landscape, but there are also references to lively streets, houses, shops and workshops (including workshops for luxury items), which remain difficult to define in physical terms. In some towns, such as Tours, Paris, Lyon, Metz and Maastricht, a measure of suburban settlement also developed outside the old wall-circuit.[31]

A good case can be made for diverse regional or local developments in this period in terms of the physical appearance of individual buildings and towns. Tours, Metz, Lyon and Marseille are physically different from one another because of their different geographical, historical and socio-political settings. Another good example is provided by the situation in the Flemish Scheldt valley in comparison to that of the Meuse valley. Both areas have polyfocal settlements with a least one nucleus of Roman origin, and bishops chose some of them

(Cambrai and Tournai in the Scheldt valley, Maastricht and Huy in the Meuse valley) as seats of both religious and secular function. But the Meuse valley had an economic and socio-political edge, as it was more closely linked with trade and with Dorestad, and it gradually became a favourite abode of the Austrasian elite. Nevertheless, Verhulst identifies this phase of the sixth and seventh centuries as the 'nadir of urban life'.[32]

It appears – in Gaul at least – that Merovingian kings were interested in towns as a basis for power and prestige; a town was probably also a well-appreciated source of income. So, in a sense, Gregory's towns still reflected the late Roman urban world.[33] By c.AD 600, however, Merovingian rulers based themselves more in the 'countryside', and this trend became increasingly marked in Carolingian times. But the sixth century also saw the gradual revival of trade, particularly long-distance trade, and possibly also of the emergence of special trading-sites. Simultaneously, old Roman towns were superseded as central stages for rituals of power by a multitude of other places and spaces where political and religious power was displayed.[34] This trend continued well into the seventh century and beyond, but may have been stronger in the North Sea region than in the southern parts of Charlemagne's realm.

On the whole, the seventh century remains obscure. But gradually major changes did occur, among them the growing role of regional territorial entities in some areas and the new social conditions this brought about.[35] Even more important was the revival of trade, particularly long-distance trade, associated in the North Sea region with the growing role of Frisian (and other) traders.[36] This influenced settlements along the Meuse and Rhine valleys, and was a factor in the contacts between the Merovingian rulers of Neustria and the Anglo-Saxon kingdoms, notably Kent, from c.550.[37]

The revival of long-distance trade may well have been instrumental in the appearance or further development of a number of town-like trading settlements, some of which later developed into major towns characterised by Hodges as 'Type B' or permanent *emporia*, of which Dorestad, in the heartland of Frisia, is the best-known and most important. Located at the confluence of the northern branch of the Lower Rhine into the Kromme Rijn and the Lek, Dorestad emerged in the first quarter of the seventh century. But archaeology has not (yet) revealed anything about the earlier phases of this settlement, which may have been eradicated by the river. The embankment, where part of the harbour area was discovered and which constitutes the northern part of the settlement, came into use c.675 and significant changes occurred about a generation later.[38] Another key site is Quentovic, located on the Canche in northern France. Coin evidence suggests that a settlement may already have existed here before c.640, but it was not until the last third of the seventh century that it became a fully-fledged *emporium*. Again, little if anything is known about physical appearance of the early phases of settlement there.[39]

Another impetus for urban development was the establishment of a series of major abbeys in the seventh century. In some places these became major players in Carolingian trade and economy, and thus important agencies in the development of towns. These abbeys were founded on Merovingian (royal) estates close to urban settlements, thereby establishing a new settlement core; they also established a topographical and economic focus, which, from the eighth century onwards, become one of the driving forces of new urban developments. This has been particularly well demonstrated for the southern Low Countries, for example at Arras in northern France and Ghent in Flanders.[40] In Arras, the old Roman *civitas* probably had a church in the late seventh century, but an earlier church may have existed by *c.*550 across the River Crinchon. This became the core of the St-Vaast abbey, thus leading to a 'dual-focus' settlement. The abbey was later fortified (presumably between 880 and 890) and became the centre of a multifunctional complex, which developed eventually into the medieval town. In Ghent, two early seventh-century monastic communities, later the abbeys of St-Peter and St-Bavo, were located on former royal estates. The first stood to the east and the other to the south of a settlement known as *Ganda* (near an old Roman *vicus*, possibly with a late *castrum*). Although very little is known about *Ganda*, it was fortified in the ninth century and eventually developed into the medieval town centre.

So, the late sixth and seventh centuries constituted another phase in the establishment of new nuclei which in some cases attracted new settlements and ultimately towns, either on their own or through coalescence with other *nuclei*, which might have been estate-centres, abbeys, strongholds or incipient trading places. The importance of the abbeys in economic and political terms should not be underestimated when discussing Carolingian towns, as Verhulst and Lebecq have emphasised.[41] It is mainly during this late Merovingian phase and the subsequent Carolingian period that the power of the abbeys grew, and that some of the conditions for the emergence of polyfocal urban settlements were put in place.[42]

It should also be emphasised that these changes (particularly the growing importance of *emporia*) do not mean that other towns with older roots disappeared. The results from the extensive excavations at places like Dorestad and Anglo-Saxon *Hamwic* (Southampton) form a considerable part of the literature, and this can give the impression to the unwary that the other urban settlements were of little significance. This situation also seems to have affected actual research into the subject, with the result that the roles of other urban settlements have been comparatively neglected, and relatively little is known about their relations with the seventh-century *emporia*. For these reasons, alternative approaches like the one offered by Verhulst – who takes into account the urban phenomenon as a whole – are particularly valuable.[43]

The eighth-century urban world

There is now a consensus that a 'medieval' urban world began to take shape in the late seventh and eighth centuries, with changes witnessed not only in Neustria and Austrasia but also beyond the north-western fringes of what was to become the Carolingian empire. This period saw the success of the settlements known as *emporia*. The nature of these settlements, their physical appearance, infra-structure, internal spatial organisation and location in relation to other (older or contemporary) settlement-centres have been the subject of many publications. Hodges has framed the theoretical characterisation and interpretation of these sites; his views have dominated the debate over the past two decades, but are now being questioned.[44] Hodges set the *emporia* within the context of long-distance trade and gift-exchange, calling them 'gateway communities', 'ports-of-trade' and 'centrally-administered settlements'. He identified two major types, A and B.

Type A *emporia* are defined as periodic markets or 'fairs', normally held on boundaries, on the coast or on a riverbank, consisting of no more than a few tent-like structures. The ephemeral nature of such sites makes them hard to detect, identify and study, and they may never have constituted a significant settlement type.[45] Major sites such as Quentovic and Dorestad may have originated as Type A *emporia* but there is currently no archaeological evidence to demonstrate this. Hodges' Type B *emporia* – now often referred to as the 'classic' *emporia* – are better documented, particularly by archaeology.[46] Best-known from the heartlands of the Carolingian empire are Quentovic and Dorestad, and Rouen might also be added to the list.[47] Other perhaps subsidiary centres include Domburg and Medem-blik (both in the Netherlands). To the south, comparable urban settlements existed, in the Po valley and at Marseille for example, though the latter had lost much of its trading role by the Carolingian period.[48]

What really characterises these Type B *emporia* is their unambiguous 'urban' character. They were all substantial agglomerated settlements, located on a river-front or on the coast, each with a harbour infrastructure, often with a grid-street layout and an organised plot system. All have yielded considerable direct or indirect evidence for long-distance contacts and trade, most clearly identifiable through the presence of imported pottery, coins, glass vessels and other items. All have revealed remains of specialised craft activities, notably metalworking and antler- and horn-working, glass-working and the production of textiles. On a cautionary note, though, all these traits can also be seen on some rural sites, particularly elite centres; the difference between 'urban' and 'rural' in this sense may be a function of scale, not character, of production.[49] But it remains unclear whether, or to what extent, one can speak at this stage of a specifically 'urban' material culture which was fundamentally different from its rural counterpart.

The size of these towns varied considerably. Dorestad was the largest, with a surface area of up to 200 hectares (500 acres). In comparison, the contemporary *emporium* of *Lundenwic* (London) stood at 50–80 hectares (120–200 acres), and *Hamwic* (Southampton) was about 45 hectares (110 acres) at its greatest extent. As to population, recent estimates range from 1,000–8,000 individuals for Dorestad, while for the other main towns an average of 1,000–3,000 is proposed. Crucially, these populations far outnumbered the average for rural settlements of the period. This is presumably why Hodges sees 'classic' Type B *emporia* as very major concentrations of urban population, in contrast to the towns of Roman origins. This explains in part why he sees them as 'dream cities', impressive phenomena which captured the imagination of their contemporaries.[50] The underlying assumption is influenced by the belief that other towns – notably those with Roman roots – had very small populations. But the size of the early medieval urban population is very much a matter of conjecture, and the 'older' towns may have been rather more populous than is so often suggested.[51]

If, as Theuws suggests, late Merovingian Maastricht was the scene of an intricate power-play between the kings, the clergy and the regional aristocracy concerning the control of its churches and their parishioners, it is not unreasonable to suppose that its population was of a size sufficient to justify this level of political activity.[52] The decree of Pope Zacharias' (741–52) that bishoprics should not be established in poorly populated settlements, because this was demeaning to episcopal standing and the status of the Church, is sometimes used to argue that those towns had a sizable population.[53] Zacharias' pronouncement may mean that, normally, the towns where bishops held their office were substantial, but it may also mean that exceptions did occur or could occur, and that those places were to be avoided. The association of a bishopric with an urban centre may suggest, but does not prove, that the town was densely populated. Nevertheless, it remains difficult to view the 'classic *emporia*' as having consistently larger concentrations of population than other, 'older' Roman towns. In population terms this means that the 'classic' *emporia* may have been less exceptional than Hodges suggests, though they may have been atypical in other ways. They may even have been something of a backwater as compared to the 'real' towns of the period which had more standing in other ways. Perhaps, therefore, the importance of *emporia* in the range of urban settlements in the Carolingian period has been overstressed.

Hodges emphasised other points that deserve attention. The first relates to the location of *emporia*. He argues that most if not all of the Type B *emporia* were totally new foundations, established on new sites with no relationship, psychological or physical, to earlier settlements in the vicinity. However, within the former Roman provinces, many of these sites were located in the immediate vicinity of a Roman predecessor which preserved at least some visible ruins or other reminders of Roman times. It is true that these *emporia* were 'places without a previous history' in the sense that their nature, context and functions were totally different from those of the nearby Roman settlements.[54] But the degree of coincidence in geographical location is too great to be devoid of significance.

Second, Hodges argued that these *emporia* were planned creations and that their regular layout implies the direct intervention of a central authority; he often uses the word 'architects' and cautiously suggests the influence of Mediterranean (Roman or Islamic) models. The regular grid of streets and plots does suggest the intervention of an authority and, when available, documentary evidence bears this out. However, it should not be forgotten that the patterns are basically very simple ones, easy to realise from a technical point of view. Furthermore, some of these settlements may have emerged first as seasonal trading-places, only to attract the attention of rulers at a subsequent stage in their development, as seems to have been the case at Dorestad. However, we still know little of the precursors or early phases of Dorestad, Quentovic or Haithabu (Hedeby). Furthermore, there is growing evidence that rural settlement patterns underwent equally significant changes in the seventh to early eighth century, contemporary with – or possibly even before – the flowering of major *emporia*. This new observation about changes in rural settlement patterns may mean that more complex interpretative models have to be developed concerning contemporaneous urban developments.

Another point concerns the linkage between *emporia* as monopolistic markets and long-distance trade in prestige goods. The early medieval gift-exchange economy is prominent in this context. As such, *emporia* are interpreted as 'royal' creations and tools to be used in prestige exchange relations. Strong links with long-distance trade are undeniable and are confirmed by documentary evidence, which records tolls and sometimes incentives and protection offered to traders (as in the case of Dorestad). This can be archaeologically conspicuous, as emphasised in *emporia* outside the Frankish realms by the presence of significant amounts of imported pottery and prestige commodities like vessel-glass and coinage. But as we learn more about these sites and their hinterlands, it is becoming increasingly clear that other roles were just as important; these *emporia* also seem to have acted as central points for craft production and regional trade, and they may also have functioned as nodal centres of regional power.

Van Es argues convincingly for multiple functions in the case of Dorestad.[55] He lists long-distance trade, regional trade relations, craft production, food supply and perhaps administrative functions (as suggested by the written evidence for the presence of Carolingian officials called *ministeriales* and *procuratores rei publicae*, literally, 'procurators of public things'). To some extent, however, these regional central-place functions remain hypothetical and it is possible that they emerged only after some of these towns had developed as trading sites. In other cases, administrative functions were still fulfilled by older towns, notably those which are not customarily seen as *emporia* but rather as older *civitates* where bishops or counts resided as the representatives of authority (Maastricht, Tournai or Tours, for example).

More certain is the role of *emporia* in regional trade and food provisioning, as has been demonstrated at Dorestad. Evidence is provided by the growing data for

270

rural settlements in their hinterlands, particularly by archaeozoological remains, and by the quantity of imported objects which were redistributed through these *emporia*. As our understanding of rural settlement expands, we will get a clearer picture of the regional settlement hierarchies and the regional interactions between the towns and their rural hinterlands.

Hodges' fourth point concerns the dating of these sites. He argued that the period *c.*670–800 was the high-point of these *emporia*; by the early ninth century, they had started to decline and many were gradually abandoned or replaced by sites nearby. The classic example is Dorestad, which was apparently in decline by the mid-ninth century, yet it remained important enough for the Vikings to sack it four times between 834 and 837, and again in 847, 850, 857 and 863, suggesting also that any damage caused to the fabric of the settlement had been repaired.[56] Quentovic may also have been largely abandoned in the early ninth century, since the historical texts imply that it had lost its functions as a major trading-place and as a gateway community, but this remains to be proven archaeologically.[57] But for other sites, the situation is less clear or simply different. At Rouen and at the sites in the southern Low Countries, the question of a terminal demise in the earlier ninth century remains open.

Inevitably, Viking attacks have often been seen as a seriously disruptive element which put an end to many Carolingian towns. But, however traumatic these attacks may have been, their long-term destructive effects on urban development should not be exaggerated. Many urban settlements were sacked but the damage often appears to have been limited and recovery was quick. This may well have been the case at Dorestad, which was perhaps already in decline before the Vikings attacked it. Nor is there much evidence of long interruptions in the development of these urban sites, although in some cases, such as Ghent, the settlement was relocated to a nearby site.[58] Elsewhere, the Viking assaults were perhaps no more than anecdotal to the history of the individual urban settlement, as Hodges indirectly suggests for London. The trading focus at *Lundenwic*, though not deserted, had been in decline from the early ninth century onwards and was already in the process of being replaced with *Lundenburh*, further to the East.[59] Others sites (often those with a *portus*), held their ground or profited from the changing conditions, and emerged anew as dynamic urban settlements.[60] The old trading networks did not necessarily disappear altogether, but these new settlements, many of them polyfocal, evolved in the tenth and eleventh centuries into the centres from which later, major medieval cities would be born.

In conclusion, all this means that the Carolingian rulers inhabited a complex world with several main traditions as far as towns were concerned. On one side, there was the old Roman world incorporating Gaul, parts of Germany and the Low Countries, with Italy and the western Mediterranean beyond. There, strongly reduced and even deserted towns were still very much part of the landscape, either as partly derelict remains or as partly used or re-used (urban) settlements.

On the other hand, in areas outside the boundaries of the old empire (parts of the Netherlands and Germany), urban settlements were essentially a new phenomenon. This complex urban world underwent a process of constant change during Carolingian times. Some of the major *emporia* disappeared, dwindled significantly or – more importantly – underwent changes that reflected changing functions and a changing socio-economic context. But the overall trend in the evolution of the urban world of the ninth century seems to be one of a growing importance of regional functions (including regional trading, provisioning and production) and, although long-distance trade did not disappear, this process culminated in the emergence of new dynamic urban settlements in the tenth and eleventh centuries.[61]

The material world of Carolingian towns

Historical and archaeological research related to Carolingian towns must also consider the physical appearance of urban settlements and their components, and the ways in which the layout of the townscape may have influenced the behaviour of the inhabitants. The limited information provided by contemporary written sources often uses generalised and elliptic descriptive terms to describe the urban environment – meaningful then but obscure now – so it is up to archaeology to offer some suggestions. However, notwithstanding numerous excavations in Carolingian-period towns, the archaeological information is still very patchy, since most of the relevant excavations have uncovered only a relatively small proportion of the original site. The subject is also complex, involving questions of general layout, street patterns and equipment, harbour infrastructure, defences, the design of house plots (including fences and access) and their internal spatial organisation, the different functional categories of buildings (both public and private) and building techniques. Beyond this, there is also the 'mobile' component: household goods of all kinds, tools and other equipment pertaining to craft production, furniture and the like.[62]

The first theme relates to the general location and topography of the towns. Again, a distinction has to be made between those towns which had direct Roman predecessors and the others, which emerged in the immediate vicinity of Roman towns or on new sites. In the first case, the sheer presence of Roman ruins – including town walls – often played some role in the general topography of the Carolingian town. Sometimes, as at Tours, a late Roman *castrum* formed one of the nuclei of the later (Merovingian, Carolingian and medieval) town. A comparable situation exists in the centre of Maastricht, where the location of the new settlement was influenced by the combination of two main factors: the location of the Roman remains and the presence of waterways. Outside the former Roman Empire, things are of course different; there, waterways seem to have been the predominant factor determining location.

By the Merovingian period, waterways had become the major means of transportation and an essential feature of trading, despite the continued existence and use of the old Roman road system.[63] Hence, it is not surprising that nearly all the Carolingian towns, whatever their origins, were located on river(s) or on the coast and had some kind of harbour infrastructure. In fact, there is a good case to be made for the hypothesis that the absence of suitable waterways played a part in the decline of some Roman towns. An example is provided by Tongeren (Belgium) which was replaced as a bishop's see by nearby Maastricht on the Meuse.[64] As to harbour infrastructure, archaeology has so far revealed several systems. Often, the early phase (seventh and sometimes eighth century) was a rather simple 'beach harbour', that is, a beach where the ships (which had a shallow draught) could be drawn and moored on dry land, as was the case at Anglo-Saxon *Hamwic*. Such 'beach harbours' require little if any investment, meaning that the harbour – and therefore the settlement which it served – could easily shift to another nearby site. This may be the explanation for the shift from *Südsiedlung* to Haithabu in seventh-century Denmark.

But from the late seventh century onwards, more elaborate harbour structures including jetties and quay structures were often erected. In London, a simple quay-like waterfront structure which shored up the riverbank has been dated dendrochronogically to 680–690. In Birka, several stone-packed and wood-encased jetties with a length of up to 4–5 m (13–16 ft) served the settlement from the ninth century onwards. In Haithabu, quay structures and a pier – which protected the harbour as well as offering shelter and mooring space – were in use in the (late) ninth century and later. Further east, on the Slavonic-Baltic coast in Germany, the site of Ralswiek on the island of Rügen (destroyed in the ninth century) revealed an even more complex structure. Here each settlement unit had a number of buildings and one or two landing places; the distinct urban characteristics of Ralswiek are reflected in the presence of craft installations (pottery, bone and antler, iron, amber-working) and ship-building.[65] The jetties at Carolingian Dorestad are a little different as they may have served also as a kind of causeways or metalling of the mudflats along the riverbank. The earliest, which can be dated to 675, were only 10–20 m (33–66 ft) long, but as the Rhine moved eastwards, they were extended until they eventually measured up to 185 m (600 ft) long or more. Ships could only be moored at the head of the individual jetties, which seem to have corresponded to single plots with a house and outbuildings, set behind a road running along the old riverbank. The complex process of construction suggests an element of community co-ordination.

Another major component was the town walls. As already indicated, urban fortifications of late Roman date were often still in existence in the Carolingian world, although perhaps in a state of disrepair or ruin. In the north-west, a number were hastily refurbished in the later ninth century (e.g. at Tournai). But little is known about these repaired structures. In their early phases, the Type B *emporia* do not seem to have been systematically defended. A ditch *c*.3 m (10 ft) wide flanked the western side and south-western corner of *Hamwic*, but it may be a boundary ditch rather than a defensive feature. At Ribe, Denmark, an eighth- or early ninth-century ditch surrounded the urban settlement but it too may be a boundary; it is only in the tenth century that Ribe acquired a defence consisting of an earthen bank and moat. This kind of town wall, the bank perhaps crowned with a wooden fence, is a simple system well illustrated at Haithabu, where the earliest such town walls are dated *c*.900–950. The defence-works protecting the other active towns date from the second half of the ninth century or slightly later, and have to be interpreted in the light of new threats, notably Viking raids. But politics may have provided another catalyst for change, with Carolingian rulers using the external threat as a means of tightening internal security.

This is reflected by the passages in the Edict of Pîtres (864) in which Charles the Bald laid down rules concerning those fortifications and strongholds that he considered to be under threat.[66] Fortification works in the form of a curved ditch and bank protected the main *castrum* site in the heart of Bruges. Though the precise date remains a matter of some conjecture, these defences pre-date 950 and it is likely that they originated around the middle of the ninth century.[67] In Ghent, a moat was dug around the new settlement constructed after the Viking attack in 879 and may also date from the late ninth century.[68] Whether this moat was the basic defence against the Vikings remains uncertain.[69] Its trajectory curved around the settlement and abutted the northern bank of the Scheldt, forming a D-shaped area. Several later towns located on a riverbank or on the coast have a town wall of comparable shape (including Haithabu and somewhat later also Birka). But a D-shaped delineation should not be taken as a dating criterion for the late Carolingian period; it is a fairly simple and functional system also employed after this period. Some of the circular strongholds in the Flemish coastal area (Souburg, Domburg, and Middelburg) have revealed a system of defensive ditch-*cum*-earthen bank which is comparable to those protecting the late Carolingian towns. It is possible that the later defence works in the Scandinavian world, for example the tenth-century Danish strongholds of Trelleborg, Fyrkat, Nonnebakken and Aggersborg, were to some extent copies of what the Vikings had encountered in the Carolingian realm, such as the late ninth-century circular strongholds in the coastal areas of the Low Countries.[70]

As for other defensive strongholds, the general picture for the Carolingian period remains obscure. In Ghent, it has been suggested that a donjon-like tower may have flanked the moat; in other places, old Roman defences may have played a part. Finally, the town wall protecting Haithabu may well have enclosed an area which was significantly larger than the actual settlement, meaning that the urban area included an 'open' area which could be used to expand the settlement, could include burial sites or could be put to other uses such as craft production. There-fore, a town as defined by its defences was not necessarily a completely built-up area. To what extent this also applies to other towns of the Carolingian period is a matter of conjecture. Reconstruction drawings of urban settlements (like *Hamwic*) show a fairly dense building pattern, but it seems quite possible that significant open spaces were in fact part of the early medieval urban experience.

Given the patchy nature of the archaeological evidence, relatively little is known about streets and street-plans. Excavations outside the Carolingian realm suggest that grid street-plans characterised some of the early towns and *emporia* (*Hamwic*, Wolin and Ribe for example), and are interpreted as reflecting the intervention of an authority. The 'Dorestad-type' layout of a central or main street, parallel to the shore or riverbank, is one that occurs often in Carolingian-age towns.[71] But the less regular street-plan at Haithabu suggests that other, perhaps more organic, developments occurred as well. In the Romanised west, the situation was undoubtedly influenced by the presence of a Roman *substratum*, occasionally also by the remains of Roman buildings and by other, more recent structures such as churches. As to the street make-up, the picture presently available is one where regional developments and traditions seem to play an important part. In England, streets with gravel metalling are more common, while in the Scandinavian world and to the East wood planking or timber logs are often used for street surfaces. Wooden surfaces occasionally also turn up in the Carolingian regions, in Ghent and somewhat later also in Antwerp.

Market places have only rarely been identified in early medieval towns. The best-known (though somewhat controversial example) case is that at Ribe (Denmark), dated to the first half of the eighth century and characterised by its regular and planned grid of rectangular plots. It had a surface of at least one hectare (2.5 acres) and was organised on a layer of sand carefully deposited to provide a level surface. It was probably seasonal in nature but had permanent buildings before the end of the eighth century. Not surprisingly, this 'market' has been interpreted as the result of the intervention of a central authority, and used to support the hypothesis that the town of Ribe as a whole was a planned creation. Whether this authority was the king or a local elite (attested at the nearby estate centre at Dankirke) remains an open question.[72] In most other cases, the commercial activities probably took place on or near the beach or harbour.

As for public buildings other than churches, data remain extremely limited. More historical and archaeological work has been done on ecclesiastical buildings – notably churches and also ecclesiastical groups.[73] This is certainly the case in the old Romanised regions, where their characteristics and significance (in social, administrative, political and even economic terms) have been the subject of considerable interest. This is also true for the Christian successors to Roman temples and other buildings, and the new churches of Merovingian and Carolingian times. However, these buildings have often been studied more or less in isolation from the surrounding urban habitat, except when they are used as reference points in the general topography of individual towns on the premise that their prominence and constancy influenced urban topographical development. There is now a wealth of literature on the technical and architectural features of these buildings, and a lot more information is gradually becoming available for rural and – far more rarely – urban wooden churches of Merovingian and Carolingian date.[74] The predominance of stone ecclesiastical buildings in the south is equally well known. But in the Carolingian north, early medieval stone churches were not necessary the norm: they were flanked by the growing number of wooden church buildings, which are not only much more difficult to apprehend archaeologically but they may also have been less permanent elements in the (urban) landscape. But on the whole, the role of such buildings as an element in Carolingian urban material, socio-economic, and socio-cultural development remains to be assessed far more thoroughly than has been done so far.

Another phenomenon of importance was the transformation of extra-mural funerary sites into religious compounds. Some of these became cores of later – including Carolingian – urban development, as for instance in the case of St-Denis near Paris or the St-Servaas compound to the west of Maastricht.[75] In Tours, the compound at St-Martin reflects a comparable development, though in that case the process started even earlier. In some cases, monasteries played a similar role.[76] The point is that through the sheer presence of monastic communities – whose economic and political power had grown since the seventh century – the buildings that went with them influenced the general spatial organisation of the area and the emerging town. They may also have influenced the material appearance of the settlement in terms of building types and techniques.

Cemeteries associated with these monasteries also had an impact on the topography of a number of Carolingian towns. One of the main changes from the sixth century onwards in the old Romanised regions, was the gradual 'entry of death' into the town in contrast to the Roman habit of burying their dead outside the walls.[77] This change was linked to the creation of ecclesiastical compounds, whether funerary ones with martyrs' graves, or monasteries and churches. The role of elite graves in this process is undeniable and some churches may have started as aristocratic funerary chapels in Merovingian times. But by the Carolingian period, cemeteries around churches within the settlement were becoming part of the urban space. As such, they not only influenced the local topography but must also have changed the perception that the inhabitants had of an urban space which no longer belonged exclusively to the living.[78]

The houses, ancillary structures and building plots constitute the main components of private space and only archaeology has the potential to provide us with information on these subjects. But in this domain, there is very considerable regional variation in tradition, local topography, regional resources (raw materials) and the general political, socio-economic and socio-cultural context. For the Carolingian regions, the information is, unfortunately, much more fragmentary than from contemporary sites in England and Scandinavia. This may be linked to the nature of the archaeological deposits, which have sometimes been subjected to heavy erosion, or the excavation techniques used. But whatever the cause, too little is known at present to allow for a general assessment of domestic spatial organisation within towns in Carolingian Francia. The system of a single row of sub-rectangular plots along a road on the riverbank and delimited by a fence is demonstrated in the harbour-zone at Dorestad, but whether this is a general characteristic or applies only to this particular area of the town remains a matter of conjecture.

By the tenth or eleventh centuries, long and narrow plots with a wattle fence were also in use in Antwerp.[79] In general, the evidence suggests that the house plots were organised rather strictly in the early phases of the life trajectory of the new early-medieval towns (though exceptions did occur). In later times, perhaps from the ninth but probably from the tenth century onwards, the plots became longer and narrower, each of them having a narrower street frontage, which again affected the spatial organisation within the plots. But this assessment is conjectural and again, there seems to be a measure of regional variation. It is possible that already by the late Carolingian period the two trends – increasingly large houses and narrower plots – started the 'densification' of the building texture, eventually leading to continuous street frontages in the Middle Ages. In Dorestad, Haithabu and *Hamwic*, the buildings and outbuildings – and sometimes also a well – are more unevenly distributed over the plot, though the buildings and particularly the houses sometimes – but certainly not always – seem to be aligned on the street. Not surprisingly, the houses and their ancillary buildings also reflect considerable regional variation, sometimes as the result of interacting traditions which still merit further attention.

A few general points can be made. First of all, wood had long since become the raw material *par excellence*, a development which started after the collapse of the Roman empire. Stone was of course still used as a building material for churches and parts of monasteries, accounting to a significant degree for the robbing of Roman buildings. Secular stone buildings did occur in the eighth and ninth cen-turies, as with some elite estate centres – such as the *aula* ('hall') in Petegem in Flanders.[80] But even some of the palace complexes built by the Carolingians (e.g. Ingelheim, Aachen, Compiègne, Quierzy) contained significant wooden buildings alongside a few major stone structures. Occasionally – notably in the south – parts of Roman buildings were still used as *spolia* in dwellings, but elsewhere stone houses are totally absent from the townscape until the eleventh century.

Secondly, in the Carolingian north there are clear structural links between rural houses and 'urban' ones. One of the main questions, then, is how and when the distinctively 'urban' house emerged. Current evidence suggests that the process seems to have been a gradual one. In the south, Roman traditions may have played a part and the change may have come as early as the sixth century, judging from the fact that shops, wooden houses and the like are mentioned in urban contexts referred to by Gregory of Tours and others. But little if anything is known about the physical features of such buildings. Further north, the change may date from the eighth to tenth centuries.

Because of exceptional conservation circumstances, the most interesting case is one of the ninth-century houses in Haithabu. Dendrochronology provides dates for the building and modification of a house, 5 × 12 m (16 × 40 ft) in size. In 870 it was built with wattle-and-daub walls on a sill-beam, with wooden buttresses and a thatched roof. It had a main room, 5 × 6 m (16 × 20 ft), with central hearth and a smaller room on each side, one of which had a clay baking-oven. The house was probably linked with craft production. But in 882, it was modified and one of the smaller rooms was equipped with a trough, presumably converting it into a stable.[81] Apart from demonstrating that such a structure could last for 15 to 20 years, this building also points to the intricate relations between craft production and agriculture within an urban context, showing that the border between the two was neither very strict nor mutually exclusive. It may be that the 870–882 house was already 'urban' in nature, but future work will have to confirm this.

Another interesting feature of the situation in the Scandinavian world (including the English Danelaw region) is that by the (late) tenth century, sunken-featured buildings – that is buildings with a floor excavated into the soil – again became more prominent. This may reflect a link with the tradition of the Mero-vingian and Anglo-Saxon sunken huts, and such structures are perhaps precursors of later buildings with a cellar or with a storey.[82] In the Carolingian regions proper, information on urban housing remains very limited, to say the least. The smallish wattle-and-daub building found in Antwerp and dated (provisionally) to the ninth century does not (yet) add much to our knowledge but, by the eleventh century, a hall-like house and later a three-aisled one replaced it.[83] At Dorestad detailed evidence is not yet available, but here too the hall-like houses without internal posts placed along the waterfront are smaller than, but closely akin to, the farmsteads in the immediate hinterland of the settlement.[84] This very rapid survey hardly does justice to the complexity of the issue and there must have been considerable variation depending on the regional context and traditions. But at present, what little can be said does suggest that in the Carolingian north the 'urban' house developed slowly, without at this time leading to a dwelling which was fundamentally different or divorced from the rural ones.[85]

The main difference between the urban and rural evidence is the limited presence of structural features indicating explicit agricultural activities in the town. But the layout of the settlements, the density of building, and some other aspects of the houses and outbuildings, reflect activities other than subsistence pro-duction. Apart from trade, craft production seems to be one of major clues as to the nature and significance of these towns. But although archaeology is a power-ful tool to study craft-working, it also has serious limitations, particularly because it is difficult to assess correctly the quantitative importance of any type of production across time, and because some major crafts, such as textile production, leave relatively limited traces. Nor is it always easy to distinguish domestic production from production for regional or supra-regional trade.[86] Nevertheless, all the evidence points to a very significant role for craft production in most of the settlements in question, and for some (such as York, Haithabu, *Hamwic* and Winchester) the information is now fairly detailed. Information is also available for Maastricht,[87] but for others, like Dorestad, it remains to be fully assessed.

The main craft-working activities detected archaeologically are metal-working (including iron-working, non-ferrous metalworking and the production of jewellery and dress accessories), some glass-working (notably the production of glass beads in the Scandinavian world), bone-, horn- and antler-working, leather production and leather-working, and a measure of textile production. The identi-fication of pottery production is more problematic because often it was located on the periphery of the settlement. Sometimes, however, as for instance in Mero-vingian Maastricht and in Huy, there is sufficient information to suggest that the better-quality pottery served more than a local or regional market.[88] This may also be the case with the glazed wares of late Carolingian and tenth-century date, probably produced in the Huy area.[89] Often the craft-working concerns high-quality if not luxury items, which is one of reasons why Hodges and others have viewed some of the *emporia* as settlements of a rather special kind. But, given the role of the *emporia* as regional distribution centres, other goods may well have been as important as craft produce.

The question is where these crafts were practised in the Carolingian urban settlements and on this issue the information available does not provide a coher-ent picture. Smaller (but not necessarily unimportant) crafts like jewellery production could easily be handled within a small workshop which did not require specialist building infrastructure. The discovery of a small workshop for specialised metalworking on one of the house-plots in Birka (Sweden) shows that craft-working was often handled within the living areas of the town.[90] Nor is there any hard evidence yet for concentrations of specific types of craft production in specific zones of the settlement, though some of those requiring a more extensive infrastructure (like leather or iron production) may occur more often at the periphery of the actual housing areas.

A final issue concerns the portable items of material culture, that is, the movable goods which the inhabitants owned and used, and which could include all manner of objects from furniture and tools to clothing, jewellery, pottery, toilet implements and foodstuffs of any kind. Again, there is considerable regional variability, and it is not clear whether a characteristically Carolingian 'urban' range of commodities and household goods can be identified. Given that much information remains to be published and that a systematic comparison with the range of commodities in rural contexts has yet to be carried out, this remains difficult. But a few possible indications can be mentioned.

Of paramount importance seems to be the presence of foreign goods, of luxury or quality products and of objects related to craft-working. All these are admittedly also found on elite sites in rural contexts but not necessarily in the same amounts or with the same regularity. Furthermore, in some cases, they may denote the presence of foreigners as well as trade. In the graveyards adjoining Birka, for instance, a significant number of these foreign commodities are found in association with non-native burial rites indicating the presence of foreigners, presumably traders. The presence of foreign pottery in *Hamwic* (Southampton) has also been explained by the presence of foreigners who may have found the local products culturally unacceptable.[91] We also need more information about the range of foodstuffs consumed in towns as compared to that available in the rural hinterland. It is more than likely that archaeozoological and palaeobotanical work will provide important evidence but, although some information is available for a number of urban sites, it still seems too early to arrive at definite conclusions.[92] In conclusion, it seems that in Carolingian towns an 'urban' material culture was developing which was not necessarily comparable to later ones, and which was reminiscent of the characteristic material culture of some contemporary elite sites.

Carolingian urban networks and the urban hinterland

As social and spatial constructs, towns cannot function in isolation, because their inhabitants necessarily interact in a variety of ways with all kinds of other settlements and with the surrounding countryside. Thus, they are also tributaries of and contributors to the broader socio-economic, socio-political and cultural context. In the north-west of the Carolingian empire, the North Sea area and the major waterways of the Rhine, Scheldt, and Meuse – the latter leading south to the Rhône-axis and to the Mediterranean – provided extensive opportunities for trade and exchange within the region and with England and Scandinavia. This certainly influenced the success of the Frisian traders and of Dorestad.[93] The urban settlements on the Meuse (Maastricht, Huy, Namur) seem to have profited from the Meuse–Rhine–Dorestad connection (as well as from the fact that this was the region were Charlemagne's ancestral dynasty had extensive personal estates), sufficiently so to gain an edge over the towns of the Scheldt region in the seventh and earlier eighth century.

But, from the mid-eighth century, the Scheldt towns developed under the economic impulse of the great abbeys and later also because of the waning of Dorestad and its network.[94] South of the Low Countries, *Hamwic* had close contacts with north-west and northern France, including Quentovic; Rouen and the Seine led to the Paris region, which was in turn linked with the eastern north–south axis of the Meuse and the Rhône. To the north, the Dorestad–Domburg link offered a gateway to England (East Anglia and the Thames valley) as well as to Scandinavia – the latter also via the Almere to the north and along the Dutch and northern German coastal area with the terp-sites as rural consumers. In Scandinavia, Ribe provided contacts with England and the north-west part of the Carolingian empire, while Haithabu, Wolin, a number of other sites on the southern Baltic coast and early trading places like Paviken, possibly also Visby, and others on Gotland covered the Baltic and the connections to the East. Birka also belonged to this network in the eighth to the tenth centuries, linking inland Sweden to the Baltic. In addition, a number of trading-places – ranging from relatively substantial ones to non-permanent landings – already formed a kind of network in southern Scandinavia and along the southern Baltic coast from c.800 onwards.[95]

Our knowledge of these links and networks is based partly on indirect documentary indicators as well as archaeology (such as the presence of foreign goods, particularly coins and pottery). Hodges and Verhulst have relied fairly heavily on the numismatic evidence to identify connections and interpret the directions, relative importance and evolution of the exchange patterns. Though far more difficult to interpret, because it is not necessarily always linked to actual trade, the non-local pottery generally points in the same direction. In Carolingian times, north-west Frankish pottery is found in *Hamwic*, while Badorf, Mayen and Tating wares are found further east on the North Sea coasts and in Scandinavia. Anglo-Saxon and Scandinavian pottery, on the other hand, does not seem to travel much if at all. The Frankish finds have often been linked with the exchange of other commodities, particularly high-quality or luxury goods, notably wines from the Rhineland and central Francia. The pottery may have been a relatively unimportant sideline, and some of it may simply have been part of the equipment of the travellers; at any rate, the quantity of pottery items thus distributed is not necessarily very high.

Assessing the quantity of such traded items necessarily remains largely conjectural, but it has been suggested that the Rhenish pottery arriving at Dorestad and traded there may not have represented more than about one shipload of c.2.5 cubic metres (3.3 cu. yd) a week.[96] The relatively limited number of Rhenish finds in Scandinavia and the Baltic also suggests that such contacts may not have been all that important in comparison with Baltic goods, and this may imply that an autonomous Baltic network existed alongside one around the North Sea. As to the other commodities, the prevailing theory as formulated by Hodges is that the major towns (his *emporia*) dealt mainly in luxury goods, but other goods – and perhaps also bulk goods that are invisible archaeologically – played an equally important part from Carolingian times onwards. This would be in keeping with the unequivocal evidence for the development of harbour infrastructures, as well as with the growing trading activities of the monasteries.

However important the overseas trade and exchange, the international urban networks are not the only ones linking the individual towns of the period. Most of them relied heavily on the countryside for basic supplies and they must also have had regional functions.[97] Furthermore, their often polyfocal nature with monasteries, administrative or ('proto'-)feudal entities and/or estate centres probably made the distinction between town and countryside less sharp than it would be in later times. And while specialist craft production no doubt fed some of the overseas trade, it also made goods for the elite sites and for the emerging monastic and feudal estates in the surrounding countryside. These estates in turn produced a surplus which could be traded. In other words, these settlements – some of which actually grew in the shadow of a monastery or an estate to which a *portus* was attached – in part also functioned as a kind of market. But given the special links between the authority involved and its traders, it was perhaps more a general trading place, not a market in the sense familiar from the high middle ages.

Conclusions

This survey of the different interpretations of the urban phenomenon in Merovingian and Carolingian times scratches the surface of the complex issues involved and the models proposed. There are several levels at which the transformation from the Late Roman to Early Medieval urban world can be discussed, ranging from the all-encompassing socio-economic and societal models to regional and inter-regional systems and networks. But although this approach may prejudice some more subtle interpretations and explanations, like those of Verhulst or Hodges, it seems clear that most of the models proposed try to explain the appearance and evolution of these settlements in a very global way. They are seen as a single phenomenon, subject to – and responding to – a given (and often rather general) set of socio-economic, socio-political and socio-cultural conditions and impulses. All of these levels of abstraction of factual data are of course needed to try and understand the early medieval urban phenomenon as a whole. But conversely, too much abstraction may be made of specific local or regional situations and developments. Furthermore, cognitive issues, such as how urban settlement and urban space – as opposed to towns as an almost purely economic and functional phenomenon – were perceived by contemporary inhabitants and local elites, are rarely acknowledged or left aside as 'unreachable' because of the dearth of written and archaeological information.

Reality was, however, far more complex. While some general factors – like the role of central authorities or more general economic developments – no doubt always played a part, the data suggest that different sets of factors and conditions also influenced developments in specific towns or regions. The situation in the old Romanised world of southern Gaul was not identical to – though not completely isolated from – that in the Low Countries. Even there, regional differences (e.g. between the Scheldt and Meuse valleys) are readily identifiable; as we have seen, the same can be argued for other regions and towns. Similarly, it becomes increasingly evident that the individual urban settlements cannot be divorced from their regional setting: they were changing parts of changing regional systems and slowly integrating economies and, as such, they played changing roles in both regional and supra-regional networks and hierarchies. This means detailed work on regional and even local situations – like the work done on Tours, Metz, London and elsewhere, or the approach taken by Verhulst – remains of paramount importance.

At the same time, and in order to render justice to the intricacies of the urban phenomenon, we will need to develop more complex and sensitive models which draw on history, archaeology, geography, anthropology and sociology. While the anthropological models that have been used to explain the early medieval economy – and notably the gift-model – have much to offer, it would seem prudent to adopt a more balanced view, which over-emphasises neither the elite nor the spirit of the age, however important these were.[98] Sensitive models such as these will have to pay more attention to the local and regional setting and to the convoluted relationships between town and rural hinterland. The emphasis that many models put on economy, and particularly on trade, is understandable from a twentieth-century point of view. But there is more than enough reason to pay more attention to production and consumption as corollary agencies of change.

At present, it is possible to sketch a first and very general picture of the town in the age of Charlemagne. In north-west Europe, a new urban world was in the process of emerging by the time the Carolingians came to power. The Merovingians and their Church had not totally forsaken the old Roman towns; but, apart from their uses as administrative centres and possibly also as settlements conferring a degree of prestige (and perhaps also legitimation of power), these Roman settlements and towns were very much a ruin from a distant past. From the seventh century onwards, however, Merovingian rulers professed a more direct interest in a number of towns and their trading activities. Whether they always actually created the newer towns – or intervened only later when the settlements were already established – remains an open question. But some of these sites did evolve into more or less monopolistic and centrally-controlled settlements. This allowed the Merovingians to profit from a revival of international and regional exchange while at the same time offering openings to other rulers and possibilities to enhance their prestige. Simultaneously, socio-economic developments provided an additional impetus for these urban settlements leading to new networks.

This, then, was the urban world that the Carolingians found: a series of different types of settlements active in trade and crafts, sometimes combined with administration, and ranging from small to relatively large sites. They may also have had an inkling of urban settlements in other parts of the world, notably the Islamic regions (Spain), the Byzantine empire, the Anglo-Saxon kingdoms and – in slightly later times – Scandinavia. But on the whole, the urban world was still very much a sideline in an essentially rural- and land-based economy and power structure. During the rule of Charlemagne and his successors, towns, such as they were, continued to evolve. Some declined, some went on, most if not all changed in terms of functions, sometimes regardless of the troubles which struck a number of them as in the case of the Viking attacks. And new towns slowly emerged, taking advantage of different circumstances, such as growing trade and particularly the growing local and regional markets for a number of commodities. Some even emerged as a kind of *bourgs castraux* ('fortified towns') in the shadow of abbeys and, later on, of strongholds too, and many developed as a result of the coalescence of the individual (rural, monastic, urban, elite and/or stronghold) settlement nuclei. Such settlements often resulted from the combination of changing circumstances and developments set in motion *before* the Carolingians came to power. By the end of the Carolingian age, things had changed so much – and were still changing – that one can indeed see this period as a crucial phase. This is the time when many of the conditions for the emergence of the 'classic' medieval town of the eleventh and twelfth century were set.

This analysis raises questions of whether an 'urban policy' was pursued by the Carolingian rulers. But the degree of direct royal intervention in this urban world and its development remains uncertain, and we still know too little about royal perceptions of, and attitudes towards, towns. Indirect intervention seems clear – notably by influencing the economy with measures related to coinage, tolls and markets – but that is about as far as we can go at present. Such interventions do not necessarily constitute a teleological urban policy. In fact, it is also quite possible that the Carolingians had only a limited or perhaps even a parasitic interest in the urban phenomenon, given their predilection for the rural world that was the basis of their power and income, and where they chose to build their palaces. And perhaps the complexity of what was to some extent a new world in constant movement may also have played a part. If we are sometimes baffled by the urban phenomenon and its socio-economic and socio-cultural settings and meanings, it is not at all implausible that the Carolingian rulers may have been so too. So they may have been 'visionaries' – though without realising what the future was actually going to look like – or more simply rulers who took pragmatic measures which suited their own more immediate concerns and interests which in turn set in motion new developments affecting their society and its towns.

Whatever the case, the towns of the Carolingian Age encompassed a whole range of units, not always easily well-defined or easily-categorised. And this urban world was in constant and even relatively rapid change. The finer details of this long and complex process, and its precise chronology, still require a lot of study. Detailed archaeological fieldwork which also pays suitable attention to taphonomic analysis and other (e.g. environmental) evidence – as opposed to 'classic' archaeological indicators like coins and pottery – will no doubt help to clarify the main issues. Among these, spatial analysis, the material and social links between town and countryside, and the production of commodities are probably the most important ones. We will also need to gain more information about the material characteristics of Carolingian towns and urban life, and we will have to develop more complex interpretative models to explain the phenomenon and its development in the age of Charlemagne and beyond.

Notes

1 Samson (1994), pp. 108–10; Hodges (1982), pp. 21–5; Scull (1997).
2 Galinié (2000).
3 Carver (1993) and (1997); Hodges (1982), (1989), (1996) and (2000).
4 Denecke (1975).
5 Moreland (2000); Scull (1997).
6 See, for example, the debate in Palliser, ed. (2000).
7 Loveluck, ch. 14 (pp. 230–58) in this volume.
8 Verhulst (1989); Hodges (1989). On these *wics*, see also Hill and Cowie, eds. (2001).
9 Galinié (2000).
10 Hodges (1982), p. 23; Scull (1997), pp. 291–2.
11 For example, Hodges (1982); Verhulst (1999) and (2002); McCormick (2001).
12 See also Samson (1994); Galinié (2000); Carver (1997).
13 Galinié (2000).
14 Ward-Perkins (1997).
15 Carver (1993), p. 61; Galinié (2000).
16 Hodges (2000), p. 119.
17 Christie (2000), p. 67; Loseby (2000).
18 Verhulst (1999); Verhaeghe (1990).
19 Hen and Innes, eds. (2000). On the use of Roman *spolia* at Aachen, see Jacobsen (1994); Nelson (2001a); Noble (2001).
20 Whittaker (1990).
21 Ward-Perkins (1984), pp. 203–29.
22 Loseby (1998) and (2000).
23 Faulkner (2000), p. 47; Loseby (2000); Verhaeghe (1990); Verhulst (1999), pp. 21–3; Ward-Perkins (1984); Balzaretti (1996a; 1996b; 2000); Brogiolo (1999; 2000).
24 For example, Hodges (2000), p. 120. On Tours, see Galinié, ed. (2000).
25 Galinié, ed. (2000); McPhail et al. (2003).
26 Halsall (1995); Reynaud (1998).
27 Samson (1994).
28 Ward-Perkins (1984), p. 16.
29 Galinié (1988), p. 61, and (1997), p. 75.
30 Loseby (1998), p. 264.
31 Galinié (1988) and (1997); Halsall (1995); Reynaud (1998); Villedieu (1990); Loseby (1998).
32 Verhulst (1999), pp. 24–43.
33 On the survival of the Roman tax system, see Durliat (1990) and Wickham (1993).
34 de Jong and Theuws, eds. (2001); Hodges and Bowden, eds. (1998).
35 Atsma, ed. (1989); Hodges and Bowden, eds. (1998).
36 Lebecq (1983); McGrail, ed. (1990).
37 Wood (1994).
38 van Es (1990), pp. 162–3.
39 Lebecq (1993); Coupland (2002).
40 Verhulst (1999).
41 Lebecq (2000).
42 Loveluck, ch. 14 (pp. 230–58) in this volume.
43 Verhulst (1999).

44 For example, Hodges (1982), pp. 47–88, and (1989), pp. 69–114.
45 Hodges (2000), p. 77.
46 Clarke and Ambrosiani (1995).
47 On Quentovic, see Lebecq (1993). On Dorestad, see van Es (1990); van Es and Verwers (1980); Coupland (1988) and (2002). On Rouen, Gauthiez (1989) and (1993); Le Maho (2001).
48 Balzaretti (1996a); Loseby (2000).
49 Loveluck, ch. 14 (pp. 230–58) in this volume.
50 Hodges (2000).
51 Samson (1994).
52 Theuws (2001).
53 Samson (1999), p. 84.
54 Hodges (2000), p. 80.
55 van Es (1990), p. 163.
56 Coupland (1988).
57 Lebecq (1993); see, however, Coupland (2002).
58 Verhulst (1999), p. 66.
59 Hodges (2000), pp. 114–16.
60 Verhulst (1999); Verslype (1999).
61 Verhulst (1999).
62 Clarke and Ambrosiani (1995), but since then the database has expanded.
63 Roman roads were still in use during the reign of Charles the Bald: Janssen (1989); Nelson (1992), p. 30.
64 Verhaeghe (1990).
65 Jensen (1991); Clarke and Ambrosiani (1995), pp. 109–10.
66 Nelson (1992), pp. 208–10. A comparable motive is likely for Alfred's decision to move Lundenwic within the walled area of Lundenburh.
67 De Witte et al. (2000).
68 Verhulst and Declercq (1989), pp. 49–52.
69 Verhulst (1999), pp. 61–2.
70 Olsen and Schmidt (1977), pp. 92–5.
71 Clarke and Ambrosiani (1995), p. 139.
72 Näsman (2000), p. 56.
73 For example, in Geneva: Bonnet (1993).
74 Heitz (1980); Bonnet (1997); Gauthier (1997).
75 Wyss (1997), (1999) and (2001); Gauthier (1997), pp. 58–61.
76 Loveluck, ch. 14 (pp. 230–58) in this volume.
77 Galinié (1996).
78 On the process in Gaul, see Galinié and Zadora-Rio, eds. (1996).
79 van De Walle (1961).
80 Loveluck, ch. 14 (pp. 230–58) in this volume.
81 Schietzel (1981), pp. 61–9.
82 Verhaeghe (1994), p. 152.
83 van De Walle (1961), pp. 128–30.
84 van Es (1990), pp. 156–7.
85 Verhaeghe (1994), pp. 150–3.
86 Verhaeghe (1995).
87 Dijkman and Ervynck (1998).

88 On Maastricht, see Dijkman (1993); Dijkman and Ervynck (1998); on Huy, see Willems (1971).
89 Verhaeghe (1995).
90 Clarke and Ambrosiani (1995), pp. 202–3.
91 Hodges (1981).
92 Loveluck, ch. 14 (pp. 230–58) in this volume
93 Lebecq (1983); McGrail, ed. (1990); Hansen and Wickham, eds. (2000).
94 Verhulst (1999).
95 Callmer (1994), p. 77.
96 van Es and Verwers (1993).
97 As argued for Dorestad by van Es (1990).
98 Moreland (2000).

BIBLIOGRAPHY

Primary sources

All primary sources mentioned more than once in the text of this book are listed here. Editions and translations mentioned only once are given in the relevant note in that chapter, with the full reference in the secondary bibliography below.

English translations

The best set of English translations of primary sources on the reign of Charlemagne is P.D. King, *Charlemagne: Translated Sources*, Kendal (1987). Also useful is H.R. Loyn and J. Percival, *The Reign of Charlemagne*, Documents of Medieval History 2, London (1975) and, for the whole Carolingian period, P.E. Dutton, *Carolingian Civilization: A Reader*, Peterborough ONT (1993), 2nd edn (2004). Also useful is D. Whitelock, *English Historical Documents* I, London (1979), a standard source.

For Merovingian sources, many key sources are translated in P. Fouracre and R. Gerberding, *Late Merovingian France: History and Hagiography 640–720*, Manchester (1996). Sources linked to Einhard are now conveniently collected in P.E. Dutton, *Charlemagne's Courtier: The Complete Einhard*, Peterborough ONT (1998).

Admonitio generalis (General Admonition). A. Boretius, ed. MGH *Capit* I, Hanover (1883), no. 22, pp. 303–7; English trans. King (1987), pp. 209–20

Alcuin, *Carmina* (Poems). E. Dümmler, ed. MGH *PLAC* I, Berlin (1881), pp. 160–351

Alcuin, *De vitiis et virtutibus* (On Vices and Virtues). J.P. Migne, ed. *PL* 101, cols 613–38

Alcuin, *Disputatio de rhetorica et de virtutibus sapientissimi regis Karli et Albini magistri* (Disputation on Rhetoric and Most Wise Virtues between King Charles and Master Alcuin). English trans. W.S. Howell, ed. *The Rhetoric of Alcuin and Charlemagne*, New York NY (1965)

Alcuin, *Epistulae* (Letters). E. Dümmler, ed. MGH *Epp.* IV, *Epistolae Karolini ævi* II, Berlin (1895), pp. 1–481; English trans. (selection) S. Allott, *Alcuin of York c.732 to 804: His Life and Letters*, York (1974)

Alcuin, *Libellus contra haeresim Felicis* (Short Book against the Heresy of Felix). G.B. Blumenshine, ed. *Libellus contra haeresim Felicis*, Studi e Testi 285, Vatican (1980)

Alcuin, *Versus de patribus, regibus et sanctis Euboricensis ecclesiae* (York Poem). English trans. P. Godman, ed. *Alcuin, The Bishops, Kings, and Saints of York*, Oxford (1982)

Annales alamannici (Alemannic Annals). G.H. Pertz, ed. MGH *SS* I, Hanover (1926), pp. 22–30

Annales Bertiniani (Annals of St-Bertin) (*AB*). G. Waitz, ed. MGH *SSRG* V, Hanover (1883) and F. Grat, J. Vielliard and S. Clémencet, Paris (1964); English trans. J.L. Nelson, *The Annals of St-Bertin*, Ninth-Century Histories 1, Manchester (1991); edn and German trans. R. Rau, ed. *QK* II, Berlin (1959), pp. 19–155

Annales Fuldenses (Annals of Fulda) (*AF*). F. Kurze, ed. MGH *SSRG* VII, Hanover (1891); English trans. T. Reuter, *The Annals of Fulda*, Ninth-Century Histories 2, Manchester (1992); edn and German trans. R. Rau, ed. *QK* III, Berlin (1960), pp. 19–155

Annales Guelferbytani (Wolfenbüttel Annals). G.H. Pertz, ed. MGH *SS* I, pp. 23–31, 40–6; English trans. (selection) King (1987), pp. 149–66

Annales Laureshamenses (Annals of Lorsch) *(AL)*. G.H. Pertz, ed. MGH *SS* I, Hanover (1829), pp. 22–39; English trans. (selection) King (1987), pp. 137–45

Annales Mettenses Priores (Earlier Metz Annals) *(AMP)*. B. de Simson, ed. MGH *SSRG* X, Hanover and Leipzig (1905); English trans. (selection) Fouracre and Gerberding (1996), pp. 330–70, and King (1987), pp. 149–66

Annales Mosellani (Moselle Annals) *(AM)*. J.M. Lappenberg, ed. MGH *SS* XVI, Hanover (1859), pp. 491–99; English trans. (selection) King (1987), pp. 132–7

Annales Nazariani (Annals of St-Nazarius). G.H. Pertz, ed. MGH *SS* I, Hanover (1926), pp. 22–44; English trans. (selection) King (1987), pp. 149–66

Annales qui dicuntur Einhardi (commonly known as the Revised Version Royal Frankish Annals) (RFA *(Rev.)*). F. Kurze, ed. MGH *SSRG* 6, Hanover (1895); edn and German translation, R. Rau, *QK* I, Berlin (1956), pp. 216–53; English translation, Scholz (1970), pp. 37–125, and, for years 768–801, in King (1987), pp. 108–31

Annales regni Francorum (commonly Royal Frankish Annals). F. Kurze, ed. MGH *SSRG* VI, Hanover (1895); English trans. Scholz (1972), pp. 37–125 and, for years 768–814, in King (1987), pp. 74–107; edn and German trans. R. Rau, ed. *QK* I, Berlin (1956), pp. 9–155

Annales Xantenses (Annals of Xanten). B. de Simson, ed. MGH *SSRG* XII, Hanover (1909); edn and German trans. R. Rau, ed. *QK* II, Berlin (1959), pp. 340–71

Anonymous, *Vita Alcuini* (Life of Alcuin). W. Arndt, ed. MGH *Scriptores* XV.i, Hanover (1887), pp. 182–97

Anonymous, *Translatio S. Germani* (Translation of [the relics of] St German). G. Waitz, ed. MGH *SS* XV.i, Hanover (1887), pp. 5–9; B. Krusch, ed. MGH *SSRM* VII, Hanover and Leipzig (1920), pp. 422–8.

Astronomer, *Vita Hludowici pii imperatoris* (Life of Emperor Louis the Pious).G. Pertz, ed. MGH *SS* II, Berlin (1829), pp. 604–48; edn and German trans. R. Rau, ed. *QK* I, Berlin (1956), pp. 257–381; English trans. A. Cabaniss, *Son of Charlemagne*, Syracuse NY (1961); E. Tremp, ed. *Astronomus, Das Leben Kaiser Ludwigs (Vita Hludowici imperatoris)*, MGH *SSRG* LXIV, Hanover (1995), pp. 280–555

Boniface, *Epistulae* (Letters). M. Tangl, ed. *Die Briefe des heiligen Bonifatius und Lullus* MGH *Epp. Sel.* I, Hanover (1916); English trans. E. Emerton, *Letters of St Boniface*, New York, NY (1940) and (selection) C.H. Talbot, *The Anglo-Saxon Missionaries in Germany*, London (1954), pp. 65–149

Capitularia regum francorum (Capitularies of the Kings of the Franks). A. Boretius and V. Krause, ed. MGH *Capit.* I, Hanover (1883); English trans. (selection), King (1987), pp. 202–68

Chronicon Moissacense (Chronicle of Moissac). G.H. Pertz, ed. MGH *SS* I, Hanover (1829), pp. 282–313; selected English trans. King (1987), pp. 145–9

Codex Carolinus (CC). W. Gundlach, ed. MGH *Epp.* III, *Epistolae Karolini ævi* I, Berlin (1892), pp. 476–653; selected English trans. King (1987), pp. 269–307

De litteris colendis (On Cultivating Letters). A. Boretius, ed. MGH *Capit.* I Hanover (1883), no. 29, pp. 78–9; English trans. King (1987), pp. 232–3

Eigil, *Vita Sturmi abbatis Fuldensis*. P. Engelbrecht, ed. *De Vita Sturmi des Eigils von Fulda: Literarkritische-historische Untersuchung und Edition*, Marburg; English trans. C.H. Talbot, 1954. *The Anglo-Saxon Missionaries in Germany*, London, pp. 181–202

Einhard, *Epistolae* (Letters). K. Hampe, ed. MGH *Epp.* V, *Epistolae Karolini ævi* III, Berlin (1899), pp. 105–45; English trans. Dutton (1993), pp. 283–311 and Dutton (1998), pp. 131–65

Einhard, *Translatio et miracula SS Marcellini et Petri* (Translation and Miracles of Saints Marcellinus and Peter). G. Waitz, ed. MGH *SS* XV, pp. 238–64; English trans. Dutton (1998), pp. 69–136

Einhard, *Vita Karoli* (Life of Charlemagne) (*VK*). O. Holder-Egger, ed. MGH *SSRG* Hanover (1911); French trans. L. Halphen, ed. *Éginhard: Vie de Charlemagne*, Paris (1938); edn and German trans. R. Rau, ed. *QK* I, Berlin (1956), pp. 164–211; English trans. Dutton (1998), pp. 15–39

Fragmentum Chesnianum (Chesne Fragment). A. Duchesne, ed. *Historiae Francorum scriptores Coaetanei ab ipsius gentis origine ad Philippi IV*, 5 vols, Paris (1636–49), II, pp. 21–3; G.H. Pertz, ed. MGH *SS* I, Hanover (1829), pp. 33–4; partial trans. in King (1987), pp. 149–66

Fredegar, *Chronicarum quae dicuntur Fredegarii scholastici libri IV cum continuationibus* (Chronicle of Fredegar, with Continuations). B. Krusch, ed. MGH *SSRM* II, Hanover (1881), pp. 1–193; English trans. J.M. Wallace-Hadrill, ed. *The Fourth Book of the Chronicle of Fredegar with its Continuations*, London (1960)

George of Ostia, *Epistola ad Hadrianum* (Letter to Pope Hadrian). E. Dümmler, eds. MGH *Epp.* IV, Berlin (1895), no. 3, pp. 20–29; partial edn, A.W. Haddan and W. Stubbs, eds. *Councils and Ecclesiastical Documents*, 3 vols, Oxford (1871), III, pp. 447–61; partial English trans., D. Whitelock, *English Historical Documents* I, London (1979), no. 191

Hincmar, *De ordine palatii* (On the Governance of the Palace). T. Gross and R. Schieffer, eds. *Hinkmar von Rheims, De ordine palatii*, MGH *Fontes NS* IV Hanover (1980); English trans. Dutton (1993), pp. 485–500.

Isidore of Seville, *Etymologiae* (Encyclopaedia of Etymologies in 20 Books). W.M. Lindsay, ed. *Isidore Hispalensis episcopi. Etymologiarum sive originum libri XX*, 2 vols, Oxford (1911)

Jonas, *De institutione regia* (On the Institution of Kingship). A. Dubreucq, ed. *Le Métier du roi = De institutione regia. Sources chrétiennes* 407, Paris (1995); English trans. R. Dyson, *A Ninth-Century Political Tract; the De Institutione regia of Jonas of Orléans*, Smithtown NY (1983)

Karolus magnus et Leo papa (Charles the Great and Pope Leo). E. Dümmler, ed. MGH *PLAC* I, Berlin (1881), pp. 366–79; English trans. (selected) in Dutton (1993), pp. 55–7 and P. Godman, *Poetry of the Carolingian Renaissance*, London (1985), pp. 197–206; W. Hentze, ed. *De Karolo rege et Leone papa: der Bericht über die Zusammenkunft Karls des Grossen mit Papst Leo III in Paderborn 799 in einem Epos für Karl den Kaiser*, Paderborn (1999)

Liber Historiae Francorum (Book of the History of the Franks) (*LHF*). B. Krusch, ed. MGH *SSRM* II, Hanover (1888), pp. 215–328; English trans. Fouracre and Gerberding (1986), pp. 79–96

Liber Pontificalis (Book of the Popes) (*LP*). L. Duchesne, ed. *Le Liber pontificalis. Texte, introduction et commentaire*, 2 vols. Rome, (1886–92), reissued with a third volume including updated commentary by C. Vogel, Paris (1955–57); English trans. R. Davis, *The Book of the Pontiffs (Liber pontificalis). The Ancient Biographies of the First Ninety Roman Bishops to AD 715*, Liverpool (1989); *The Lives of the Eighth-Century Popes*, Liverpool (1992); *The Lives of the Ninth-Century Popes*, Liverpool (1995)

Libri Carolini. *See* Theodulf of Orléans.

Lupus of Ferrières, *Epistolae* (Letters). L. Levillain, ed. *Loup de Ferrières: correspondance*, Les Classiques de l'Histoire de France au Moyen Âge, 10 and 16, Paris (1927–35); P.K. Marshall, ed. *Epistulae*, Leipzig (1984); G.W. Regenos, trans. *The Letters of Lupus of Ferrières*, The Hague (1966)

Nithard, *Historiarum libri IV* (Four Books of History). E. Müller, ed. MGH *SSRG* XLIV, Hanover (1907); P. Lauer, ed. *Nithard: Historie des fils de Louis le Pieux*, Les Classiques de l'Histoire de France au Moyen Âge 7, Paris (1926); English trans. Dutton (1993), pp. 333–63, and Scholz (1970), pp. 129–74; edn and German trans. R. Rau, ed. *QK* I (1956), pp. 385–461

Notker Balbulus, *Gesta Karoli Magni imperatoris* (Deeds of the Emperor Charles the Great). G.H Pertz, ed. MGH *SS* II, Berlin (1829), pp. 726–63; H. Haefele, ed. MGH *SSRG NS* XII, Berlin (1959); German trans. R. Rau, ed. *QK* III, Berlin (1960), pp. 321–427; English trans. L. Thorpe, *Einhard and Notker the Stammerer, Two Lives of Charlemagne*, Harmondsworth (1969), pp. 93–172

Paul the Deacon, *Gesta episcoporum Mettensium* (Deeds of the Bishops of Metz). G.H. Pertz, ed. MGH *SS* II, Berlin (1929), pp. 260–8

Paul the Deacon, *Historia Langobardorum* (History of the Lombards). L. Bethmann and G.H. Waitz, eds. MGH *SSRL*, Hanover (1878), pp. 12–187; English trans. F.W. Foulke, *Paul the Deacon. History of the Langobards*, Philadelphia PA (1907, repr. 1974).

Poeta Saxo, *Annalium de gestis Caroli Magni imperatoris libri quinque* (Annals of the Deeds of the Emperor Charles the Great in Five Books). P. von Winterfeld, ed. MGH *PLAC* IV, Berlin (1899), pp. 1–71

Regino of Prüm, *Chronicon* (Chronicle). F. Kurze, ed. MGH *SSRG* 50, Hanover (1890); edn and German trans. R. Rau, ed. *QK* III, Darmstadt (1960), pp. 180–318

Thegan, *Gesta Hludowici imperatoris* (Deeds of the Emperor Louis). G.H. Pertz, ed. MGH *SS* II, Berlin (1829), pp. 585–604; German trans. R. Rau, ed. *QK* I, Berlin (1955), pp. 213–53; E. Tremp, MGH *SSRG* LXIV, Hanover (1995), pp. 168–277

Theodulf of Orléans, *Libri Carolini / Opus Caroli regis contra synodum*. H. Bastgen, ed. MGH *Conc.* II, Supp. , Hanover (1924); A. Freeman with P. Meyvaert, eds. *Opus Caroli regis contra synodum*, MGH *Concilia* II, Supplementum I, Hanover (1998)

Theophanes Confessor, *Chronicle*. Mango, C. and Scott, R. trans, *The Chronicle of Theophanes Confessor: Byzantine and Near Eastern History AD284–813*, Oxford (1997)

Translatio S. Germani and *Vita Alcuini. See* Anonymous.

Widukind of Corvey, *Rerum gestarum Saxonicarum libri III* (Achievements of the Saxons, in Three Books). A. Bauer and R. Rau, ed. *AQ* VIII, Darmstadt (1969), pp. 1–183

Secondary Sources

Authors' names are filed by the first capital letter in the author's preferred form – De Boe is under D, de Jong under J.

A.A.V.V. 2001. *Paolo Diacono e il Friuli Altomedievale (secc. VI–X). Atti del XIV Congresso Internazionale di Studi sull'Alto Medioevo*, Centro di Studi sull'Alto Medioevo, Spoleto

Airlie, S. 1990. 'Bonds of power and bonds of association in the court circle of Louis the Pious', in Godman and Collins, eds. (1990), pp. 191–204

Airlie, S. 1992. 'The anxiety of sanctity: St Gerald of Aurillac and his maker', *JEH* 43, pp. 372–95.

Airlie, S. 1995. 'The aristocracy', in McKitterick, ed. (1995), pp. 431–50

Airlie, S. 1999. 'Narratives of triumph and rituals of submission: Charlemagne's mastering of Bavaria', *TRHS* 6th series 9, pp. 93–119

Airlie, S. 2000. 'The palace of memory: the Carolingian court as political centre', in S. Rees Jones, R. Marks and A. Minnis, eds. *Courts and Regions in Medieval Europe*, York, pp. 1–20

Airlie, S. 2001. 'True teachers and pious kings: Salzburg, Louis the German, and Christian order', in Gameson and Leyser, eds. (2001), pp. 89–105

Albanes, J. and Chevalier, U., eds. 1899. *Gallia Christiana novissima* II, Marseille

Alberi, M. 1998. 'The evaluation of Alcuin's concept of the *Imperium Christianum*', in J. Hill and M. Swann, eds. *The Community, the Family and the Saint*, Turnhout, pp. 3–17

Althoff, G. 1997. *Spielregeln der Politik im Mittelalter. Kommunikation in Frieden und Fehden*, Darmstadt.

Althoff, G. 1990. *Verwandte, Freunde und Getreue. Zum politische Stellenwert der Gruppenbindung im früheren Mittelalter*, Darmstadt; English translation, Cambridge (2004)

Anderson, B. 1991. *Imagined Communities: Reflections on the Origin and Spread of Nationalism*, London

Angenendt, A. 1997. 'Karl der Grosse als "Rex et sacerdos"', in Berndt, ed. (1997), pp. 255–78

Atsma, H. ed. 1989. *La Neustrie: les Pays au Nord de la Loire de 650 à 850*, Beihefte der Francia 16, Sigmaringen

Balzaretti, R. 1996a. 'Cities, emporia and monasteries: local economies in the Po valley, c.700–875', in Christie and Loseby, eds. (1996), pp. 212–34

Balzaretti, R. 1996b. 'Cities and markets in the early Middle Ages', in G. Ausenda, ed. (1996), *After Empire: Towards an Ethnology of Europe's Barbarians*, Studies in Historical Archaeoethnology 1, Woodbridge, pp. 113–42

Balzaretti, R. 1999. 'Review article: San Vincenzo al Volturno. History rewritten?', *EME* 8, pp. 387–99

Balzaretti, R. 2000. 'Monasteries, towns and the countryside: reciprocal relationships in the archdiocese of Milan, 614–814', in Brogiolo et al. eds. (2000), pp. 235–57

Barbé, H., Barret, M., Routier, J.-C., and Roy, E. 1998. 'Aménagement du réseau hydrographique et urbanisation aux bords de l'abbaye Saint-Bertin. Données récentes de l'archéologie à Saint-Omer', *Revue du Nord – Archéologie de la Picardie et du Nord de la France* 80, pp. 7–50

Barbero, A. 2000. *Carlo Magno. Un padre dell' Europa*, Rome

Barrandon, J.-N. and Dumas, F. 1990. 'Minéral de Melle et monnaies durant le haut Moyen-Age: relations établies grâce aux isotopes de plomb', *BSFN* 45, pp. 901–6

Bartonková, D. ed. 1966–76. *Magnae Moraviae fontes historici*, 5 vols, Brno

Bately, J.M. ed. 1986. *The Anglo-Saxon Chronicle. A Collaborative Edition: Vol. 3 MS A*, Cambridge

Becher, M. 1989. 'Drogo und die Königserhebung Pippins', *Frühmittelalterliche Studien* 23, pp. 131–52

Becher, M. 1992. 'Neue Überlieferungen zum Geburtsdatum Karls des Grossen', *Francia* 19, pp. 37–60

Becher, M. 1993. *Eid und Herrschaft. Studien zum Herrscherethos Karls des Großen*, Sigmaringen

Becher, M. 1999a. *Karl der Grosse*, Munich; translated as *Charlemagne* (2003), New Haven, CT

Becher, M. 1999b. 'Karl der Große und Papst Leo III', in Stiegemann and Wemhoff, eds. (1999a), pp. 22–36

Bendixen, K. 1988. 'Nyere danske fund af merovingiske, karolingiske og ældre danske mønter', in *Commentationes numismaticae 1988: Festschrift für Gert und Vera Hatz*, Hamburg, pp. 37–50

Bentley, M. ed. 1997. *Companion to Historiography*, London

Béranger, J. 1948. 'Le refus de pouvoir', *Museum Helveticum* 5, pp. 178–96

Berndt, R. ed. 1997. *Das Frankfurter Konzil von 794. Kristallisationspunkt karolingischer Kultur*, 2 vols. Quellen und Abhandlungen zur mittelrheinischen Kirchengeschichte 80, Mainz

Bertelli, C. and Brogiolo, G.P. eds. 2000. *Il futuro dei Longobardi. L'Italia e la costruzione dell'Europa di Carlo Magno*, Milan

Bertelli, C., Brogiolo, G.P. , Jurkovic, M., Matejcic, I., Milosevic, A. and Stella, C. eds. 2001. *Bizantini, Croati, Carolingi. Alba e tramonto di regni e imperi*, Milan

Best, W., Genson, R., and Hömberg, P. 1999. 'Burgenbau in einer Grenzregion', in Stiegemann and Wemhoff, eds. (1999b), pp. 328–45

Besteman, J., Bos, J., and Heidinga, H. eds. 1990. *Medieval Archaeology in the Netherlands: Studies presented to H.H. van Regteren Altena*, Assen and Maastricht

Bianchi, L. 2000. 'Le *scholae peregrinorum*', in Pani Ermini, ed. (2000), pp. 211–15

Bischoff, B. 1940. *Die südostdeutschen Schreibschulen und Bibliotheken der Karolingerzeit*: I. *Die Bayrischen Diözesen*, Leipzig, 3rd edn (1974) Wiesbaden

Bischoff, B. 1957. 'Die Kölner Nonnenhandschriften und das Skriptorium von Chelles', in F. Gerke, G. von Opel, H. Schnitzler, eds. *Karolingische und Ottonische Kunst: Werden, Wesen, Wirkung*, Wiesbaden, pp. 395–411; reprinted Bischoff (1966), I, pp. 16–34

Bischoff, B. 1965. 'Die Hofbibliothek Karls des Großen', in Braunfels, ed. (1965), III, pp. 42–62, revised in Bischoff (1966–81), III, pp. 149–70; English trans. in Bischoff (1994), pp. 56–75

Bischoff, B. 1966, 1967, 1981. *Mittelalterliche Studien. Ausgewählte Aufsätze zur Schriftkunde und Literaturgeschichte*, 3 vols, Stuttgart

Bischoff, B. 1974. *Lorsch im Spiegel seiner Handschriften*, Munich, 2nd edn (1989) Lorsch

Bischoff, B. 1980. *Die südostdeutschen Schreibschulen und Bibliotheken in der Karolingerzeit, 2: Die vorwiegend österreichischen Diözesen*, Wiesbaden

Bischoff, B. 1994. *Manuscripts and Libraries in the Age of Charlemagne*, trans. M. Gorman, Cambridge Studies in Palaeography and Codicology 1, Cambridge

Bischoff, B. 1998 and 2004. *Katalog der festländischen Handschriften des neunten Jahrhunderts*, Vol. 1 *Aachen–Lambach*, and Vol. 2 *Laon–Paderborn* Wiesbaden

Bitterauf, T. ed. 1905. *Die Traditionen des Hochstifts Freising, 744–926*, Quellen und Erörterungen zur bayerischen Geschichte Neue Folge 4, Munich

Blackburn, M.A.S. ed. 1986. *Anglo-Saxon Monetary History*, Leicester

Boe, G. De *See* De Boe, G.

Blake, H. ed. 1995. *Archeologia urbana a Pavia*, I, Pavia

Bonnet, C. 1993. *Les Fouilles de l'ancien groupe épiscopal de Genève (1976–1993)*, Cahiers d'archéologie genevoise 1, Geneva

Bonnet, C. 1997. 'Les églises en bois du haut Moyen Age d'après les recherches archéologiques', in Gauthier and Galinié, eds. (1997), pp. 217–36

Borgolte, M. 1983. 'Die Geschichte der Grafengewalt im Elsass von Dagobert I bis Otto dem Grossen', *Zeitschrift der Geschichte des Oberrheins* 131, pp. 3–54

Borgolte, M. 1984. *Geschichte der Grafschaften Alemanniens in früischer Zeit*, Sigmarigen

Borst, A. 1991. *Medieval Worlds: Artists, Barbarians and Heretics in the Middle Ages*, Cambridge

Borst, A. 1993. 'Alcuin und die Enzyklopädie von 809', in Butzer and Lohrmann, eds. (1993), pp. 53–78

Borst, A. 1998. *Die karolingische Kalenderreform*, MGH Schriften 46, Hanover

Boshof, E. 1996. *Ludwig der Fromme*, Darmstadt

Boüard, M. De. *See* De Boüard, M.

Bowlus, C.R. 1995. *Franks, Moravians and Magyars. The Struggle for the Middle Danube, 788–907*. Philadelphia, PA

Braunfels, W. ed. 1965. *Karl der Grosse: Werk und Wirkung*, Aachen

Braunfels, W. ed. 1965–67. *Karl der Grosse. Lebenswerk und Nachleben: I, Persönlichkeit und Geschichte; II, Das geistige Leben; III, Karolingische Kunst; IV, Das Nachleben*, Düsseldorf

Brogiolo, G.P. 1989. 'Brescia: building transformations in a Lombard city', in K. Randsborg, ed. *The Birth of Europe: Archaeology and Social Development in the First Millennium A.D.*, Rome, pp. 156–65

Brogiolo, G.P. 1993. *Brescia Altomedievale. Urbanistica ed edilizia dal IV al IX secolo*, Documenti di Archeologia 2, Mantua

Brogiolo, G.P. 1999. 'Ideas of the town in Italy during the transition from Antiquity to the Middle Ages', in Brogiolo and Ward-Perkins, eds. (1999), pp. 99–126

Brogiolo, G.P. 2000. 'Towns, forts and the countryside: archaeological models for northern Italy in the early Lombard period (568–650)', in Brogiolo et al. eds. (2000), pp. 299–323

Brogiolo, G.P. 2001. 'Urbanistica di Cividale longobarda', in A.A.V.V. (2001), pp. 357–85

Brogiolo, G.P. ed. 1999. *S. Giulia di Brescia. Gli scavi dal 1980 al 1992. Reperti preromani, romani e alto medievali*, Florence

Brogiolo, G.P. and Ward-Perkins, B. eds. 1999. *The Idea and Ideal of the Town in Late Antiquity and the Early Middle Ages*, The Transformation of the Roman World 4, Leiden

Brogiolo, G.P. , Gauthier, N. and Christie, N. eds. 2000. *Towns and their Territories between Late Antiquity and the Early Middle Ages*, The Transformation of the Roman World 9, Leiden

Brooks, N.P. 1984. *The Early History of the Church of Canterbury*, Leicester

Brooks, N.P. 1999. *Bede and the English*, Jarrow Lecture, Jarrow

Brown, P. 1996. *The Rise of Western Christendom. Triumph and Diversity, AD 200–1000*, Oxford

Brown, T.S. 1990. 'Louis the Pious and the papacy. A Ravenna perspective', in Godman and Collins, eds. (1990), pp. 297–307

Brown, T.S. 1995. 'Byzantine Italy, c. 680–c. 876', in McKitterick, ed. (1995), pp. 320–48

Brown, W. 2001. *Unjust Seizure. Conflict, Interest and Authority in an Early Medieval Society*, Ithaca NY

Brunner, K. 1979. *Oppositionelle Gruppen im Karolingerreich*, Vienna

Brunner, K. 1983. 'Auf den Spuren verlorenen Traditionen', *Peritia* 2, pp. 1–22

Buc, Ph. 2000. 'Ritual and interpretation: the early medieval case', *EME* 9, pp. 183–210

Buc, Ph. 2001. *The Dangers of Ritual. Between Early Medieval Texts and Social Scientific Theory*, Princeton, NJ

Bullough, D.A. 1970. 'Charlemagne and his achievement in the light of recent scholarship', *EHR* 85, pp. 59–105

Bullough, D.A. 1971. *The Age of Charlemagne*, London

Bullough, D.A. 1985a. '*Alboinus deliciosus Karoli regis*. Alcuin of York and the shaping of the Carolingian court', in L. Fenske, W. Rösener and T. Zotz, eds. *Institutionen, Gesell-schaft und Kultur im Mittelalter: Festschrift J. Fleckenstein*, Sigmaringen, pp. 73–92

Bullough, D.A. 1985b. '*Aula renovata*: the Carolingian court before the Aachen palace', *Proceedings of the British Academy* 71, pp. 267–301; reprinted in Bullough (1991), pp. 121–60

Bullough, D.A. 1991. *Carolingian Renewal*, Manchester

Bullough, D.A. 1995. 'Reminiscence and reality: text, transmission and testimony of an Alcuin letter', *JML* 5, pp. 174–201

Bullough, D.A. 1997. 'Alcuin before Frankfort', in Berndt, ed. (1997), pp. 571–85

Bullough, D.A. 2004. *Alcuin: Reputation and Achievement*, Leiden

Bult, E. and Hallewas, D. 1990. 'Archaeological evidence for the early medieval settlement around the Meuse and Rhine deltas up to c. AD1000', in Besteman et al. eds. (1990), pp. 71–89

Bur, M. 1999. *Le Château*, Typologie des Sources du Moyen Âge Occidental, Fasc. 79, Turnhout

Busch, R. 1995. *Domplatzgrabung in Hamburg*, Teil 1, Hamburg

Butzer, P.L. and Lohrmann, D. eds. 1993. *Science in Western and Eastern Civilization in Carolingian Times*, Basel

Butzer, P.L., Kerner, M. and Oberschelp, W. eds. 1997. *Karl der Grosse und sein Nachwirken: 1200 Jahre Kultur und Wissenschaft in Europa*, Turnhout

Callebaut, D. 1994. 'Résidences fortifiées et centres administratifs dans la vallée de l'Escaut (IXe–XIe siècle)', in Demolon et al. eds. (1994), pp. 93–112

Callmer, J. 1994. 'Urbanization in Scandinavia and the Baltic region c. AD700–1100: trading places, centres and early urban sites', in Ambrosiani, B. and Clarke, H. eds. *The Twelfth Viking Congress: Developments around the Baltic and the North Sea in the Viking Age*, Birka Studies 3, Stockholm, pp. 50–90

Camps, J. ed. 1999. *Cataluña en la época carolingia. Arte y cultura antes de románico (siglos IX y X)*, Barcelona

Cantino Wataghin, G. 2000. 'Monasteri tra VIII e IX secolo: evidenze archeologiche per l'Italia settentrionale', in Bertelli and Brogiolo, eds. (2000), pp. 129–41.

Cantino Wataghin, G. 2001. 'Istituzioni monastiche nel Friuli altomedievale: un'indagine archeologica', in A.A.V.V. (2001), pp. 281–319

Caroli, M. 2000. 'Bringing saints to cities and monasteries: *translationes* in the making of a sacred geography (9th–10th centuries)', in Brogiolo et al. eds. (2000), pp. 259–74

Carré, F. 1996. 'Le site de Portjoie (Tournedos, Val-de-Reuil, Eure), VIIe–XIVe siècles: organisation de l'espace funéraire', in Galinié and Zadora-Rio, eds. (1996), pp. 153–62

Carver, M. 1993. *Arguments in Stone: Archaeological Research and the European Town in the First Millennium*, Oxford

Carver, M. 1997. 'Town and anti-town in the first millenium AD. Keynote lecture', in De Boe and Verhaeghe, eds. (1997a), pp. 379–389

Catteddu, I. 1997. 'Le site médiéval de Saleux 'les Coutures': habitat, nécropole et églises du haut Moyen Age', in De Boe and Verhaeghe, eds. (1997d), pp. 143–8

Cavadini, J.C. 1993. *The Last Christology in the West: Adoptionism in Spain and Gaul, 785–820*, Philadelphia, PA

Chazelle, C. 2001. *The Crucified God in the Carolingian Era. Theology and Art of Christ's Passion*, Cambridge

Chazelle, C. ed. 1992. *Literacy, Politics and Artistic Innovation in the Early Medieval West*, London and New York, NY

Chélini, J. 1962. 'Alcuin, Charlemagne et Saint-Martin de Tours', in *Mémorial de l'anneé martinienne, DCCCLX–MDCCCLXI*, Paris, pp. 19–50

Chijs, P.O. van der, 1866. *De munten der frankische en duitsch-nederlandsche vorsten*, Haarlem

Christie, N. 1995. *The Lombards. The Ancient Longobards*, Oxford

Christie, N. 2000. 'Construction and deconstruction: reconstructing the late-Roman townscape', in Slater, ed. (2000), pp. 51–71

Christie, N. ed. 1991. *Three South Etrurian Churches. Santa Cornelia, Santa Rufina and San*

Liberato. Archaeological Monographs of the British School at Rome 4, London

Christie, N. and Loseby, S. eds. 1996. *Towns in Transition: Urban Evolution in Late Antiquity and the Early Middle Ages*, Aldershot

Christie, N. and Kipling, R. 2000. 'Structures of power or structures of convenience? Exploiting the material past in late Antiquity and the early Middle Ages', in S. Pearce, ed. *Researching Material Culture*, Leicester Archaeology Monographs 8, Leicester, pp. 21–35

Clarke, H. and Ambrosiani, B. eds. 1995. *Towns in the Viking Age*, London

Classen, P. 1988. *Karl der Große, das Papsttum und Byzanz*, Sigmaringen

Clercq, C. de, ed. 1963. *Concilia Galliae (A.511–A.695)*, CCSL 148A, Turnhout

Coates-Stephens, R. 1997. 'Dark age architecture in Rome', *PBSR* 65, pp. 177–232

Colgrave, B. and Mynors R.A.B. 1986. *Bede's Ecclesiastical History of the English People*, Oxford

Collins, R. 1990. 'Charles the Bald and Wifred the Hairy', in M. Gibson and J.L. Nelson, eds. *Charles the Bald: Court and Kingdom*, 2nd edn, London, pp. 169–88

Collins, R. 1994. 'Deception and misrepresentation in early eighth-century Frankish historiography: two case studies', in Jarnut et al. eds. (1994), pp. 227–47

Collins, R. 1996. *Fredegar*, Authors of the Middle Ages 13, Aldershot

Collins, R. 1998a. 'The 'Reviser' revisited: another look at the alternative version of the *Annales Regni Francorum*', in Murray, ed. (1998), pp. 191–213

Collins, R. 1998b. *Charlemagne*, London

Collins, R. 2002. 'Frankish past and Carolingian present in the age of Charlemagne', in Godman et al. eds. (2002), pp. 301–22

Conant, K. 1979. *Carolingian and Romanesque Architecture, 800–1200*, London

Contreni, J.J. 1992. *Carolingian Learning, Masters and Manuscripts*, Aldershot

Coupland, S. 1985. 'L'article XI de l'Edit de Pîtres du 25 juin 864', *BSFN* 40, pp. 713–14

Coupland, S. 1986. '*In palatio nostro*: les monnaies palatines de Charlemagne', *BSFN* 41, pp. 87–9

Coupland, S. 1988. 'Dorestad in the ninth century: the numismatic evidence', *JMP* 75, pp. 5–26

Coupland, S. 1990. 'Money and coinage under Louis the Pious', *Francia* 17, pp. 23–54

Coupland, S. 1991. 'The early coinage of Charles the Bald, 840–864', *NChr* 151, pp. 121–58

Coupland, S. 2002. 'Trading places: Quentovic and Dorestad reassessed', *EME* 11, pp. 209–32

Courson, A. de, ed. 1863. *Cartulaire de l'abbaye de Saint-Sauveur de Redon*, Paris

Coville, A. 1928. *Recherches sur l'histoire de Lyon du Vme siècle au IXme scièle (450–800)*, Paris

Cramer, P. 1993. *Baptism and Change in the Early Middle Ages, c. 200–1150*, Cambridge

Crosby, S. McK. 1987. *The Royal Abbey of Saint Denis from its Beginnings to the Death of Suger, 475–1151*, London and New Haven, CT

Crusafont i Sabater, M. 1983. 'Tipo inédito de Carlomagno de la ceca de Roda', *Acta numismatica* 13, pp. 125–35

Cubitt, C. 1995. *Anglo-Saxon Church Councils, c. 650–c. 850*, London

Dam, R. Van. *See* Van Dam, R.

Damminger, F. 1998. 'Dwellings, settlements and settlement patterns in Merovingian southwest Germany and adjacent areas', in I. Wood, ed. *Franks and Alamanni in the Merovingian Period – An Ethnographic Perspective*, Woodbridge, pp. 33–89

Davies, R.R. 2002. 'The medieval state: the tyranny of a concept?', *Journal of Historical Sociology* 16, pp. 280–300

Davies, W. 1988. *Small Worlds: the Village Community in Early Medieval Brittany*, London

Davies, W. and Fouracre, P. eds. 1986. *The Settlement of Disputes in Early Medieval Europe*, Cambridge

Day, W. 1997. 'The monetary reform of Charlemagne and the circulation of money in early medieval Campania', *EME* 6, pp. 25–45

De Boe, G. and Verhaeghe, F. eds. 1997a. *Urbanism in Medieval Europe*. Papers of the 'Medieval Europe Brugge 1997' Conference 1, Zellik

De Boe, G. and Verhaeghe, F. eds. 1997b. *Death and Burial in Medieval Europe*. Papers of the 'Medieval Europe Brugge 1997' Conference 2, Zellik

De Boe, G. and Verhaeghe, F. eds. 1997c. *Religion and Belief in Medieval Europe*. Papers of the 'Medieval Europe Brugge 1997' Conference 4, Zellik

De Boe, G. and Verhaeghe, F. eds. 1997d. *Rural Settlements in Medieval Europe*. Papers of the 'Medieval Europe Brugge 1997' Conference 6, Zellik

De Boe, G. and Verhaeghe, F. eds, 1997e. *Military Studies in Medieval Europe*. Papers of the 'Medieval Europe Brugge 1997' Conference 11, Zellik

De Boüard, M. 1974: 'De l'aula au donjon – Les fouilles de la motte de La Chapelle à Doué-la-Fontaine (Xe–XIe siècle)', *Archéologie Médiévale* 3–4, pp. 5–110

De Witte, H., Van Strydonck, M. and Ervynck, A. 2000. 'Sint-Donaas en de Brugge Burg: dendrochronologisch onderzoek en radiokoolstofdateringen', in *Jaarboek 1997–1999. Brugge Stedelijke Musea* (2000), Bruges, pp. 179–87

Delaporte, J. 1989. 'Un denier de Charlemagne frappé à Rouen', in Atsma, ed. (1989), pp. 41–3

Delogu, P. 1988. 'The rebirth of Rome in the 8th and 9th centuries', in Hodges and Hobley, eds. (1988), pp. 32–42

Delogu, P. 1995. 'Lombard and Carolingian Italy', in McKitterick, ed. (1995), pp. 290–319

Delogu, P. 1998. 'L'importazione di tessuti preziosi e il sistema economico romano nel IX secolo', in Delogu, ed. (1998), pp. 23–41

Delogu, P. 2000. 'The papacy, Rome and the wider world in the seventh and eighth centuries', in Smith, ed. (2000), pp. 197–220

Delogu, P. ed. 1998. *Roma Medievale. Aggiornamenti*, Florence

Demolon, P. 1972. *Le village mérovingien de Brebières*, Arras

Demolon, P. and Louis, E. 1994. 'Naissance d'une cité médiévale flamande. L'exemple de Douai', in Demolon, et al. (1994), pp. 47–58

Demolon, P. , Galinié, H. and Verhaeghe, F. eds. 1994. *Archéologie des villes dans le Nord-Ouest de l'Europe (VIIe–XIIIe siècle)*, Actes du IVe Congrès International d'Archéologie Médiévale, Douai

Denecke, D. 1975. 'Der geographische Stadtbegriff und die räumlich-funktionale Betrach-tungsweise bei Siedlungstypen mit zentraler Bedeutung in Anwendung auf historische Siedlungsepochen', in Jankuhn, H., Schlesinger, W. and Steuer, H. eds. (1975) *Vor-und Frühformen der europäischen Stadt im Mittelalter. Bericht über ein Symposium in Reinhausen bei Göttingen vom 18. bis 24. April 1972*, Abhandlungen der Akadamie der Wissenschaften zu Göttingen, Philologisch-Historische Klasse, 3. Folge, 83–4, Göttingen, pp. 33–55

Depeyrot, G. 1993. *Le numeraire carolingien: corpus des monnaies*, Paris

Depreux, Ph. 1997. 'L'expression *statum est a domno rege et sancta synodo* annonçant certaines dispositions du capitulaire de Frankfort (794)', in Berndt, ed. (1997), pp. 81–101

Detmold, C.E. 1882. *The Historical, Political and Diplomatic Writings of Niccolò Machiavelli*, 4 vols, Boston

Dijkman, W. 1993. 'La céramique du haut moyen-age à Maastricht: tradition et innovation', in Piton, ed. (1993), pp. 217–25

Dijkman, W. and Ervynck, A. 1998. *Antler, bone, horn, ivory and teeth: the use of animal skeletal material in Roman and early medieval Maastricht*, Archaeologica Mosana 1, Maastricht

Doll, M. 1999. 'Im Essen jedoch konnte er nicht enthaltsam sein – Fleischverzehr in der Karolingerzeit', in Stiegemann and Wemhoff, eds. (1999b), pp. 445–9

Duby, G. 1962. *L'Economie rurale et la vie des campagnes*, Paris

Duby, G., 1991. *France in the Middle Ages, 987–1460: from Hugh Capet to Joan of Arc*, Cambridge, Mass.

Durliat, J. 1990. *Les Finances publiques de Dioclétien aux Carolingiens (284–889)*, Beihefte der Francia 21, Sigmaringen

Dutton, P.E. 1993. *Carolingian Civilization. A Reader*, Peterborough, ONT, 2nd edn (2004)

Dutton, P.E. 1994. *The Politics of Dreaming in the Carolingian Empire*, Lincoln, NE

Dutton, P.E. 1998. *Charlemagne's Courtier. The Complete Einhard*, Peterborough, ONT

Early, R. 2001. 'Les origines du château de Mayenne apports archéologique', in Renoux, ed. (2001), pp. 273–87

Edwards, C. 1994. 'German vernacular literature: a survey', in McKitterick, ed. (1994), pp. 141–70

Ervynck, A. 1992. 'Medieval castles as top-predators of the feudal system: an archaeo-zoological approach', *Château Gaillard* 15, pp. 151–9

Ervynck, A., Baeteman, C., DeMiddele, H., Hollevoet, Y., Pieters, M., Schelvis, J., Tys, D., Van Strydonck, M. and Verhaeghe, F. 1999. 'Human occupation because of a regression or the cause of a transgression?', *Probleme der Küstenforschung im südlichen Nordseegebiet* 26, pp. 97–121

Es, W.A. van, 1990. 'Dorestad centred', in Besteman et al. eds. (1990), pp. 151–82

Es, W.A. van, and Verwers, W. 1980. *Excavations at Dorestad 1: The Harbour, Hoogstraat 1*, Nederlandse Oudheden 9, Amersfoort

Es, W.A. van, and Verwers, W. 1993. 'Le commerce de céramiques carolingiennes aux Pays-Bas', in Piton, ed. (1993), pp. 227–36

Esposito, M. ed. (1907). 'An unpublished astronomical treatise by the Irish monk Dicuil', *Proceedings of the Royal Irish Academy*, 26C Dublin

Estey, F. 1951. 'The *scabini* and the local courts', *Speculum* 26, pp. 119–29

Ettel, P. 1998. 'Karlburg – Entwicklung eines königlich-bischöflichen Zentralortes am Main mit Burg und Talsiedlung vom 7. bis zum 13. Jahrhundert', *Château Gaillard* 18, pp. 75–85

Faulkner, N. 2000. 'Change and decline in late Romano-British towns', in Slater, ed. (2000), pp. 25–50

Favier, J. 1999. *Charlemagne*, Paris

Federici-Schenardi, M. and Fellner, F. 1997. 'L'habitat rural du haut moyen âge de Develier-Courtételle (Jura, Suisse)', in De Boe and Verhaeghe, eds. (1997d), pp. 121–30

Fichtenau, H. 1953. 'Karl der Große und das Kaisertum', *Mitteilungen des Instituts für österreichische Geschichtsforschung* 61, pp. 257–334

Folz, R. 1974. *The Coronation of Charlemagne*, London

Fouracre, P. 1984. 'Observations of the outgrowth of Pippinid influence in the "Regnum Francorum" after the Battle of Tertry (687–715)', *Medieval Prosopography* 5:2, pp. 1–31

Fouracre, P. 1992. 'Cultural conformity and social conservatism in early medieval Europe', *HWJ* 33, pp. 152–60

Fouracre, P. 1995a. 'Eternal light and earthly needs: practical aspects of the development of Frankish immunities', in W. Davies and P. Fouracre, eds. (1995), *Property and Power in the Early Middle Ages*, Cambridge, pp. 43–81

Fouracre, P. 1995b. 'Carolingian justice: the rhetoric of reform and the contexts of abuse', *Settimane di Studio* 42 (1995), pp. 771–803

Fouracre, P. 2000. *The Age of Charles Martel*, London

Fouracre, P. and Gerberding, R. 1996. *Late Merovingian France. History and Hagiography 640–720*, Manchester

Fried, J. 1982. 'Der karolingische Herrschaftsverband im 9. Jht. Zwischen Kirche und Königshaus, *HZ* 235, pp. 1–43

Fried, J. 1998. 'Elite und Ideologie oder die Nachfolgerordnung Karls des Grossen vom Jahre 813', in Le Jan, ed. (1998), pp. 70–109

Fried, J. 2000. 'Wann verlor Karl der Grosse seinen ersten Zahn?', *DA* 56, pp. 573–83

Fried, J. 2001. 'Papst Leo III besucht Karl den Großen', *HZ* 272, pp. 289–326

Gai, S. 1999a. 'Die Pfalz Karls des Großen in Paderborn – Ihre Entwicklung von 777 bis zum Ende des 10. Jahrhunderts', in Stiegemann and Wemhoff, eds. (1999b), pp. 183–96

Gai, S. 1999b. 'Karolingische Glasfunde der Pfalz Paderborn', in Stiegemann and Wemhoff, eds. (1999b), pp. 212–17

Galinié, H. 1988. 'Reflections on early medieval Tours', in Hodges and Hobley, eds. (1988), pp. 57–62

Galinié, H. 1996. 'Le passage de la nécropole au cimetière: les habitants des villes et leurs morts du début de la christianisation à l'an Mil', in Galinié and Zadora-Rio, eds. (1996), pp. 17–22

Galinié, H. 1997. 'Tours de Grégoire, Tours des archives du sol', in Gauthier and Galinié, eds. (1997), pp. 65–80

Galinié, H. 1999. 'Tours from an archaeological standpoint', in C.E. Karkov, K.M. Wickham-Crowley and B.K. Young, eds. *Spaces of the Living and the Dead: An Archaeological Dialogue*, American Early Medieval Studies 3, Oxford, pp. 87–105

Galinié, H. 2000. *Ville, espace urbain et archéologie*, Collection Sciences de la Ville 16, Tours

Galinié, H. ed. 2000. *Terres Noires – 1*, Documents Sciences de la Ville 6, Tours

Galinié, H. and Zadora-Rio, E. eds. 1996. *Archéologie du cimetière chrétien. Actes du 2e colloque A.R.C.H.E.A. (Orléans, 29 septembre–1er octobre 1994)*, Revue Archéologique du Centre de la France, Supplément 11, Tours

Gameson, R. ed. 1994. *The Early Medieval Bible. Its Production, Decoration and Use*, Cambridge

Gameson, R. and Leyser, H. eds, 2001. *Belief and Culture: Studies presented to Henry Mayr-Harting*, Oxford

Ganshof, F.L. 1959. *Recherches sur les capitulaires*, Paris

Ganshof, F.L. 1968. *Frankish Institutions under Charlemagne*, New York, NY

Ganshof, F.L. 1970. 'L'historiographie dans la monarchie franque sous les Mérovingiens et les Carolingiens', *Settimane di Studio* 17, pp. 631–750

Ganshof, F.L. 1971. *The Carolingians and the Frankish Monarchy*, New York, NY

Ganz, D. 1989. 'Humor as history in Notker's *Gesta Karoli Magni*', in E.B. King, ed. *Monks, Friars and Nuns in Medieval Society*, Sewanee, TE, pp. 171–83

Ganz, D. 1990. *Corbie in the Carolingian Renaissance*, Beihefte der Francia 20, Sigmaringen

Ganz, D. 1997. 'The preface to Einhard's "Vita Karoli"', in H. Schefers, ed. (1997), *Einhard: Studien zu Leben und Werk*, Darmstadt, pp. 299–310

Ganz, P. ed. 2000. *Jacob Burckhardt Werke: kritische Gesamtausgabe* 10, Munich and Basel, pp. 274–305

Garrison, M. 1997, 'English and Irish at the court of Charlemagne', in P.L. Butzer, M. Kerner, and B. Oberschelp, eds. *Karl der Grosse und sein Nachwirken. 1200 Jahre Kultur und Wissenschaft in Europa. I. Wissen und Weltbild*, Turnhout, pp. 97–124

Garrison, M. 1998a. 'Letters to a king and biblical exempla: the examples of Cathuulf and Clemens Peregrinus', *EME* 7, pp. 305–28

Garrison, M. 1998b. 'The social world of Alcuin: nicknames at York and at the Carolingian court', in Houwen and MacDonald, eds. (1998), pp. 59–80

Garrison, M. 2000a. 'The Franks as the new Israel'? in Hen and Innes, eds. (2000), pp. 114–61

Garrison, M. 2000b. 'Send more socks: on mentality and the preservation context of early medieval letters', in M. Mostert, ed. (2000), *New Approaches to Medieval Communication*, Turnhout, pp. 69–100

Garrison, M., Nelson, J.L., and Tweddle, D. eds. (2001), *Alcuin and Charlemagne: the Golden Age of York*, York

Gasparri, S. 2000. 'Il passaggio dai Longobardi ai Carolingi', in Bertelli and Brogiolo, eds. (2000), pp. 25–43

Gatto, L. 1998. 'Riflettando sulla consistenza demografica della Roma altomedievale', in Delogu, ed. (1998), pp. 143–59

Gauthier, N. 1997. 'Le paysage urbain en Gaule au VIe siècle', in Gauthier and Galinié, eds. (1997), pp. 49–61

Gauthier, N. and Galinié, H. eds. 1997. *Grégoire de Tours et l'espace gaulois*, Revue archéologique du Centre de la France, 13e supplement, Tours

Gauthiez, B. 1989. 'Rouen pendant le Haut Moyen Age' in Atsma, ed. (1989), pp. 1–20

Gauthiez, B. 1993. 'La réoccupation planifiée de la cité de Rouen au Haut Moyen Âge', in J. Stratford, ed. *Medieval Art, Architecture and Archaeology at Rouen*, The British Archaeological Association Conference Transactions 12, pp. 12–19

Geary, P. 1985. *Aristocracy in Provence: The Rhône Basin at the Dawn of the Carolingian Age*, Stuttgart

Geary, P.J. 1990. *Furta Sacra. Thefts of Relics in the Central Middle Ages*, Princeton, NJ

Geary, P.J. 1994. 'Die Provence zur Zeit Karl Martells', in Jarnut, et al. (1994), pp. 381–92

Geary, P.J. 1995. 'Extra-judicial forms of conflict resolution', *Settimane di Studio* 42, pp. 569–605

Geary, P.J. 2002. *The Myth of Nations: The Medieval Origins of Europe*, Princeton, NJ

Gerberding, R. 1987. *The Rise of the Carolingians and the 'Liber Historiae Francorum'*, Oxford

Gerchow, J. 1988. *Die Gedenküberlieferung der Angelsachsen, mit einem Katalog der Libri Vitae und Necrologien*, Berlin

Geuenich, D., Ludwig, U. and Angenendt, A. eds. 2000. *Der Memorial und Liturgiecodex von San Salvatore / Santa Giulia in Brescia*, MGH Lib. Mem. NS 4, Hanover

Gibson, S. and Ward-Perkins, B. 1983. 'The surviving remains of the Leonine wall. Part II: The Passeto', *PBSR* 51, pp. 222–39

Gilles, K.-J. 1985. 'Fundmünzen der sächsischen Kaiserzeit aus dem Trierer Land', *Funde und Ausgrabungen im Bezirk Trier* 17, pp. 40–7

Gillingham, J. 1999. *Richard I*, New Haven, CT

Glöckner, K. ed. 1929–36. *Codex Laureshamensis*, 3 vols, Darmstadt

Godman, P. 1985a. *Poetry of the Carolingian Renaissance*, London

Godman, P. 1985b. 'Louis "the Pious" and his poets', *FS* 19, pp. 239–89

Godman, P. and Collins, R. eds. 1990. *Charlemagne's Heir. New Perspectives on the Reign of Louis the Pious*, Oxford

Godman, P. , Jarnut, J. and Johanek, P. eds. 2002. *Am Vorabend der Kaiserkrönung. Das Epos 'Karolus Magnus et Leo papa' und der Papstbesuch in Paderborn 799*, Berlin

Goffart, W. 1986. 'Paul the Deacon's "Gesta episcoporum Mettensium" and the early design of Charlemagne's succession', *Traditio* 42, pp. 59–93

Goffart, W. 1988. *The Narrators of Barbarian History*, Princeton, NJ

Goldberg, E.J. 1995. 'Popular revolt, dynastic politics and aristocratic factionalism in the early middle ages: the Saxon *Stellinga* reconsidered', *Speculum* 70, pp. 467–501

Gorman, M. 1982. 'The encyclopaedic commentary on Genesis prepared for Charlemagne by Wigbod', *Recherches Augustiniennes* 17, pp. 173–201

Gorman, M. 1997. 'Wigbod and Biblical Studies under Charlemagne', *Revue Bénédictine* 107, pp. 40–76

Grewe, H. 1999. 'Die Pfalz Ingelheim' and ' Die Königspfalz zu Ingelheim am Rhein', in Stiegemann and Wemhoff, eds. (1999a), pp. 100–7

Grierson, P. 1965. 'Money and coinage under Charlemagne', in Braunfels, ed. (1965), I, pp. 501–36

Grierson, P. and Blackburn, M.A.S. 1986. *Medieval European Coinage*, Vol. 1, *The Early Middle Ages (5th–10th Centuries)*, Cambridge

Grothe, A. 1999. 'Zur Karolingischen Keramik der Pfalz Paderborn', in Stiegemann and Wemhoff, eds. (1999b), pp. 207–11

Grothe, A. and König, A. 1999. 'Villa Huxori – Das Frühmittelalterliche Höxter', in Stiegemann and Wemhoff, eds. (1999b), pp. 374–9

Guérard, B. ed. 1845. *Polyptyque de l'abbé Irminon*, 2 vols, Paris

Guérard, B, ed. 1859. *Cartulaire de l'abbaye de St-Victor de Marseilles*, Paris

Haertle, C.M. 1997. *Karolingische Münzfunde aus dem 9 Jahrhundert*, 2 vols, Cologne, Weimar and Vienna

Hägermann, D. 2000. *Karl der Grosse, Herrscher des Abendlandes: Biographie*, Munich

Hallinger, K. ed. 1963. Corpus Consuetudinum Monasticarum, I. *Initia Consuetudinis Benedictinae. Consuetudines Saeculi Octavi et Noni*, Sieburg

Halphen, L. 1921. *Études critiques sur l'histoire de Charlemagne*, Paris

Halsall, G. 1995. *Settlement and Social Organisation: the Merovingian Region of Metz*, Cambridge

Hamerow, H., Hollevoet, Y. and Vince, A. 1995. 'Migration period settlements and "Anglo-Saxon" pottery from Flanders', *Medieval Archaeology* 38, pp. 1–18

Hannig, J. 1983. 'Pauperiores vassi de infra palatio? Zur Entstehung der karolingischen Königsbotenorganisation', *MIÖG* 91, pp. 309–74

Hannig, J. 1984. 'Zentralle Kontrolle und regionale Machtbalanz. Beobachtungen zum System der karolingischen Köngsboten am Beispiel des Mittelrheingebiets', *AKG* 66, pp. 1–46

Hansen, I.L. and Wickham, C. eds. 2000. *The Long Eighth Century: Production, Distribution and Demand*, The Transformation of the Roman World 11, Leiden

Hanusse, C. 1999. 'L'habitat rural du haut Moyen Âge (VIe–Xe s.) de "La Sente" à Grentheville (Calvados): premiers éléments de synthèse', in J. Decaëns and A-M. Flambard Héricher, eds. *Actes du IIIe Colloque Européen des Professeurs d'Archéologie Médiévale, III*, Université de Caen, Centre de Michel de Boüard, C.R.A.M., Caen, pp. 85–93

Hardt, M. 1998. 'Royal treasures and representation in the early middle ages', in Pohl and Reimitz, eds. (1998), pp. 255–80

Hartmann, W. 1989. *Die Synoden der Karolingerzeit im Frankenreich und in Italien*, Paderborn, Munich and Vienna

Hatz, V. 1985. 'Nachlese zum Krinkberg-Fund', *Hikuin* 11, pp. 125–32

Heeringen, R. van, Henderikx, P.A. and Mars, A. eds. 1995. *Vroeg-Middeleeuwse ringwalburgen in Zeeland*, Amersfoort

Heil, J. 2000. '"Nos nescientes de hoc velle manere" – "We wish to remain ignorant about this": Timeless end, or approaches to reconceptualizing eschatology after A.D. 800 (A.M. 6000)', *Traditio* 55, pp. 73–103

Heinzelmann, M. 1979. *Translationsberichte und andere Quellen des Reliquienkultes*, Typologies des Sources du Moyen Âge Occidental 33, Turnhout

Heitz, C. 1980. *L'Architecture religieuse carolingienne*, Paris

Hellmann, S. 1932. 'Einhards literarische Stellung', *Historische Vierteljahresschrift* 27, pp. 40–110; reprinted in S. Hellmann (1961) *Ausgewählte Abhandlungen zur Historiographie und Geistesgeschichte des Mittelalters*, Darmstadt, pp. 159–229

Hellmuth Andersen, H., Madsen, H.J. and Voss, O. 1976. *Danevirke*, 2 vols, Copenhagen

Hen, Y. 2000. 'Paul the Deacon and the Frankish liturgy', in P. Chiesa, ed. *Paolo Diacono: una scrittore fra tradizione longobarda e rinnovamento carolingio. Atti del convegno internazionale di studi, Cividale de Friuli, Udine, 6–9 maggio 1999*, Udine (2000), pp. 205–21

Hen, Y. 2001. *The Royal Patronage of Liturgy in Frankish Gaul to the Death of Charles the Bald (877)*, London

Hen, Y. and Innes, M. eds. 2000. *The Uses of the Past in the Early Middle Ages*, Cambridge

Henderikx, P.A. 1995. 'De ringwalburgen in het mondingsgebied van de Schelde in historisch perspectif', in Heeringen et al. eds. (1995), pp. 71–112

Henderson, G. 1994. 'Emulation and invention in Carolingian art', in McKitterick, ed. (1994), pp. 248–73

Hendy, M. 1988. 'From public to private: the western barbarian coinages as a mirror of the disintegration of late Roman state structures', *Viator* 19, pp. 29–78

Hentze, W. ed. 1999. *De Karolo rege et Leone papa*, Paderborn

Hill, D. and Cowie, R. eds. 2001. *Wics. The early mediaeval trading centres of northern Europe*, Sheffield Archaeological Monographs, 14, Sheffield

Hodges, R. 1981. *The Hamwih Pottery*, CBA Res. Rpt. 37, London

Hodges, R. 1982. *Dark Age Economics: The Origins of Towns and Trade, AD600–1000*, London

Hodges, R. 1989. *The Anglo-Saxon Achievement: Archaeology and the Beginnings of English Society*, London

Hodges, R. 1996. 'Dream cities: emporia and the end of the Dark Ages', in Christie and Loseby, eds. (1996), pp. 289–305

Hodges, R. 2000. *Towns and Trade in the Age of Charlemagne*, London

Hodges, R. ed. 1995. *San Vincenzo al Volturno 2: The 1980–86 Excavations, Part II*, London

Hodges, R. and Bowden, W. eds. 1998. *The Sixth Century: Production, Distribution and Demand*, The Transformation of the Roman World 3, Leiden

Hodges, R. and Hobley, B. eds. 1988. *The Rebirth of Towns in the West AD700–1050*, CBA Res. Rpt. 68, London

Hodges, R. and Whitehouse, D. 1983. *Mohammed, Charlemagne and the Origins of Europe*, London

Hoek, C. 1986. 'La Maison forte aux Pays-Bas', in M. Bur, ed. (1986), *La Maison Forte au Moyen Age*, Paris, pp. 113–36

Hoffmann, D., Meier, D. and Müller-Wille, M. 1997. 'Geologische und archäologische Untersuchungen zur Landschafts- und Siedlungsgeschichte des Küstengebietes von Norderdithmarschen', *Germania* 75, pp. 223–63

Hoffmann, H. 1958. *Untersuchungen zur karolingischen Annalistik*, Bonn

Horst, K. van der, Noel, W. and Wüstefeld, W. 1996. *The Utrecht Psalter in Medieval Art. Picturing the Psalms of David*, London

Houts, E. van, 1999. *Memory and Gender in Medieval Europe, 900–1200*, Basingstoke

Houts, E. van, ed. 2001. *Medieval Memories. Men, Women and the Past 700–1300*, Harlow

Houwen, L.A.J.R. and MacDonald, A.A. eds. 1998. *Alcuin of York. Scholar at the Carolingian Court*, Germania Latina 3, Gröningen

Howell, W.S. ed. 1941. *The Rhetoric of Alcuin and Charlemagne*, Princeton, NJ

Hudson, P. 1981. *Archeologia urbana e programmazione della ricerca: l'esempio di Pavia*, Florence

Hyde, J. 1966. 'Medieval descriptions of cities', *Bulletin of the John Rylands Library* 48, pp. 308–40

Innes, M. 1997a. 'The classical tradition in the Carolingian renaissance: ninth-century encounters with Suetonius', *International Journal of the Classical Tradition* 3, pp. 265–82

Innes, M. 1997b. 'Charlemagne's will: inheritance, ideology and the imperial succession', *EHR* 112, pp. 833–55

Innes, M. 1998a. 'Memory, orality and literacy in an early medieval society', *P&P* 158, pp. 3–36

Innes, M. 1998b. 'Kings, monks and patrons: political identities and the abbey of Lorsch', in Le Jan, ed. (1998), pp. 301–24

Innes, M. 2000a. *State and Society in the Early Middle Ages: The Middle Rhine Valley, 400–1000*, Cambridge

Innes, M. 2000b. 'Teutons or Trojans? The Carolingians and the Germanic past', in Hen and Innes, eds. (2000), pp. 227–49

Innes, M. 2001. 'People, places and power in Carolingian society: a microcosm', in de Jong and Theuws, eds. (2001), pp. 397–437

Innes, M. 2003. '*A Place of Discipline*: aristocratic youth and Carolingian courts', in C. Cubitt, ed. (2003), *Court Culture in the Early Middle Ages*, Turnhout, pp. 59–76

Innes, M. and McKitterick, R. 1994. 'The writing of history', in McKitterick, ed. (1994), pp. 193–220

Jacobsen, W. 1994. 'Die Pfalzkonzeptionen Karls der Grossen', in L.E. Saurma-Jeltsch, ed. (1994), *Karl des Grosse als vielberufener Vorfahr*, Sigmaringen, pp. 23–48

Jackson, R.A. 1995. *Ordines Coronationis Franciae*, Philadelphia, PA

Jäggi, C. 2001. 'Il tempietto di Cividale del Friuli nell'ambito dell'architettura longobarda', in A.A.V.V. (2001), pp. 407–28

Jan, R. L. *See* Le Jan, R.

Jankuhn, H. 1965. 'Karl der Grosse und der Norden', in Braunfels, ed. (1965), I, pp. 699–707

Jankuhn, H. 1986. *Haithabu: Ein Handelsplatz der Wikingerzeit*, Neumünster

Janssen, W. 1989. 'Reiten und Fahren in der Merowingerzeit', in H. Jankuhn, W. Kimmig and E. Ebel, eds. *Untersuchungen zum Handel und Verkehr der vor- und frühgeschichtlichen Zeit in Mittel- und Nordeuropa. Teil V. Der Verkehr. Verkehrswege, Verkehrsmittel, Organisation*, Abhandlungen der Akademie der Wissenschaften zu Göttingen, Philologisch-Historische Klasse, 3. Folge, 180, Göttingen, pp. 174–228

Jarnut, J., Nonn, U., and Richter, M. eds. 1994. *Karl Martell in seiner Zeit*, Beihefte der Francia, 37, Sigmaringen

Jeanne-Rose, O. 1996. 'Trouvailles isolées de monnaies carolingiennes en Poitou', *RN* 151, pp. 258–83

Jensen, S. 1991. *The Vikings of Ribe*, Ribe

Jones, L.W. 1932. *The Script of Cologne from Hildebald to Hermann*, Cambridge, Mass.

Jong, M. de, 1992. 'Power and humility in Carolingian society: the public penance of Louis the Pious', *EME* 1, pp. 29–51

Jong, M. de, 1995. 'Carolingian Monasticism: the Power of Prayer', in McKitterick, ed. (1995), pp. 622–53

Jong, M. de, 1996. *In Samuel's Image. Child Oblation in the Early Medieval West*, Leiden and New York, NY

Jong, M. de, 1998. 'Imitatio morum. The cloister and clerical purity in the Carolingian world', ed. M. Frassetto, *Medieval Purity and Piety. Essays in Medieval Clerical Celibacy and Religious Reform*, New York, NY and London, pp. 49–80

Jong, M. de, 2000. 'The empire as *ecclesia*; Hrabanus Maurus and biblical *historia* for rulers', in Hen and Innes, eds. (2000), pp. 191–226

Jong, M. de, 2001a. 'Religion', in McKitterick, ed. (2001), pp. 131–64

Jong, M. de, 2001b. 'Exegesis for an empress', in E. Cohen and M. de Jong, eds. *Medieval Transformations. Texts, Power and Gifts in Context*, Leiden (2000), pp. 69–100

Jong, M. de and Theuws, F. with Rhijn, C. van, eds. 2001. *Topographies of Power in the Early Middle Ages*, The Transformation of the Roman World 6, Leiden

Kaczynski, B.E. 1995. 'Edition, translation, and exegesis: the Carolingians and the Bible', in Sullivan, ed. (1995), pp. 171–85

Katz, E. ed. 1889. *Laureshamensium editio emendata secundum codicem St. Paulensem XXV c/ 32=CA*, St Paul in Lavanttal, Carinthia

Kempshall, M. 1995. 'Some Ciceronian models for Einhard's "Life of Charlemagne"', *Viator* 26, pp. 11–37

Kershaw, I. 2000. *Hitler, 1936–1945: Nemesis*, London

Keynes, S. 1997. 'Anglo-Saxon entries in the "Liber Vitae" of Brescia', in J. Roberts, J.L Nelson, and M. Godden, eds. *Alfred the Wise. Studies in honour of Janet Bately on the Occasion of her Sixty-Fifth Birthday*, Cambridge, pp. 99–120

Keynes, S. 1998. 'King Alfred and the Mercians', in M.A.S. Blackburn and D.N. Dumville, eds. *Kings, Currency and Alliances. History and Coinage of Southern England in the Ninth Century*, Cambridge, pp. 1–46

Keynes, S. ed. 1996. *The Liber Vitae of the New Minster and Hyde Abbey*, Early English Manuscripts in Facsimile 26, Copenhagen

King, P.D. 1987. *Charlemagne: Translated Sources*, Kendal

Kluge, B. 1999. 'Nomen imperatoris und Christiana Religio', in Stiegemann and Wemhoff, eds. (1999b), pp. 82–90

Kluge, B. 2002. 'Die Bildnispfennige Karls des Großen', in B. Paszkiewicz, ed. *Moneta Mediævalis: studia numizmatyczne i historyczne ofiarowane Profesorowi Stanislawowi Suchodolskiemu w. 65 rocznic_ urodzin*, Warsaw, pp. 367–77

Köhler, W. 1958. *Die karolingischen Miniaturen, II. Die Hofschule Karls des Grossen*, Berlin

Krautheimer, R. 1980. *Rome: Profile of a City, 312–1308*, Princeton, NJ

Krüger, K.H. 1998. 'Neue Beobachtungen zur Datierung von Einhards Karlsvita', *FS* 32, pp. 124–45

Kurze, F. 1913. *Die karolingischen Annalen bis zum Tode Einhards*, Berlin

Lafaurie, J. 1972. 'Le trésor carolingien de Sarzana-Luni', in *Monnaies et médailles racontent l'histoire de France*, Paris, pp. 23–38

Lafaurie, J. 1974. 'Numismatique: des Mérovingiens aux Carolingiens. Les monnaies de Pépin le Bref', *Francia* 2, pp. 26–48

Lafaurie, J. 1976. 'Moneta palatina', *Francia* 4, pp. 59–87

Lafaurie, J. 1978. 'Les monnaies impériales de Charlemagne', *Comptes-rendus de l'Académie des Inscriptions et Belles-lettres*, pp. 154-76

Lambech, P. ed. 1665–79. *Commentariorum de Augustissima Bibliotheca Caesarea Vindobonensi*, 8 vols, Vienna

Lambot, C. ed. 1945. *Œuvres théologiques et grammaticales de Godescalc d'Orbais*, Louvain

Lauwerier, R. 1995. 'Veeteelt in Oost-Souburg', in Heeringen et al. (1995), pp. 213–18

Lebecq, S. 1983. *Marchands et navigateurs frisons du haut moyen âge*, 2 vols, Lille.

Lebecq, S. 1993. 'Quentovic: un état de la question, *Studien zur Sachsenforschung*, 8, pp. 73–82

Lebecq, S. 1997. 'Routes of change: production and distribution in the West (5th–8th century)', in L. Webster and M. Brown, eds. *The Transformation of the Roman World AD400–900*, London, pp. 67–78

Lebecq, S. 2000. 'The role of monasteries in systems of production and exchange of the Frankish world between the seventh and ninth centuries', in Hansen and Wickham, eds. (2000), pp. 123–39

Le Jan, R. 1995. *Famille et pouvoir dans le monde franc, VIIIe–Xe siècles*, Paris

Le Jan, R. 1997. 'Justice royale et pratiques sociales dans le royaume franc au IXe siècle', *Settimane di Studio* 44, pp. 47–87

Le Jan, R. 2001. 'Convents, violence and competition for power in seventh-century Francia', in de Jong and Theuws, eds. (2001), pp. 243–69

Le Jan, R. ed. 1998. *La royauté et les élites dans l'Europe carolingienne (début du IXe siècle aux environs de 920)*, Paris

Le Maho, J. 2001. 'Les destins comparés de deux cités de fond d'estuaire: Rouen et Nantes du VIe au Xe siècle', in Manneville, P. ed. *Des villes, des ports, la mer et les hommes. 124e Congrès des sociétés historiques et scientifiques, Nantes, 19–26 avril 1999*, Paris, pp. 13–25

Lendi, W. 1971. *Untersuchungen zur frühalemannischen Annalistik. Die Murbacher Annalen*, Freiburg

Lepetz, S., Méniel, P. and Yvinec, J-H. 1995. 'Archéozoologie des installations rurales de la fin de l'âge de fer au debut du Moyen âge', in G. Brunel and J-M. Moriceau, eds. (1995), *Histoire & sociétés rurales — l'histoire rurale en France* 3, pp. 169–82

Levillain, L. 1932. 'Le couronnement impérial de Charlemagne', *Revue d'Histoire de l'Église de France* 18, pp. 5–19

Levison, W. 1946. *England and the Continent in the Eighth Century*, Oxford

Leyser, K. 1979. *Rule and Conflict in an Early Medieval Society*, London

Leyser, K. 1992. 'Concepts of Europe in the early and high middle ages', *Past and Present*, 137, pp. 25–47, reprinted in Leyser (1994), *Communication and Power in Medieval Europe: The Carolingian and Ottonian Centuries*, pp. 1–18

Llewellyn, P. 1993. *Rome in the Dark Ages*, London

Lorren, C. and Périn, P. 1997. 'Images de la Gaule rurale au VIe siècle', in Gauthier and Galinié, eds. (1997), pp. 93–109

Loseby, S. 1998. 'Marseilles and the Pirenne thesis I: Gregory of Tours, the Merovingian kings and "un grand port"', in Hodges and Bowden, eds. (1998), pp. 203–30

Loseby, S. 2000. 'Marseilles and the Pirenne thesis II: "ville morte"', in Hansen and Wickham, eds. (2000), pp. 167–93

Lošek, F. 1997. *Die Conversio Bagoariorum und Carantanorum und der Brief des Erzbischofs Theotmar von Salzburg*, MGH *Studien und Texte* XV, Hanover

Louis, E. 1997. 'Archéologie et bâtiments monastiques, VIIème–IXème siècles. Le cas de Hamage (France, Département du Nord)', in De Boe and Verhaeghe, eds. (1997c), pp. 55–63

Löwe, H. 1951. 'Studien zu den Annales Xantenses', *DA* 8, pp. 59–99

Löwe, H. 1956. 'Zur *Vita Hadriani*', *DA* 2 (1956), pp. 493–8

Löwe, H. 1973. *Von Cassiodor zu Dante*, Berlin

Löwe, H. 1974. 'Religio Christiana: Rom und das Kaisertum in Einhards Vita Karoli Magni', in *Storiografia e Storia. Studi in onore di E. D. Theseider*, Rome, pp. 1–20

Löwe, H. 1983. 'Die Entstehungszeit der Vita Karoli Einhards', *DA* 39, pp. 85–103

Loyn, H.R. and Percival, J. 1975. *The Reign of Charlemagne*. Documents of Medieval History 2, London.

Ludowici, B., 2001. 'Archäologische Quellen zur Pfalz Ottos I in Magdeburg: Erste Ergebnisse der Auswertung der Grabungen 1959 bis 1968 auf dem Magdeburger Domplatz', in Schneidmüller and Weinfurter, eds. (2001), pp. 71–84

MacLean, S. 2003. *Kingship and Politics in the Late Ninth Century. Charles the Fat and the End of the Carolingian Empire*, Cambridge

Maho, J. Le. *See* Le Maho, J.

Malmer, B. 1966. *Nordiska mynt före år 1000*, Lund

Marazzi, F. 1993. 'Roma, il Lazio, il Mediterraneo: relazioni fra economia e politica dal VII al IX secolo', in Paroli and Delogu, eds. (1993), pp. 267–85

Markus, R.A. 1968. 'Gregory the Great's rector and his genesis', in J. Fontaine, R. Gillet and S. Pellistrandi, eds. *Grégoire le Grand*, pp. 137–46, Paris

Markus, R.A. 1990. *The End of Ancient Christianity*, Cambridge

Markus, R.A. 1991. 'Gregory the Great on kings: rulers and preachers in the Commentary I on Kings', in D. Wood, ed. *The Church and Sovereignty*, Studies in Church History, Subsidia 9, Oxford, pp. 7–21; reprinted in Markus (1994) *Sacred and secular. Studies on Augustine and Latin Christianity*, Aldershot, ch. XII

Markus, R.A. 1997. *Gregory the Great and his World*, Cambridge

Martin, P.-H. 1997. 'Eine Goldmünze Karls des Großen', *Numismatisches Nachrichtenblatt* 46, pp. 351–55

Martínez Díez, G. and Rodríguez, F. ed. 1992. *La Collecíon canónica hispana 5. Concilios Hispanos: segunda parte*, Monumenta Hispaniae Sacra, Serie Canónica, Madrid

Matthys, A. 1991. 'Les fortifications du bassin de la Semois ardennaise du VIe au XVIIIe siècle', in H. Remy, ed. (1991), *Archéologie en Ardenne de la préhistoire au XVIIIe siècle*, Brussels, pp. 207–22

McCormick, M. 1984. 'The liturgy of war in the early middle ages: crisis, litanies and the Carolingian monarchy', *Viator* 15, pp. 1–23

McCormick, M. 1986. *Eternal Victory: Triumphal Rulership in Late Antiquity, Byzantium and the Early Medieval West*, Cambridge

McCormick, M. 2001. *Origins of the European Economy. Communications and Commerce AD300–900*, Cambridge

McCulloch, J. 1976. 'The cult of relics in the letters and *Dialogues* of Pope Gregory the Great', *Traditio* 32, pp. 145–84

McGrail, S. ed. 1990. *Maritime Celts, Frisians, and Saxons*, CBA Res. Rpt. 71, London

McKitterick, R. 1977. *The Frankish Church and the Carolingian Reforms, 789–895*, London

McKitterick, R. 1983. *The Frankish Kingdoms under the Carolingians, 751–987*, London

McKitterick, R. 1985. 'Knowledge of canon law in the Frankish kingdoms before 789: the manuscript evidence', *Journal of Theological Studies* n.s. 36, pp. 97–117; reprinted in McKitterick (1994), ch. 2

McKitterick, R. 1989. *The Carolingians and the Written Word*, Cambridge

McKitterick, R. 1991. *Anglo-Saxon Missionaries in Germany: Personal connections and local influences*, Eighth Brixworth Lecture, Vaughan Paper 36, Leicester

McKitterick, R. 1993. 'Zur Herstellung von Kapitularien: die Arbeit der Leges-Skriptorium', *Mitteilungen des Instituts für Österreichische Geschichtsforschung* 101, pp. 1–16

McKitterick, R. 1994. *Books, Scribes and Learning in the Frankish Kingdoms, 6th–9th Centuries*, Aldershot

McKitterick, R. 1995. 'England and the Continent', in McKitterick, ed. (1995), pp. 64–84

McKitterick, R. 1997. 'Constructing the past in the early middle ages: the case of the Royal Frankish Annals', *TRHS* 6th ser. 7, pp. 101–29

McKitterick, R. 1999. 'Paul the Deacon and the Franks', *EME* 8, pp. 319–39

McKitterick, R. 2000. 'The illusion of royal power in the Carolingian Annals', *EHR* 115, pp. 1–20

McKitterick, R. 2004. *History and Memory in the Carolingian World*, Cambridge

McKitterick, R. ed. 1990. *The Uses of Literacy in Early Mediaeval Europe*, Cambridge

McKitterick, R. ed. 1994. *Carolingian Culture: Emulation and Innovation*, Cambridge

McKitterick, R. ed. 1995. *The New Cambridge Medieval History, II: c.700–c.900*, Cambridge

McKitterick, R. ed. 2001. *The Early Middle Ages*. Short Oxford History of Europe 2, Oxford

McPhail, R.I., Galinié, H. and Verhaeghe, F. 2003. 'A future for Dark Earth?', *Antiquity* 77, pp. 349–58

Mecke, B. 1999. 'Die Pfalzen in Paderborn' in Stiegemann and Wemhoff, eds. (1999b), pp. 176–82

Meens, R. 1998. 'Politics, mirrors of princes and the Bible. Sins, kings and the well-being of the realm', *EME* 7, pp. 345–57

Meens, R. 1999. 'Questioning ritual purity: the influence of Gregory the Great's answers to Augustine's queries about childbirth, menstruation and sexuality', in R. Gameson, ed. *St Augustine and the Conversion of England*, Stroud, pp. 174–86

Melzer, W. 1999. 'Soest zur Karolingerzeit', in Stiegemann and Wemhoff, eds. (1999b), pp. 365–73.

Metcalf, D.M. 1988. 'North Italian coinage carried across the Alps. The Ostrogothic and Carolingian evidence compared', *Rivista Italiana di Numismatica e Scienze Affini* 90, pp. 449–56.

Metcalf, D.M. and Merrick, J. 1967. 'Studies in the composition of early medieval coins', *NChr* 127, pp. 167–81

Metcalf, D.M., Merrick, J. and Hamblin, L. 1968. *Studies in the Composition of Early Medieval Coins*, Newcastle-upon-Tyne

Metcalf, D.M. and Northover, P. 1989. 'Coinage alloys from the time of Offa and Charlemagne to *c.* 864', *NChr* 149, pp. 101–20

Meulemeester, J. de, 1983. 'Castrale motten in België', *Archaeologia Belgica* 255, pp. 199–225

Meulemeester, J. de, Matthys, A. and Poisson, J.-M. 1997. 'Structures emmottées: une comparaison d'exemples fouillés récemment en Belgique et en Rhône-Alpes', in De Boe and Verhaeghe, eds. (1997e), pp. 139–48

Milella, A. 2000. 'Le diaconie', in Pani Ermini, ed. (2000), pp. 192–9

Milosevic, A. ed. 2000. *Hrvati I Karolinzi*. 2 vols, Muzej Hrvatskih Arheoloskih Spomenika, Split

Mitchell, J. 1999. 'Karl der Grosse, Rom und das Vermächtnis der Langobarden', in Stiegemann and Wemhoff, eds. (1999b), pp. 95–108

Mitchell, J. 2000a. 'Artistic patronage and cultural strategies in Lombard Italy', in Brogiolo et al. eds. (2000), pp. 47–70

Mitchell, J. 2000b. 'L'arte nell'Italia longobarda e nell'Europa carolingia', in Bertelli and Brogiolo, eds. (2000), pp. 73–87

Molinier, M.A. ed. 1902. *Obituaires de la province de Sens* I: *Diocèses de Sens et de Paris*, Paris

Mordek, H. 1990. 'Some newly discovered capitulary texts belonging to the legislation of Louis the Pious', in Godman and Collins, eds. (1990), pp. 437–54

Mordek, H. 1995. *Bibliotheca capitularium regum Francorum manuscripta. Überlieferung und Traditionszusammenhang der fränkischen Herrscherserlasse*. MGH *Hilfsmittel* 14, Munich

Mordek, H. 1999. 'Von Paderborn nach Rom – der Weg der Kaiserkrönung', in Stiegemann and Wemhoff, eds. (1999b), pp. 47–54

Mordek, H. ed. 1986. *Überlieferung und Geltung normativer Texte des frühen und hohen Mittelalters*, Sigmaringen

Moreland, J. 2000. 'Concepts of the early medieval economy', in Hansen and Wickham, eds. (2000), pp. 1–34

Morrison, K.F. and Grunthal, H. 1967. *Carolingian Coinage*, New York, NY

Morrissey, R. 2003. *Charlemagne and France: A Thousand Years of Mythology*, trans. C. Tihanyi, Notre Dame, IN

Murray, A. ed. 1998. *After Rome's Fall. Narrators and Sources of Early Medieval History. Essays presented to Walter Goffart*, Toronto ONT

Nardi, S. 1992. 'Cencelle: tipologia delle strutture murarie di una città medievale abbandonata nel Lazio settentrionale (Tarquinia, VT)', in E. Herring, R. Whitehouse and J. Wilkins, eds. (1992), *Papers of the Fourth Conference of Italian Archaeology. New Developments, Part 2*, London, pp. 219–29

Näsman, U. 2000. 'Exchange and politics: the eighth–early ninth century in Denmark', in Hansen and Wickham, eds. (2000), pp. 35–68

Nees, L. 1991. *A Tainted Mantle. Hercules and the Classical Tradition at the Carolingian Court*, Philadelphia, PA

Nelson, J.L. 1983. 'Legislation and consensus in the reign of Charles the Bald', in C.P. Wormald, D.A. Bullough and R. Collins, eds. (1983), *Ideal and Reality in Frankish and Anglo-Saxon Society: Studies presented to J.M. Wallace-Hadrill*, Oxford, pp. 202–27; reprinted in Nelson (1986a), pp. 91–116

Nelson, J.L. 1986a. *Politics and Ritual in the Early Medieval World*, London

Nelson, J.L. 1986b. 'Queens as Jezebels: Brunhild and Balthild in Merovingian history', in Nelson (1986a), pp. 1–48

Nelson, J.L. 1987a. 'Making ends meet: wealth and poverty in the Carolingian church', *Studies in Church History* 24, pp. 25–36; reprinted in Nelson (1996a), pp. 145–53

Nelson, J.L. 1987b. 'The Lord's anointed and the people's choice: Carolingian royal ritual', in D. Cannadine and S. Price, eds. *Rituals of Royalty: Power and Ceremonial in Traditional Societies*, London, pp. 137–80, reprinted in Nelson (1996a), pp. 99–132

Nelson, J.L. 1988. 'Kingship and empire', in J.H. Burns, ed. (1988), *The Cambridge History of Medieval Political Thought*, Cambridge, pp. 211–51

Nelson, J.L. 1990. 'Literacy in Carolingian government', in McKitterick, ed. (1990), pp. 258–96; reprinted in Nelson (1996a), pp. 1–36

Nelson, J.L. 1991. 'La famille de Charlemagne', *Byzantion* 61, pp. 194–212, reprinted in Nelson (1999), ch. XII

Nelson, J.L. 1992. *Charles the Bald*, London and New York, NY

Nelson, J.L. 1993. 'Women at the court of Charlemagne: a case of monstrous regiment?', in J.C. Parsons, ed. (1993) *Medieval Queenship*, Stroud, pp. 43–61; reprinted in Nelson (1996a), pp. 99–132

Nelson, J.L. 1995. 'Kingship and royal government', in McKitterick, ed. (1995), pp. 383–430

Nelson, J.L. 1996a. *The Frankish World 750–900*, London

Nelson, J.L. 1996b. 'Gender and genre in women historians of the early middle ages', in Nelson (1996a), pp. 183–98

Nelson, J.L. 1997. 'The siting of the council at Frankfort. Some reflections on family and politics', in Berndt, ed. (1997), pp. 149–66

Nelson, J.L. 1998. 'Making a difference in eighth-century politics: the daughters of Desiderius', in Murray, ed. (1998), pp. 171–90

Nelson, J.L. 1999. *Rulers and Ruling Families in Early Medieval Europe*, Aldershot

Nelson, J.L. 2000a. 'Viaggiatori, pellegrini e vie commerciali', in Bertelli and Brogiolo, eds. (2000), pp. 163–72

Nelson, J.L. 2000b. 'Writing early medieval biography', *HWJ* 50, pp. 129–36

Nelson, J.L. 2001a. 'Aachen as a place of power', in de Jong and Theuws, eds. (2001), pp. 217–42

Nelson, J.L. 2001b. 'Carolingian contacts', in M. Brown and C. Farr, eds. (2001), *Mercia. An Anglo-Saxon Kingdom in Europe*, London, pp. 126–43

Nelson, J.L. 2001c. 'The voice of Charlemagne', in Gameson and Leyser, eds. (2001), pp. 76–88

Nelson, J.L. 2002a. 'England and the continent in the ninth century, I: ends and beginnings', *TRHS* 6th ser. 12, pp. 1–21

Nelson, J.L. 2002b. 'Charlemagne — *pater optimus?*', in Godman et al. eds. (2002), pp. 269–81

Nice, A., 1988. 'La nécropole mérovingienne de Goudelancourt-les-Pierrepont (Aisne)', *Revue Archéologique de Picardie*, 3–4, pp. 127–43

Nice, A., 1994. 'L'habitat mérovingien de Goudelancourt-les-Pierrepont (Aisne) – Aperçu provisoire d'une unité agricole et domestique des VIe et VIIe siècles', *Revue d'Archéologique de Picardie*, 1–2, pp. 21–63

Noble, T.F.X. 1976. 'The monastic ideal as a model for empire: the case of Louis the Pious', *Revue Bénédictine* 86, pp. 235–50

Noble, T.F.X. 1980. 'Louis the Pious and his piety re-reconsidered', *Revue Belge de Philologie et d'Histoire* 58, pp. 297–316

Noble, T.F.X. 1984. *The Republic of St. Peter. The Birth of the Papal State, 680–825*, Philadelphia, PA

Noble, T.F.X.1990. 'Louis the Pious and the frontier of the empire', in Godman and Collins, eds. (1990), pp. 333–48

Noble, T.F.X. 1992. 'From brigandage to justice: Charlemagne, 785–794', in Chazelle, ed. (1992), pp. 49–76

Noble, T.F.X. 1995. 'The papacy in the eighth and ninth centuries', in McKitterick, ed. (1995), pp. 563–86

Noble, T.F.X. 2000. 'Paradoxes and possibilities in the sources for Roman society in the early middle ages', in Smith, ed. (2000), pp. 55–84

Noble, T.F.X. 2001. 'Topography, celebration and power: the making of a papal Rome in the eighth and ninth centuries', in de Jong and Theuws, eds. (2001), pp. 45–92

Olsen, O. and Schmidt, H. 1977. *Fyrkat. En jysk vikingeborg. I. Borgen og bebyggelsen*, Nordiske Fortidsminder, Serie B – in quarto 3, Copenhagen

Osborne, R. 1987. 'The atrium of S. Maria Antiqua, Rome: a history in art', *PBSR* 55, pp. 186–223

Palliser, D. ed. 2000. *The Cambridge Urban History of Britain, 1: 600–1540*, Cambridge

Pani Ermini, L. ed. 2000. *Christiana Loca. Lo spazio cristiano nella Roma del primo millennio*, Rome

Parker, G. 1998. *The Grand Strategy of Philip II*, New Haven, CT

Paroli, L. 1993. 'Ostia nella tarda antichità e nell'alto medioevo', in Paroli and Delogu, eds. (1993), pp. 153–75

Paroli, L. 1998. 'La scultura in marmo a Roma tra l'VIII e il IX secolo', in Delogu, ed. (1998), pp. 93–122

Paroli, L. and Delogu, P. eds. 1993. *La storia economica di Roma nell'alto medioevo alla luce dei recenti scavi archeologici*, Biblioteca di Archeologia Medievale 10, Florence

Patzold, S. 2000. *Konflikte im Kloster: Studien zu Auseinandersetzungen in monastischen Gemeinschaften des ottonische–salischen Reichs*, Historische Studien, 463, Husum

Payer, P. 1984. *Sex and the Penitentials. The Development of a Sexual Code*, Toronto ONT

Peacock, D. 1997. 'Charlemagne's black stones. The re-use of Roman columns in early medieval Europe', *Antiquity* 71, pp. 709–15

Pierfitte, G. 1933. 'Numismatique toulousaine: les monnaies de Charlemagne et de Charles le Chauve', *RN* 4.36, pp. 49–54

Pierpaoli, M. 1986, *Storia di Ravenna. Dalle origini all'anno Mille*, Ravenna

Piton, D. ed. 1993. *Travaux du Groupe de Recherches et d'Etudes sur la Céramique dans le Nord–Pas-de-Calais. Actes du colloque d'Outreau (10–12 avril 1992). La Céramique du Vème au Xème siècle dans l'Europe du Nord-Ouest*, Nord-Ouest Archéologie, numéro hors-série 1, Berck-sur-Mer

Pohl, W. 1988. *Die Awaren. Ein Steppenvolk in Mitteleuropa, 567–822 n. Chr*, Munich

Pohl, W. 2001, 'The *regia* and the *hring* – barbarian places of power', in de Jong and Theuws, eds. (2001), pp. 439–66

Pohl, W. and Reimitz, H. eds. 1998. *Strategies of Distinction. The Construction of Ethnic Communities*, Transformation of the Roman World 2, Leiden

Proos, R. 1997. 'Venray-'t Bruske, an early medieval settlement on the sandy soils of Limburg', in De Boe and Verhaeghe, eds. (1997e), pp. 149–56

Prou, M. 1892. *Catalogue des monnaies françaises de la Bibliothèque Nationale. Les monnaies carolingiennes*, Paris

Ramsey, B. ed. and trans. 2000. *John Cassian: The Institutes*, New York, NY

Rand, E.K. 1929. *A Survey of the Manuscripts of Tours*, Studies in the Script of Tours 1, Cambridge, Mass.

Rand, E.K. 1934. *The Earliest Book of Tours*, Studies in the Script of Tours 2, Cambridge, Mass.

Ranke, L. von, 1854. *Zur Kritik fränkisch-deutscher Reichsannalisten*, Abhandlung der königlichen Akademie der Wissenschaften, Berlin, pp. 415–58

Rankin, S. 1994. 'Carolingian music', in McKitterick, ed. (1994), pp. 274–316

Rau, R. ed. 1972, 1974, 1975. *Quellen zur karolingischen Reichsgeschichte*, 3 vols, Darmstadt

Rauch, C. and Jacobi, H.J. 1976. *Die Ausgrabungen in der Königspfalz Ingelheim, 1909–1914*, Mainz

Reimitz, H. 2000a. 'Ein karolingisches Geschichtsbuch aus Saint-Amand: Der Codex Vindobonesis palat. 473', in C. Egger and H. Weigl, eds. *Text-Schrift-Codex. Quellenkundliche Arbeiten aus dem Institut für Österreichische Geschichtsforschung*, Munich, pp. 34–89

Reimitz, H. 2000b. 'Conversion and control: the establishment of liturgical frontiers in Carolingian Pannonia', in W. Pohl, I. Wood, and H. Reimitz, eds. (2000), *The Transformation of Frontiers from Late Antiquity to the Carolingians*, The Transformation of the Roman World 10, Leiden, pp. 189–207

Renoux, A. 1997. 'Le château des comtes de Champagne à Montfélix (Chavot) et son impact sur l'environnement (Xe–XIIIe siècle)', in De Boe and Verhaeghe, eds. (1997e), pp. 119–30

Renoux, A. 1999. 'Karolingische Pfalzen in Nordfrankreich (751–987)', in Stiegemann and Wemhoff, eds. (1999b), pp. 130–7

Renoux, A. 2001: 'Le vocabulaire du pouvoir à Mayenne et ses implications politiques et architecturales (VIIe–XIIIe siècle)', in Renoux, ed. (2001), pp. 247–72

Renoux, A. ed. 2001. 'Aux Marches du Palais'. Qu'est-ce-qu'un palais médiéval? Actes du VIIe Congrès international d'Archéologie Médiévale Le Mans – Mayenne, 9–11 septembre 1999, Le Mans

Reuter, T. 1985. 'Plunder and tribute in the Carolingian empire', TRHS 5th ser. 35, pp. 75–94

Reuter, T. 1990. 'The end of Carolingian expansion', in Godman and Collins, eds. (1990), pp. 391–405

Reuter, T. 1991. Germany in the Early Middle Ages, 800–1056, Harlow

Reuter, T. 1992. The Annals of Fulda, Ninth-Century Histories 2, Manchester

Reuter, T. 1994. '"Kirchenreform" und "Kirchenpolitik" im Zeitalter Karl Martells: Begriffe und Wirklichkeit', in Jarnut et al., eds. (1994), pp. 35–59

Reuter, T. 1997. 'The medieval nobility in twentieth-century historiography', in Bentley, ed. (1994), pp. 177–202

Reuter, T. 2000. '"You can't take it with you": testaments, hoards and moveable wealth in Europe, 600–1100', in E.M. Tyler, ed. Treasure in the Medieval West, Woodbridge, pp. 11–24

Reuter, T. ed. 1979. The Medieval Nobility. Studies on the Ruling Classes of France and Germany from the Sixth to the Twelfth Century, Amsterdam, New York, NY and Oxford

Reuter, T. ed. 1980. The Greatest Englishman, Exeter

Reynaud, J.-F. 1998. Lugdunum Christianum: Lyon du IVe au VIIIe s.: Topographie, Nécropoles et Édifices Religieux, Documents d'Archéologie Française 69, Paris

Reynolds, L.D. 1983. Texts and Transmission: A Survey of the Latin Classics, Oxford

Reynolds, L.D., and Wilson, N.G. 1991. Scribes and Scholars. A Guide to the Transmission of Greek and Latin Literature, Oxford

Reynolds, S. 1994. Fiefs and Vassals, Oxford

Romana Strassola, F. 2000. 'Xenodochia', in Pani Ermini, ed. (2000), pp. 189–91

Romanelli, P. and Nordhagen, P.J. 1964. S. Maria Antiqua, Rome

Rosenwein, B.H. 1999. Negotiating Space. Power, Restraint and Privileges of Immunity in Early Medieval Europe, Manchester

Ross, J.B. 1945. 'Two neglected paladins of Charlemagne: Erich of Friuli and Gerold of Bavaria', Speculum 20, pp. 212–35

Rovelli, A. 2000a. 'Monetary circulation in Byzantine and Carolingian Rome: a reconsideration in the light of recent archaeological data', in Smith, ed. (2000), pp. 85–100

Rovelli, A. 2000b. 'Some considerations on the coinage of Lombard and Carolingian Italy', in Hansen and Wickham, eds. (2000), pp. 195–223

Samson, R. 1994. 'Populous dark-age towns: the Finleyesque approach', Journal of European Archaeology 2, pp. 97–129

Samson, R. 1999. 'Illusory emporia and mad economic theories', in M. Anderton, ed. (1999), Anglo-Saxon Trading Centres; Beyond the Emporia, Glasgow, pp. 76–90

Santangeli Valenzani, R. 2000. 'Residential building in early medieval Rome', in Smith, ed. (2000), pp. 101–12

Sarfatij, H. 1977. 'Die Frühgeschichte von Rijnsburg (8–12 Jahrhundert), ein historisch-archäologischer Bericht', in Beek, B. Van, Brandt, R., and Groenman van Waateringe, W. eds. (1977), Ex horreo, pp. 290–302, Amsterdam

Scheers, S. ed. 1991. Numismatiek en archeologie in West-Vlaanderen, Westvlaamse Archaeologica 7, pp. 31–42

Schefers, H. ed. 1997. Einhard: Studien zu Leben und Werk, Darmstadt

Schieffer, R. 2000. 'Charlemagne and Rome', in Smith, ed. (2000), pp. 279–95

Schietzel, K. 1981. *Stand der siedlungsarchäologischen Forschung in Haithabu: Ergebnisse und Probleme*, Berichte über die Ausgrabungen in Haithabu 16, Neumünster

Schneidmüller, B. and Weinfurter, S. eds. 2001. *Ottonische Neuanfänge*, Mainz

Scholz, B. trans. 1970. *Carolingian Chronicles*, Ann Arbor, MI

Schramm, P.E. 1951. 'Die Annerkennung Karls des Großen als Kaiser', *HZ* 172, pp 449–515

Schramm, P.E. 1964. 'Karl der Große. Denkart und Grundauffassungen: Die von ihm bewirkte Correctio ("Renaissance")', *HZ* 198, pp. 306–45

Scull, C. 1997. 'Urban centres in pre-Viking England?', in J. Hines, ed. *The Anglo-Saxons from the Migration Period to the Eighth Century: An Ethnographic Perspective*, Studies in Historical Archaeoethnology 2, Woodbridge, pp. 269–98

Slater, T.R. ed. 2000. *Towns in Decline, AD 100–1600*, Aldershot

Smith, J.M.H. 1992. *Province and Empire. Brittany and the Carolingians*, Cambridge

Smith, J.M.H. 1995a. '*Fines Imperii*: the marches', in McKitterick, ed. (1995), pp. 169–89

Smith, J.M.H. 1995b. 'Religion and lay society', in McKitterick, ed. (1995), pp. 654–78

Smith, J.M.H. 2000. 'Old saints, new cults: Roman relics in Carolingian Francia', in Smith, ed. (2000), pp. 317–40

Smith, J.M.H. 2003. 'Einhard: the sinner and the saints', *TRHS* 6th ser. 13, pp. 55–77

Smith, J.M.H. ed. 2000. *Early Medieval Rome and the Christian West. Essays in Honour of Donald A. Bullough*, Leiden

Spera, L. 1997. 'Cantieri edilizi a Roma in età carolingia: gli interventi di papa Adriano I (772–795) nei santuari delle catacombe. Strategie e modalità di intervento', *Rivista di Archeologia Cristiana* 1.lxxiii, pp. 185–254

Staerk, A. 1910. *Les manuscrits latins du Ve au XIIIe siècle conservés à la Bibliothèque Impériale de Saint-Petersbourg*, 2 vols, St Petersburg

Stafford, P. 1998. *Queen Emma and Queen Edith*, Oxford

Staubach, N. 1984. '"*Cultus divinus*" und karolingischen Reform', *FS* 18, pp. 546–81

Staubach, N. 1990. '"Des grossen Kaisers kleiner Sohn": Zum Bild Ludwig des Frommen in der älteren deutschen Geschichtsforschung', in Godman and Collins, eds. (1990), pp. 701–23

Steine, H.E. ed. and trans. 1981. *Wandalbert von Prüm: Vita et miraculi santi Goaris*, Frankfurt

Stengel, E. ed. 1913–58. *Urkundenbuch des Klosters Fulda*, 2 vols, Marburg

Stephan, H.-G. 1994. 'Archäologische Erkenntnisse zu karolingischen Klosterwerkstätten in der Reichsabtei Corvey', *Archäologisches Korrespondenzblatt* 24, pp. 207–16

Steuer, H. 1999. 'Handel und Wirtschaft in der Karolingerzeit', in Stiegemann and Wemhoff, eds. (1999b), pp. 406–16

Stevens, W.S. 1997. 'Astronomy in Carolingian schools', in Butzer et al. eds. (1997), pp. 417–88

Stiegemann, C. and Wemhoff, M. eds. 1999a. *799: Kunst und Kultur der Karolingerzeit. Karl der Grosse und Papst Leo III in Paderborn*, 2 vols, Mainz

Stiegemann, C. and Wemhoff, M. eds. 1999b. *799: Kunst und Kultur der Karolingerzeit. Beiträge zum Katalog der Ausstellung Paderborn 1999*, Handbuch zur Geschichte der Karolingerzeit, Mainz

Stocking, R. 2001. *Bishops, Councils and Consensus in the Visigothic Kingdoms, 589–633*, Ann Arbor, MI

Stoclet, A. 1980. 'La *Clausula de unctione Pippini regis*. Mises au point et nouvelles hypothèses', *Francia* 8, pp. 1–42

Stoclet, A. 2000. 'La *Clausula de unctione Pippini regis*, vingt ans après', *Revue Belge de Philologie et d'Histoire* 78, pp. 719–71

Stork, I. 1993. 'Zum Fortgang der Untersuchungen im frühmittelalterlichen Gräberfeld. Adelshof und Hofgrablege bei Lauchheim, Ostalbkreis', *Archäologische Ausgrabungen in Baden-Württemberg 1992*, Stuttgart, pp. 231–39

Story, J. 1999. 'Cathwulf, kingship, and the royal abbey of Saint-Denis', *Speculum* 74, pp. 1–24

Story, J. 2003. *Carolingian Connections: Anglo-Saxon England and Carolingian Francia, c. 750–870*, Aldershot

Sullivan, R.E. ed. 1995. *"The Gentle Voices of Teachers": Aspects of Learning in the Carolingian Age*, Columbus, OH

Tessier, G., Lot, M., Prou, M. and Giry, A. eds. 1952. *Recueil des actes de Charles II le Chauve, roi de France*, Chartes et Diplômes relatifs à l'Histoire de France, Paris

Tierney, J.J. ed. 1967. *Liber de mensura orbis terrae*, Dublin

Tischer, M.M. 2001. *Einharts 'Vita Karoli': Studien zur Entstehung Überlieferung und Rezeption*, Hanover

Theuws, F. 1990. 'Centre and periphery in Northern Austrasia (6th–8th centuries). An archaeological perspective', in Besteman et al. eds. (1990), pp. 41–69

Theuws, F. 1991. 'Landed property and manorial organisation in Northern Austrasia: some considerations and a case study', in N. Roymans and F. Theuws, eds. (1991), *Images of the Past: Studies on Ancient Societies in Northwestern Europe*, Amsterdam, pp. 299–407

Theuws, F. 1999. 'Changing settlement patterns, burial grounds and the symbolic construction of ancestors and communities in the late Merovingian southern Netherlands', in C. Fabech and J. Ringtved, eds. (1999), *Settlement and Landscape*, Aarhus, pp. 337–49

Theuws, F. 2001. 'Maastricht as a centre of power in the early middle Ages', in de Jong and Theuws, ed. (2001), pp. 155–216

Tys, D. 1997. 'Landscape and settlement: the development of a medieval village along the Flemish coast', in De Boe and Verhaeghe, eds. (1997d), pp. 157–67

Unterkircher, F. ed. 1967. *Das Wiener Fragment der Lorscher Annalen*, Codices Selecti Phototypice Impressi 15, Graz

Urbanczyk, P. ed. 1997. *Early Christianity in Central and East Europe*, Warsaw

Ussermann, A. 1790. *Germaniae Sacrae Podromus seu Collectio Monumentorum Res Alemannicas Illustrantium* 1, St-Blasien, Carinthia

Van Dam, R. 1985. *Leadership and Community in Late Antique Gaul*, Berkeley, CA

Verhaeghe, F. 1990. 'Continuity and change: links between medieval towns and the Roman substratum in Belgium', in R. De Smet, H. Melaerts and C. Saerens, eds. (1990), *Studia Varia Bruxellensia ad orbem graeco-latinum pertinentia* 2, Leuven, pp. 229–53

Verhaeghe, F. 1994. 'L'espace civil et la ville. Rapport introductif', in P. Demolon, H. Galinié and F. Verhaeghe, eds. 1994 *Archéologie des villes dans le Nord-Ouest de l'Europe (VIIe–XIIIe siècle). Actes du IVe Congrès International d'Archéologie Médiévale (Douai, 1991)*, Archaeologia Duacensis 11, and Maison des Sciences de la Ville de l'Université de Tours 7, Douai, pp. 145–90

Verhaeghe, F. 1995. 'Industry in medieval towns: the archeological problem. An essay', in J-M. Duvosquel and E. Thoen, eds. (1995), *Peasants and Townsmen in Medieval Europe: Studia in honorem Adriaan Verhulst*, Ghent, pp. 271–93

Verhulst, A. 1989. 'The origins and development of medieval towns in northern Europe', *P&P* 122, pp. 3–35

Verhulst, A. 1999. *The Rise of Cities in North-West Europe*, Cambridge

Verhulst, A. 2002. *The Carolingian Economy*, Cambridge

Verhulst, A. and Declercq, G. 1989. 'Het vroeg-middeleeuwse Gent tussen de abdijen en de grafelijke versterking', in Decavele, J. ed. 1989 *Gent. Apologie van een rebelse stad*.

Geschiedenis. Kunst. Cultuur, Antwerp, pp. 37–59

Verslype, L. 1999. 'La topographie du haut moyen age à Tournai. Nouvel état des questions archéologiques', in *Revue du Nord – Archéologie de la Picardie et du Nord de la France* 81, pp. 143–62

Villa, C. 1995. 'Die Horazüberlieferung und die Bibliothek Karls des Großen. Zum Werkverzeichnis der Handschrift Berlin Diez B.66', *DA* 51, pp. 29–52

Villedieu, F. 1990. *Lyon St-Jean. Les fouilles de l'avenue Adolphe Max,* Documents d'Archéologie en Rhône-Alpes 3, Lyon

Vogüé, A. de, ed. 1971–72. *La Règle de Saint Benoît,* 6 vols. Sources chrétiennes 181–6, Paris

Völckers, H.H. 1965. *Karolingische Münzfunde der Frühzeit (751–800),* Göttingen

Waddell, H. 1976. *More Latin Lyrics from Vergil to Milton,* London

Wallace-Hadrill, A. 1995. *Suetonius,* London

Wallace-Hadrill, J.M. 1965. 'Charlemagne and England', in Braunfels, ed. (1965), I, pp. 683–98; reprinted in Wallace-Hadrill (1975), pp. 155–80

Wallace-Hadrill, J.M. 1967. *The Barbarian West 400–1000,* 3rd edn, London

Wallace-Hadrill, J.M. 1971. *Early Germanic Kingship in England and on the Continent,* Oxford

Wallace-Hadrill, J.M. 1975. *Early Medieval History,* Oxford

Wallace-Hadrill, J.M. 1983. *The Frankish Church,* Oxford

Walle, A.L.J. van de, 1961. 'Excavations in the ancient centre of Antwerp', *Medieval Archaeology* 5, pp. 123–36

Wamers, E. 1994. *Die frühmittelalterlichen Lesefunde aus der Löhrstraße (Baustelle Hilton II) in Mainz,* Mainz

Ward-Perkins, B. 1984. *From Classical Antiquity to the Middle Ages: Urban Public Building in Northern and Central Italy, AD 300–850,* Oxford

Ward-Perkins, B. 1997. 'Continuitists, catastrophists, and the towns of post-Roman Northern Italy', *PBSR* 65, pp. 157–76

Wartmann, H. 1863–66. *Urkundenbuch der Abtei St-Gallen,* 3 vols, St Gall

Wattenbach, W. and Levison, W. 1953. *Deutschlands Geschichtquellen im Mittelalter. Vorzeit und Karolinger* 2, Weimar

Werner, K.F. 1980. '*Missus-Marchio-Comes.* Entre l'administration centrale et l'administration locale de l'empire carolingien', in W. Paravicini and K.F. Werner, eds. (1980), *Histoire Comparée de l'Administration (IVe–XVIIIe siècles),* Beihefte der *Francia* 9, Munich, pp. 191–239

Werner, K.F. 1990. '*Hludovicus Augustus:* Gouverner l'empire Chrétien – idées et réalités', in Godman and Collins, eds. (1990), pp. 28–36

Werner, K.F. 1995, 'Karl der Grosse oder Charlemagne? Von der Aktualität einer überholten Fragestellung', Sitzungsberichte der Bayerischen Akademie der Wissenschaften, Phil.-hist. Klasse, Hft. 4

West, G.V.B. 1999. 'Charlemagne's involvement in central and southern Italy: power and the limits of authority', *EME* 8, pp. 241–67

Whitelock, D. 1979. *English Historical Documents,* London

Whittaker, R. 1990. 'The consumer city revisited: the *vicus* and the city', *JRA* 3, pp. 110–18

Wickham, C. 1981. *Early Medieval Italy. Power and Society, 400–1000,* London

Wickham, C. 1984. 'The other transition: from the ancient world to feudalism', *P&P* 103, pp. 3–36

Wickham, C. 1993. 'La chute de Rome n'aura pas lieu', *Le Moyen Age* 99, pp. 107–126; trans. as C. Wickham (1998a), 'The Fall of Rome will not take place', in L. Little and B. Rosenwein, eds. (1998), *Debating the Middle Ages,* Oxford, pp. 45–57

Wickham, C. 1998b. 'Ninth-century Byzantium through western eyes', in L. Brubaker, ed. (1998), *Byzantium in the Ninth Century: Dead or Alive?*, Aldershot, pp. 245–56

Wieczorek, A. 1996. *Die Franken: Wegbereiter Europas vor 1500 Jahren: König Chlodwig und seine Erben*, Mainz. For an abbreviated version see, Musée du Petit Palais (1997), *Les Francs: précurseurs de l'Europe*, Paris

Wigh, B. 1998. 'Animal bones from the Viking town of Birka, Sweden', in E. Cameron, ed. (1998), *Leather And Fur: Aspects of Early Medieval Trade and Technology*, London, pp. 81–90

Willems, J. 1971. 'Le quartier artisanal gallo-romain et mérovingien de "Batta" à Huy', *Bulletin du Cercle archéologique Hesbaye-Condroz* 11, pp. 7–62

Witte, H. De. *See* De Witte, H.

Witvrouw, J. 1999. 'Le centre domanial du haut moyen âge du Thier d'Olne à Engis / Hermalle-sous-Huy', *Bulletin de Liaison de l'Association Francaise d'Archéologie Mérovingienne* 23, pp. 105–8

Wolfram, H. 1995a. *Österreichische Geschichte 378–907: Grenzen und Räume. Geschichte Österreichs vor seiner Entstehung*, Vienna

Wolfram, H. 1995b. *Salzburg, Bayern, Osterreich: Die Conversio Bagoariorum et Carantanorum und die Quellen ihrer Zeit*, Vienna

Wood, I. 1990. 'Administration, law and culture in Merovingian Gaul', in McKitterick, ed. (1990), pp. 63–81

Wood, I. 1994. *The Merovingian Kingdoms 450–751*, London

Wood, I. 2000. 'Before and after the mission: social relations across the middle and lower Rhine in the seventh and eighth centuries', in Hansen and Wickham, eds. (2000), pp. 149–66

Wood, I. 2001. *The Missionary Life. Saints and the Evangelisation of Europe, 400–1050*, Harlow

Wormald, C.P. 1999. *rly Romance in Spain and Carolingian France*, Liverpool

Wright, R. ed. 1991. *Latin and the Romance Languages in the Early Middle Ages*, London

Wyss, M. 1997. 'Saint-Denis (France): Du mausolée hypothétique du Bas-Empire à l'ensemble basilical carolingien', in De Boe and Verhaeghe, eds. (1997c), pp. 111–14

Wyss, M. 1999. 'Saint-Denis', in Stiegemann and Wemhoff, eds. (1999b), pp. 138–41.

Wyss, M. 2001. 'Un établissement Carolingien mis au jour à proximité de l'abbaye de Saint-Denis: la question du palais de Charlemagne', in Renoux, ed. (2001), pp. 191–200

Yvinec, J.-H. 1993. 'La part du gibier dans l'alimentation du haut moyen âge', in J. Desse and F. Audoin-Rouzeau, eds. (1993), *Exploitation des Animaux Sauvages à Travers le Temps*, Juan-les-Pins, pp. 491–504

Zadora-Rio, E. 1995. 'Le village des historiens et le village des archéologues', in E. Mornet, ed. (1995), *Campagnes médiévales: l'homme et son espace. Etudes offertes à Robert Fossier*, Paris, pp. 145–53

Zadora-Rio, E. and Galinié, H. eds. 2001. 'La fouille du site de Rigny, 7e–19e s. (commune de Rigny-Ussé, Indre-et-Loire): l'habitat, les églises, le cimetière. Troisième et dernier rapport préliminaire (1995–1999)', *Revue Archéologique du Centre de la France* 40, pp. 167–242

Zanini, E. 1998. *Le Italie Bizantine. Territorio, insediamenti ed economia nella provincia bizantina d'Italia (VI–VIII secolo)*, Bari

INDEX

Towns, bishoprics and royal vills are listed as main entries; otherwise place-names are listed under *monasteries, nonneries, palaces* or *rural settlements*

Aachen *see* palaces
Abodrites 47, 185–6
Adalhard, count and abbot of Corbie 97, 202, 207, 247
Adalung, abbot of Lorsch 92
Admonitio Generalis (789) 30, 77, 104–5, 115–16, 118, 122, 138, 153–4, 156
Adoptionism 111, 127, 139, 140–1, 157, 203
Æthelred, king of Northumbria (774–78 and 790–96) 140, 201–4
Agilolfing dynasty *see* Bavaria
Aistulf, Lombard king (749–56), 168, 178
Alcuin 92, 95, 136–42, 112–13, 118, 120, 125, 136–43, 146, 155, 157–8, 162, 195, 197, 201–7
  audience and 45
  biblical scholar 114, 155, 162
  career in York 136–8, 140, 199
  classical texts 39–40, 137
  death 142
  discussion of empire 141
  eschatological anxieties 105
  jealously of 138–9
  letters by 53, 67, 117, 124–7, 130, 139–41, 146–8, 159, 197, 202–3, 207
  poetry 137–41, 143, 145, 163
  pupils and disciples 40, 115, 139, 141–2, 148
  teacher 39–40, 115, 137–8, 140, 158–9, 162
  at Tours 125, 139–40, 142, 159
  Vita Alcuini 137
Aldric, bishop of Le Mans 42
Aldulf, papal legate 197, 207–8
Alemannia 17, 47, 83, 97, 160, 162, 186–8, 192

Alhred, king of Northumbria (765–74) 199–200, 202
Alpaida, mother of Charles Martel 12
Aluberht, missionary to the Saxons 197, 199
Angilbert 157, 163
  court poem by 144
Angilramn, bishop of Metz 32, 143–4, 157
Anglo-Saxon England 5, 108–9, 112, 136–9, 151, 155, 159, 162, 172, 192, 195–208, 215, 224, 230, 260, 266–7, 275–6, 278, 280–1
  letters 139, 141, 197–202, 204, 207
  see also Alcuin; Alhred; Æthelred; Boniface; Eardwulf; Offa
Annals and chronicles 59, 63, 72, 139, 162
  Anglo-Saxon Chronicle 195–6, 201, 205–6
  Annals of Fulda 163, 193
  Annals of St-Bertin 163, 198
  Chronicle of Fredegar and its continuations 7, 10, 12, 15, 25, 32, 56
  Chronicle of Moissac 60, 116, 185
  Chronicle of Theophanes 8
  composition of 54, 58, 60, 63–4
  definition of 43
  Earlier Annals of Metz 6–15, 19
  Fragmentum Chesnianum 56–7, 59
  as *gesta* ('official history') 41–2
  Historia regum (Symeon of Durham) 197
  Lorsch Annals 54–69, 186, 200–1
    account of imperial coronation 64–9
    'Lorsch Annals of 785' 57–9

manuscripts 55–6, 59–64
minor 55, 58–9
Moselle Annals 56–7, 59
Royal Frankish Annals 7, 25, 41–3, 45,
47, 53–9, 64–6, 68–9, 94, 109–
10, 113, 126, 128, 162–3, 184,
196–7, 207
Revised version 17, 19, 42, 47–8,
90, 109
anointing (consecration) 9, 17, 25, 28–9,
66, 93, 97, 106–7, 111–12, 116,
168
Ansegisus, abbot of St Wandrille,
compiler of capitularies 43, 77,
88
Antwerp 262, 275, 277–8
Aquileia 111, 127, 148, 257
Aquitaine 17–18, 47, 76, 96, 100–1, 109,
190, 203–4, 215
Arabs 8, 10–11, 47, 66, 164, 173–4, 178,
270, 283
aristocracy 28, 90–101, 131, 146, 189,
234, 239, 269
co-operation with ruling dynasty 18,
86, 91, 93, 99, 101
kingmaking powers 100, 106–8
marriage alliances 98–9, 187–8, 192
patronage of churches and
monasteries 18, 121, 234
see also rural settlement
royal patronage of 92–6
tension with ruling dynasty 90–1, 98–
100
see also counts
Arn (abbot of St-Amand 782–821,
archbishop of Salzburg 785–
821) 67, 92, 125–7, 139, 146–8
Arnulf, bishop of Metz 15, 32–3, 163
Arras 267
assemblies 6–8, 10, 25, 29, 48, 55, 72, 75–
8, 85, 109, 139–40, 183–4, 238
Aachen (802) 118, 148
Aachen (813) 129
ecclesiastical issues within 109
Frankfurt (794) see Synods
Mainz (800), 65–7

Thionville (806) 128, 186
Rome (800) 55, 65–9
Astronomer, biographer of Louis the
Pious 38, 40, 43–4, 163
Audulf, count in Britanny and Bavaria
92–3
Augustine, St (bishop of Hippo) 42, 44,
114, 126, 130, 144, 158–9, 162,
Austrasia 6, 11, 14, 17, 74, 198, 230, 266,
268
Autchar, follower of Carloman 97–8
Avars 64, 141, 183–5
campaigns against 67, 75, 94–5, 126–
7, 128, 143, 147, 183–6, 190,
200–1
conversion of 126–7, 141, 147, 186
Hring fortress 184, 200
paganism 96, 126
treasure 95, 147, 200–3
tribute taken by 184

baptism 93, 104, 114, 122–3, 125–8, 141
Bavaria 11, 17, 92–4, 96, 100, 139, 146,
148, 162–3, 183–92, 230
Agilolfing dynasty 14, 16, 47, 76, 81,
93–4, 184, 188–9
incorporation into Francia 187, 189
law-code 189
ninth-century sources for 185
Odilo, father of Tassilo 16
see also Tassilo
Bede 42, 114, 137, 162, 197–8, 200, 207
Benevento see Italy
Bernard, Charlemagne's grandson 101
Bertha, Charlemagne's daughter 206–7
Bible, correction of 114, 138, 154–5, 162
biography 22–4, 38, 41, 43–44, 49
see also Astronomer; Einhard; Thegan
Birka 224, 273–4, 279–81
bishops
Charles Martel and 12–13
'correct' prayer and 104
duties of 104, 107, 110, 122–3
links with Carolingian kings 106, 111
link between palace and regions 104
as missi dominici 85

role in local government 73, 84–5, 169, 175, 237

towns and 104, 176, 265, 269–70

Boethius 44, 140, 160

Bohemians 47, 185

Boniface, archbishop of Mainz 108–9, 125, 187, 189, 192, 197, 200

book-lists 144, 149, 156, 161–2

book production 142–5, 154–6, 160

  at court 156

  in monasteries 156, 160

Boso, duke (rebel, 879) 92, 99

Brescia 3, 122, 175, 180, 213

Brevium Exempla 237

Brittany 64, 92, 95, 142, 163, 187, 197, 211–13

Bruges 216, 274

buildings

  materials of manufacture 276–7

  upper floors 104, 131, 173

  see also rural settlement; towns

Bulgarians 185

Burgundy 13, 17, 193, 230

burials and cemeteries 25–6, 43, 56, 142, 172, 174, 177, 231–4, 237–8, 243–6, 248–9, 253, 274, 280

Byzantine empire 8, 45, 47, 64, 68, 112, 151, 168, 172, 177–8, 184–5, 249, 283

  Charlemagne's recognition as emperor by 2, 68, 212, 224

  see also Constantinople; Iconoclasm; Irene; Nicephorus I

Cambrai 262, 266

Candidus 142

capitularies 58, 76–84, 86, 95, 105, 107–10, 118–19, 138, 156, 164–5, 175, 217–18, 221

  collections 43

  definition 76–7

  First Saxon (787) 188

  General capitulary to the *missi*, 'Programmatic' (802) 79, 81, 83, 148

  Herstal (779) 76

links between landowners, officials and court 78–80, 82, 270

manuscripts 78

oral and written pronouncement 77–8, 80

replies from officials 79–80

Thionville (806) 128, 186

see also Admonitio Generalis

Capracorum, papal estate 173–4

Carinthia 55, 185–7, 189

Carloman, brother of Charlemagne 5, 28–9, 31, 44, 48, 93, 96–7, 99, 169, 212–13

Carloman, brother of Pippin III 11, 14, 16–17, 24–5, 75, 108–9, 115, 189

cathedrals 103, 120, 121, 136–7, 142–4, 146, 148, 153, 156

  size of 'chapters' 145

Cathwulf 1, 3, 112

cemeteries *see* burials

Charles Martel 5, 10–17, 25, 48, 74, 92, 183, 187, 245

  wives and children 16, 92, 189

Charles the Bald 41, 87, 106, 156, 213, 216, 218–21, 237, 239, 243, 245–6, 250, 274

Charles the Younger, eldest son of Charlemagne and Hildegard 32–3, 64, 206

charters 79, 81–4, 93, 96, 146, 176, 191, 216, 237, 243, 260

  local affairs 79, 83–4, 176, 178, 237–8, 243

  Merovingian 10, 12, 14, 16–18

Childeric III (743–51) 6, 14, 16

Chrodegang, bishop of Metz 121

chronicles *see* Annals

Church, the 103–31

  Aachen as a central place 119

  Charlemagne's concerns for 1, 71–2, 106, 115, 203–4

  concept of *ecclesia* 106–11, 114–15

  government and 84–5

  Merovingian elites and 85

  'ministry' and salvation 108

  'State' and 106–8, 111

see also Rome; papacy
churches
  land lost to nobles 13
  restoration and building of 44, 103–4,
    106, 121, 145, 170–3, 176, 179,
    233–4, 237–8, 243
  rural 233–4, 237–8
  urban 138, 275
  see also monasteries
Cividale 176–8, 180
clerics, canons and canonesses 106, 108,
  111, 119, 120–2, 136, 246
Codex Carolinus 9, 171, 179
coins 18, 23, 170, 172, 175, 178, 205, 211–
  27, 244–5, 270, 281, 284
  gold coins
    Carolingian Italy 170, 175, 216,
      226–7
    Merovingian 211, 217
  hoards 172, 214–15, 218, 220
  issued by counts 213
  legislation
    capitulary (808) 221
    capitulary of Mantua (781) 217
    edict of Pîtres (864) 213, 220
    synod of Frankfurt (794) 218
  mint sites 213, 216, 218, 223–4
    Aachen ('the palace') 217, 221,
      226, 227
    Dorestad 214–20, 223–4, 226
    Italy 216, 223
    Mainz 214, 216–17, 218–19, 223–4,
      226
    Melle 214–7, 220, 223–4, 226–7
    Quentovic 216, 219, 224, 226–7
    St-Denis 246, 248
  monetary reforms 211, 212
    Charles the Bald 213, 218, 219–20
    Louis the Pious (*Christiana religio*)
      215, 223, 224, 226–7
    monogram 218–23
    portrait coins 211, 212, 224–7
    pre-772 213–18
  rural sites 244, 246
  silver content 216–17, 221, 223–4
  use of coins

    local 212–13, 227
    long-distance 217
Cologne 142–5, 164, 203, 216, 218, 224,
  226, 239, 241, 262, 264
  see also manuscripts
Compiègne 239, 242, 247, 250, 277
Constance 188, 190, 192
computus 145, 147, 153, 159, 163
Concilium Germanicum (742) 109, 115
confraternities of prayer (*Libri Vitae*,
  'Books of Life') 125, 140, 156,
  199–200, 202
Constantinople 2, 47, 68, 93, 168, 177,
  204, 224
Corbeny 239, 251
correctio 35, 105, 115, 122, 124, 129, 165
counts 73–87, 90, 92–3, 107, 110, 191, 270
  authority east of Rhine 191–2
  duties of 73–4, 83–4, 107, 110
  fortified settlements of 239–40
  in Germany 18
  in Italy 175
  links with *missi* 84
  local government and 73–4, 79, 82,
    93, 191, 169, 175, 237
  role in towns 270
  royal offices 83–4
Court 72, 77, 84, 93, 112–13, 125–6, 129,
  131, 138–40, 142, 163–4, 170,
  206, 208, 221
  competition for offices at 32–3, 73–5,
    87, 90, 104, 110
  court-based politics 49, 75–6, 119
  mediating local power 6, 74, 77–80,
    85, 87, 94, 147
  poetry at 10, 112, 140, 143–4, 157–8,
    163
  see also Aachen
craft-working 233, 235–6, 243, 245, 252–
  4, 259–60, 268, 270, 272–4, 278–
  80, 282–3
cultus divinus – cult of God 104, 119–26,
  129

De litteris colendis 153, 156
Desiderius, king of the Lombards (757–

74) 28–9, 97, 151, 169, 175
Dijon 214–15, 217, 265
Domburg 214–15, 217, 219, 223, 262,
    268, 274, 280
donation of Constantine 31, 44, 68
Dorestad 213–21, 223–4, 226–7, 236, 254,
    262, 266, 268–71, 275, 277–81
Douai 240, 243, 251, 254
Doué-La-Fontaine, *vill* 239, 251
Drogo, son of Carloman, nephew of
    Pippin III 16–17

Eardwulf, king of Northumbria (796–806
    and 808–10) 196–7, 207–8
Ebroin, Merovingian mayor of the
    palace 9, 11–13
Edict of Pîtres (864) 220, 238, 274
education 137, 153, 156–60, 199
    canon of knowledge 161–2
    Charlemagne's involvement in 38
    Charlemagne's learning 113–14, 158
    classical texts, survival of 160–1
    at court 140
    early Christian writers 159–60
    pagan writers 159
    schools 103, 113, 137, 140, 148, 153,
        156–60, 162, 165, 199
    seven liberal arts 38, 49, 137, 158–9
Einhard 2, 38–51, 52, 131, 156–7
    eastern Frank, an 128, 193
    epitaph by Hraban Maur 40
    national pride 48–9, 95, 190–1
    relationship with Charlemagne 15,
        22, 24, 38, 42
    Vita Karoli 3, 45, 52–3, 69, 72, 95, 106,
        136, 140, 158, 162, 192
    audience 3, 40–1
    Carolingian administration 71
    chapter divisions in 38–9
    Charlemagne's childhood 15–16
    Charlemagne, description of 23,
        34, 48–9, 71–2, 130, 158, 164
    Charles Martel 11, 13
    classical sources 34, 39–40, 43–9
    early Christian sources 39, 41–2,
        46–7

early manuscripts 39–41
    Merovingian dynasty 5–8
    modern criticism 22
    originality 38, 40
    papacy 31, 52, 167, 170, 179
    reliability 22, 28, 39, 52–3, 72
    style and vocabulary 39, 41–2, 44–6
Elipand, bishop of Toledo 127
epitaphs
    Alcuin 142
    Charlemagne 43
    Einhard 40
    Eric, duke of Friuli 94
    Gerold, count of Bavaria 94
Eric, duke of Friuli 94–5
Ermold the Black 163
eschatological anxieties (800) 105, 113
ethnicity
    archaeology and 185
    contemporary terminology 47, 185,
        190–1, 197–9
    ethnogeography 47–8, 183
    expansion of Francia, impact on 191
    gentes beyond the Rhine 183
    language and 190–1
    law 187–90
    modern views of Charlemagne's
        identity 22–3
Eucherius, bishop of Orléans 12–13
exile 8–9, 12–13, 64, 97, 147, 175, 195,
    199, 203–8
    Charlemagne's protection of Anglo-
        Saxon exiles 204–8

false prophets 105
Fastrada, Charlemagne's queen (783–94)
    32, 46, 99–100, 128
Felix of Urgel 127, 141
    see also Adoptionism
feud 81
fideles ('faithful men') 80, 110, 120, 128,
    136, 200–1
Frankfurt *see* palaces; synods
Fridugis 148, 157
Frisia 10, 17, 126, 172, 179, 187, 191, 199,
    211, 215, 266, 280

General Admonition (789) *see Admonitio Generalis*

George, bishop of Amiens and Ostia 198

Gerald of Aurillac 94–5

Gerberga, wife of Carloman 28

Gerold (brother of Hildegard), count of Bavaria 56, 94, 101, 188

Gervold, abbot of St-Wandrille 206

Gerward, librarian 41, 50

Ghent 213, 262, 267, 271, 274–5
see also monasteries

gift-giving 69, 81, 167, 171, 177, 199–201, 268, 270, 283

Gisela, Charlemagne's daughter 158, 162

Gisela, Charlemagne's sister and abbess of Chelles 42, 119–20, 158

Gottschalk 40

Gregory I 'the Great', pope (590–604) 31, 56, 114–15, 118, 159, 162, 198, 201

Gregory III, pope (731–41) 197

Gregory, bishop of Tours (573–94) 162, 265–6, 277

Grifo, half-brother of Pippin III 16–17, 189

Gundoin, Merovingian rival to Pippin of Herstal 6

Hadrian I, pope (772–95) 29–31, 117–18, 122, 145, 147, 170–4, 177–9, 198–9, 201–3

Haithabu (Hedeby) 270, 273–5, 277–9, 281

Hamburg 250

Hamwic (Southampton) 267, 269, 273–5, 277, 279–81

harbours (*portus*) 254, 260, 266, 268, 271–3, 275, 277, 281–2

Hardrad, count and rebel 98–9

Harun al-Rashid, Abbasid caliph, 66, 164

Hedeby *see* Haithabu

Heiric of Auxerre, scholar 157

Helmgaud, count and envoy to Constantinople 93

heresy 105, 111, 127, 139, 141, 157, 203–4
see also Adoptionism

Hildebald, head of palace chapel and archbishop of Cologne 142–8, 164

Hildebrand, count and uncle of Pippin III 25

Hildegard, Charlemagne's queen (d. 783) 32–3, 94, 99–100, 188

Hilduin, archchaplain 131

Himiltrude, mother of Pippin the Hunchback 33

Hincmar, archbishop of Rheims (845–82) 13, 72, 111

hostages 95, 102, 169, 175, 188

Höxter, royal *vill* 241–3, 251–2

Hraban Maur 40, 115, 123, 157–8, 162

Hugh, count of Tours and envoy to Constantinople 93

hunting 81–2, 87, 241–2, 251

Huy 262, 266, 279–80

Iconoclasm 112, 157, 172, 203–4
see also Libri Carolini

imagined communities 112, 114, 191, 198

imperial coronation 46, 52–3, 64, 141, 146, 167
refusal of office 52–3

Ingelheim *see* palaces

Ireland 112, 147, 152–3, 157, 197, 203

Irene, Byzantine empress 66, 68, 203–4

Irmino, abbot of St-Germain 27

Isidore of Seville 27, 42–3, 47, 160, 162

Israel
Franks as 'New Israel' 15, 113–14

Italy 167–80
Benevento 47–8, 65–6, 117, 122, 168–9, 173, 175, 177–8, 213
Byzantine territories 177–8
coinage 170, 175, 213, 216
Lombard Italy
Charlemagne's conquest of (773/4) 28, 98, 122, 168–9, 173, 175, 184, 189
cultural achievements 161, 176–8, 180
Frankish alliances with 168
papal alliance with 29

Pippin's campaigns against 28
see also Desiderius; Paul the Deacon;
    Pippin III
see also monasteries; Paulinus of
    Aquileia; Peter of Pisa; Rome
itineraries, royal 30, 65–6, 75, 138, 164,
    183, 239

Jerusalem 64–6, 115
Johannes, follower of Louis the Pious 96
Jonas, bishop of Orléans 44
justice 8–9, 13, 15, 18, 43, 74, 81–4, 94–5,
    125, 130
    loss of under Merovingians 8–9
    trial by ordeal 100
    see also Law

Karlburg, fort 239, 241–3, 248, 251–3, 255
Karolus magnus et Leo papa 1, 53, 162–3
kingship
    Carolingian 7–8, 13, 72–3, 106, 242,
        · 249
    granting offices 86–7
    Hincmar of Rheims on 72
    ideology of Christian kingship 1, 3,
        44, 48, 107, 111, 113, 115
    Merovingian 6–8, 73–4
    model rulers 11, 13
    Old Testament models 15, 112–13, 115
    rex et sacerdos 111, 116, 127
    tonsuring of opponents 17

language 47, 153
    Latin 48, 107, 154
    vernacular 48, 148, 154, 158, 190–1,
        196–7
Laon 157, 218, 223, 237, 239, 251
law 71, 77–9, 81–3, 112, 160–1
    Alemannic 188
    Bavarian 188–9
    canon law 28, 109, 117, 143, 155–6, 162
    Dionysio-Hadriana 30, 117
    codification as form of Frankicisation
        71, 187–8, 190
    Frisian 187
    Lex Salica 113–14

Old Testament 109, 112, 115
    Saxon 188
    see also Justice
Leidrad, archbishop of Lyon 103–4, 106,
    118–19, 121, 125, 127, 130–1
Leo III, pope (795–816) 171–3, 179, 196–
    7, 200, 205–8
    attack on (799) 53, 64–8, 117, 141,
        144, 148, 170–1, 173, 179
    reception at Paderborn 3, 75, 67
    see also Assemby of Rome (800)
Leudgar, bishop and martyr of Autun 9,
    11–12
Levison, Wilhelm 195
Liber Historiae Francorum, pro-
    Merovingian source 9–11
Liber Pontificalis (Book of the Popes) 53,
    116, 146, 163, 170–4, 179–80
library catalogues *see* book lists
Libri Carolini see Theodulf of Orléans
libri vitae see confraternities of prayer
Liège 122, 144, 157, 255,
literacy 77, 107, 112, 122, 153–4, 161,
    241–2, 245, 252
liturgy 103, 118–19, 127, 137, 140, 145,
    163–4
    Gregorian Sacramentary 118, 138,
        145
    Rome 118
    Sacramentary of Gregory (the
        Hadrianum) 118
Liudger, bishop of Münster (805–9) 199
Liutgard, Charlemagne's queen (d. 800)
    65, 141
Liutprand, Lombard king (712–44) 151,
    168, 176, 178
London (*Lundenwic*) 269, 271, 273, 283,
    286
Lothar, emperor (840–55) 114, 175–6,
    216
Lothar, king of West Francia (954–86)
    240
Louis the Pious 38, 40–3, 65, 72, 76–7,
    93, 96, 106, 111, 115, 120–1,
    155, 163, 183, 192, 198, 215,
    220–3, 226–7, 239, 241, 246

imperial coronation (813) 46, 87, 100
king in Aquitaine 100
see also coins
Lucca 176
Lul, bishop of Mainz 199–200, 202
Lupus of Ferrières 40–1, 49, 156–7
Lyon 103–4, 106, 119, 127, 131, 161, 217,
    220, 224, 226, 264–5

Maastricht 255, 262, 265–6, 269–70, 272–
    3, 276, 279–80
Mægenfrith, chamberlain 202
Magyars 184–5
Mainz 144, 188, 192, 199, 216
manuscripts 78–80, 142–3, 155, 160–2,
    164, 247
    Benediktinerstift St-Paul im Lavanttal
        8/1 55–6, 59
    Berlin, Preussiche Kulturbesitz Diez
        B Sant.66 161
    British Library, Cotton Domitian
        A.viii 202, 209
    British Library, Cotton Tiberius C.XI
        41
    Cologne, Dombibliothe 103 145
    Cologne, Dombiblothek 83.II 145
    St-Petersburg, National Library of
        Russia O.v.IV.1 56, 69
    Vienna, ÖNB 473 40–1
    Vienna, ÖNB 515 59–64
    Vienna, ÖNB 1861 145
marriage alliances 28, 32, 45, 93, 98–9,
    169, 187–9, 206–7
Marseilles 220, 265, 268
Martin, abbot of Laon 157
Mayenne 239, 251
mayors of the palace 6–7, 9, 12–13, 15–
    16, 18, 24, 48, 74, 108–9, 120
Medemblik 268
Mellier, royal *vill* 239, 251
memory 10, 13, 24, 27, 34, 41–2, 45, 94,
    198
Merovingian dynasty 5–19, 24, 41, 48,
    73–4, 76, 108, 120, 151, 189–90,
    207, 245, 266, 283
    see also Childeric III

Francia under the, 3, 39, 76, 80, 85,
    155, 159, 187, 211, 217, 231–2,
    234, 240, 259, 260, 262, 267,
    269, 273, 275–6, 279, 282
Metz 15, 32, 48, 119, 121, 143, 157, 163,
    264–5, 283
Meuse valley
    Carolingian lands in 266, 280
    settlements 232, 235, 237–8, 253, 262,
        265–6, 273, 280
Milan 176, 214, 216–17, 219, 223, 226
ministry (*ministerium*) 72, 83, 103, 107–8,
    270
miracles 25–7, 33, 42–3, 48, 68
missi dominici 64–5, 67, 80–1, 83–5, 107,
    144, 148, 169, 175, 177, 191
mission and missionaries 140–1, 147–8,
    188–90, 185–6, 192, 197–8
    Danes, Slavs and Avars 125, 141, 147–
        8, 186
    east of the Rhine 186, 190, 192
    Frisia 125, 187, 199
        see also Liudger
    Saxons 44, 125–6, 140, 187, 197–9
    see also Boniface
monasteries 18, 25–7, 42, 48, 104–5, 111,
    119–23, 129, 176–8, 231, 238
    243–8
    centres of learning 153, 156–7, 160–1,
        165
    duty of prayer 120–1
    foundation as form of Frankicisation
        18, 187, 190, 198
    in Francia
        Corbie 156–7, 160–1, 203, 213, 247
        Corvey 156, 192, 241, 243, 246–9,
            252
        Freising 81, 104, 146
        Fulda 79, 98, 121, 123, 125, 130,
            156–8, 160–1, 188, 192–3, 195
        Ghent, St-Peter and St-Bavo 213,
            267
        Gorze 56, 121
        Hamage 243–4, 247–52
        Lorsch 56–7, 60, 92, 96, 98, 121,
            156, 160–1, 188

foundation of 121
    royal patronage of 121
Mondsee 144
Murbach 59, 70, 149
Prüm 40, 45, 100
Reichenau 56–7, 60, 157, 160–1, 188
St-Amand 146–7, 155–7, 207
St-Bertin 252
St-Denis 13, 93, 97, 100, 116, 213,
    223, 238–9, 243, 245–7, 249–50,
    252, 276
St-Gallen 40, 94, 152, 156–7, 160–
    2, 188
St-Martin, Tours 53, 125, 140–2,
    155, 157–61, 213, 216–17, 237–8
St-Médard, Soissons 131
St-Riquier 65, 163
St-Servaas, Maastricht 276
St-Vaast 267
St-Wandrille 77, 206
Weißenburg 188
in Italy
    Farfa 122, 169–70
    Monte Cassino 17, 24, 122, 169–70
    San Vincenzo 122, 169–70
link between core and peripheral
    regions 121
mission, and 125, 192, 198
model for empire 131
obedience to a rule 111–12, 118, 130,
    146
relationship with bishops 104
royal patronage 26, 42, 85, 120, 125,
    169, 199, 245, 267
services owed to kings 121
urban 267
Montfélix-Chavot, fort 240, 251
Moravia 185
mosaics 167, 172, 175, 177, 180, 245
music 103, 118–19, 121, 153, 157, 159, 164

Namur 262, 280
Neustria 7–8, 10–12, 14, 17, 74, 151, 215,
    230, 266, 268
Nicephorus I, Byzantine emperor (802–
    11) 68

Nithard 49
nobility see aristocracy
northmen see Vikings
Notker Babulus (the Stammerer), monk
    of St-Gall 24, 34, 40, 94, 98, 113,
    116, 130–1, 152–3, 169, 193
nunneries
    Chelles 119–20, 144, 158, 219
    Nivelles 15

oaths 30, 65–8, 80–2, 84, 99, 122, 205
Offa, king of Mercia (757–96) 138, 151,
    200–7
Oost-Souburg, fort 240–1, 243
Opus Caroli regis see Libri Carolini
orality 26, 32–3, 77–8, 80, 98, 140, 154
Orléans 12–13, 44, 94, 122–4

Paderborn Epic see Karolus magnus et Leo
    papa
Paderborn see palaces
Palace, the
    centre of reform 104, 118
    links between 'the palace', bishoprics
        and the regions 104
    sacrum palatium – the sacred palace
        103, 105, 129–31
palaces 164, 183, 191, 237–9, 247, 277
    Aachen 64, 75, 118, 129–30, 140, 143–
        4, 147, 163–4, 208, 217, 226–7,
        237–8, 242, 247, 277
    central place 94, 119, 122, 130,
        140, 148, 200
    chapel 44, 46, 129–30, 142–3, 224
    Charlemagne's presence at 64, 94,
        130–1
    monastic model 130–1
    Old Testament model 129–30
    Frankfurt 75, 109, 127–8, 139, 164,
        183, 224, 226
    Ingelheim 75, 143, 183, 238–9, 242,
        247, 277
    Paderborn 1, 3, 64–5, 67, 141, 144,
        148, 164, 183, 192, 238–9, 240–
        2, 252
    Quierzy 239, 251, 277

Regensburg 100, 128, 139, 183, 191
  see also coins; Soest; Mellier
Palaiseau, royal villa of 26–7
papacy see Gregory I; Gregory III,
    Stephen II; Stephen III;
    Stephen IV; Hadrian I; Leo III;
    Paschal I; Zacharias I
  see also Rome
Paris 3, 25, 79–80, 93, 96, 108, 144, 213,
    217, 219, 224, 243, 245, 262,
    265, 276, 280
Paschal I, pope (817–24) 173–4, 196
Paul the Deacon 32–3, 48, 118, 157, 163,
    178, 198
Paulinus of Aquileia 111, 127, 157
Pavia 28–9, 31, 66, 95, 116, 137, 169,
    175–7, 180, 217, 219, 220, 223,
    226
penance 32–3, 105, 115, 123, 128
Peter of Pisa 137, 157–8, 178
pilgrims 81, 111–12, 116, 126, 171–4,
    178–9
Pippin III (751–68) 26–8, 47, 74–6, 96,
    108–9, 111–13, 116–17, 121,
    168, 183, 187, 189, 221, 223,
    227, 239, 245
  accession 6–11, 16–18, 24–5, 30, 41,
    44, 74, 93, 168
  Donation of 30–1, 116, 170
  Italy and 9, 28, 168, 170
  papal anointing (754) 8–9, 17, 25, 93,
    116, 169
Pippin of Herstal 6–7, 10–15, 17, 19, 187,
    190
Pippin of Italy 65, 161, 163
Pippin the Hunchback, eldest son of
    Charlemagne 33, 96, 99–100, 128
Plectrude, wife of Pippin of Herstal 11,
    14
plunder and tribute see Warfare
Poeta Saxo 193
populus christianus – the 'Christian
    people' 67, 72, 105, 107–10,
    115, 121, 124–6, 129
pottery 232, 236–7, 242–4, 246, 252, 263,
    270, 279–81, 284

prayer 105–6, 109, 111, 114, 116–17, 119–
    23, 125, 127–9, 137, 144, 148,
    156, 199, 201–2
priests 65, 67, 109, 111–12, 115, 119, 122–
    4, 126, 203, 204–6, 212
  celibacy and clerical marriage 123–4
Prudentius, bishop of Troyes 198
pseudo-writings (Letters from Heaven)
    105

Quentovic 206, 216, 219, 224, 226–7,
    236, 254, 266, 268, 270–1, 280
  see also coins

Ralswiek, Rügen 273
Ravenna 65–6, 117, 168, 177
rebellion
  against Charlemagne (785) 80, 90, 98,
    188–9
  against Charlemagne (792) 96, 99–
    100, 128
  in Italy (776) 169, 175–6, 189
  Stellinga revolt (841–3) 188
reform see correctio
Regensburg see palaces
Regino of Prüm 45
relics 31, 49, 64, 80, 119, 121, 131, 80,
    131, 174, 179
renaissance, renovatio 42, 48, 151–66,
    167, 178, 180
  royal patronage 151, 160, 164–5
Rhine 28, 47–8, 143, 243–4, 246, 273, 280
  Frankish policy beyond 75, 80, 85,
    183–93, 189–90, 250–1
  frontier 75, 142, 154, 183–93, 215, 218
  Merovingian policy beyond 190
  palaces beyond 183, 191
  settlements 121, 232–5, 237, 250, 253
Ribe 274–5, 281
Richbod, abbot of Lorsch and bishop of
    Trier (791–804) 56–7
Rigobert, bishop of Rheims 13
ritual purity 110, 112, 119, 123–4, 130
Rome 116–17, 167–74, 196–8, 262
  Charlemagne's
    patronage of 44, 71, 95, 106, 117,

130, 167–8, 170–1, 174, 177–9, 200
  visits to 29–31, 52–3, 55, 65–8, 116, 167, 178
classical
  Carolingian as heirs of 152–4, 161, 163
diaconae (deaconries) 172, 179
domuscultae (papal estates) 173–4
foreign *scholae* 172–3, 196
lands belonging to 117, 168, 172–3
Lombards, threat from 9, 29, 169
papacy
  relationship with Carolingian kings 1–2, 7, 114, 116–17, 141, 167–8, 170, 178–80, 201, 207–8
  patronage of 170–4
  revival 167, 170–4
St-Peter's 1, 30–1, 44, 46, 55, 656, 141, 146, 170–1, 178–9
xenodochia (pilgrim hostels) 171–2
see also donation of Constantine; donation of Pippin; *Liber Pontificalis*; liturgy; papacy
Rotrud, Charlemagne's daughter 158, 162
Rouen 79, 206, 224, 226, 236, 262, 268, 271, 280
rural settlements
  Brebières 233
  Develier-Courtételle 233, 236, 252–3
  Dommelen 232–3, 252
  Ename 254
  Geldrop 232–3, 252
  Goudelancourt-les-Pierrepont 233
  Grentheville 233
  Hulsel 232–3
  Laucheim 232
  Mondeville 233–4
  Oostburg 240
  Petegem 237–8, 249–50, 277
  Poortugaal 250
  Portjoie 233–4
  Reusel-De Mierden 232
  Rigny-Ussé 233–4, 238, 250
  Rijnsburg 233, 235–6

Saleux-les-Coutures 233–7, 241, 250, 252–3
Serris 234
Sugny, fort 240–2, 251
Thier d'Olne 237–8, 250
Valkenburg De Woerd 232–7, 250, 252
Venray-'t Brukske 232, 252
Veurne 240, 251
Villiers-le-Bacle 233
rural settlement 230–55
  animal husbandry 235, 240–1, 248, 251, 253
  archaeological deposits 230–1, 235, 240, 243, 247–8, 252
  churches 233–4, 237–8, 243
  ecclesiastical-secular complexes 237–9, 242–6, 248–9
  elite 26–7, 237–9, 242–51
  estate-centres 231, 237–41, 249
  farmsteads 173, 231–5, 278
  fortified 231, 237–40, 246, 250–1
  hamlets 231–3, 236–8, 253, 255
  hierarchy 230–1, 237, 240–1, 248–53
  house plots and building types 231, 233–4, 237, 243
  Merovingian 6, 18, 231–2
  ninth-century change 237, 240, 244, 249
  nucleated 231, 234, 238, 250, 252
  poly-focal 231, 254, 281
  settlement shift 232–3
  seventh-century change 231–3, 237
  site continuity 232–3, 236
  social ranking within 232–5, 237–8, 241, 246, 251, 253
  specialist craft production 236, 242–3, 247–8, 252
  trade networks 236, 242–3, 247
  watermills 234

St Denis 25
St Germain 25–6
St Martin 25
Salzburg 67, 92, 125, 127, 139, 144, 146–8, 157, 192

Saxons 44, 65, 142, 184, 187, 196–7, 201
    bishops 192, 196–7
    conversion 44, 125, 140, 187
    Frankish defeat by (782) 90, 195–6
    incorporation into Francia 187, 190
    massacre of (782) 2, 90–1, 195–6, 201
    Merovingian campaigns against 187
    paganism 125–6, 187–8, 200
    peace with Franks 188
    resettlement of Saxony beyond the
        Elbe 184
    source of plunder 28
    Stellinga revolt (841–43) 188
    tenth-century hostility 190
    tribute and plunder 95, 187
    war against 28–9, 44, 46–7, 90, 184,
        187–8
    see also Widukind
scabini, officers of local justice 82, 191
Scheldt valley
    towns 262, 265, 280
script
    caroline minuscule 155
    at Tours 142
Slavs 47, 64, 90, 183–6, 190–1, 193
    East Frankish hegemony over 193
    slaves 186
    war against 90
    see also Abodrites; Bohemians;
        Carinthia; Sorbs; Wends;
Smaragdus 44
Soest, *vill* 239, 241–3, 251–2, 255
Sorbs 47, 185
Spain 3–4, 45, 47, 91, 96, 127, 139, 155,
    160, 162, 283
Spoleto 64, 117, 168, 170–1
spolia 173, 245, 247–50, 277
Stephen II, pope (752–57) 8–9, 15, 17, 25,
    30, 93, 116
Stephen III, pope (768–72) 28–9, 31
Stephen IV, pope (816–17) 196
Stephen, count of Paris 80, 93
subkingdoms 76
    see also Aquitaine; Austrasia; Bavaria;
        Burgundy; Neustria; Italy
synods 85, 108–10, 127, 139–40, 198, 204

Aachen (813) 101, 129
Frankfurt (794) 110, 125, 128, 139–40,
    143, 164, 203–4, 218
frequency of 110
Merovingian 108–9
public meetings 108–9, 111
reform synods (813) 129
Regensburg (792) 127
royal involvement in 108–9, 129
terminology 109–10
Ver (755) 76, 111
see also assemblies

Tassilo, duke of Bavaria 16, 42, 45, 99,
    147, 184, 188–90
taxation 73–4, 206, 235, 241, 251,
Thegan (*Gesta Hludowici*) 38, 40, 44, 114,
    163
Theoderic, king of the Ostrogoths (454–
    526) 151, 179
Theoderic, vassal 90, 92
Theodulf, bishop of Orléans 94, 112,
    122–5, 143, 155, 157–8, 163
    biblical scholar 114, 155
    episcopal statutes 123–4
    Libri Carolini 112, 139, 157
    poetry 94, 143–4, 157, 163
Theudald, count 100
Thuringia 17, 47, 98, 187–8
Tongeren 255, 273
Tournai 221, 237, 250, 254, 262, 266 270,
    273
Tours 141, 129, 155, 157, 159–61, 237–8,
    262, 264–5, 272, 276
    see also monasteries
towns
    beyond the Roman frontier 263, 272
    building types 175, 260, 265, 272,
        278
    churches in 123, 138, 172, 179, 262,
        264–5, 267, 269, 275–6, 283
    continuity of Roman towns 175, 262–
        3, 265, 272, 275
    dark earth 262, 264
    definition and functions of 231, 254,
        259–61, 263, 265, 268

demise of Roman towns 175–6, 259, 261–5, 271, 273, 283
emergence of medieval towns 173, 175–6, 231, 254, 259, 261–2, 265, 268, 284
emporia 226, 236, 254, 260, 263, 266–72, 274, 275, 279, 281,
links with rural settlements 231, 240, 254, 260, 268, 277, 281–2
monasteries in 176, 267
physical size 268–9, 275
political prestige 168, 176, 260, 262, 266
population size 171–2, 264, 268
private space 104, 131, 276–7
royal authority in 176, 218, 221, 259, 262, 266–7, 270, 274–5, 283–4
social factors 260–1, 269, 280, 283
street systems and house plots 260, 263, 265, 270, 272–4, 275, 277–8
terminology 260–1
trade and 261, 265–6, 270, 275, 279–81
urban material culture 263, 268, 270, 272, 278–9
Viking attacks on 271, 274, 283
walls and defences 172–4, 176, 179–80, 265, 272–4, 276, 284
waterways 272–3, 280
see also Vikings
trade 23, 152, 179, 186, 199–200, 206–7, 236 261, 266–8, 270, 272, 275, 278–84
in weapons 186
treasure 14, 91, 94–6, 170, 184, 200–3
Trier 57, 144, 214, 224, 226, 262, 264–5

Utrecht 144, 187

Valenciennes 254, 262
vassi dominici 79, 83–4, 90
Verona 29, 161, 176, 217
Vikings 47, 139, 142, 173, 183–5, 201, 206, 211, 215, 221, 240, 254, 271, 274, 283
Danewerk 184
Danish forts 274

Frankish policy towards 184
Frisia, rulers of 187
Gottfried, king of the Danes 47, 184
mission 186
support for Saxon resistance 184
towns 275, 281, 283
Vita Karoli see Einhard

Wala, count 92, 100
Walahfrid Strabo, abbot of Reichenau 38–41, 46, 49, 156–7
Wandalbert of Prüm 40
warfare 14, 38, 46–8, 74, 84, 86, 90–1, 94, 112, 126, 159, 168, 251
Battle of Tertry (687) 6–8, 12–13, 17
bond between king and nobility 75–6, 84, 86
Christian warriors 94–5, 126
Frankish defeats 91
orders for mobilisation 84–5
plunder 28, 47, 74, 76, 94–6, 183, 190, 200–1, 221
religion and ideology as motive for 95
social mobility 74–5, 84, 86, 95–6
Treaty of Verdun (843) 193
tribute 74, 95, 184, 187, 190, 221, 241
see also Avars; Benevento; Saxons; Vikings
Warin, count of Alemannia 97
weights and measures 112, 221
Weltabi 47
Wends 185
Wido, count in Brittany 95, 142
Widukind of Corvey, scholar 190
Widukind, Saxon rebel 90, 188, 195 *see also* Saxons
Wigbod, scholar 114, 157, 162
wills
Charlemagne's 91–2, 104, 177
Willicarius, bishop of Vienne 13
Winchester 279
Wolin 275, 281
Würzburg 188, 192, 239

York 3, 197, 199, 297
archbishops 137–8, 199, 208

books to Francia 138, 199–200
cathedral chapter 136, 145
liturgy 137
poem about 137
school 137, 199
see also Alcuin

Youth
    Charlemagne's 15–16, 24–8, 30, 44

Zacharias I, pope (741–52) 7, 15–16, 25,
    117, 172–3, 176, 269

Lightning Source UK Ltd.
Milton Keynes UK
UKOW021148180212

187491UK00001BB/31/P